Preaching and Teaching
with Imagination

Highly recommended as a beginning text in preaching. A very solid and substantive yet spritely contribution to the discussions being held today as to our direction in preaching.

— David L. Larsen

Biblical preachers are often anxious when "imagination" and "preaching" appear in the same sentence. They worry that imaginative preaching means departing from the text and thus becoming unbiblical. The result is often "biblical" preaching that is unimaginative, lifeless, and dull. The fact that Warren Wiersbe—a preacher whose biblical credentials are impeccable—has written saying that imagination is not only permissible, but necessary, should allay some fears and greatly enhance a lot of preaching.

— Stuart Briscoe

This book should be a winner! As a significant evangelical contribution on the role of imagination in preaching, it is long overdue. . . . While holding uncompromisingly to sound hermeneutical control in preaching, Wiersbe chases away the scare-bears of those who fear that imagination is threatening, if not fatal, to truth. . . . The book itself is a model of imaginative art. I found it nearly as delicious as a Father Brown whodunit.

— Richard A. Bodey

His words have already stimulated one of his *sons* in the ministry to make the creative connections that get the video of the imagination turned on about spiritual reality. Thanks for the courage to carefully wrestle with the need to understand figurative language.

— David Wyrtzen

After presenting an excellent overview of the need for imaginative preaching and an overview of imagination in the Bible, Wiersbe discusses how to use imagery in various kinds of sermons. This book trumpets a significant message that preachers need to read and heed.

— Roy B. Zuck

Preaching and Teaching with Imagination

The Quest for Biblical Ministry

Warren W. Wiersbe

BakerBooks

A Division of Baker Book House Co.
Grand Rapids, Michigan 49516

© 1994 by Warren W. Wiersbe

Published by Baker Books
a division of Baker Publishing Group
P.O. Box 6287, Grand Rapids, MI 49516-6287
www.bakerbooks.com

Printed in the United States of America

Library of Congress Cataloging-in-Publication Data
Wiersbe Warren W.
  Preaching and Teaching with imagination : the quest for biblical ministry / by Warren W. Wiersbe.
       p.   cm.
    Includes bibliographical references and index.
    ISBN 10: 0-8010-5757-4 (pbk.)
    ISBN 978-0-8010-5757-1 (pbk.)
    1. Preaching. I. Title.
  BV4211.2.W474 1994
  251—dc20   94-1710

Dedicated with affection and appreciation
to the congregations of the three churches I have been
privileged to pastor:

Central Baptist Church, East Chicago, Indiana
Calvary Baptist Church, Covington, Kentucky
The Moody Church, Chicago, Illinois

and to the many conferences and congregations in various
parts of the world where I've been privileged to minister.

Thank you for listening, for praying, and for encouraging.
I wish that I had preached better sermons,
but I know I couldn't have preached a better Gospel.

"The great teacher is the one
who turns your ears into eyes
so that you can see the truth."
Eastern Proverb

"Ears that hear and eyes that see —
the Lord made them both."
Proverbs 20:12

"For this people's heart has become calloused;
they hardly hear with their ears,
and they have closed their eyes.
Otherwise they might see with their eyes,
hear with their ears,
understand with their hearts and turn,
and I would heal them."
Matthew 13:15

Contents

III. Imagination and Biblical Preaching

APPENDICES

Preface

First of all, I want to thank my wife Betty for all the help and encouragement she gave me in the writing of this book. Most authors put this at the end of the Preface, but since this is a book on imagination, I'm putting it at the beginning to show the reader how creative I can be.

This is a book about preaching and teaching the Word of God. Its aim is to help us so proclaim the Word that the people who hear us will experience the power of God's truth changing their lives.

I'm sharing with you the burden of a preacher, writer, and occasional seminary instructor who got weary of bringing skeletons into the pulpit and producing cadavers in the pews. I have a concern to challenge our preachers—and those who train preachers—to move out of the academy into the marketplace and to start communicating God's truth the way God communicated it to us in His Word. We've analyzed and outlined the Bible to death. Now it's time we released the *living* Word to accomplish its powerful ministry in our needy world.

These chapters record the attempt of an amateur to bring together insights from many disciplines to help us find out how to do biblical preaching. Biblical preaching is far more than the proclamation of Bible truth, although that's certainly an important part of it. Biblical preaching means declaring God's truth *the way He declared it,* and that means *with imagination.*

I repeat: this book is the work of an amateur. I readily admit that I'm not an expert in the disciplines from which I've drawn material for this book. If I had waited until I mastered semiotics, hermeneutics, and all that's involved in modern literary theory, this book would never have been written. I'd become like the fellow who attended university year after year and kept postponing his graduation. When his father was asked what his son would be when he graduated, the father replied, "An old man." At my age, I can't afford to play such a waiting game.

So I send this book forth. I trust that others, better qualified than I, will catch the vision and write better books that will correct my mistakes, explain things more precisely, and teach us how to be more effective preachers and teachers of God's truth. This book is a courageous attempt on the part of a novice to point out some neglected paths on the homiletical landscape. My prayer is that better guides will also come along.

It was Dr. Warren S. Benson, Vice-president of Professional Doctoral Programs at Trinity Evangelical Divinity School, Deerfield, Illinois, who first challenged me to investigate this subject and then to teach it in Trinity's Doctor of Ministry program; I'm grateful to him for his encouragement. I'm also grateful to the students whose varied responses and insightful questions helped me find my way through the frightening maze. Some of them taught me far more than I taught them, for it's in the give-and-take of honest discussion that all of us learn more. Obviously, Dr. Benson, Trinity, and the doctoral students are not responsible for the errors and deficiencies in this book, although they can certainly take credit for making it a better book.

I also owe a sincere thank-you to my friend Mark Sweeney, Corporate Vice-president of Scripture Press Publications and Publisher of Victor Books. Mark often discussed the book with me and encouraged me during the difficult process of writing it, and I'm grateful. Some publishers don't seem to know what authors go through, but Mark is an exception. Thanks too to Robert Hosack who oversaw the editing of the manuscript and gave me many valuable suggestions.

Our pastor son David W. Wiersbe read the manuscript carefully and gave me many excellent suggestions. I find that as I get older, I need to keep in touch with the ideas and insights of the younger generation of preachers; David has helped me do that. I'm also grateful for the help given by other friends who read the manuscript and graciously shared their suggestions.

Let me add one word of caution: if you're tempted to skip Parts I and II and dive immediately into the "practical discussion" in Part III, don't yield to temptation. It's important that you get the theoretical and biblical foundation first; so keep reading, and you will see that all of the text relates to what we're all seeking: more effective communication of the Word of God.

I'm only too conscious of the shortcomings of this book. But if what I've written helps you strive toward preparing and preaching more effective sermons, then it has been worth it all.

Warren W. Wiersbe

Part One
Imagination and Life

"... the imagination is one of the
essential ministries in nurturing the life of faith."

—Eugene Peterson

"Many a promising sermon is stultified
because it is woven of concepts
rather than of pictures. . . ."

—George A. Buttrick

"God was pleased through the foolishness
of what was preached to save those who believe."

—1 Cor. 1:21

Chapter One
The Tale of Two Preachers

Delivering God's message is serious business. In fact, it could be a matter of life or death. Consider with me two men who used two different approaches in communicating their messages and in doing so witnessed two different results. The message from the first speaker was rejected, and he went out and committed suicide. The message from the second speaker was accepted, and he helped to suppress a rebellion and save the life of a king.

This fascinating story is found in 2 Samuel 17. King David had been forced out of Jerusalem by his son Absalom who now possessed his father's throne, his father's wives, and the leadership of all of his father's army. But in the wake of all this unbridled success, Absalom had a serious problem: what should he do about his father who had fled into the wilderness to escape?

He turned for help to his trusted counselor Ahithophel, whose reply was:

> I would choose twelve thousand men and set out tonight in pursuit of David. I would attack him while he is weary and weak. I would strike him with terror, and then all the people with him will flee. I would strike down only the king and bring all the people back to you. The death of the man you seek will mean the return of all; all the people will be unharmed (2 Sam. 17:1-3).

Absalom and his advisers liked the plan and, had they followed it, they probably would have routed David and his forces and put down all opposition. But Absalom wanted to hear Hushai's counsel as well. Hushai, of course, was on David's side; and David had prayed that God would turn Ahithophel's counsel into foolishness (15:31). This is what Hushai said.

> The advice Ahithophel has given is not good this time. You know your father and his men; they are fighters, and as fierce as a wild bear robbed of her cubs. Besides, your father is an experienced fighter; he will not spend the night with the troops. Even now, he is hidden in a cave or some other place. If he should attack your troops first, whoever hears about it will say, "There has been a slaughter among the troops who follow Absalom." Then even the bravest soldier, whose heart is like the heart of a lion, will melt with fear, for all Israel knows that your father is a fighter and that those with him are brave.
>
> So I advise you: Let all Israel, from Dan to Beersheba — as numerous as the sand on the seashore — be gathered to you, with you yourself leading them into battle. Then we will attack him wherever he may be found, and we will fall on him as dew settles on the ground. Neither he nor any of his men will be left alive. If he withdraws into a city, then all Israel will bring ropes to that city, and we will drag it down to the valley until not even a piece of it can be found (2 Sam. 17:7-13).

After hearing Hushai's plan, Absalom and the elders changed their minds; *and humanly speaking, this is what saved David's life.* To be sure, it was the Lord who changed Absalom's mind (v. 14; Prov. 21:1). But the same God who ordains *the end* also ordains *the means* to the end. In this case, the means to the end — convincing Absalom not to accept Ahithophel's plan — was the speech that Hushai made.

Read the two speeches again and notice the two different approaches. Apart from the fact that Hushai's speech is three times longer than Ahithophel's (and for a good reason), the

16

contrast between the two approaches is obvious. In modern terms, Ahithophel used a cerebral "left brain" approach and Hushai, a visceral "right brain" approach. Absalom *heard* what Ahithophel was saying, but he *saw* and *felt* what Hushai was saying. Ahithophel's counsel was wise, but it was rejected, and this led to his humiliation and death. Hushai's counsel was weak in military strategy, but it was accepted and led to Absalom's defeat.

"If we have learned anything else," wrote Norman Cousins in his book *Human Options,* "it is that the ideas of the poets and artists penetrate where everything else has failed."[1] The movers and shakers in history have usually been people like Hushai who can turn people's ears into eyes so that they see and feel the message and respond positively to it. In the United States in the '60s, the folk songs of the "flower people" probably did more to influence government policy about Vietnam and civil rights than did all the speeches given in Congress. Why? Because, like Hushai's speech, these songs painted pictures and stirred the imagination. Songs such as "Where Have All the Flowers Gone?" and "Blowin' in the Wind" affected more people in a deeper way than did press releases from the White House.

I realize that "right brain" and "left brain" are popular terms used to describe a phenomenon that isn't totally accepted by everybody in the scientific community. Nevertheless, using these terms is helpful in discussing recognized human approaches and behaviors. Physiologists and psychologists tell us that, generally speaking, each half of the brain performs specific functions, although these functions are not monopolized by that half of the brain. The "right brain" specializes in things creative, such as artistic patterns and shapes, the writing of poetry and the painting of pictures; while the "left brain" deals with things cognitive and logical, such as language and numbers and scientific concepts. Musicians and artists would especially use their right brain, while scientists and architects would lean heavily on the left brain.[2]

Read Ahithophel's speech again and notice the "left-brain" flavor. Four times he says "I would" and focuses attention on himself as an authority figure. He presents a logical plan for killing the king and capturing the people, a plan that probably would have worked. But listening to his plan is like reading the road map when you'd rather be looking at the scenery. *Like some of our preaching today, Ahithophel's speech has authority, precision, logic, and wisdom, but it doesn't have what it takes to make people see and feel the message and want to obey it.*

Now consider Hushai's speech. To begin with, the emphasis is on the listener, not the speaker. Hushai spoke to Absalom personally and wasn't afraid to say "you" or "your." At the close of his speech, he used the pronoun "we" so that Absalom got the feeling that "all Israel" was behind him. Hushai enabled Absalom to picture himself at the head of the victorious army. "Let all Israel . . . be gathered to you, with you yourself leading them into battle." What did Absalom know about leading an army? Probably very little. But Hushai convinced him he could do it and, in his imagination, Absalom had already won the victory.

Hushai used words to paint pictures. Look at the similes and metaphors he used: "as fierce as a wild bear robbed of her cubs"; "whose heart is like the heart of a lion"; "melt with fear"; "as numerous as the sand on the seashore"; "as dew settles on the ground." These are expressions that turned Absalom's ears into eyes so that he could see what Hushai was saying. I especially like the images of the sand (v. 11) and the dew (v. 12). When Absalom imagined the sand on the seashore, it gave him a false sense of security, and the image of the falling dew made the whole enterprise look easy.

Hushai's *coup de grace* was his description of Absalom supervising the destruction of David's city of refuge, dragging every stone into the valley. By the time Hushai had finished his speech, Absalom had turned his left brain off and his right brain to "high" and had already crowned himself the conquering hero.

I mentioned earlier that there was a good reason why Hushai's speech was longer than Ahithophel's. Remember Sgt. Joe Friday of the popular "Dragnet" radio and TV series?

18

Remember his famous saying, "Just the facts, ma'am, just the facts"? Well, Ahithophel followed that line of thinking: "Here's the plan. It's logical. It will work. Now, get with it!" In police work, I suppose, Sgt. Friday's approach is the best; but it isn't the best way to prepare and deliver a sermon.[3]

It takes time to paint pictures. It takes time for our listeners to see those pictures and in their imagination place themselves in the scene. I can't prove it from the text, but I get the impression that Hushai spoke deliberately, pausing to let each simile sink in. When he got to that last sentence, he saw Absalom smile and nod his head as the usurper visualized himself leading the army of Israel and defeating Israel's greatest soldier.

I fear that too many of us who speak professionally—and this includes schoolteachers, politicians, and university lecturers as well as preachers—have the wrong idea of what it means to deliver a message. Too often we are guilty of unconsciously accepting what Michael J. Reddy calls "the conduit metaphor." We envision ourselves as fountains of knowledge and our listeners as empty receptacles ready to receive what we know. As we speak, our words are supposed to build an invisible conduit between us and our listeners, so the information we have automatically moves from one mind to the other, and communication is successful. To "conduit speakers," thoughts are "things" that are "contained" in "words" and transferred to "minds" by the spoken word. Dr. Reddy summarizes this viewpoint by saying that "language functions like a conduit, transferring thoughts bodily from one person to another."[4]

This approach to preaching is more prevalent than most of us realize. You accepted "the conduit metaphor" the last time you said to a congregation or a class, "I hope this doesn't go over your head!" Statements such as "I trust this idea is coming across" or "Let me drop this thought into your mind" are also wedded to the "conduit" approach to communication, the approach that Ahithophel used to his own destruction.

If you don't respond to the picture of a sermon as a "conduit," try seeing your sermons as "conveyor belts." You study hard all week, do your exegesis, apply all the rules of hermeneutics, and come up with a lot of helpful biblical materi-

19

al that you want your congregation to know. You organize it on your homiletical "conveyor belt" and, as soon as the choir finishes its anthem, you throw the switch and start the belt moving. All of this marvelous material passes from the pulpit to the pew and the worshipers are supposed to pick it up and make it their own. *But it just doesn't work that way.*

During a question-and-answer session at a pastors' conference, one of the pastors suddenly stood to his feet, marched down the center aisle of the auditorium, arrived at the microphone, took a deep breath, and said: "My preaching sounds like a commentary! I'm dull! I have all the biblical facts but there's no life! What should I do?" It was the "conduit/conveyor" error all over again. My distraught preacher friend needed to discover that an outline is no more a message than a menu is a meal or a road map is a journey.

What did Hushai know that we need to know? That is what we will look at next.

"A theologian takes God seriously. . . .
A poet takes words seriously. . . . .
A pastor takes actual persons seriously. . . ."

—Eugene Peterson

"Do you know what makes man the most suffering of all
creatures? It is that he has one foot in the finite
and the other in the infinite,
and that he is torn between two worlds."

—Anonymous

Chapter Two
What Hushai Knew: People

Hushai knew some basic truths about three important areas of life: people, the world, and words. Because he knew these truths and applied them, he was able to outmaneuver both Ahithophel and Absalom. Hushai was an effective communicator.

What did Hushai know about people? He knew that people think in pictures and respond with their hearts as well as their heads. He would have agreed with Pascal's famous statement, "The heart has its reasons which reason does not know."[1]

What did Hushai know about the world? That the world is a vast theater, always presenting to us the drama of truth that makes it possible for us to learn and teach. In this, Hushai agreed with David, who wrote: "The heavens declare the glory of God; the skies proclaim the work of his hands" (Ps. 19:1).

What did Hushai know about words? That words began as pictures, and that language is metaphorical and helps to build the bridge between the world around us and the world within us. Here Hushai was in full agreement with the prophets, the psalmists, the apostles, and our Lord Himself, all of whom used word pictures to help us see spiritual truth.

Understanding and applying these three truths helps to make possible the miracle that we call *communication*. Somewhere, columnist Sidney J. Harris wrote, "The two words 'information' and 'communication' are often used interchangeably, but they signify quite different things. Information is giving out; communication is getting through." Ahithophel gave out, but Hushai got through. Ahithophel manufactured a conduit, but Hushai painted a picture.

The Mind—Our Inner Picture Gallery

Ponder this fact: *we think in pictures even though we speak and write with words.* In his book *The Human Situation*, W. Macneile Dixon wrote:

> If I were asked what has been the most powerful force in the making of history, you would probably judge me of unbalanced mind were I to answer, as I should have to answer, metaphor, figurative expression. It is by imagination that men have lived; imagination rules all our lives. The human mind is not, as philosophers would have you think, a debating hall, but a picture gallery. Around it hang our similes, our concepts. . . . Metaphor is the essence of religion and poetry.[2]

Especially lay hold of that one statement: "The human mind is not . . . a debating hall, but a picture gallery." This doesn't mean that we avoid arranging our thoughts in a logical manner in order to reason with people. After all, Paul did admonish us to do all things "in a fitting and orderly way" (1 Cor. 14:40). It simply means that reasoning alone—talking to the left brain—will not always accomplish our purpose.

God gave each of us an imagination—the picture gallery of the mind—and He expects us to use it. "It is by imagination that men have lived," said Dixon; "imagination rules all our lives." In fact, Napoleon said that "imagination governs the world." Because many preachers (and some who teach preachers) have forgotten that basic fact, hermeneutics has become analyzing, homiletics has become organizing, and preaching has become catechizing. The sermon is a logical outline, a lecture buttressed with theology, that majors on explanation and application but ignores visualization. *We have forgotten that the bridge between the mind and the will is the imagination, and that truth isn't really learned until it's internalized.* "The purpose of preaching," wrote Halford Luccock, "is not to make people see reasons, but visions."[3]

Needed — A Healthy Imagination

Imagination is the image-making faculty in your mind, the picture gallery in which you are constantly painting, sculpting, designing, and sometimes erasing. "God is the Supreme artist," Clyde S. Kilby reminds us[4]; and since we are made in the image of God, we share in His creative ability. That creative gift resides for the most part in the imagination.

Dwight E. Stevenson defines imagination as "the capacity to see old and familiar things in new associations from new perspectives, to combine things not previously put together."[5] Leland Ryken says, "The imagination is the human faculty that allows us to create something new, to see or feel something familiar in a fresh way, to express an old truth in a new manner, to make a new application of truth to life."[6]

Recalling, perceiving, and *combining* seem to be the major functions of the imagination, and they add up to *creating*. "The *Imagination* is one of the highest prerogatives of man," wrote Charles Darwin. "By this faculty he unites former images and ideas, independently of the will, and thus creates brilliant and novel results."[7] The house you live in, the chair you're sitting on, the car you drive, the book you're now reading, and the computer on which it was written, were all first of all "born" in somebody's imagination.

Imagination is a womb that is impregnated with the old so that it might give birth to the new. It is the bridge that links the world around you with the world within you. It's also one of the bridges between your right brain and your left brain, so that *vision* has *supervision* and doesn't become just *visionary*.

> **Imagination is the image-making faculty in your mind, the picture gallery in which you are constantly painting, sculpting, designing, and sometimes erasing.**

As the French moralist Joseph Joubert said, "He who has imagination but no knowledge has wings but no feet."

Very often when you start to talk about the imagination, orthodox Christians start to get nervous.[8] This fear arises because many fine Christian people are prone to confuse *imagination* with *the imaginary,* what I call *fancy.* They don't want their preacher dabbling in daydreams, illusions, and whimsy. After all, Paul warned preachers, "Have nothing to do with godless myths and old wives' tales" (1 Tim. 4:7); and the admonition is, "Preach the Word" (2 Tim. 4:2).

Fancy—the imaginary—is only one product of the imagination, and we must have great respect for people such as Walt Disney and J.R.R. Tolkien who can invent whole new universes to the delight and entertainment of the world. But there's a vast difference between imagination and fancy. Imagination helps us penetrate reality and better understand it, while fancy helps us temporarily escape reality and better endure it. Fancy builds an alternate world (Middle Earth, Lilliput, Oz), usually related in some recognizable way to the real world; but imagination sees a deeper world right where we are.[9] Samuel Johnson was right when he wrote to Boswell back in 1774, "We may take Fancy for a companion, but we must follow Reason as our guide."[10]

C.S. Lewis wrote: "For me, reason is the natural organ of truth; but imagination is the organ of meaning. Imagination, producing new metaphors or revivifying old, is not the cause of truth, but its condition."[11] In other words, a healthy imagination is essential if we ever hope to understand how one truth relates to another and how both of them relate to life. It takes more than a dictionary and a grammar to grasp the message of *King Lear* or "Tintern Abbey," and it takes more than a set of Kittel's *Theological Dictionary of the New Testament* and a copy of Robertson's *Shorter Greek Grammar* to see meaning in the exciting images shared by John in the Book of Revelation.

Some Christians have a second mistaken idea about imagination, an idea that usually shows up in books on "how to improve your preaching" or "how to be more creative in the ministry." The idea is that God gave us imagination only so that

26

we can embellish things and appear clever. The emphasis is on thinking up striking sermon titles, finding arresting illustrations, and developing unusual outlines. The approach is purely cosmetic. It sees imagination as skill in decorating the cake with no thought given to improving the recipe. Imagination in preaching is not a new technique to be learned but a radical new attitude and outlook to be cultivated. If in reading this book, you're hoping to find six easy steps toward more imaginative preaching, now is the time to stop reading because you're only wasting your time.

Why is it important that you cultivate a healthy imagination and, guided by the Spirit of God, use it in your ministry? This effort results in essential benefits for you as a human being, for your ministry, and for the people to whom you minister.

Let's begin with what a healthy imagination means to you personally as a human being. You were created in the image of God, created by an imaginative God who is infinitely original. You were created to assist Him in caring for His creation and in building His church. You were created to enjoy all that God's artistic mind has conceived and His powerful hands have made. You were created to cultivate your inner person—including your imagination—and use all that you are to the glory of God.

Christians who ignore or neglect the cultivating of their imagination can't enter into the full enjoyment of all that God has for them. A sanctified imagination opens the door to so much that is beautiful and enriching that it's a pity more believers don't realize what they are missing and do something about it. Horace Bushnell said, "God gave man imagination that He might have a door to enter by."[12] The English poet and mystic Thomas Traherne wrote in his book *Centuries of Meditations,* "For God hath made you able to create worlds in your own mind which are more precious to Him than those which He created."[13] Our thoughts of Him, our meditations on His Word, our seasons of prayer—all are related to the imagination and can help us grow in grace. Remember, I'm referring to *imagination* and not *fancy;* for entertaining fanciful thoughts about God is just as idolatrous as making an image of God and bowing before it.

The imagination must be fed just as the mind and heart must be fed. William Temple defined "worship" as "the quickening of conscience by His holiness; the nourishment of mind with His truth; *the purifying of imagination by His beauty;* the opening of the heart to His love; the surrender of will to His purpose...."[14] The imagination must be captivated by the beauty of God as revealed in the Word of God. If not, it will be captivated by some lesser beauty; and this is the first step toward idolatry.

Even if you and I were not in the ministry, we would still need to cultivate the imagination in order to be full and complete human beings, created in the image of God. But because we are in ministry, we have an even greater reason for opening the imagination to God's truth and beauty: we must communicate God's truth to others, and we can't do this effectively unless we understand the important part imagination plays in all that we do. Once again, we see the choice between the approach of Ahithophel and the approach of Hushai.

Consider this matter of Bible study. "The Bible is, in the finest sense, the most imaginative book ever written," said Clyde S. Kilby.[15] People who study the Word of God with only a left-brain outlook will miss much of what this marvelous Book has to say. They will be like those people in the Gospel of John who couldn't understand the spiritual language Jesus used because they lacked imagination: When Jesus spoke about His resurrection, the Jews thought He was talking about rebuilding the temple (John 2:19-21); Nicodemus was perplexed when Jesus spoke about a new birth (3:1-12); the Samaritan woman wondered where He would get the water He was offering her (4:1-15); the disciples didn't understand what kind of food He ate (4:31-33); and the Jewish crowd was offended when He told them to eat His flesh and drink His blood (6:52-59).[16] These and other examples demonstrate that it takes more than left-brain exegesis and analysis, important as they are, to open up the treasures of the Bible. Said R.W. Dale, "There is hardly a page of Holy Scripture which will not become more intelligible to us if we read it with an active imagination."[17]

Now, the frightening thing is this: very few current books

written about hermeneutics and exegesis even mention the imagination. They explain how to approach the figurative language of the Bible and how to deal with types and symbols, but they fail to explain the important part the imagination plays in *pulling the whole thing together so that we can see what the writer is saying.* To quote Halford Luccock again:

> The tragedy often is that the more a man studies, the worse he gets; his mind becomes subdued to what he works in, and the textbook style of language hardens on him like a shell. He becomes a literary and vocal crustacean. The preacher who is too busy to read poetry, fiction, drama and the naturalists is too busy. While he is busy here or there with Kant or John Dewey or Karl Barth or Karl Marx or other Olympians, the opportunity of speaking for God to people in their native tongue is gone.[18]

We find all kinds of literature in the Bible — narrative, poetry, proverbs, riddles, songs, parables, symbols, drama, paradoxes, epigrams — and these various *genre* must be recognized and approached in the right spirit if we hope to discover their treasures. We don't deal with the imagery of Psalm 23 as we do the theology of Romans 8.[19] Blessed is that Bible student who comes to God's Word with an open mind, a loving heart, a submissive will, *and a sensitive imagination.* I agree with A.J. Gossip: "Of all possessions, few are more serviceable to the preacher than a wise and schooled imagination."[20] And Henry Ward Beecher told the preachers at Yale that "the first element on which your preaching will largely depend for power and success, you will probably be surprised to learn, is *Imagination,* which I regard as the most important of all the elements that go to make the preacher."[21]

Imagination and Pastoring

So, we need imagination to study the Bible accurately and be able to enter into its message sympathetically. We also need imagination to build a bridge between that ancient Book and the needs of people today. Our preaching must be in the present tense so that we're not just lecturing to our people about what happened to Noah, David, and Paul. Harry Emerson Fosdick's wry comment is still true—that nobody ever goes to church to find out what happened to the Hittites.

I've often recommended to ministerial students what I will now recommend to you: after you have prepared the sermon, carefully review it and bravely ask yourself, "So what?" Imagine your congregation before you—the executive who just lost his job, the teenager struggling against peer pressure, the young mother worried about her child's illness, the single parent trying to balance the budget, and just about everybody fighting temptation and some besetting sin—and see if what you're planning to share with them will mean anything to them. *Imagine yourself in their situation, responding to what you are saying.* Anticipate their objections, their misunderstandings of your words, their hidden defenses, and then prepare for them.[22] On more than one occasion, when I have examined a sermon in this way, I have ended up scrapping the entire sermon and starting over again; and I should have done so more often.

This is where pastoral work comes in—getting to know your people, how they think, what they need, and what they want God to do in their lives. With the emphasis today on the megachurch and the minister as CEO, the very mention of pastoral ministry, except for counseling, makes some people smile and automatically relegate you to the age of the ministerial dinosaur. When I was in seminary, the professors assured us that "a home-going pastor makes for a church-going people." That may not be as true today as it was in the '40s and '50s, but I do know this: a pastor with a shepherd's heart and a healthy imagination, one who knows his sheep and loves them, will do a better job communicating God's love and truth than the ivory-tower executive who, unlike Jesus Christ, has no time for people. Churches grow when people care, and that caring has to be modeled by the pastor, personally and from the pulpit.

Hushai knew people. He knew that Absalom's mind was a picture gallery, not a debating chamber; so he spoke to him about wild bears, lions, the sand on the seashore, the dew settling, and a city being destroyed. Hushai knew that *the imagination of every man and woman has an appetite and must be fed*. Many of the people who attend church today have starved imaginations for one reason or another, and they can never have healthy imaginations unless they change their diets.

In a later chapter, I will deal with the tragedy of starved imaginations and what the church must do about it. But now we move to the second thing Hushai knew: he knew the world around him.

"A rock pile ceases to be a rock pile
the moment a single man contemplates it,
bearing within him the image of a cathedral."

—Antoine de Saint-Exupéry

"Learn to associate ideas worthy of God
with all that happens in Nature—
the sunrises and the sunsets,
the sun and the stars, the changing seasons,
and your imagination will never be at the
mercy of your impulses,
but will always be at the service of God."

—Oswald Chambers

Chapter Three
What Hushai Knew:
The World around Him

Hushai hung some pictures in the gallery of Absalom's mind, pictures taken from the world that both of them knew personally. It was a world in which she-bears protected their cubs and roaring lions fought courageously, a world in which nobody could number the sand grains on the seashore or hear the dew fall on the grass. Hushai didn't invent a new world (fantasy); he simply used the world that he and Absalom already knew (imagination); and that's how Hushai won the battle. John Calvin called creation "the book of the unlearned."[1] The person unable to read a printed book can learn much from studying the heavens and the earth and how God works in His creation. In his *Institutes,* Calvin calls God's creation "a dazzling theater," "a most glorious theater," and "this magnificent theater of heaven and earth."[2] Along with David, Calvin believed that the heaven and earth declare the glory of God.

God has so arranged things that there is a connection between the facts of the natural world and the *truths* of the spiritual world. Ralph Waldo Emerson rejected Calvinism, but he would have agreed with Calvin's view of nature as the "theater of God." Emerson wrote in his seminal book *Nature,* "The world is emblematic. Parts of speech are metaphors because the whole of nature is a metaphor of the human mind."[3] In his "Divinity School Address," given at Harvard in 1838, Emerson boldly announced: "I once heard a preacher who sorely tempted me to say I would go to church no more. . . . A snow storm was falling around us. The snow storm was real, the preacher merely spectral, and the eye felt the sad contrast in looking at him, and then out of the window behind him into the beautiful metaphor of the snow."[4]

In a profound sermon based on Deuteronomy 29:29, Campbell Morgan says this about the relationship of the natural world to God's truth and His nature:

> Have you ever noticed that in our Lord's teaching He made use of figures and symbols, but never hinted that the figure was the fact? He always gives us to understand that, after all, the things seen are only symbols of something else. Let me give you an illustration. He says, "I am the true Vine." Now, we make a mistake if we say that Jesus borrowed the figure of the vine to teach us what He is. The deeper truth is this. God planted the vine in the world and let it grow through the centuries on the pattern of the infinite Christ.[5]

In the Incarnation, God announced that matter is not evil and that He would use material things as vehicles for revealing Himself and His truth. Christians take a sacramental view of nature, not a Gnostic view. The Gnostic philosophy is that matter is evil; and the closer you get to the spiritual, the farther you move from the material. The Christian philosophy, however, is that matter is not evil but a gift from God for our benefit and our learning; and the closer you get to God, the more you see His hand in the world around you. The Gnostic sees only tree branches waving in the wind, but the Christian sees "the trees of the field clapping their hands" (see Isa. 55:12).

Unfortunately, the Gnostic view of nature has crept into our thinking. We no longer sincerely sing "This Is My Father's World" because the world is wicked and under the condemnation of God, and we must be separated from it. We think that the poet Gerard Manley Hopkins is a bit odd when he shouts, "The world is charged with the grandeur of God!" or when he chuckles and writes, "Glory be to God for dappled things!"

34

On Sunday morning, July 25, 1858, Charles Haddon Spurgeon read an unusual text to his London congregation: "I have multiplied visions, and used similitudes" (Hosea 12:10, KJV). He then preached what I think is one of his most creative sermons, pointing out that "God is every day preaching to us by similitudes. The things which we see about us are God's thoughts and God's words to us; and if we were but wise there is not a step that we take, which we should not find to be full of mighty instruction."[6] He then expounded this truth by applying it to four areas of life: God speaks to us *every day*, in *every season* of the year, in *every place* and in *every calling*. Interestingly, Spurgeon's friend and fellow Londoner Joseph Parker said to his City Temple congregation some years later, "The whole year, from spring to winter, is a long parable, a curious symbol, a marvelous revelation of divine purpose; he that hath eyes to see, let him see; he that hath ears to hear, let him hear."[7]

Every Bible reader knows that Jesus used images from the visible world to teach truths about the invisible world. As a master teacher, He followed the principle of starting with the known and moving to the unknown, but His use of natural images meant more than that. Our Lord not only saw God's truth revealed all around Him, but He touched the common things of life and sanctified them: bread and wine, water, seeds, yeast, vines, birth, lamps, dogs, sparrows, cups, coins, even crosses. Our Lord had a sacramental view of nature and could joyfully have sung, "This Is My Father's World." The world in which Jesus lived was "charged with the grandeur of God."

In our noble attempt to be biblical preachers, we have so emphasized the analytical that we've forgotten the poetic. We see the trees waving their branches, but we hold the branches still, examine them scientifically, leaf and twig, and all the while fail to hear the trees clapping their hands at the glory of God.

In our noble attempt to be biblical preachers, we have so emphasized the analytical that we've forgotten the poetic. We see the trees waving their branches, but we hold the branches still, examine them scientifically, leaf and twig, and all the while fail to hear the trees clapping their hands at the glory of God. To preach biblically means much more than to preach the truth of the Bible accurately. It also means *to present that truth the way the biblical writers and speakers presented it, and that means addressing the imagination.* Both the world around us and the Word of God before us are "charged with the grandeur of God," but too often we fail to bring them together and take them into the pulpit. Like Ahithophel, we put our dry facts into the conduit and then wonder why nothing happens when we preach.

Imagination and Spiritual Vision

In one of his finest essays, "The Value of Sanctified Imagination," A.W. Tozer wrote:

> The value of the cleansed imagination in the sphere of religion lies in its power to perceive in natural things shadows of things spiritual. It enables the reverent man to "See the world in a grain of sand. . . . And eternity in an hour."
>
> The weakness of the Pharisee in days of old was his lack of imagination, or what amounted to the same thing, his refusal to let it enter the field of religion. He saw the text with its carefully guarded theological definition and he saw nothing beyond. "A primrose by the river's brim/A yellow primrose was to him/And it was nothing more."
>
> When Christ came with His blazing spiritual penetration and His fine moral sensitivity, He appeared to the Pharisee to be a devotee of another kind of religion, which indeed He was if the world had only understood. He could see the soul of the text while the Pharisee could see only the body, and he could always prove Christ wrong by an appeal to the letter of the law or to an interpretation hallowed by tradition.

I long to see the imagination released from its prison and given to its proper place among the sons of the new creation. What I am trying to describe here is the sacred gift of seeing, the ability to peer beyond the veil and gaze with astonished wonder upon the beauties and mysteries of things holy and eternal.[8]

As Halford Luccock reminded us in chapter 2, the purpose of preaching "is not to make people see reasons, but visions."[9]

In his essay, Dr. Tozer quoted from two poets who were trailblazers in breaking the shackles of tradition and using words to unveil pictures. The first quotation is from the opening four lines of "Auguries of Innocence" by William Blake (1757–1827), and the complete opening stanza reads like this:

To see a World in a Grain of Sand
And a Heaven in a Wild Flower,
Hold Infinity in the palm of your hand
And Eternity in an hour.

The poem goes on for 128 more lines to survey the "inner meaning" of animals, birds, plants, people, and various miscellaneous things that we all take for granted. Like Emerson, Blake had little to do with organized religion; and, also like Emerson, Blake opposed the "system makers" whose definitions and formulas analyzed everything to death and turned God's beautiful world into a laboratory.

In a letter written in 1803, Blake said, "May God us keep from single vision and Newton's sleep." The "single vision" was the scientific approach to life as personified by Isaac Newton, the great mathematician and physicist whose formulas explained everything in the universe. But Newton put people to sleep with a false confidence—because of Newton's formulas, men and women were convinced that they understood the world and could manipulate it as they pleased. If Blake were living today, he would rejoice to learn that Newton's formulas are no longer the last word in physics.[10]

Tozer's second quotation comes from the poem "Peter Bell"

by William Wordsworth (1770–1850). You may recall from your days in English Literature 101 that Wordsworth and his friend Coleridge were part of what the textbooks call "the romantic era" in literature. Of course, the word "romantic" has nothing to do with Hollywood movies, daytime TV serials, or garish paperback novels. The writing in the "romantic era" was a right-brain reaction against "the enlightenment" with its left-brain emphasis on science, logic, authority, and formulas. The romantic writers claimed that truth was something to *experience* as well as to *explain,* and in this they antedated the existentialists. The romantic writers felt that to explain nature but not experience it was to rob it of its power and beauty. They agreed with Blake that there's more to the world than Newtonian mechanics and the logic of Kant and Locke.

Along with "Peter Bell," many of Wordsworth's poems were a call to a sensuous (not sensual) experience of nature, something that just can't be found in books. "The Tables Turned" is one of my favorites.

Up! up! my Friend, and quit your books;
Or surely you'll grow double:
Up! up! my Friend, and clear your looks;
Why all this toil and trouble?
The sun, above the mountain's head,
A freshening lustre mellow
Through all the long green fields has spread,
His first sweet evening yellow.
Books! 'tis a dull and endless strife:
Come, hear the woodland linnet,
How sweet his music! on my life,
There's more of wisdom in it.
And hark! how blythe the throstle sings!
He, too, is no mean preacher:
Come forth into the light of things,
Let Nature be your teacher.
She has a world of ready wealth,
Our minds and hearts to bless—
Spontaneous wisdom breathed by health,

Truth breathed by cheerfulness.
One impulse from a vernal wood
May teach you more of man,
Of moral evil and of good,
Than all the sages can.
Sweet is the lore which Nature brings;
Our meddling intellect
Mis-shapes the beauteous forms of things: —
We murder to dissect.

"We murder to dissect." What a line — and what an indictment! I must confess that I've been guilty many times of treating the Bible the way Wordsworth's bookish student treated nature. Instead of allowing the living words of Scripture to express themselves in their own natural way, I've taken them apart and organized them so severely that my "meddling intellect" has mangled the text and robbed it of its beauty and its power.

This isn't a plea for the abandonment of an intelligent and reverent critical study of the Scriptures, using all the helps we can get. I'll have more to say about this later, but I want to assure any troubled seminary professors reading this book that I do not in any way advocate eliminating biblical languages, exegesis, hermeneutics, or homiletics from the curriculum. *I'm only asking that we include something that's been left out for too long: the proper use of a sanctified imagination in the study and preaching of the Word of God.* It's important to know the Book and books, but it's also important to know the book of nature and the book of human nature if we hope to penetrate the picture gallery of the human mind with the truth of God's Word.

Hushai knew *people* and *the world around him.* But he also knew *words,* those mysterious sounds and symbols that convey meanings and powerfully influence what people think and do. We now turn our attention to *words.*

"In the beginning was the Word,
and the Word was with God,
and the word was God."

—John 1:1

"[The Bible's] most customary way of expressing
God's truth is not the sermon or theological outline
but the story, the poem, the vision, and the letter,
all of them literary forms and products of the imagination."

—Leland Ryken

"Words are the physicians of a mind diseased."

—Aeschylus

Chapter Four
What Hushai Knew: Words

Inescapably, preaching is a work of metaphor."[1] David Buttrick says this in *Homiletic: Moves and Structures,* one of the most creative books on preaching that's been published since H. Grady Davis' *Design for Preaching.*[2] Buttrick goes on to say, "Theological meaning must always be embodied in images drawn from life."[3] Hushai had never read Buttrick's book, but he followed Buttrick's principles. That's why he talked to Absalom about bears, lions, sand, and dew. Ahithophel expressed only concepts while Hushai presented his concepts in *images.*

Theologian Sallie McFague writes: "Images 'feed' concepts; concepts 'discipline' images. Images without concepts are blind; concepts without images are sterile."[4] I suggest you read that statement again, ponder it, and then think about Ahithophel and Hushai. Ahithophel presented concepts without images, so his words were sterile. They failed to give birth to life-changing pictures in Absalom's mind. Hushai, on the other hand, combined concepts and images and won the contest.

One of the bridges between the world around us and the world within us is a system of symbols that we call language; and language is basically metaphorical. It communicates in *pictures.* God's creation is a theater and the human mind is a picture gallery, and we link the two by using *words.*

"Every word which is used to express a moral or intellectual fact, if traced to its root, is found to be borrowed from some

41

material appearance," wrote Emerson in *Nature.* The word *right,* he points out, originated from *straight* (Latin, *rectus*); and *wrong* came from a root meaning "twisted" (from *wrong* to *wring* [twist]). He reminds us that the word *supercilious* is Latin for "raising the eyebrows," something that haughty people are prone to do when they disapprove of something.[5]

"Metaphor is a primary way in which we accommodate and assimilate information and experience to our conceptual organization of the world," writes philosopher Eva Feder Kittay. "In particular, it is the primary way we accommodate new experience. Hence it is at the source of our capacity to learn and at the center of our creative thought."[6] Since preachers want their people to learn, to think, and to have new and maturing experiences, they had better get acquainted with this thing called *metaphor.*

Metaphor—the Way Language Works

Today we have an exploding literature on metaphor. When you start reading it, you soon discover that linguists and philosophers don't always agree on what constitutes a metaphor or how a metaphor actually works. But the linguists and philosophers seem to agree that the word *metaphor* comes from the two Greek words *meta* (trans, across) and *pherein* (to carry), and that together they mean "to carry across, to transfer." A metaphor is a "verbal transfer" that connects two seemingly unrelated things and creates from this union something new.

> **It's by using metaphorical language that you turn people's ears into eyes and help them see the truth. The task of the preacher is not unlike the task of the writer.**

One scholar defines a metaphor as "a figure of speech whereby we speak about one thing in terms which are seen to be suggestive of another."[7] When Isaiah cried, "All flesh is grass!" he was using a metaphor and was inviting his listeners to ponder seriously the relationship between grass and people. Jesus spoke metaphorically when He said, "The seed is the word of God." His listeners knew what seeds were, but did they know the relationship between seeds and God's Word?

It's by using metaphorical language that you turn people's ears into eyes and help them see the truth. The task of the preacher is not unlike the task of the writer. Novelist Joseph Conrad said, "My task . . . is, by the power of the written word to make you hear, to make you feel—it is, before all, to make you see."[8] However, using metaphors means much more than following the principles of wise pedagogy and going from the known to the unknown. Metaphor is not simply a "function" of language; metaphor is the way language works. We don't use similes and metaphors to "embellish" our speech and impress people, the way eighteenth-century Britons put lace on their clothes and silver buckles on their shoes. Many scholars believe that metaphor is the fundamental way language is structured and that we use metaphorical expressions as we communicate simply because language is made that way. Like the man in Moliere's play who discovered he'd been speaking prose for forty years, we've been speaking metaphorically all our lives and perhaps didn't realize it.[9]

In their fascinating book *Metaphors We Live By*, Lakoff and Johnson give scores of examples of how metaphors are used in everyday speech.[10] For example, when people talk about "half-baked ideas" or "warmed-over theories," they're comparing ideas to food. Ideas are also plants, as in statements such as "The idea died on the vine" or "The idea finally came to fruition." "I've lived life to the fullest" pictures life as a container, as does "I can't cram one more activity into my life." Each of these statements involves metaphors, even though we don't always recognize them. Metaphor is so much a part of everyday speech that we take it for granted.

I've already introduced you to the "conduit metaphor," which unfortunately seems to govern so much of our preaching and teaching. Questions such as "Am I coming across?" or "Am I getting through?" betray the fact that the speaker has the "conduit metaphor" in mind as he or she speaks. Many seemingly tame statements are really metaphors that belong to the "conduit" category. For example: "What are you trying to get into my head?" "What he says doesn't carry much weight." "That idea flew right past me." "Words just keep pouring out of her!" "Stop throwing out so many new ideas!" These statements picture ideas as "things" that are dropped into the conduit of speech and "delivered" (we hope) to the people listening.

Get the point? (Ideas are also like swords or arrows!) Even in our everyday conversations, we use metaphorical language, because *language is metaphorical.* "All language originated in metaphor. Literal language is a pruning away and a rationalization of our figurative thought."[11]

As far back as the third century before the birth of Christ, the Greeks were discussing metaphor, and Aristotle wrote in his *Poetics:*

> It is a great thing, indeed, to make a proper use of these poetical forms, as also of compounds and strange words. But the greatest thing by far is to be a master of metaphor. It is the one thing that cannot be learned from others; and it is also a sign of genius, since a good metaphor implies an intuitive perception of the similarity in dissimilars.[12]

I agree with the great philosopher that we can't go to school and earn a master of metaphor degree; but I humbly disagree with him when he claims that the understanding and use of metaphors can't be learned. (The fact that Aristotle discussed metaphor in both his *Poetics* and his *Rhetoric* suggests that he may have made that statement tongue-in-cheek.) Certainly, with every ability there must be an accompanying intuition that turns the skill into an art; and education alone can't supply that intuition. But since metaphor involves the use of the imagination, and imagination is a part of the divine image in men and women, then all of us must have within us the basic materials to work with to develop metaphorical skills. Preachers of the Word especially need to focus on mastering metaphor, for that's the way language is made, the way people think, and the way the Bible was written.

44

The Power Is in Showing, Not Telling

When I was pastoring the Moody Church in Chicago, I received an invitation to speak to a high school social studies class about "the biblical view of sex ethics." It was a glorious opportunity, but I turned it into an embarrassing disaster by making two mistakes. First, I took the "conduit" approach and unloaded a lot of theological baggage on them, most of which stayed in the conduit and was never picked up by the students. My second mistake was in presenting my case through argument, aiming at the left-brain students while the right-brain students — the majority — folded their mental tents and silently stole away.

A better approach would have been to show the teenagers the biblical pictures of what happened to people who practiced sex outside the boundaries established by God. Proverbs 5 pictures sanctified sexual love as a beautiful stream of refreshing water, and sex outside of marriage as a sewer running in the streets.[13] Proverbs 6 reminds us that sex is like fire: beautiful and powerful when kept under control, but destructive when out of bounds (vv. 27-29). Proverbs 7 presents a vivid picture of a young man *turning into an animal* and going to the slaughter as he falls into the traps of the prostitute (vv. 22-27). Nathan's "ewe lamb" story to David (2 Sam. 12:1-6) makes the point that sex outside of marriage turns people into thieves, and they end up robbing both themselves and others.[14]

So, according to Scripture, when it comes to the matter of sex, everybody must choose either the stream or the sewer, warmth and power or burning destruction, the human or the animal, investment or robbery. If, instead of lecturing, I had shared these pictures with the students, I might have made the kind of impact that would have stayed with them and made a difference in their lives.

C.S. Lewis said, "All our truth, or all but a few fragments, is won by metaphor."[15] And H. Richard Niebuhr believed that "we are far more image-making and image-using creatures than we usually think ourselves to be and . . . our processes of perception and conception, of organizing and understanding the signs that come to us . . . are guided and formed by images in

45

our mind. Our languages, we are reminded, are symbolic systems."[16]

We have now reached a key question in our investigation: What is there about metaphorical language that gives it so much power? Contrary to popular belief, not every picture is worth a thousand words, but some words carry a dynamic that is greater than that of many pictures. When Sir Winston Churchill offered the people of Great Britain "blood, toil, tears, and sweat," why did they follow him instead of run him out of office? What is the secret, if there is one, of the power of metaphor?

Part of the answer is found, I think, in the fact that metaphors affect *the whole personality* and are not like routine concepts that touch only the mind. Metaphors challenge us and make us think. They arouse our curiosity and force us to adjust our perspective and try to see two things at one time. Then we have to figure out why the two things are put together when they are so different. Sallie McFague is right when she says that "good metaphors shock, they bring unlikes together, they upset conventions, they involve tension, and they are implicitly revolutionary."[17]

Notice the Puritan poet John Milton's use of this powerful device. When he received word that his friend Edward King had drowned in the Irish Sea, he wrote the elegy *Lycidas* in King's honor. In it, Milton wrestled with the problem of why a good man such as King died young while godless ministers lived long and prospered. He draws a vivid picture of the "false shepherds" of the seventeenth-century English church, calling them men who "for their bellies' sake creep and intrude, and climb into the fold," an obvious reference to John 10:1 and Philippians 3:19. But when, in line 119, Milton calls these false shepherds "blind mouths," we are immediately arrested. We stop and ask, "How can mouths be blind?" The metaphor has done its work![18]

I like Eva Kittay's statement that metaphors "rearrange the furniture of the mind."[19] When two seemingly contrary ideas such as "blindness" and "mouths" are brought together, the union creates a dynamic tension that excites the mind and arouses the emotions; and the will is held captive until the tension is either resolved or dismissed. The late physician-novelist Walker Percy wrote, "Metaphors are very strange because when you put two things together it's a way of discovering meanings which haven't been discovered before."[20] And Aristotle wrote in his *Rhetoric* that "strange words simply puzzle us; ordinary words convey only what we know already; it is from metaphor that we can best get hold of something fresh."[21]

Metaphors are something that we *experience*. Hearing a live metaphor and understanding it is a *transaction* that involves more than the intellect; and it can lead to a changed perspective on life. When that happens, our response to the preacher is, "Yes, now I *see* what you're saying!" And with this response comes an emotional and spiritual experience that makes the truth of the metaphor a part of our inner person. We may find ourselves echoing the words of the Emmaus disciples, "Were not our hearts burning within us while he talked with us on the road and opened the Scriptures to us?" (Luke 24:32)

In the last paragraph, I used the phrase "live metaphor," so I had better pause to explain it. Semantic scholars have decided that there are three kinds of metaphors: *live* or *vivid, sick* or *pale,* and *dead* or *faded.* Live metaphors are the kind that powerfully "connect" the mind and heart of the hearers so that they want to do something in response to what they learn. *Sick* or *pale* metaphors may affect the mind, but they have no effect on the emotions or the will. *Dead* or *faded* metaphors bore the mind and may even create a negative "So what?" response from the heart and will. Dead metaphors are clichés; and when we hear speakers use them, we respond negatively with boredom and with pity.[22]

One of the interesting things about metaphors is that they touch different people in different ways at different levels of life. The child's response to Psalm 23 is different from that of the veteran missionary; but both individuals can respond to the same metaphor, *and the response of each can be authentic and rewarding.* The people in our congregations come from different backgrounds, have different IQs and educational experiences, and are at different levels of emotional and spiritual maturity; yet each one of them can "plug into" a metaphor and be enriched spiritually. Metaphors are something like our Lord's seamless garment: people can even touch the hem of the garment and experience life-changing power.[23]

Next we will meet another preacher who, like Hushai, used "power words" to save King David's life.

"A story-formed community . . .
will not be so sure it has all the answers.
Such a community will listen for surprises,
for strangers, and for imaginative
new ideas which it cannot control."

—Philip S. Keane

"Expositors tend to look on sermon or lesson preparation
in terms of doing research for a lecture or paper.
They should view it more like writing a story or poem."

—Leland Ryken

". . . we need not allow ourselves
to be abashed by any suggestion that the
old metaphors are out of date
and ought to be superseded."

—Dorothy Sayers

"Imagining is a fundamental quality
of being human, engaged in by
all people everywhere."

—Philip S. Keane

Chapter Five
Preacher, Tell Me a Story

The Lord sent Nathan to David" (2 Sam. 12:1). Is that an assignment you would eagerly accept? After all, David was an adulterer, a murderer, and a liar; and he was working overtime to keep his sins hidden from everybody, including God. Besides that, he was the king, wielding absolute authority; and there are indications that David at times could be impulsive and hot-headed, such as the time he intended to kill Nabal (1 Sam. 25). Nathan's job wasn't an easy one. This might well have been the last pastoral visit of his ministry.

"He was a happy preacher whose pulpit awakened David and brought David back to God," said Alexander Whyte. "Nathan took his life in his hand that day. But he had his reward."[1]

Listen to Nathan's story as though you'd never heard it before.

There were two men in a certain town, one rich and the other poor. The rich man had a very large number of sheep and cattle, but the poor man had nothing except one little ewe lamb he had bought. He raised it, and it grew up with him and his children. It shared his food, drank from his cup and even slept in his arms. It was like a daughter to him.

Now a traveler came to the rich man, but the rich man refrained from taking one of his own sheep or cattle to prepare a meal for the traveler who had come to him. Instead, he took the ewe lamb that belonged to the poor man and prepared it for the one who had come to him. (2 Sam. 12:1-4)

In telling David a story, Nathan took the wise approach. Most of us enjoy hearing stories because there's usually somebody or something in the story that we can identify with. Once we're caught up in the story, the possibilities of self-discovery are numerous. Nathan's story is really a parable, and parables start off like *pictures,* then become *mirrors,* and then become *windows.* First there's *sight* as we see a slice of life in the picture; then there's *insight* as we see ourselves in the mirror; and then there's *vision* as we look through the window of revelation and see the Lord. As he went to the palace, Nathan prayed that David would see himself, judge himself, and then turn himself over to the Lord in repentance.

Nathan and Hushai both deserved Aristotle's "master of metaphor" degree, for both of them knew how to turn the listener's ear into an eye. David had been a shepherd; and as he listened to his chaplain's story, he saw the rich man's flocks and herds and the poor man's ewe lamb. He knew how it felt to have a lamb in his arms. He also knew how a shepherd responded when somebody tried to steal one of his sheep. For David, the setting was perfect.

David clearly saw the *picture,* but he failed to see the *mirror* until Nathan said, "You are the man!" and preached him a sermon. Then the king capitulated, looked through the *window* at God's mercy and said, "I have sinned against the Lord." The use of metaphor in ministry is not a substitute for "Thus says the Lord!" Recall my quotation from Sallie McFague: "Images 'feed' concepts; concepts 'discipline' images. Images without concepts are blind; concepts without images are sterile."[2] Nathan's story made David angry at *another man's sin;* Nathan's sermon made David confess his own sin. A balanced ministry of the Word requires both concept and image.

The imagery in Nathan's story fascinates me. Uriah's wife is a cuddly ewe lamb. Temptation is an unexpected traveler who stops for a visit. Adultery is robbery. Sexual sin is like eating a meal. These images are not limited to Nathan's parable; they're found often in Scripture.

Bathsheba is pictured as a loving ewe lamb. A husband should look upon his wife as a beloved lamb who shares his house, his table, his arms, and his bed. Proverbs 5:19 compares the wife to a doe who brings her husband satisfaction. First Thessalonians 4:4 and 1 Peter 3:7 (NKJV) picture the wife as a vessel that should be kept pure and beautiful. Peter suggests that this vessel should be treated like a delicate and valuable vase. Proverbs 5:15-18 compares the love of a faithful wife to a refreshing fountain, but adultery to drinking at a filthy sewer.

The biblical image of sheep is a familiar one. Israel was Jehovah's flock (Pss. 74:1; 79:13; 100:3; Matt. 15:24), just as the church is the flock of which Jesus is the shepherd (John 10; Acts 20:28-30; Heb. 13:20). Sinners are lost sheep who need to be found (Isa. 53:6; Luke 15:4-6), and believers are weak sheep who need to be led and protected (Ps. 23; John 10:1-18; 1 Peter 2:25). When God's people suffer, they are like sheep destined for the slaughter (Ps. 44:22; Rom. 8:36).

Temptation is pictured many ways in Scripture. To Cain, temptation was like a hungry beast lurking at the door (Gen. 4:7); and God warned him not to open the door. James describes temptation as the bait on a hook or in a trap (James 1:14), and as a womb pregnant with evil (James 1:15; see also Ps. 7:14 and Isa. 59:4, 16). But in Nathan's story, temptation is a friendly traveler who drops in for a visit.

When we consider this image of the traveler, we can see that the working of temptation is subtle. The traveler comes as a guest but soon becomes the master of the house. So influential is this visitor that the host is even willing to steal and kill in order to please him! Welcoming the visitor is the first step toward sin and death. Whoever "entertains" temptation will pay dearly for the feast.

Adultery is equated with robbery in 1 Thessalonians 4:6, for the verb "take advantage" means "to defraud" or "to exploit." The Greek word translated "take advantage" is related to the word for *covetousness,* and the two concepts obviously go together (Eph. 4:19; 5:3; Col. 3:5). Proverbs 6:30-35 also presents the picture of adultery as robbery and shows the tragic consequences.

No matter how much personal pleasure David experienced with Bathsheba, God compared what he did to the killing and eating of another man's only lamb. It isn't a pretty picture. In Scripture, sin is often pictured as eating. "This is the way of an adulteress: she eats and wipes her mouth and says, 'I've done nothing wrong' " (Prov. 30:20). Zophar described the sinner as somebody who enjoys the taste of sin but doesn't realize that it will eventually produce sickness (Job 20:12-19). Eliphaz talked about the person who "drinks up evil like water" (Job 15:16).

The first temptation involved desiring food and eating it (Gen. 3:6). "Stolen water is sweet; food eaten in secret is delicious" (Prov. 9:17; and see 20:17). In Proverbs 9, Wisdom and Folly, personified as women, both prepare feasts; but Folly's feast leads to death. The lips of the adulteress drip honey; but in the end, the sweetness becomes bitterness (Prov. 5:3-4). The adulteress pleads, "Come, let's drink deep of love till morning" (Prov. 7:18). For a description of sanctified married love, see Song of Songs 4:10-15, where images of wine, honey, milk, water, and fragrant fruits are all involved in the enjoyment of the relationship.

Nathan's parable was brief, but it was rich in images to hang in the picture gallery of the king's mind. David didn't realize how Nathan's story quietly penetrated and worked in his inner being. As a shepherd, David identified with the poor man's love for his ewe lamb. As a king, he was incensed by the injustice of the rich man's action in stealing and killing his neighbor's lamb. As a husband, David knew the blessing of married love; and as a human being and one-time fugitive in the wilderness, he knew the joy of satisfying both hunger and thirst. He also knew what it was like to entertain guests. The cumulative effect of these images prepared David for Nathan's, "You are the man!"

But suppose Nathan had preached a doctrinal homily to David, dealing with such abstractions as sin, marriage, and injustice? Would the king have responded as he did? Probably not. The abstractions might have reached the king's mind, but they would never have touched his heart. As we shall see in a later chapter, the imagination has a powerful role to play in building character and changing life. Walter Brueggemann was right when he wrote, "The link of obedience to imagination suggests that the toughness of ethics depends on poetic, artistic speech as the only speech that can evoke transformed listening."[3]

Such "transformed listening" is what preaching is all about—using words to turn ears into eyes so that people see the truth and want their lives to change. If it worked with a tough case like David, with God's blessing, it will work with anybody.

"A fact stated barely is dry.
It must be the vehicle of some humanity
in order to interest us.
It is like giving a man a stone
when he asks you for bread."

—Henry David Thoreau

"I caution against communication
because once language exists
only to convey information,
it is dying."

—Richard Hugo

Chapter Six
Skeletons in the Pulpit,
Cadavers in the Pews

Grandma Thatcher was in church Sunday morning in her usual place on the aisle, fifth pew back, piano side of the sanctuary, the place that's been hers for over thirty years. She had smiled at everybody as she hobbled in; and when they asked her how she was, she said, "Oh, fine—just fine!"

But she wasn't fine. As usual, her unsaved husband, George, had sent her off to church with curses ringing in her ears. Before slamming the front door, he had uttered his standard Lord's Day malediction: "Why don't you just move down there!" But that wasn't all. Grandma Thatcher's body hurt in some new places that day, and she was hoping that her visit to the doctor on Wednesday would help bring relief. She dreaded the arrival of winter and was praying that fuel prices wouldn't go up again. If it weren't for her Lord, her large-print Bible, and her Christian friends, Grandma Thatcher would have given up a long time ago.

When Pastor Bowers stepped into the pulpit to preach, Grandma Thatcher silently prayed, "Father, give him something special for me. I need it!" The text was Genesis 9, and the message was the twenty-second in a series on Genesis that Pastor Bowers called "Beginning at the Beginnings." (Some of the members were wishing he would start thinking about ending at the endings.) The sermon was entitled, "God Talks to Noah." Pastor Bowers read the chapter and then, rather proud of his wordsmanship, gave the congregation his main points:

I. Creation Presented — 9:1-3
II. Capital Punishment — 9:4-7
III. Covenant Promised — 9:8-17
IV. Carnality Practiced — 9:18-23
V. Consequences Prophesied — 9:24-29

As some of the saints dutifully wrote the outline in the space provided on the back page of their worship folders, Grandma Thatcher breathed a disappointed sigh, "Last week it was all S's. Today it's all CP's." She settled back in the pew, turned the preacher off and began meditating on the psalm she'd read early that morning before George had gotten up to menace her day.

A few weeks later, Pastor Bowers was away at District Conference; and the guest preacher was a retired missionary who had served many years in the Andean mountains of South America. Oddly enough — or providentially — his text was from Genesis 9, and the title in the worship folder was "Always Look for the Rainbow." Grandma Thatcher hoped the sermon would be as interesting as the title.

The speaker began his sermon by describing a rainstorm he'd experienced while on a missionary trip in the mountains. The congregation chuckled when he said, "I wish Noah had been with us. We could have used him!"

Then he started talking about the storms in human lives, and the compassion in his voice convinced the congregation that he'd been through more than one storm himself. "Storms are a part of life; God made it that way," he said. "But I've learned a secret that's helped me all these years, and it's still helping me: *Always look for the rainbow.* The world looks for the silver lining and sings 'Somewhere over the Rainbow,' but we Christians have something far better than that. Did you ever meet the three men in the Bible who saw rainbows?"

He talked about Noah who saw the rainbow *after* the storm. "Maybe you're going through a storm right now and you're wondering if the Lord even cares about you. Trust Him! The day will come when you'll see the rainbow and know that He's been faithful to work out His purposes for you."

Then he had them turn in their Bibles to Ezekiel 1, and he spoke about how Ezekiel saw the rainbow *in the midst of* the storm. It was a difficult day. Ezekiel had been exiled to Babylon, and the city of Jerusalem and the temple were about to be destroyed, but God was still on the throne. "You can't close your eyes to the storm and pretend it's not there," said the preacher, "but you can look for the rainbow in the storm. It's there!"

His third example was from Revelation 4:1-3, where he read to them of the Apostle John's experience. "Noah saw the rainbow *after* the storm, Ezekiel saw it *in the midst of* the storm, but John saw it *before* the storm. And John saw a complete circle, not just a bow. He saw that God was on His throne, and that meant that everything was under control." Then the speaker turned to Revelation 6 and showed them Jesus Christ at the throne, and he preached the Gospel to them.

He closed his Bible, smiled at the listening congregation, and said: "Dear friends, you and I will experience storms until we are called to heaven; and then all storms will cease. Expect the storms and don't be afraid of them, because God is always faithful. Just remember God's message to us today: *Always look for the rainbow.* Depend on the faithfulness of God. Sometimes He'll show you the rainbow after the storm, sometimes during the storm, and sometimes before the storm. *But He will never fail you.*"

As Grandma Thatcher limped home, she asked herself, "Why do I feel so nourished and satisfied down inside? Why is my heart so calm and joyful? I'm not even afraid to meet George when I get home, and the doctor's appointment doesn't bother me now. *What has happened to me?*"

What had happened to her and to other members of the congregation, including the young people, who left the sanctuary that morning sensing that God had met with them? True, their minds had been instructed; but Pastor Bowers always gave them plenty of Bible facts to think about, sometimes using Hebrew and Greek. True, their wills had been challenged; but this time they really wanted to practice what the preacher challenged them to do. Trusting the faithfulness of God seemed the most natural thing to do. What was different about the guest speaker's sermon? *He had fed their imaginations.*

Starved Imaginations and Disobedience

In his preaching ministry, Pastor Bowers took skeletons into the pulpit and ended up with cadavers in the pews — undernourished saints who had nothing to chew on but outlines. The guest missionary speaker took both concepts and images into the pulpit and wove them together in such a way that his listeners' ears became eyes and they saw the truth. In seeing the truth, their imagination was cleansed and nourished; and they were spiritually satisfied and encouraged within.

I can't prove it statistically, but I have a feeling that many, if not most, of the people in our churches suffer from starved imaginations. In fact, most people outside the church are also afflicted; and the evidences of this malady in our society aren't difficult to discover. The most glaring evidence that something is wrong in our churches is the great gulf that exists between what the church preaches and what the church practices. "Religious sin" and starved imaginations go together.

In recent years, the media have been having a heyday exposing the sins of religious leaders; and they aren't finished yet. Reporters have uncovered everything from embezzlement and outright lying to extramarital affairs and child sexual abuse. But what the media people may not realize is that their discoveries are just the tip of the iceberg. Local congregations are having their share of quiet scandals among Bible-studying church members who have professed to be Christians for a long time. In one evangelical church after another, men and women who have listened to biblical sermons since childhood are admitting to filthy sins that they've covered up for years. One youth leader said to me, "The kids I work with claim to be saved; but if they're saved at all, it's only from the waist up."

Why is it that professed Christians dutifully sit in church and listen to Bible sermons and then go out and live like pagans? Pastors grieve over this dilemma and wonder if it's really worthwhile to study, pray, and preach. There may be no one simple answer to this complex problem, but I have a suspicion that one factor is the *starved imagination* of congregations. These people have studied the Bible and listened to sermons, but the truths of Scripture have never penetrated their imaginations. They've packed a lot of Bible facts into their heads and are able to regurgitate these facts on demand, but the truths about God and the Christian life have never affected their imaginations. While the responsibility for their disobedience is totally their own, the responsibility for making the proclamation of God's truth exciting and personal rests with those of us who preach. The "hearers of the Word" can't easily become "doers" if their "hearing" doesn't become "seeing."

"When you stop to think about it," wrote Northrop Frye in *The Educated Imagination,* "you soon realize that our imagination is what our whole social life is really based on. . . . In practically everything we do, it's the combination of emotion and intellect that we call imagination that goes to work."[1] Scripture compares the imagination to a womb in which we give birth to the images that direct our lives. When we yield to temptation, it's because we hunger for "the bait" and imagine what it would be like to enjoy it. "Then, after desire has conceived, it gives birth to sin; and sin, when it is full-grown, gives birth to death" (James 1:15).

It's possible to be "pregnant with evil" (Ps. 7:14), and the womb is the imagination that is impregnated by temptation. "They conceive trouble and give birth to evil," said Job's friend Eliphaz; "their womb fashions deceit" (Job 15:35). The Prophet Isaiah echoed these words in Isaiah 59:4. But it's also possible for the imagination to be "impregnated" with the holy and the beautiful! When the truth of God's Word penetrates our listeners' imaginations so they can see it and feel it, then the Holy Spirit can use our sermons to bring about the inner changes necessary for the development of spiritual character.

Balanced Preaching and Balanced Spiritual Growth

In her fascinating book, *Metaphor and Meaning in Psychotherapy,* Ellen Y. Siegelman explores the connection between metaphors and psychological healing. She maintains that the inner life can't be changed unless feeling ("affect") and understanding ("cognition") are connected. My conviction is that this connection involves the use of the imagination and metaphorical images. Dr. Siegelman writes: "Cognition without affect is simply an intellectualization that will not hold; affect without cognition is just a feeling-state without a home."[2]

Right-brain religion generates a lot of heat, and left-brain religion generates a lot of light; and it's through the imagination that the twain can meet. Preaching that involves the imagination as well as the mind and the emotions will encourage balanced spiritual growth.

Let's examine that statement and see how it applies to preaching. If a person's life is to be manageable and meaningful, the intellect and the emotions must be united; and this union is formed partly by the imagination. Religion that's all feeling is shallow and extremely unpredictable, "a feeling-state without a home." The person lives on a roller coaster and is spiritually "high" one day and down in the depths the next day, and the depths keep getting deeper. However, religion that's all cognition is cold and calculating and lacks the excitement and enjoyment that ought to accompany faith in the living God.

Right-brain religion generates a lot of heat, and left-brain religion generates a lot of light; and it's through the imagination that the twain can meet. Preaching that involves the imagination as well as the mind and the emotions will encourage balanced spiritual growth. Grandma Thatcher understood the Grand Canyon of difference between reading an outline on the back of the bulletin and seeing the rainbow in the storm.

Further, we must not separate personal morality from the image-making faculty within us that we call imagination. No Christian rises any higher than the beauty and quality of the pictures that hang in the gallery of his or her mind. I agree with Philip Keane that "we need a moral theology for the right side of the brain (visual imagination) as well as for the left side of the brain (logical principles)."[3] It's significant that the reasonable lectures people are giving about sexual promiscuity and AIDS are doing very little to change attitudes or habits. When it comes to these matters, many people think with their glands and not with their brains. Imagination is on the throne and reason is in the dungeon.

During the "Pearly Gate" scandals, I heard a television reporter say about a media preacher, "I guess it's *Elmer Gantry* all over again." He was referring to the 1927 Sinclair Lewis novel about a hypocritical preacher who lived a scandalous life and used religion as the cover-up. "You've picked the wrong book," I said to my TV set. "Sure, there's some of *Elmer Gantry* involved, but the real explanation of the scandals is in *The Picture of Dorian Gray*."

Dorian Gray was a handsome, wealthy, young Londoner who sold his soul to the devil provided the evil one would keep him young and handsome. As he became more and more wicked, Dorian Gray noted that a beautiful portrait of himself was gradually becoming ugly, so he hung it in an attic room and locked the door. As his diabolical life brought defilement and death to several innocent people, the hidden portrait became even more repulsive, his face revealing a record of the hideous condition of his own soul. Dorian Gray decided that the portrait must be destroyed, so he plunged a knife into it. When he did, the face in the portrait lost its ugliness and became the face of a handsome youth. But Dorian Gray was found dead on the floor, a withered and ugly old man with a knife in his heart.

People see different messages in Oscar Wilde's novel, but to me, among other things, it's an allegory about the imagination, the picture gallery of the mind. It dramatically illustrates the warning in 1 John 1: Don't claim to be obedient to God if you're walking in the darkness. The longer we pretend, the uglier our true character becomes and the more the light becomes darkness. *But the truth will come out.* The picture hanging in the attic is what we really are, and one day that locked door will be opened.

We cannot emphasize too much the power of metaphor to affect personal morality. In her insightful article, "The Moral

Necessity of Metaphor," novelist Cynthia Ozick reminds us that "metaphor is one of the chief agents of our moral nature, and . . . the more serious we are in life, the less we can do without it."[4] Harvey Cox writes, "The picturing, symbolizing, world-view-making faculty of human beings appears to interact with an individual's moral reasoning at every stage of human growth. People tend to make moral choices on the basis of what are often vague, precognitive images of what the world is like and how they fit into it."[5]

Our preaching must help people put into the gallery of their minds pictures that reveal "the beauty of holiness" (Ps. 29:2, KJV). We must help them see the glory of God's truth and the beauty of the Savior who is the standard of holiness for all of us. It isn't enough that we explain the Bible and exhort people to obey it. Remember what Halford Luccock said? "The purpose of preaching is not to make people see reasons, but visions."[6]

Walter Brueggemann speaks for all of us when he says, "I have found myself discovering that mostly I do not need more advice, but strength. I do not need new information, but the courage, freedom and authorization to act on what I already have been given in the gospel."[7] Telling people what they ought to do without motivating them to do it is only to add to their burdens. That was the approach of the scribes and Pharisees; it was not the approach of Jesus (Matt. 23:1-4).

Then Brueggemann adds: "The deep places in our lives—places of resistance and embrace—are not ultimately reached by instruction. Those places of resistance and embrace are reached only by stories, by images, metaphors and phrases that line out the world differently, apart from our fear and hurt."[8] That explains why Jesus so often said, "The kingdom of heaven is like. . . . " It also explains why the common people heard Him gladly and why so many lives were transformed when He preached the Word of God.

"Television is chewing gum for the eyes."

—*Frank Lloyd Wright*

"In the age of television,
image becomes more important than substance."

—*S.I. Hayakawa*

"I find television very educating.
Every time somebody turns on the set
I go into the other room
and read a book."

—*Groucho Marx*

Chapter Seven
The Hidden Destroyers

Why are many of the people we minister to suffering from starved imaginations? Our anemic skeletal preaching might contribute to their plight, but it certainly doesn't cause it. Most of these people had starved imaginations before they joined our congregations. But, what is the cause of the malady?

North American sociologist Robert H. Bellah gives one answer, based on his interpretation of American history. He believes that the American society early abandoned the poetic and embraced the pragmatic; and this has "dried up" the American imagination.

According to Bellah, Jonathan Edwards was "the last Protestant theologian before the twentieth century to have in his control the entire imaginative resources of the Christian tradition. Edwards' use of imagery was unparalleled and he stood at the beginning of the American tradition of revivalist preaching." But after Edwards, says Bellah, "such a union of persuasion and thought tends to fall apart." Bellah calls this decline the "gradual drying up of the Protestant imagination in America."[1]

What made the American Protestant religious imagination "dry up"? Bellah suggests as the major cause, the American emphasis on science and reason, leading to the loss of the "vision long nurtured in the religious and poetic traditions of the West."[2] Instead of having the "double vision" that sees both the facts and the truths behind the facts (what Sallie McFague calls "concept" and "image"), the American people focused on whatever was scientific, technical, industrial, practical, and financially profitable. They gradually abandoned the inner vision and fell prey to what William Blake called "the single vision and Newton's sleep."[3] Unfortunately, this pragmatic approach to life infected the churches, and many of them replaced the Bible's sacramental view of creation with the more "scientific" outlook.

From the theological point of view, it was a replication of the sin of God's ancient people Israel when they turned from the true God and worshiped idols. Israel lost the sacramental view of creation and centered their attention and affection on the gifts rather than the Giver. They began to live on substitutes and to see the world as a place filled with treasures to exploit, with no sincere consideration of the God who gave these treasures to them. They ceased to be stewards and became consumers. This was the ancient version of the "consumer mentality" that has affected all of us today.

Oswald Chambers had this to say about idolatry and starved imaginations:

> The people of God in Isaiah's day had starved their imagination by looking on the face of idols, and Isaiah made them look up at the heavens, that is, he made them begin to use their imagination aright. Nature to a saint is sacramental. If we are children of God, we have a tremendous treasure in nature.[4]

In short, we and the people we preach to live in the kind of society that quietly defiles and destroys the imagination of the unsuspecting victim. In today's world, if you want to have a healthy imagination, you have to work at it. Your inner person is constantly being assaulted by artificial images that dim your view of God's creation and erode your imaginative faculty. People with starved imaginations usually don't know what's wrong with them; and sometimes in their attempt to solve the problem, they only plunge deeper into difficulty.

The emphasis on technology and consumerism in Western society has created some powerful industries to protect and promote what the announcer on the old "Superman" television program called "the American way of life." These industries have created for us an artificial environment of imaginary needs that keep us from enjoying the real world that God gave us. Enjoyment *without God* is impoverishment; enjoyment *with God* is enrichment.

The technological world is a world of manufactured experiences that leave both the wallet and the imagination empty. If you have enough money, you can buy almost any kind of experience today, from a day in a medieval castle to a simulated space flight. Products and services are rarely presented on the basis of their merits; they're promoted by *advertising images*: the cigarette-smoking macho cowboy riding his horse, the whiskey-drinking banker lounging by the fireside, the sexy woman leaning against the new automobile. According to former advertising executive Jerry Mander, "The role of *advertising* . . . is to create a world of mirrors in which people can obtain new images of themselves that fit the purposes of the overall system."[5]

"Technology is the knack of so arranging the world that we can't experience it," said Swiss novelist and playwright Max Frisch.[6] He might have added, "And having so arranged the world, the technocrats can now market artificial experiences to us, experiences we wouldn't need if we'd just get back to experiencing the world God created for us." A fantasy world replaces a real world and starves the imagination. Chesterton was right: "The world will never starve for want of wonders, but only for want of wonder."

Pornography and "Realism"

One of the symptoms of the starved imagination malady may be the success of pornography in our country—both the hardcore kind and the more sophisticated varieties—as well as the emphasis on so-called "realism" in the arts. Sometimes the two are united in a joint assault on the picture gallery of the mind.

Feminist leader and author Midge Decter calls pornography

"a vision of anonymous, faceless sex, sex without personality and without consequences."[7] Because pornography is that kind of an experience, it leaves people excited but empty, their inner hunger not satisfied. Because their inner hunger persists, they must find ways to generate greater sexual excitement; and thus the appetite feeds on itself but doesn't feed the imagination. It eventually defiles and destroys that which it hoped to satisfy.

So-called "realism" in the arts is sometimes only a more socially accepted form of pornography. Indeed, some social critics see "artistic realism" as a sign of decay rather than of progress. North American novelist and biographer Mark Schorer wrote: "When we feel that we are no longer in a position to say what life means, we must content ourselves with telling how it looks."[8] "Realism" may give fantasy sufficient food to build a titillating alternate world, but it can only starve the imagination and keep it from understanding and enjoying the real world. It takes imagination to penetrate reality and discover the truths behind it.

This explains why the biblical writers handled with delicacy, and often with symbolism, matters relating to sex. The Bible deals with these matters in a "slanted way," as Emily Dickinson expresses it in her poem #1129.

Tell all the Truth but tell it slant—
Success in circuit lies
Too bright for our infirm Delight
The Truth's superb surprise.

As lightning to the Children eased
With explanation kind
The Truth must dazzle gradually
Or every man be blind.

I'll have more to say about this perceptive poem in later chapters. Just keep in mind that the "realism" in today's society isn't feeding the imagination, but destroying it.

People don't have to get involved in pornography or technological traps to starve their imaginations. All they have to do is attend school and the educational system may do the job for them. Children are born with healthy imaginations; but by the time they've been in the school system for a few years, they start thinking and speaking very conventionally. According to Ellen Y. Siegelman, a child's ability for making metaphors "seems to wane when the child enters school and throughout the elementary school years." When children enter school, their drawings become "less imaginative and more literal."[9]

This reminds me of a story told about the artist Picasso. Late in life, he visited an exhibition of drawings made by children; and he said: "When I was their age, I could draw like Raphael, but it took me a lifetime to learn to draw like them."[10]

Too many public schools are only outmoded factories for turning out citizens who are conformists. Fortunate are those students who have at least one teacher who can help them discover and develop their creative gifts. When I was in the sixth grade, I had such a teacher; and I will always be grateful for her. She encouraged me to read and write, and she took time to criticize my little essays and stories. By the time I entered junior high school, I was hooked on books, and I knew I wanted to be a writer.

Educator Kieran Egan reminds us that "the imagination is not simply a capacity to form images, but is a capacity to think in a particular way. It is a way that crucially involves our capacity to think of the possible rather than just the actual."[11] If all that education does is encourage us to swallow an approved meal and later regurgitate it, without offering us the opportunity to question either the recipe or the menu, then it's no surprise that we're destroying imaginations while dispensing information. Why do we make "concept" and "image" competitors, even enemies, when God made them to be friends and coworkers?

Television

When it comes to starving the imagination, many social critics think that the greatest single culprit is *television*.[12] "Though television passes for experience," says Jerry Mander, "it is more like 'time out.' "[13] He cites evidence from researchers proving that watching television is "antiexperience" rather than experience. "Television information seems to be received more in the unconscious than the conscious regions of the mind where it would be possible to think about it."[14]

One of our leading North American experts on television is Dr. Neil Postman, professor of communication arts and sciences at New York University, author of *Amusing Ourselves to Death* and *Conscientious Objections*. Postman's emphasis is that television is an entertainment medium; therefore, everything we watch on television comes across as entertainment even if it's serious. Whether we're watching the bombing of a Vietnam village or the funeral of an assassinated president, we're "amusing ourselves" rather than educating ourselves. Postman claims that "the form in which ideas are expressed affects what those ideas will be."[15]

Postman and other critics are especially concerned about the way television presents the news—in forty-five second "bites" that together resemble propaganda more than they do reporting. As activist Jerry Rubin said, "On the television screen news is not so much reported as created."[16] When we watch presidential candidates campaign or debate, the important thing isn't how they address national and international issues but *what kind of image is coming across to the viewing public.* There was a time in American politics when the speech writer was the most important member of the presidential team. Now, it's the media expert, the man or woman who can "sell" the image of the candidate the way advertisers sell beer or mouthwash. Whether the viewers realize it or not, says Postman, "television has achieved the power to define the form in which news must come, and it has also defined how we shall respond to it."[17]

The British television political commentator Robin Day has also expressed concern about the way the medium handles the news. "Though the main facts are covered," he writes in his book *Day by Day,* "their news value is liable to be affected by an overemphasis on what is available by way of direct visual coverage of events. This tends to be edited so as to select the most visibly emotive or violent part for transmission."[18]

Along with Mander, Postman, and Day, British media pioneer Malcolm Muggeridge expressed concern over the influence of television on human life. His insightful book *Christ and the Media* contains three lectures he gave at All Souls Church, London, in 1976, along with reports of the discussion periods and the responses of the men who chaired the lectures. His thesis is simply that "this medium [television], *by its nature*, doesn't lend itself to constructive purposes."[19]

Television, of course, is a means of transmitting *images*; but, says Muggeridge, "The Christian faith has come to us in words, not images. . . . If it had come to us in images instead of words, it would not have lived as it has."[20] When asked if he thought Jesus Christ would have consented to be interviewed on television, he replied in the negative. "The wonder, you see, of the Word which became flesh, and dwells among us, cannot get on to film, cannot get on to video, cannot get into a camera, Mother Teresa notwithstanding. In the beginning was the *Word*, and the Word became flesh, not celluloid."[21]

The imagination is fed primarily by words and concepts, not by visual images. When we watch images, the messages they convey tend to bypass our thinking and influence us subjectively in ways we may not comprehend. But when we hear words, we can create our own images in our imagination; and these images are more meaningful to us than the ones manufactured by the media experts.

The imagination is fed primarily by words and concepts, not by visual images. When we watch images, the messages they convey tend to bypass our thinking and influence us subjectively in ways we may not comprehend. But when we hear words, we can create our own images in our imagination; and these images are more meaningful to us than the ones manufactured by the media experts. An interviewer asked a little girl if she preferred listening to the radio or watching television, and she replied, "Listening to the radio." When asked why she preferred radio, she said, "Because the pictures are clearer." That says it all.

Both children and adults are being deeply affected by what they watch on television; *and they don't realize the damage that's being done.* By the time the average child in the United States finishes elementary school, he or she has watched 8,000 murders on television.[22] From first grade to graduation, she will spend 13,000 hours in school but will watch television more than 15,000 hours; and she will watch over 1,000 commercials a week. By the time she is twenty, she will have seen over 1 million commercials.[23]

Radio—a Better Choice

Three recent developments in radio have caught my attention. The first is the success of Garrison Keillor, the man who invented the little Minnesota town of Lake Wobegon and the people who populate it. Keillor made these people so real that millions of listeners would sit by their radios weekly to hear the latest "news from Lake Wobegon." One Saturday evening, I sat in the World Theater in St. Paul and listened to Keillor give the "news," and all the while I was wishing I could make my sermons and books as captivating as he makes his mythical town. Keillor may well be the most gifted and imaginative communicator in radio today. At least he's proving that people will forsake television and listen to a radio storyteller as he feeds their imagination.[24]

The second development is the popularity of the old radio programs such as "Amos and Andy," "The Shadow," "Burns and Allen," "Jack Benny," "Bob and Ray," "The Lux Radio Theater," and a host of others. Local radio stations are airing these programs to appreciative and growing audiences; and in Chicago, Chuck Shaden has turned old-time radio (and other forms of nostalgia) into a profitable industry. I note that many gift catalogs now list cassettes of the old radio shows. Nostalgia as such isn't one of my special interests, but I must confess that my imagination thrives on listening to these voices from the past.

When our family lived in Chicago, one of my daily tasks was to transport our children to school each morning as I made my way to the Moody Church where I was serving as senior pastor. I sometimes tuned in to a local station that played old-time radio programs; and at first the children laughed at the old-fashioned music and commercials, and some of the humor. But gradually they became interested and started to enjoy the programs. I was one happy father when one morning our younger daughter said, "You know, I like this better than television!"

The third development is the new emphasis in radio on drama and readings. National Public Radio has given us excellent versions of *The Hobbit, Winnie the Pooh, Charlotte's Web*, and numerous short stories either read or dramatized, including my favorite Sherlock Holmes mysteries. If our children would devote thirty minutes a day to listening to radio drama, it might feed their imagination and cure them of television addiction.

To be fair all around, I must admit that I have pastor friends who tell me they couldn't preach effectively if they didn't watch television. Apparently the experience helps them better understand the mind-set of the congregation, and it even gives them material for illustrations.

So be it. "Each one should be fully convinced in his own mind" (Rom. 14:5). I just hope that they compensate for whatever damage occurs in their inner person, because you can't devote time to watching television without being affected by it. Robert Murray M'Cheyne's warning about the Greek and Roman classics is applicable here: "True, we ought to know them; but only as chemists handle poisons—to discover their qualities, not to infect their blood with them."[25]

You may disagree with me about some of these matters, but one thing I'm sure we agree on: the imagination of the average church attender is starved, and if people are to mature spiritually, we must feed the imagination as we expound the Word of God.

"Ears that hear and eyes that see—the Lord has made them both" (Prov. 20:12).

"But blessed are your eyes because they see, and your ears because they hear" (Matt. 13:16).[26]

"The greatest thing by far
is to be a master of metaphor."

—Aristotle

"Whole works of scientific research,
even entire schools, are hardly more
than the patient repetition, in all its ramifications,
of a fertile metaphor."

—Kenneth Burke

"A philosophical treatise has never been written
which did not depend upon the use of metaphor."

—D. Berggren

"All thinking is metaphorical."

—Robert Frost

Chapter Eight
The Mystery of Metaphor

Metaphors are very strange," wrote novelist Walker Percy, "because when you put two things together it's a way of discovering meanings which haven't been discovered before."[1]

When Jesus said to His disciples, "You are the salt of the earth," He brought together *salt* and *disciples* and planted a seed that's been growing for centuries and producing fruit. But He went on to say, "You are the light of the world." Now we have a three-way connection: Christ's followers are like salt and like light, but they also create some kind of new relationship between salt and light. Indeed, metaphors are "very strange."

What's supposed to happen to you when you hear a metaphor? If the metaphor is merely embellishment ("He was as frustrated as a termite in a yo-yo"), you might think to yourself, "Now wasn't that clever!" But that kind of response turns the metaphor into a distraction instead of a discovery. Instead of focusing on *what's* being said, you start paying more attention to how it's being said; and that kind of response can be lethal to good communication.

If the metaphor is "dead" ("He's a bull in a china shop"), you might groan inwardly and perhaps even turn the speaker off. But if the metaphor is alive and vivid ("Why have you made me your target?" [Job 7:20]), you will probably find yourself *connecting* and saying to yourself, "I see something! I feel something! I understand something!"

"Connecting" is a term I've borrowed from psychotherapy. It describes what happens when a person "puts together" things that previously seemed unrelated, and thus gains new insight into life and the problems he or she is trying to solve. Says Ellen Y. Siegelman, "Much of psychotherapy consists in identifying previously unconscious metaphors and discovering how we unwittingly live by them."[2] She quotes Edgar Levenson, "The significant insights in therapy . . . are not solutions but *connections*—connections drawn between previously unrelated events."[3]

But what is actually "connected" within our listeners when they're confronted by a biblical metaphor? I'm not trained in psychotherapy, but I'll hazard a suggestion. I suspect that a successful "connection" would involve the building of at least three bridges.

The first bridge is between *the contemporary listener and the ancient Book.* On hearing the metaphor and "seeing" the picture it conveys, the listener says, "The Bible is speaking to *me*. It has something to say to me *today!*" The Word is heard, not simply as the text of a sermon, but as the voice of God coming to the worshiper in a living way. Biblical metaphors are timeless and can convey their messages to people in the age of computers just as they did to people in the age of clay tablets.

"Every great literature has always been allegorical," wrote G.K. Chesterton, "allegorical of some view of the universe. The *Iliad* is only great because all life is a battle, the *Odyssey* because all life is a journey, the Book of Job because all life is a riddle."[4] The many metaphors of life found in the Bible are "living links" that connect God's Word to the hearts and minds of people today. In these moments the truth is transported to human hearts. The listener sees the relationship between the ancient text and the modern situation, and this opens the way for the Spirit to apply the Word. *We want people to hear the voice of God, not just the voice of the preacher.*

It's something like watching a video of your neighbors' recent vacation trip. It's all rather bland until you see a place that you've visited; and you say to your wife or husband, "Remember when we were there?" All sorts of memories and emotions surface within you, some happy and perhaps some painful ("Isn't that where you sprained your ankle?"); and suddenly the video takes on new interest.

In one sense, preaching is a travelogue that introduces us to the people, places, and events that make up salvation history. God has so recorded the story in the Bible that, if it's properly presented, people will say, "I've been there!" or "That's where I am right now!" One of the goals of preaching is to help people meet themselves in the Bible and discover the contemporary significance of that ancient Book.

A.W. Tozer used to remind us that "the Bible world is the real world."⁵ Too many people think that when they open the Bible, they have to set their watch back several thousand years; but just the opposite is true. It's the Bible that brings us up-to-date so that we know what's going on in today's world. That's one reason why Scripture contains so many biographies, because human nature doesn't really change from one age to another. And that's also why your Bible is filled with metaphors and images that transcend time and space and speak to people of every age.

Let me suggest secondly that metaphors can help people build a bridge between *their past and their present*. All of us have had difficult experiences that we'd like to bury and forget, but using the "Memory Gardens Cemetery" only makes the situation worse. It's amazing how many people are being controlled by hurts and angers they thought they'd interred long ago. Metaphor has a way of bringing together the experiences of the past and the potential of the present and giving the listener new hope and encouragement.

Most of the people we know can describe their lives in a metaphor. A friend of mine used to ask me regularly, "Well, how goes the battle?" To him, life was a battleground, not a playground; and he took it all very seriously. Many people talk about being in "the rat race," or about being "trapped" in their job or their marriage, or perhaps about "tough sailing" or "tough sledding."

The metaphor we choose not only reveals our interpretation of life, but it also helps us choose the way we'll respond to life.

If life is a battle, then I'll have to be a brave soldier and stick it out to the end. If life is a cage in which I'm trapped, then I'll either resign myself to my fate or figure out some way to break out. If the sailing is tough, I'll adjust the sails to try to make the winds work for me and not against me. The picture in our mind often determines the course of our life.

Metaphors help listeners build bridges between the ancient text and their own contemporary situation, and between their past and present. The third bridge is built between *the person's mind and heart.* Recall the quotation from Sallie McFague: "Good metaphors shock, they bring unlikes together, they upset conventions, they involve tension, and they are implicitly revolutionary."[6] In other words, a good metaphor is an explosive thing that shakes our inner person and forces us into a confrontation with the truth. Even before we mentally grasp what the metaphor is saying, we can feel the impact of it. T.S. Eliot claimed that "genuine poetry can communicate before it is understood."[7]

When confronted by a metaphor, you might find yourself remembering forgotten experiences and unearthing buried feelings, and then bringing them together to discover new insights. Your mind says, "I see!" Your heart says, "I feel!" Then in that transforming moment your imagination unites the two and you say, "I'm beginning to understand!" Then you're challenged to take a step forward in spiritual and emotional maturity. "True insight is always connection," says Ellen Y. Siegelman, "a simultaneous experience of feeling and thought, of 'passion and prose.' "[8]

This kind of experience doesn't happen when the preacher or teacher is only imparting information. A lecture may connect a teacher's notebook with a student's notebook, but a sermon must connect God's mind and heart with the mind and heart of the listener. It's when we penetrate the imagination with metaphors that we assist the listener in "putting things together." Information is important, but we have to package that information in such a way that the listener has a confrontation with truth that produces an "experience explosion" within.

Welding Imagination with Experience

What philosopher and educator Alfred North Whitehead had to say about university education applies to our ministry of the Word.

> The university imparts information, but it imparts it imaginatively. At least, this is the function which it should perform for society. A university which fails in this respect has no reason for existence. This atmosphere of excitement, arising from imaginative consideration, transforms knowledge. A fact is no longer a bare fact: it is invested with all its possibilities. It is no longer a burden on the memory: it is energizing as the poet of our dreams, and as the architect of our purposes.[9]

Read that paragraph again, but substitute "church" for "university" and see how you respond. Whitehead goes on to say:

> The tragedy of the world is that those who are imaginative have but slight experience, and those who are experienced have feeble imaginations. Fools act on imagination without knowledge; pedants act on knowledge without imagination. The task of a university is to weld together imagination and experience.[10]

The task of Christian ministry—preaching in particular—is to "weld together imagination and experience"; and metaphor is one of the tools we can use to accomplish this purpose. This doesn't mean that the experience of "connecting" will occur every time we preach metaphorically. But this kind of preaching will give the Holy Spirit something to work with as He seeks to make the truth of Christ meaningful through our exposition of the Word.

> **The task of Christian ministry—preaching in particular—is to "weld together imagination and experience"; and metaphor is one of the tools we can use to accomplish this purpose.**

Very few people can deal practically with abstractions such as truth, beauty, faith, and mercy. These abstractions must be "fleshed out" before we can really get ahold of them and put them to work in our lives. "The truth must conquer," said Phillips Brooks, "but it must first embody itself in goodness."[11] The Incarnation of our Lord is evidence of this and is a reminder to us that the Word must always "become flesh" if the Father's glory is to be seen (John 1:14). A metaphor is a kind of "verbal incarnation" that enables us to make concrete in the minds of our listeners that which would otherwise be abstract and unreal.

The expositor doesn't have to manufacture these pictures because they're usually right there in the passage, sometimes hidden in the original text.[12] Since the Holy Spirit put these images into the Scriptures, we can assume that He wants us to use them as we preach the Word.

As I have already stated, biblical preaching is more than simply preaching the truth of the Bible or explaining and applying the Bible in an organized way. Biblical preaching means proclaiming the truth of the Bible *the way the Bible presents it*. The Spirit wants to use us to help our listeners translate paper and ink into the living truth of God, and then transfer that truth, in concept and image, to the heart and mind of the listener. If we approach the Bible only as a text to be analyzed, we may completely miss both its message *and the most effective way to present that message*.

Keeping Image and Concept in Perspective

Before we leave this topic, I want to issue a caveat that the biblical preacher must heed: *the metaphor is not the subject of the sermon*. If handled properly, the metaphor expands the subject, illumines it and helps to make it vivid and personal to our listeners; but the metaphor is not the message. To turn a metaphor into an allegory is a dangerous step for the biblical preacher to take.

For example, most commentators would apply the title "the sun of righteousness" to our Lord Jesus Christ (Mal. 4:2), and would contrast the healing rays of the sun with the consuming flames of the furnace (Mal. 4:1), which seems to be the emphasis in the text. In his book *Tropologia: A Key to Open Scripture Metaphors,* Benjamin Keach gives thirty-four parallels between Jesus Christ and the sun, most of which have no relationship to the passage in which the metaphor is found.[13] It is this approach to metaphor that must be avoided.

Metaphor must never replace precise definition of doctrine. I realize that all definitions have their weaknesses and none of them is perfect; but there is a "faith that was once for all entrusted to the saints" (Jude 3), and our pictures must not be substituted for theological precepts. In American church history, it was Horace Bushnell who wanted to replace "dogmatism" with "imaginative insight." He wrote:

> The Gospel is no dogma . . . the gospel is a revelation made up of fact and form and figure, and offered as a presentation to faith. . . . What is given to faith is put forth in some fact-form or symbol to be interpreted by imaginative insight, or the discerning power of faith.[14]

The crucial question, of course, is, "Whose 'imaginative insight' do we follow as we interpret these 'faith symbols' in the Bible?" It appears that Bushnell is encouraging us to abandon a biblical hermeneutic that keeps "images" and "concepts" in their proper place. The result is a very subjective approach to Scripture that leads ultimately to a dilution and then a desertion of the faith. "He who has imagination but no knowledge has wings but no feet," wrote the French essayist Joseph Joubert, a warning that Bushnell didn't heed.

The American naturalist John Burroughs said a very wise thing when he wrote in his journal on October 24, 1907, "To treat your facts with imagination is one thing, to imagine your facts is quite another."

Part Two
Imagination and Scripture

INTERLUDE: The Ten Assumptions
A Summary

1. The mind of man is a picture gallery, not a debating chamber (Macneile Dixon).

2. Seeing the world around us helps us to see God's truth. "I have multiplied visions, and used similitudes" (Hosea 12:10, KJV). "Every natural fact is a symbol of some spiritual fact" (Emerson).

3. Language is visual, words are pictures, and metaphorical language is the link between the world within us (imagination) and the world around us (creation).

4. The Bible is a picture book that often uses imagery to reveal God's truth. Bible words are often picture words.

5. "Fancy" escapes the real world and makes an alternate world, while "imagination" penetrates the real world and creatively makes it into a new world.

6. "Images feed concepts; concepts discipline images. Images without concepts are blind; concepts without images are sterile" (Sallie McFague).

7. People come to church to see visions, not to hear reasons (Halford Luccock).

8. Lasting moral changes in human personality must involve the imagination.

9. In preaching a text, we begin with truth as a picture (sight), which then becomes a mirror (insight), which then becomes a window (vision). We preach the truths behind the pictures in the text, not the pictures themselves.

10. When you study a text, ask first, "What is the point?" Then ask, "Where are the pictures and how do both fit together?"

"Language is the house of being."

—*Martin Heidegger*

"Let it not be said that I have said nothing new.
The arrangement of the material is new."

—*Blaise Pascal*

Chapter Nine
Pictures in the Pentateuch

In the next eight chapters, I want to walk leisurely with you through the Scriptures and point out some of the more important images that are found there. Our purpose is simply to get acquainted with and be excited by the imagery in the Bible. During most of this journey, we'll only be sightseers. However, here and there we'll pause to become prospectors and dig a little deeper. Occasionally I'll drop some homiletical hints, but we'll save most of the sermonizing for Part 3.

I suggest you keep your *New International Version* handy so you can read for yourself the verses referred to but not quoted. You'll be tempted to skip over these references; but if you do, you'll rob yourself of the exposure you may need to the richness of biblical metaphor and symbolism. Please take time to read each passage and to ponder how it fits into the scheme of things. Your personal contact with the Word will do you more good than your reading of what I have to say about it. Keep your notebook handy so you can write down the ideas that come to you during this adventure.

Genesis

Since Genesis is the book of beginnings, you would expect to find many of the major biblical images first mentioned here. As we saw earlier in chapters 3 and 4, God has seen fit to use the things in creation to reveal spiritual truth to us; and He has also seen fit to embody these truths in words, many of which were originally born as pictures.

In Genesis 1, we are confronted by, among other things, darkness and light, water, seeds, dust, breath, and heavenly bodies—all of which are used imaginatively throughout Scripture to convey spiritual truth. In chapter 2, we are introduced to the Sabbath, a garden, trees, rivers, sleep, marriage, and human nakedness; while in chapter 3, we discover a serpent, clothing, thorns and thistles, sweat, pregnancy, and a sword. Later in Genesis, we will find Babel, Sodom and Gomorrah, a lamb, a ladder (or staircase), a stench, and various animals, all of which show up in other parts of the Word.[1]

Creation (Gen. 1:1-2) is sometimes presented metaphorically. The heavens are "the work of [God's] fingers" (Ps. 8:3), and the earth was laid on "foundations," like a building (Pss. 102:25; 104:5; Isa. 48:13; 51:13, 16; Jer. 31:37; Amos 9:6). Sometimes creation is pictured, not as a building on foundations, but as a tent that God "stretched out" (Pss. 19:4; 104:2; Job 9:8; 37:18; Isa. 40:22; 44:24; 45:12; Jer. 10:12; 51:15). To a people who knew something of the nomadic life, the tent was a meaningful image. However, one day the heavens and earth of the old creation "will all wear out like a garment. Like clothing you will change them and they will be discarded" (Ps. 102:26).

But *building* isn't the only picture used for creation. We also find creation pictured as *birth*. The mountains were born (Job 15:7; Ps. 90:2), and so is the precipitation season by season (Job 38:28-29). God's words to Job about His creation combine images both of *building* and of *birth*:

> Where were you when I laid the earth's foundation? Tell me, if you understand. Who marked off its dimensions? Surely you know! Who stretched a measuring line across it? On what were its footings set, or who laid its cornerstone—while the morning stars sang together and all the angels shouted for joy? Who shut up the sea behind doors when it burst forth from the womb, when I made the clouds its garment and wrapped it in thick darkness. (Job 38:4-9)

The Apostle Paul used creation to picture God's great work of salvation, the "new creation" in Christ Jesus (2 Cor. 5:17). He alluded to the creation of light: "For God, who said, 'Let light shine out of darkness,' made his light shine in our hearts to give us the light of the knowledge of the glory of God in the face of Christ" (2 Cor. 4:6). Paul described Jesus Christ as "the last Adam" (1 Cor. 15:45) who brought us deliverance from the judgment caused by the first Adam (Rom. 5:12-21; 1 Cor. 15:20-22, 45-49). The church is the "new man" in Christ (Eph. 2:14-15), and the believer is "God's workmanship, created in Christ Jesus to do good works" (Eph. 2:10). God's people can experience a "renewal" day by day as they share in this new creation (Eph. 4:20-24; Col. 3:1-11).

Darkness and light (Gen. 1:2-3) are familiar images in the Bible. Darkness is associated with sin (John 3:19-21; Prov. 4:19; Acts 26:18; Eph. 5:8), Satan's kingdom (Col. 1:13), the godless world system (2 Cor. 6:14), and eternal judgment (Matt. 8:12). "God is light" (Ps. 27:1; 1 John 1:5) and His Word is a lamp (Pss. 19:8; 119:105, 130; Prov. 6:23). Jesus is "the light of the world" (John 8:12), and believers are lights in the world (Matt. 5:14-16; Phil. 2:14-16; Eph. 5:8-15; 2 Cor. 6:14). The obedient Christian walks in the light and radiates light in the form of love (1 John 1:5-10; 2:7-11). When Christ came into the world, it was like the dawning of a new day (Luke 1:78; Matt. 4:15-16). When sinners trust Christ, they are delivered from the darkness (Eph. 5:8; Acts 26:18). Darkness is associated with death, but light is associated with life (John 1:4-9). Darkness is also connected with trials and testings (Pss. 18:28; 44:19; 91:6; 107:10ff; 143:3). "The night" is usually described as a time of sorrow and suffering (Pss. 6:6; 30:5; 77:2, 6; 91:5).

Both the Gospel of John and the First Epistle of John make much of the metaphors of darkness and light. Nicodemus is known as the man who "came to Jesus at night" (John 3:2; 19:39), but he eventually came out into the light and identified with Jesus (John 19:38-42; 3:21). Judas, however, had the opportunity of walking in the light of the Lord (John 12:35-36), but he went out into the darkness. "As soon as Judas had taken the bread, he went out. And it was night" (John 13:30). What

91

an ominous statement: "And it was night."

Soil, seed (1:11-13), and *gardens* (2:8-9) play an important role in the biblical revelation. Man is made from the ground, and his body returns to the soil (3:19). Of itself, the dust is dead, but the breath of God gave it life (2:7; Acts 17:25). The Hebrew and Greek words for "breath" and "wind" are also the words for the spirit of man and the Spirit of God (*ruach* and *pneuma*). Passages like Psalm 104:29-30 combine these meanings.

> When you hide your face, they are terrified; when you take away their breath, they die and return to the dust. When you send your Spirit, they are created, and you renew the face of the earth.

Jesus breathed on His disciples after His resurrection (John 20:22), and the breath of God produced the Word of God (2 Tim. 3:16; 2 Peter 1:20-21). Among the other signs at Pentecost was the "sound like the blowing of a violent wind" (Acts 2:2).

In the Parable of the Sower (Matt. 13:1-23), Jesus compared the human heart to soil; and He described four different hearts according to their responses to the Word of God (the seed). Paul said that the local church is "God's field" with the potential for a harvest (1 Cor. 3:5-9). In the Parable of the Weeds (Matt. 13:24-30, 36-43), Jesus used soil to picture the lost world. "The field is the world." In this parable, the seed no longer represents God's Word; it pictures God's children scattered across the world by the Lord of the harvest. "Those who had been scattered preached the word wherever they went" (Acts 8:4, and see 8:1 and 11:19). The Greek word translated "scattered" is *diaspeiro*, which means "to scatter seed." God's people are a "spiritual dispersion" in the world (*diaspora*, James 1:1; 1 Peter 1:1).

Seed has life in it, and fruit has seed in it that can produce more fruit. The "harvest" theme is a vast one in Scripture, too big to cover in a brief paragraph. The harvest pictures spiritual maturity (Gal. 5:22-23), effective ministry (John 4:31-38; 15:1-

8), winning the lost (Matt. 9:37-38; Rom. 1:13), joy after labor (Ps. 126:5-6; Isa. 9:3), faithful giving to the Lord (Gal. 6:6-10; 2 Cor. 9:6-11), and final judgment to the lost (Matt. 13:39; Rev. 14:14-20).

In Scripture, "fruit" speaks of that which results from life. We manufacture golf balls but we grow apples. Because Christians have the life of God within them, they can bear fruit to the glory of God. The "emergency offering" for the Jerusalem Jews is compared to fruit (Rom. 15:27-28) as is the blessing accrued to the Philippian church because of their gifts sent to Paul (Phil. 4:17, Greek text). When God's people offer praise to the Lord, it's called "the fruit of lips that confess his name" (Heb. 13:15).

Human history began in a garden (Gen. 2:8-9) and will end with the saved entering a "garden city" that has a river and a fruitful tree of life (Rev. 22:1-5). Because he became a thief and took what God had forbidden, man was cast out of a garden and the entrance closed and guarded (Gen. 3:23-24). Our Lord Jesus opened paradise to a thief shortly before He died and was buried in a garden (Luke 23:39-43; John 19:41-42). Remember too the Garden of Gethsemane where Jesus prayed (Matt. 26:36-46). The image of the garden is also applied in Scripture to the home and family (Ps. 128:3; 144:12).

Two key images must be noted in Genesis 2, the *river* (2:10-14) and *marriage* (2:21-25). Water is a basic necessity of life everywhere and is especially prized in the East. We're told specifically about the wells that were dug by Abraham and Isaac (Gen. 21:25-34; 26:16-33). Water for drinking symbolizes the Spirit of God (John 7:37-39), while water for washing symbolizes the Word of God (John 15:3; Eph. 5:26-27; Ps. 119:9). The refreshing rain and dew from heaven are like God's life-giving Word (Deut. 32:2; Isa. 55:10-11; and see Hosea 14:5).

Storms and "troubled waters" speak of the tribulations of life (Pss. 18:16; 42:7; 46:3; 88:7; 93:3) and the tumult of the nations (Ps. 46:1-3; Isa. 17:12-13; 57:20-21; Dan. 7:1-3, 15-17; Luke 21:25; Rev. 13:1; 17:15). Psalm 46:4-7 contrasts the quiet but powerful "river of God" with the roaring waters of the nations (vv. 1-3), a contrast also used by the Prophets Isaiah (Isa. 8:1-10) and Jeremiah (Jer. 2:18). Judah had to choose between the help of Jehovah God ("the gently flowing waters of Shiloah") and the help of Assyria ("the mighty floodwaters of the River").

The prophets used the image of *marriage* to illustrate the relationship between Jehovah and Israel (Isa. 43:4; 49:14ff; 62:4ff; 63:9; Jer. 2:2, 20-25; 3:6, 13; 30:14; Ezek. 16:23, 33-37; 23:5, 9, 22). Hosea's unhappy marriage with Gomer formed the background for his entire book in which he pleaded with the people to abandon their idolatry (prostitution) and return to the Lord. Paul used Christian marriage to picture the relationship between Christ and the church (Eph. 5:22-33; and see Rev. 21:1-4). More than one expositor has seen in the Song of Songs an illustration of the loving communion that ought to be experienced between God's people and their Savior.

Genesis 3 presents us with the images of the *serpent, food,* and *clothing.* As the *serpent* (Gen. 3:1), Satan is the deceiver (2 Cor. 11:3); as the lion, he is the destroyer (1 Peter 5:8-9). In Revelation 12, the serpent and lion unite to produce the dragon. Genesis 3:15 informs us that Satan has a family ("your offspring"). This ties in with the Parable of the Weeds, where Jesus sees the weeds as "the sons of the evil one" (Matt. 13:38).

It's significant that there is no record that Jesus ever called the publicans and sinners "children of the devil," but He did apply that title to the Pharisees (Matt. 12:24, 34; 23:13, 33; John 8:44); and so did John the Baptist (Matt. 3:7). Satan is a masquerader (2 Cor. 11:13-15) who encourages people to cultivate a "religious self-righteousness" that becomes a substitute for the righteousness of Jesus Christ (Rom. 9:30–10:13).

Throughout Scripture, you see the conflict between the true people of God and those who have religion but not saving faith. It begins with Cain, "who belonged to the evil one" (1 John 3:12) and, like Satan, was both a liar and a murderer (Gen. 4:8-9; John 8:44). The conflict climaxes with the religious leaders who arrested Jesus, abused Him, and then crucified Him. It was the unbelieving religious leaders who persecuted the early church and their successors continue to persecute God's people today (Matt. 23:33-36).

The image of *eating* (Gen. 2:16-17; 3:1ff) is associated in

Scripture with both sin and sanctity. God's people should "hunger and thirst for righteousness" (Matt. 5:6), but sinners have an appetite for evil. Tasting, eating, swallowing, and digesting are common metaphors today for receiving something into your being. We ask, "Do you expect me to swallow that?" Or we might say, "Let me chew on that for a while" or "I'm so anxious to do that, I can just taste it!"

Describing the evil man, Zophar said to Job:

> Though evil is sweet in his mouth and he hides it under his tongue, though he cannot bear to let it go and keeps it in his mouth, yet his food will turn sour in his stomach; it will become the venom of serpents within him. He will spit out the riches he swallowed; God will make his stomach vomit them up. He will suck the poison of serpents; the fangs of an adder will kill him. He will not enjoy the streams, the rivers flowing with honey and cream. What he toiled for he must give back uneaten; he will not enjoy the profit from his trading. (Job 20:12-18)

Eliphaz used a similar image when he described the corrupt person as one "who drinks up evil like water" (Job 15:16). And Solomon wrote, "Food gained by fraud tastes sweet to a man, but he ends up with a mouth full of gravel" (Prov. 20:17).

Proverbs 6:20-35 is a warning to the young man against committing adultery, and verse 30 compares the adulterer with a hungry thief. (In chapter 5, we discussed adultery as depicted by stealing and eating.) Committing adultery satisfied the man's hunger, but the adulteress was also fed. "This is the way of an adulteress: She eats and wipes her mouth and says, 'I've done nothing wrong' " (Prov. 30:20).

"For the lips of an adulteress drip honey" (Prov. 5:3); but love sanctified by God in marriage satisfies this hunger with wine, honey, milk, and fragrant fruits (Song 4:10-15). In other words, temptation is Satan's "meal" to satisfy the normal hungers that people have within. Wisdom invites all of us to her banquet (Prov. 8:1ff), but the wicked woman also has her table spread (Prov. 7:6ff).

What you and I eat becomes a part of us. The evil person eats and drinks what's evil and becomes even more evil. The righteous person has an appetite for righteousness, and God can satisfy that hunger. When Jesus told the Jews they had to eat His flesh and drink His blood in order to have eternal life, they missed the metaphor completely and accused Him of violating the Mosaic Law (John 6:53ff). He was simply saying, "Just as your food becomes a part of you, so you must receive me by faith so that I can enter in and become a part of you."

"Taste and see that the Lord is good" (Ps. 34:8; see 1 Peter 2:3). The writer of Hebrews described believers as those "who have tasted the heavenly gift . . . who have tasted the goodness of the word of God and the powers of the coming age" (Heb. 6:4-5).[2] God's Word is compared to bread (Matt. 4:4; Deut. 8:3), milk and "solid food" (Heb. 5:11-14; 1 Cor. 3:1-2; 1 Peter 2:2) and honey (Ps. 119:103), all of which must be received within if they're to do you any good physically. For, you can starve if you only admire the beautiful pictures in the cookbook and analyze the recipes.

Jesus equated doing the will of God with eating food (John 4:31-34). God's will is nourishment, not medicine! The Lord tested Israel's obedience each morning by sending them manna to eat (Ex. 16:4-5). He reminded them of His grace each year by commanding them to celebrate Passover, a feast that included a menu of lamb, bread, and bitter herbs.[3] Jesus Christ gave His church a feast of remembrance (1 Cor. 11:17-34) involving eating bread and drinking wine. He also compared the coming messianic kingdom to a joyful feast (Matt. 8:11-12; Luke 13:28-29; 22:29-30; see Isa. 25:6-12; 55:1-5).

It's evident that the early church often met together to eat, and 1 Corinthians 10:31 makes it clear that even such ordinary activities as eating and drinking can be done to the glory of God. When Moses and his associates met God on Mt. Sinai, "they saw God, and they ate and drank" (Ex. 24:11). You would expect the text to read, "And they saw God and fell on their faces in worship." In the placing of the table of "show-bread" in the tabernacle and temple, in the eating of the sacrifices by the worshipers and priests, and in the directions concerning the various Jewish feasts, God sanctified eating and drinking.

However, the act of eating sometimes pictures defeat at the hand of the enemy. The Egyptians boasted that they would "gorge" themselves on the Israelites (Ex. 15:9), but instead the waters of the sea swallowed them up (15:12). David prayed that his foes wouldn't swallow him up (Ps. 35:25) or devour his people "as men eat bread" (53:4; and see 124:3). Babylon devoured Judah (Jer. 51:34) and Israel was devoured by the nations (Hosea 8:8). Sinners plot how to swallow their victims alive (Prov. 1:12), and soldiers devour the enemy with their swords and arrows (Deut. 32:42; 2 Sam. 2:26; 11:25; Isa. 1:20; Jer. 46:10, 14; Nahum 2:13; 3:15). Of course, the ultimate devourer is death (Ps. 49:14). The teachers of the law "devoured widows' houses" (Mark 12:38-40; Luke 20:47).

Our next image is that of *clothing*. When they were in their state of innocence, Adam and Eve were not ashamed to be naked (Gen. 2:25); but after they had sinned, they felt ashamed and sought for a covering (Gen. 3:7). God rejected their coverings and gave them skins to wear (Gen. 3:21), implying that blood had to be shed for them to be acceptable to God.

The Apostle Paul saw in clothing a picture of character and conduct. He admonishes us to "put off" the things of the old life, the way we would take off dirty clothes, and then "put on" the graces of the new life (Rom. 13:11-14; Eph. 4:17–5:21; Col. 3:1-17). He also exhorts us to take our stand against the devil by putting on the spiritual armor that God has provided (Eph. 6:10-18). In the references in Ephesians and Colossians, Paul's imagery seems to come from the graveclothes that Jesus left behind in the tomb. There may also be an allusion to John 11:43-44.

"All of us have become like one who is unclean," wrote Isaiah, "and all our righteous acts are like filthy rags" (Isa. 64:6). But what can sinners do about their unacceptable garments? When Messiah ushers in the Year of Jubilee, He gives His people "a garment of praise instead of a spirit of despair" (Isa. 61:1-3); He dresses them like brides and bridegrooms adorned for the wedding (Isa. 61:10; and see 2 Cor. 5:17 and

Rev. 19:8). The Prodigal Son comes home and is dressed in the best garment in the house (Luke 15:22).

Sometimes in Scripture, a new beginning is marked by people washing themselves and changing their clothes. This was true of Jacob's family when Jacob returned to Bethel (Gen. 35:1-3) and of Joseph when he left the prison (Gen. 41:14). The people of Israel prepared to meet Jehovah at Sinai by washing their clothes (Ex. 19:10, 14), and the priests and Levites prepared themselves for ministry by having a thorough cleansing and receiving special garments (Ex. 29; Num. 8:5-7, 21). Personal purification for any Jew who was ceremonially unclean involved bathing and wearing clean garments (Num. 19:17-22). "Wash and make yourselves clean" (Isa. 1:16; and see 2 Cor. 7:1).

The ceremonial cleansing of Joshua the high priest illustrates the point (Zech. 3). The high priest was never to appear before the Lord wearing dirty clothes; so Joshua's plight was a serious one. He pictured the defilement of the Jewish remnant that had returned to the land to rebuild the temple. The filthy garments gave Satan an opportunity to accuse, but God saw this as an opportunity to magnify His grace. Joshua was cleansed and reclothed and his ministry restored. Isn't this what the Lord promised His people in 1 John 1:9? Paul saw in the transformation of the body at the coming of Christ an experience of "being clothed upon" with the new body (1 Cor. 15:53-54; 2 Cor. 5:1-4). The Twelve were "clothed with power from on high" (Luke 24:49), and the Holy Spirit "clothed himself" with Gideon (Jud. 6:34), Amasai (1 Chron. 12:18), and Zechariah (2 Chron. 24:20). Shame and disgrace are compared to clothing (Ps. 35:26; Job 8:22); so are righteousness and justice (Job 29:14; Ps. 132:9) and strength and splendor (Isa. 52:1).

Before leaving the theme of garments, we should look at two occasions in Bible history when garments played significant roles. The first is recorded in 1 Samuel 15 when the Lord rejected Saul as king. "As Samuel turned to leave, Saul caught hold of the hem of his robe, and it tore. Samuel said to him, 'The Lord has torn the kingdom of Israel from you today' " (1 Sam. 15:27-28). The second is found in 1 Kings 11:26-39, when the Prophet Ahijah tore his new robe into twelve pieces and gave ten of them to Jeroboam, signifying that he would be ruler over the ten tribes that would secede from the kingdom. Because garments are so closely identified with the person, these "action sermons" wouldn't have been so effective had Samuel and Ahijah used some other object. In this regard, we're reminded of our Lord's seamless robe (John 19:23-24).

Genesis 4:1 introduces us to the first *pregnancy* in the Bible and therefore to the theme of pregnancy and birth. Jesus used birth to illustrate spiritual rebirth (John 3:1-21). Just as pregnancy involves two parents, so spiritual birth involves the Spirit of God (John 3:5-6) and the Word of God (1 Peter 1:22-25). Our Lord's travail in suffering would make possible the joy of birth (John 16:16-22).

But pregnancy and birth also tell us something about sin. "He who is pregnant with evil and conceives trouble gives birth to disillusionment" (Ps. 7:14). Eliphaz said of the godless, "They conceive trouble and give birth to evil; their womb fashions deceit" (Job 15:35). This sounds a good deal like James 1:15. Isaiah wrote, "You conceive chaff, you give birth to straw" (Isa. 33:11); and in 59:4-14, Isaiah gives a vivid picture of the terrible plight of Jerusalem, including people in court who "conceive trouble and give birth to evil" (Isa. 59:4).

When we studied 2 Samuel 12, we saw that temptation was pictured as a visitor who came to a rich man's house. The rich man forgot how rich he was and stole a pet lamb from his poor neighbor and fed it to his guest. In Genesis 4:7, temptation is pictured as a wild beast poised at the door, waiting to spring. "But if you [Cain] do not do what is right, sin is crouching at your door; it desires to have you, but you must master it." To yield to temptation is to open the door. But why was the beast crouching at the door of *Cain's* life? Because the deception and anger in Cain's heart attracted it. Paul's admonition, "And do not give the devil a foothold" is preceded by a warning against deception and anger (Eph. 4:25-27). James pictures temptation as the bait on a hook or in a trap (James 1:13-15); but in Genesis 4, it was Cain who put out the bait to attract temptation!

Let's leave the animal at the door for a moment and give some consideration to the image of the *door* itself. By his unbelief and disobedience, Cain closed the door on the Lord when he went to the altar to worship. By his anger, he closed the door on his brother; and by his deception, he closed the door on himself. Cain knew where his brother was, but he tried to fool God. By his despair, Cain closed the door to his future. Cain opened the wrong door; and when he did, he closed the doors that should have stayed open.

One final picture should be noted in Genesis 4, that of *"the ground* which opened its mouth" to receive Abel's blood (Gen. 4:11). God commanded His people to show reverence for blood (Gen. 9:4-6; Lev. 17:11; Deut. 12:23; Ps. 72:14) and not to eat blood as a food, or meat that still had the blood in it (Lev. 3:17; Deut. 12:16). There were probably hygienic reasons behind this law, but primarily it pointed to the "precious blood" of the Son of God who would die for the sins of the world (1 Peter 1:18-19). Abel's blood cried out for vengeance (Gen. 4:10), but the blood of Christ speaks of forgiveness (Heb. 12:24).

When Abel died, the ground "opened its mouth" to receive the martyr's blood. People were not allowed to drink or eat blood, but the ground could "drink" it. In fact, for a dead body (with the blood) to remain unburied was a great humiliation (Isa. 14:18-20; 66:24; Jer. 22:18-19). But there comes a time when "the earth will disclose the blood shed upon her; she will conceal her slain no longer" (Isa. 26:21; see Num. 35:33-34). Job prayed that, after he died, his blood would cry out for the justice that had been denied him in life (Job 16:18-22).

The land bears witness to the sins committed upon it. If the people defile the land with their sins, the land will vomit them out (Lev. 18:24-28; 20:22). Man's sins make God's earth sick! The earth cried out to God about Abel's murder. Job invited his land to bear witness of any sin he'd committed against the earth (Job 31:38). In these days of ecological crisis, we wonder what the land would say about the sins of those who exploit God's creation.

Let's look at only a few more images in Genesis, and then

we'll move on to the rest of the Pentateuch. The *cities of Sodom and Gomorrah* (Gen. 13:10-13; 14; 18–19) represent that which is evil in God's sight and so deserves to be destroyed. The phrase "like Sodom and Gomorrah" describes people who are morally filthy and deserve to experience the wrath of God (Deut. 29:23; Isa. 1:9-10; 3:9; 13:19; Jer. 23:14; 49:18; 50:40; Lam. 4:6; Amos 4:11; Zeph. 2:9; Rom. 9:29; 2 Peter 2:6). Ezekiel 16:44ff traces Israel's ancestry to Sodom, and Jesus used the two wicked cities to show how unbelieving the Jews were in His day (Matt. 10:15; 11:23-24; Luke 10:12). Sodom and Gomorrah "serve as an example of those who suffer the punishment of eternal fire" (Jude 7). Revelation 11:8 uses Sodom as a code word for the city of Jerusalem, which ties in with Isaiah 1:10. The mention of Sodom and Gomorrah in Deuteronomy 32:32 refers to the enemies of Israel.

Jacob's act of *pouring oil* on the rock at Bethel (Gen. 28:18), an act of worship that he repeated years later (Gen. 35:14-15), depicts sacrificial offering. The Jews had their drink offerings which accompanied their sacrifices (Num. 15:1-12). Our Lord's death on the cross meant that He "poured out his life unto death" (Isa. 53:12) and was "poured out like water" (Ps. 22:14). The act of pouring out a liquid speaks of sacrifice and service. Mary's act of devotion to Christ comes to mind (John 12:1-8), and also the devotion shown by the woman who was a forgiven sinner (Luke 7:36-50).

Just as the Jewish drink offerings accompanied their other sacrifices, so God's servants by their giving of themselves share in the ministry of others. Paul was "poured out like a drink offering on the sacrifice and service coming from [the Philippians'] faith" (Phil. 2:17). He used the same image when describing his impending death in Rome (2 Tim. 4:6). To the Corinthians he says, "So I will very gladly spend for you everything I have and expend myself as well" (2 Cor. 12:15; see Ecc. 2:19).

In times of great agony, God's people pour out their souls to God in prayer (Ps. 42:4; 62:8; 142:1-2). Job's groans poured out like water (Job 3:24; see Lam. 2:11, 19), and his eyes poured out tears before the Lord (Job 16:20).

We also see the image of a *stench* (Gen. 34:30). Because of

101

what Simeon and Levi did to the men of Shechem, Jacob was in danger. "You have brought trouble on me by making me a stench to the Canaanites and Perizzites, the people living in this land" (Gen. 34:30; and see Ex. 5:21; 1 Sam. 13:4; 2 Sam. 10:6; 16:21; 1 Chron. 19:6). Even today, we say things like "His name stinks" or "His reputation smells." What is the connection between names and odors?

"A good name is better than fine perfume, and the day of death better than the day of birth" (Ecc. 7:1). Solomon wasn't suggesting that the burial of a body is better than the birth of a baby, but that, as far as a person's name is concerned, his funeral is better than his birthday. Why? Because after people die, their names and reputations are sealed. A good name will remain good and the deceased won't be able to hurt it. When the baby is named, nobody knows what will happen to that name; but after a person dies, the reputation is known and settled. "The memory of the righteous will be a blessing, but the name of the wicked will rot" (Prov. 10:7). And whatever rots usually smells.

Judas Iscariot was given a good name, for "Judah" means "praise" and belonged to the kingly tribe in Israel. But he ruined that name by his sins, and I doubt that any parents today would call a son Judas. On the other hand, Mary of Bethany, the woman that Judas criticized, has a fragrant name that is honored wherever the Gospel is preached (Mark 14:1-9; John 12:1-8).

When the priest ministered at the golden altar of incense in the holy place (Ex. 30:1-10, 34-38), he certainly picked up some of the fragrance and carried it with him. Prayer ought to make our lives fragrant. Our Lord's death on the cross was "a fragrant offering and sacrifice to God" (Eph. 5:2), and the lives of God's people should follow His example. Godly living is beautiful and fragrant. Paul looked upon the gifts sent by the Philippians as "a fragrant offering, an acceptable sacrifice, pleasing to God" (Phil. 4:18).

The image in 2 Corinthians 2:14 relates to the "Roman Triumph," the parade that was given to honor any Roman general who had won a great victory in foreign territory, gained new lands for Rome, and brought home valuable spoils from the battle. The general rode in a golden chariot, and with him were his soldiers and the captives they had taken. The Roman priests would have their censers filled with burning incense, and this fragrance would mean life to the victorious soldiers but death to the captives heading for the arena. Jesus Christ has won a complete victory over the enemy (Col. 2:15), and His people march with Him in this triumphal procession. No matter where we go, we should be surrounded by the fragrance of His victory. After all, we march in triumph!

I suggest you study Genesis 49 and note the images Jacob used as he unveiled for his sons the future of the twelve tribes of Israel. Most of his images relate to animal life, but he knew his sons better than we do! Note two images of the Lord: He is the Shepherd and the Rock of Israel (Gen. 49:24).

The shepherd image in Scripture begins with Abel (Gen. 4:2), and continues through the patriarchs, Moses and David, and climaxes with Christ the Shepherd (John 10; Heb. 13:20; 1 Peter 2:25; 5:4; Rev. 7:17). Pastors of local flocks of believers are also shepherds (Acts 20:28). The civil rulers in Israel were looked upon as shepherds (2 Sam. 5:2; 7:7; 1 Chron. 11:2; 17:6; Ps. 78:71; Jer. 3:15; 10:21; 23:1ff; Ezek. 34).

Jacob told Joseph that God had been his shepherd all the days of his life (Gen. 48:15). References to God the Shepherd include: Psalms 23:1; 28:9; 80:1; Isaiah 40:11; Jeremiah 31:10; Zechariah 13:7; Matthew 2:6; 26:31.

The image of God as the Rock speaks of His stability and dependability, the unchangeableness of His nature, and the faithfulness of His dealings. We may go to Him for refuge because He is ever the same and His Word never fails. First Corinthians 10:4 authorizes us to see Christ symbolized in the rock that gave Israel water (Ex. 17:1-7; Num. 20:1-13). In Moses' farewell song, five times he compared Jehovah to a rock (Deut. 32:4, 15, 18, 30-31). See 1 Samuel 2:2; 2 Samuel 22:2-3, 32, 47; 23:3; Psalms 18:2, 31, 46; 19:14; 28:1; 31:2-3; 42:9; 62:2, 6-7; 71:3; 78:35; 89:26; 92:15; 94:22; 95:1; 144:1; Isaiah 8:14 (Rom. 9:33; 1 Peter 2:8); 17:10; 26:4; 30:29; 44:8; 51:1; Habakkuk 1:12.

Exodus

The first fifteen chapters focus on the theme of redemption, Israel's going out (exodus) from Egypt. The *exodus* image is related to our Lord's death in Luke 9:31 and to the death of the believer in 2 Peter 1:15.[4]

Redemption is an important theme in the development of New Testament soteriology. The Song of Zechariah (Luke 1:67-79) majors on it, and it's the emphasis of Anna's witness to the Jewish remnant waiting for the Savior (Luke 2:36-38; and see 24:21). Paul deals with the doctrine of redemption in Romans (3:24; 8:23), Galatians (3:13-14) and Ephesians (1:7, 14; 4:30; and see Col. 1:13-14); and Peter mentions it in 1 Peter 1:18-19. Jesus Christ has set us free by paying a tremendous price, His own precious blood.[5]

Pharaoh's officials asked him, "How long will this man [Moses] be a snare to us?" (Ex. 10:7) Moses later warned the Jews that the gods of the Canaanites would be a *snare* to them if Israel didn't destroy them (Ex. 23:33; 34:12; Deut. 7:16, 25; 12:30; Jud. 2:3). The psalmists saw the ploys and plots of the enemy as snares to trip up the godly (Pss. 25:15; 91:3; 119:110; 140:5; 142:3). Israel was delivered from her enemies like a bird set free from a trap (Ps. 124:7).

Two other images from the first part of Exodus should be mentioned: the *lamb* (Ex. 12:1-13, 21-23) and the *leaven* (Ex. 12:14-20). More than one expositor has pointed out that the lamb might well be called the theme of the whole Bible.[6] Isaac asked, "Where is the lamb for the burnt offering?" (Gen. 22:7), and his question was answered by John the Baptist, "Look, the Lamb of God, who takes away the sin of the world!" (John 1:29, 36) Other Scriptures to consider are Isaiah 53:7, 1 Peter 1:19, and Revelation 5:6-14. The word "lamb" is used twenty-eight times in the Book of Revelation to refer to Jesus Christ.

In the Passover scenario, *leaven* represents that which is evil. Passover is called the Feast of Unleavened Bread because leaven (yeast) was to be put out of the Jewish homes for the full week of the celebration (Ex. 12:15ff; 13:6-7; 23:15; 34:18; see also Lev. 23:6; Num. 28:17; Deut. 16:3). In the first Passover, the leaven was left out of the dough because the people were leaving in a hurry and couldn't wait for the dough to rise; but from the New Testament usage, leaven symbolizes various kinds of evil: false teaching (Matt. 16:5-12; Gal. 5:9), hypocrisy (Luke 12:1), and "malice and wickedness" (1 Cor. 5:6-8). Like yeast, sin enters quietly, grows secretly, and soon permeates the whole mass. *yeast also puffs up!*

The "Song of Moses" in Exodus 15 abounds with imagery.[7] The Egyptian soldiers were "hurled into the sea" like so many dead stones that "sank like lead" (vv. 1, 5, 10). The army was shattered like clay pots (v. 6, and see Ps. 2:9) and burned up like stubble (v. 7). Instead of the Egyptians swallowing Israel (v. 9), the waters swallowed the Egyptians (v. 12). All God had to do was exhale and the water congealed into a wall, and then the wall fell on the pursuing army (vv. 8, 10). This great victory assured Israel that their enemies in Canaan would "melt away" and become "as still as a stone" (vv. 15-16; see Josh. 2:9, 24). God would "plant" His people in their land where they would grow and prosper (v. 17).[8]

Like the image of the vine, the image of the *eagle* (Ex. 19:4) is often used with reference to Israel. In this text, the entire Exodus experience is compared to an eagle swooping down and carrying away its prey. In spite of their bondage, the Jews had gotten too content in Egypt;[9] and God had to "shake up the nest" and teach them to fly by faith (Deut. 32:11). Centuries later, when the Jewish remnant returned to the land to rebuild their nation and their lives, God promised to help them "soar on wings like eagles" (Isa. 40:31).[10] Revelation 12:13-14 describes a future eagle-like deliverance for God's people.[11]

Israel is not only a vine and a people miraculously delivered on eagles' wings, but she is God's "treasured possession. . . . a kingdom of priests and a holy nation" (Ex. 19:5-6). Peter applied these images to Christians in 1 Peter 2:5 and 9.[12] The image of the treasured possession or inheritance is repeated often by Moses in Deuteronomy (4:20; 7:6; 9:26, 29; 14:2; 26:18; 32:9) and by the psalmists (28:9; 33:12; 74:2; 79:1; 94:14; 106:5, 40). Solomon refers to it in his prayer of dedication (1 Kings 8:51, 53), and the prophets use it too (Isa. 19:25;

63:17; Jer. 10:16; 51:19; Micah 7:18; Zech. 2:12). Since Israel is God's "treasured possession," two things are true: the people ought to love God and obey Him; and God must take care of His people, especially when the enemy invades His inheritance.[13]

Numbers

The Book of Hebrews uses Israel's experience at Kadesh Barnea (Num. 13–14) to emphasize the importance of obeying God by faith and claiming our spiritual inheritance (Heb. 3–5). The bondage in Egypt illustrates the plight of the lost sinner who can be delivered only through faith in the blood of the Lamb and the power of God. Canaan represents the believer's inheritance in Jesus Christ, an inheritance claimed by faith as depicted in the Book of Joshua. Canaan is not a picture of heaven, and crossing the Jordan is not a picture of death, in spite of what the song writers say. Crossing the Jordan illustrates the believer's death to the old life and entrance by faith into the rich *present* inheritance in Christ (Eph. 1:3). In heaven, there will be no enemies or wars!

Israel came to Kadesh Barnea and refused to trust God for the power to defeat the enemy and claim their God-given inheritance (Num. 13–14). "So we see that they were not able to enter, because of their unbelief" (Heb. 3:19). As a consequence, they wandered in the wilderness for thirty-eight years until that older unbelieving generation died off; and during those years of wandering, they did a great deal of rebelling and complaining! It appears that most professing Christians today are between Egypt and Canaan. They had enough faith to be delivered from Egypt, but they do not have enough faith to enter into Canaan and become "more than conquerors."

In Numbers 13:32 and 14:9 we find the image of eating: the land will swallow up the people, but the people can swallow up their enemies. Balak, king of Moab, was afraid that Israel would "lick up everything . . . as an ox licks up the grass of the field" (Num. 22:4). Balaam the prophet saw Israel as a wild ox and a lioness (Num. 23:22, 24; 24:9), their camp spread out "like gardens beside a river" (Num. 24:6).

The familiar phrase "like sheep without a shepherd" is introduced in Numbers 27:17 and is found again in 1 Kings 22:17, 2 Chronicles 18:16, Ezekiel 34:5-6, Zechariah 10:2, and Matthew 9:36.

Deuteronomy

The Lord "carried" Israel like a strong eagle (Ex. 19:4; Deut. 32:10-11), a concerned father (Deut. 1:31; Isa. 46:3-4; 63:9; Hosea 11:3), and a loving shepherd (Ps. 28:9).

Egypt was "the iron-smelting furnace" (Deut. 4:20) where God allowed His people to suffer (Gen. 15:13-14; 1 Kings 8:51; Jer. 11:4). Hell is compared to a furnace (Matt. 13:42, 50; and see Gen. 19:28).

"For the Lord your God is a consuming fire, a jealous God" (Deut. 4:24; 9:3; Heb. 12:29) and His anger "burns like fire" (Ex. 15:7; 32:10-11; Deut. 6:15; 7:4; 11:17; Josh. 23:16; 2 Kings 22:17; Job 19:11; 20:23; Pss. 79:5; 89:46; Isa. 5:25; 9:5; 13:13; 42:25; Jer. 4:4; 21:12; 15:14; 17:4; 21:12; Hosea 8:5; Zech. 10:3). Fire not only symbolizes God's holy anger against sin, but it also speaks of God's protection of His people as "a wall of fire" around them (Zech. 2:5).

Moses' song in Deuteronomy 32 opens with a comparison of the Word of God to rain and dew (32:2; and see Job 29:23 and Isa. 55:10-11). Just as the land needs the rain and dew in order to be fruitful, so mankind needs God's Word to produce spiritual fruit for His glory. Unlike the land of Egypt, where the farmers used irrigation, the Promised Land depended on rain and dew to water the crops; and God sent the rain if His people were obedient (Deut. 11:8-15). Proverbs 16:15 compares the favor of the king to the refreshing rain on the earth.

Moses' prophetic blessing of the twelve tribes should be compared with the blessing Jacob gave his sons (Gen. 49). Note that both Moses and Jacob use comparisons with animals. God is compared to a *shield* and a *sword* in Deuteronomy 33:12 and 29 (images that are also found in Gen. 15:1; Deut. 32:10; 2 Sam. 22:3, 31; Pss. 3:3; 7:10; 18:2, 30; 28:7; 33:20; 59:11;

84:11; 115:9-11; 119:114; 144:2; Prov. 2:7; 30:5; Isa. 31:5; Zech. 9:15; 12:8). Psalms 84:9 and 89:18 refer to Israel's king as "our shield," and Paul used the image of the shield to illustrate the protective power of faith (Eph. 6:16). According to 1 Peter 1:5, God's people are "shielded by God's power" through their faith in Him. I've devoted more attention to some of the images found in the Pentateuch because they are repeated frequently in Scripture and are basic to our understanding of biblical symbolism.

I've passed over some of the minor images, but you can locate them and trace them for yourself. Whenever you find a figurative expression in the Bible, trace the cross references[14] and see how they relate to each other. I'll have more to say about this kind of Bible study when we get to Part III.

"We learn nothing rightly
until we learn the symbolical
character of life."

—*Ralph Waldo Emerson*

"The capacity for wonder
presupposes a certain childlikeness
that has lost its value today
in both literature and art."

—*Van Wyck Brooks*

Chapter Ten
Pictures in the Historical Books

Joshua

Metaphorical expressions in the historical books of the Old Testament are found primarily in conversations and occasional excursions into poetry. Some of them are common expressions that are almost clichés, such as Rahab's statements that "all who live in this country are melting in fear because of you" and "our hearts melted" (Josh. 2:9, 11; and see 5:1). In Joshua 7:5 and 14:8, it was Israel whose hearts melted from fear and discouragement. You'll recall that Hushai used this metaphor when addressing Absalom (2 Sam. 17:10), and it is found in the prophets (Isa. 13:7; 19:1; Ezek. 21:7, 15; Nahum 2:10; and see Ps. 107:26).

In Joshua 2:19, the two spies equate "blood" with "life," a reference to Leviticus 17:11. To have blood on one's head or one's hands is to be guilty of taking someone's life (see Gen. 42:22; Lev. 20:11-13, 16, 27; 2 Sam. 1:16; 3:29; 4:11; 1 Kings 2:31, 33, 37; Isa. 59:3). This image also relates to Ezekiel's picture of the watchman who was responsible for the lives (blood) of those in the city (Ezek. 3:17-20; 23:37, 45; 33:4-8). Paul used the image in Acts 18:6 and 20:26, and Jesus used it in Luke 11:50-51 and Matthew 23:35-36. The Jewish religious leaders well understood what it meant (Acts 5:28) and so did Pilate (Matt. 27:24). Deuteronomy 22:8 informs us that it's possible to have blood "on your house" as well as on your hands.

Judges

The Song of Deborah (Jud. 5) pictures God's victory over Sisera in a dramatic way and closes with a poetic description of God's people: "But may they who love you be like the sun when it rises in its strength" (Jud. 5:31). God had sent a terrific storm to help Deborah and Barak defeat Sisera; and when the sun rose the next day and the storm was over, that sunrise was God's announcement of His victory. David compared godly leaders to the sunrise, because they brought light and hope for a new day (2 Sam. 23:4).

I wonder how Samson's wife reacted when she heard him compare her to a cow: "If you had not plowed with my heifer, you would not have solved my riddle" (Jud. 14:18). Amos used the same image when describing the lazy, indulgent women of Samaria, and he warned them that they would all be led away like cattle (Amos 4:1-3). The image of hooks that Amos uses is also found in 2 Kings 19:28 and Ezekiel 29:4. In addition, see what God allowed to happen to evil King Manasseh (2 Chron. 33:11). If people will not act like human beings, made in the image of God, then the Lord has to treat them like animals.

Ruth

The words of Boaz in Ruth 2:12 are both beautiful and full of spiritual meaning: "May you be richly rewarded by the Lord, the God of Israel, under whose wings you have come to take refuge." The image of wings usually makes us think of little chicks being protected by the mother hen (Matt. 23:37; Luke 13:34; and see Pss. 17:8; 57:1; 91:4), but there is another image involved: the wings of the cherubim in the holy of holies (Ex. 25:17-22). This seems to be the picture in references such as Psalms 36:7-8, 61:4, and 63:7. (Note the reference to God's sanctuary in Ps. 63:2.) As a Gentile, Ruth was outside the covenants of God and therefore condemned; but her faith in the God of Israel brought her into the very holy of holies! (Eph. 2:11-22)

The image of wings appears again in Ruth 3:9, where the

word "corner" is the Hebrew word "wing." (See also Ezek. 16:8.) Ruth asked Boaz to "spread the wings of his protection" over her, something he was most willing to do.

Samuel

God "weighs" our actions (1 Sam. 2:3), our motives (Prov. 16:2), and our hearts (Prov. 21:2; 24:11-12). In fact, He weighs us and isn't impressed with the weight of our wealth (Ps. 62:9) or our splendor (Dan. 5:27). Job wanted his anguish weighed (Job 6:2; see Prov. 12:25).

It's worth noting that the Greek word *axios*, translated "worth" and "worthy" in the New Testament, comes from a root that implies *weight*. According to Werner Foerster, the picture is that of "bringing up the other beam of the scales."[1] Worthy people are those who "balance the scales" and are "equivalent" to the measure God has placed on the other side. We are "weighed" by our calling (Eph. 4:1), the Gospel (Phil. 1:27), the Lord (Col. 1:10), God (1 Thes. 2:12), and the glory yet to come (Rom. 8:18). Worthy people are people of "weight" and not chaff that blows away in the wind.

The Hebrew word *kabed* means "to be heavy, to have weight," and is sometimes translated "honorable" and "glorious." Distinguished people are "people of weight" (Num. 22:15). When Paul wrote about "an eternal glory that far outweighs them all [all our sufferings]" (2 Cor. 4:17), he was probably referring to the Hebrew concept that united "weight" and "glory."

In her speech to David in 1 Samuel 25:23-31, Abigail contrasts the security of the godly ("bound securely in the bundle of the living") with the insecurity of God's enemies who are hurled away "as from the pocket of a sling" (1 Sam. 25:29), a metaphor that would be especially meaningful to a man who was an expert with a sling (1 Sam. 17:50). Hurling people out of the land is often used as an image of judgment. Jeremiah applied it to the people of Judah (Jer. 10:18) and to King Jehoiachin (Jer. 22:26), and Isaiah used it to warn selfish Shebna (Isa. 22:15-19).

In his lament over the deaths of Saul and Jonathan, David compared them to *eagles* for their swiftness and *lions* for their strength, metaphors that are rather lifeless today (2 Sam. 1:23). But David also compared Saul and Jonathan to "weapons of war" (2 Sam. 1:27). They not only knew how to *use* weapons (1:22), but they themselves were the weapons. Messiah is compared to a polished arrow in Isaiah 49:2, and the army of Zion is pictured as bows, arrows, and "a warrior's sword" in Zechariah 9:13. Paul adopts a similar image when he admonishes God's people to yield the members of their bodies as "instruments of righteousness" (Rom. 6:13), where the word translated "instruments" can also mean "weapons" (John 18:3; Rom. 13:12; 2 Cor. 6:7; 10:4). God not only *gives* us spiritual weapons to use in the battle (Eph. 6:10-17), but He wants to *make us* His weapons as we yield to Him.[2]

In 2 Samuel 14, the wily woman of Tekoa used two interesting metaphors when she tried to trick David into being reconciled to Absalom: a burning coal (v. 7) and water spilled on the ground (v. 14). If her only son should be slain, her last burning coal, there could be no more "family" because the fire would go out. This image parallels that of "the lamp going out." When David was almost slain by the Philistine giant, his men said to him, "Never again will you go out with us to battle, so that the lamp of Israel will not be extinguished" (2 Sam. 21:17; and see 1 Kings 11:36; 15:4; 2 Kings 8:19; 2 Chron. 21:7; Ps. 132:17). The woman saw Absalom as the only hope for the continuing of the "light of Israel" after David's death.[3]

"Water spilled on the ground" (2 Sam. 14:14) is a vivid picture of something vanishing that could never again be reclaimed. Job used a similar image (Job 14:10-12), and see Psalms 22:14-15 and 58:7. Only God could reclaim water spilled on the ground, but David could recall his son and guarantee the perpetuation of the royal line. If he didn't do so, it would be a terrible waste that could not be repaired.[4] Perhaps the image of "water spilled on the ground" reminded David of his experience in the cave when his three mighty men brought him water from the well of Bethlehem (2 Sam. 23:13-17).

David's song of praise in 2 Samuel 22, repeated in Psalm 18, reflects the natural imagery seen by a man who was both an outdoorsman and a soldier. Five times he refers to God as "a rock" (vv. 2-3, 32, 47) and three times as "a refuge" (vv. 3, 31). The metaphors of the storm (vv. 5-16) and David's deliverance from drowning (vv. 17-20) remind us of his years of exile in the wilderness of Judea when Saul attempted to kill him. God is a lamp (v. 29) and a shield (vv. 3, 31, 36), so that neither darkness nor danger can frighten His servant. After living in "tight places," David was brought out "into a spacious place" (v. 20); and God broadened his path for him (v. 37). One of the Hebrew words for "trouble" means "to be in a tight place" (*sarar* — to make narrow, to be in distress, to bind). God disciplines us in the "tight places" of life and then delivers us into broad places. In the New Testament, the Greek words *thlibo* and *thlipsis* carry a similar image of a person being straitened and pressured. Sometimes God enlarges our troubles so that He might enlarge us and put us in a larger place! That's what He did for David.

The poem entitled "The Last Words of David" (2 Sam. 23:1-7) focuses on the kind of leaders God wants for His people. A godly ruler is like the dawning of a new day after the storm (v. 4), which may suggest the contrast between Saul's kingship and David's. The godly leader brings forth grass (vv. 4-5), but the ungodly leader produces thorns (v. 6).[5]

Kings

The image of the *yoke* (1 Kings 12:4, 9-11, 14, 19, 21) is first found in Genesis 27:40. Israel's enslavement in Egypt was the wearing of a yoke (Ex. 6:6-7), and God used the same imagery to announce Judah's deliverance from Assyria (Isa. 10:24-27; 14:25). While it certainly was motivated by humane concerns for the animals, the prohibition against yoking an ox and an ass together (Deut. 22:10) was used by Paul to enforce the believer's separation from sin (2 Cor. 6:14). Israel's apostasy meant breaking off God's yoke (Jer. 2:20) and taking the yoke of foreign gods (see Ps. 106:28). As we shall see later, Jeremiah is preeminently "the prophet of the yoke."

115

"Jezebel's body will be like refuse on the ground." That was Elijah's prophecy and it came true (2 Kings 9:34-37). The ultimate in humiliation was to have one's corpse treated like garbage and especially like manure, which is what Israel sometimes did to their enemies (Ps. 83:9-10). This was the way Jehovah humiliated His rebellious people in Judah (Jer. 8:1-3; 9:22; 16:4; 25:33). The image in Isaiah 25:10-11 is especially vivid: first Moab is trodden into the manure, and then the people have to *swim through it*. What a way to bring down a nation's pride! Jesus said that tasteless salt wasn't even fit for the manure pile (Luke 14:35), which shows how tragic it is when a professed disciple loses his or her character. Manure is at least good for something, but tasteless salt "is no longer good for anything" (Matt. 5:13).

Isaiah's prophecy concerning Assyria (2 Kings 19:20-34; Isa. 37:21-35) speaks of Jerusalem as "the Virgin Daughter of Zion," a title used almost exclusively by Jeremiah (Jer. 14:17; 18:13; 31:4, 21; Lam. 1:15; 2:13; and see Amos 5:2). Like a virgin daughter protected by her father, Jerusalem would be protected by Jehovah; and her walls would not be breached by the invading Assyrian army. Jeremiah saw the "virgin city" invaded by Babylon, violated and crushed like grapes in a winepress (Lam. 1:15). But he also saw the day coming when the city would be restored and the Lord would treat Jerusalem like a "virgin daughter" again (Jer. 31:4, 21).

Isaiah compared the Assyrian army to shoots of grass in the field and on the housetops (2 Kings 19:26; and see Ps. 129:5-7). They had no deep roots and would be scorched by the rising sun. The Assyrian soldiers were like animals who would be led away in humiliation (2 Kings 19:28; see vv. 35-37). But see what Assyria would do to King Manasseh (2 Chron. 33:10-11).

There are two images in 2 Kings 21:13, the first relating to building construction and the second, to the domestic task of washing and drying dishes. The measuring line and plumb line were used for *construction*, but the Lord would use them for *destruction*. (See Isa. 34:11, Lam. 2:8, and Amos 7:7-9.) People wash dishes so they can use them again, and God would cleanse Jerusalem of its evil rulers so that He might eventually start anew with a godly remnant.

Chronicles

We have already noted the metaphor of lions (1 Chron. 12:8; see 2 Sam. 17:10). The image of the breaking of a dam (1 Chron. 14:11) is found in 2 Samuel 5:20. God's people as "aliens and strangers" (1 Chron. 29:15) is an image that begins with Abraham (Gen. 17:8; 23:4; and see 28:4; Ex. 6:4; Heb. 11:13) and continues into the New Testament (1 Peter 2:11). The patriarchs lived in tents because they were looking for a permanent city and didn't want to get too settled down in this world (Heb. 11:13-16). When Lot abandoned his tent and moved into the city of Sodom, he took the first step toward ruin (Gen. 13).

"The most effective poetry is that which leaves you with an emotion or sense of its potential in your own thinking."
—*Luci Shaw*

"For the poet's trade is not to talk about experience, but to make it happen."
—*John Ciardi*

"And what therefore is truth? A mobile army of metaphors. . . ."
—*Nietzsche*

Chapter Eleven
Pictures in the Poetical Books

Then, Sir, what is poetry?" James Boswell asked the great British essayist and lexicographer, Samuel Johnson.
"Why, Sir, it is much easier to say what it is not," Johnson replied. "We all know what light is not; but it is not easy to tell what it is."[1] Even so, Johnson did a fine job of defining poetry as "the art of uniting pleasure with truth, by calling imagination to the help of reason."[2] The more you ponder that definition, the more sense it makes.

The poetry of the Bible conveys divine truth in an imaginative way that nourishes the heart and stimulates the mind.[3] God has seen fit to give us part of His revelation in poetical form, and we must recognize this. Students who treat the speeches of Job or the songs of David as they would the narratives of the Gospels or the doctrinal arguments of Paul are sure to miss the meanings wrapped up in these poetical packages.

The Book of Job[4]

The overriding image in the Book of Job is that of a court of law, with Job challenging Jehovah to declare his crime and present the evidence necessary to convict him. (See Job 9:3, 14-16, 32-35; 10:2; 13:3, 18-19; 23:6; 31:35-37.) Job pleads for an umpire or arbitrator who could bring him and God together to settle the case once and for all (9:33; and see 16:19 and 19:25).[5] Job's complaint is that the Lord had convicted him and

119

sentenced him before declaring his crime and giving him a fair trial.

Job saw himself as a target at which God aimed His arrows, against which Job had no protection (6:4; 7:20). God had declared war on Job and unleashed "wave after wave" of His forces against him (10:17; 16:14). Because of the way God treated him, Job felt like a dry leaf, chaff in the wind, a shackled prisoner, and a rotting garment (13:24-28). In 19:6-12, Job pictures himself as a snared animal, a prisoner treated unjustly, a man fenced in, a king dethroned, a building destroyed, a tree uprooted, and a city besieged! Job couldn't fight back because God had unstrung his bow (30:11).[6] Job was a man in the furnace, but he had faith that all would turn out well (23:10).

When people suffer, they think about life and death, and Job was no exception. He saw his life as that of a weary hired man waiting for his salary (7:1-5). For him, life was as swift as a weaver's shuttle (7:6),[7] only a breath that comes and goes (7:7), or a cloud that quickly vanishes (7:9). His days were "swifter than a runner" (9:25), and they skimmed past like papyrus boats and eagles swooping upon their prey (9:26). Man is a flower that quickly withers and a shadow that disappears (14:2). If a tree is cut down, new shoots can spring from the stump; but when man is cut down, that's the end (14:7-10). He's gone like evaporating water (14:11-12), and his hopes disappear like a rock being eroded by a river (14:18-19). Man is weak and transient because he lives in a house of clay (4:19; 10:9), a cheap hut that isn't any stronger than a cocoon (27:18).

Job 18 is a vivid description of death that uses the images of a light put out (vv. 5-6; see 21:17), a traveler trapped (vv. 7-10), a criminal pursued (vv. 11-15), and a tree uprooted (vv. 16-21; see 24:20). Death is "the king of terrors" (v. 14). The Apostle Paul saw death as a king that "reigned" in this world because of Adam's sin (Rom. 5:14, 21). Death is also compared to a harvest (Job 5:26; 24:24), which suggests that death is indeed "the grim reaper."[8]

Job's descriptions of his three friends illustrate how useless their "comfort" was to him. To a thirsty man, they were empty

120

streams (6:15-17); to a sick man, they were worthless physicians giving him ashes for medicine (13:4, 12); to a hurting man, they were long-winded, miserable comforters (16:1-3) who crushed him with their words (19:1-2); and to a weary man, they were barking dogs that yelped at his heels (19:28).

In chapter 29, Job gives a description of the blessings he enjoyed during his days of prosperity when he reigned as a king (v. 25) and ministered to others like a father (v. 16). He bravely rescued the poor from the beastly evil men who would exploit them (v. 17), and his words were like the rain that brought hope to the needy (vv. 22-23).

There are several agricultural images in the Book of Job. Eliphaz had observed that "those who plow evil and those who sow trouble reap it" (Job 4:8). This reminds us of Paul's words about reaping and sowing in Galatians 6:7-9; see also Proverbs 11:18; 22:8; Hosea 8:7; 10:13. Death is like a harvest (Job 5:26); and the wicked, though they look like luxurious plants, will one day be barren (Job 15:27-35).

In his description of the wicked in Job 20, Zophar sees them perishing like dung (v. 7) and vanishing like a dream (v. 8). The wicked eat evil like they eat food, enjoying every morsel; but what they swallow will turn into poison in their stomachs and have to be vomited up (vv. 12-19). See Job 3:24 and 34:7, and Psalm 10:7.

We have already mentioned the Lord's poetic description of creation in Job 38: building a house (v. 4) and giving birth to a baby (vv. 8-9). As the morning light moves across the earth, things become visible like the image caused by a seal pressed on the clay (vv. 12-14). Sinners hate the light (John 3:19-21), and the rising sun takes the earth "by the skirts" and shakes the wicked out! The rain and ice come from a hidden womb (vv. 28-29) and the rain storms from the tipping over of jars (v. 37). Jehovah's description of leviathan in Job 41 is one of the most poetic pictures of a creature found anywhere in literature: his mouth like a door, his back like shields, his breathing like fire that produces smoke and boiling water, his chest like a rock, and his strength able to turn iron into straw and bronze into rotten wood.

The Psalms

Eugene Peterson says, "The Psalms, by profuse and insistent use of metaphor, make it as difficult as they possibly can for us to sally off into vague abstractions, contemptuous of the actual grass under our feet, and call this verbal woolgathering prayer."[9] He is right!

How people can read the psalms and not end up with their feet of faith solidly on the ground of divine revelation is a mystery to me. The psalmists use imagery from agriculture, warfare, nature, geography, the temple, meteorology, and a variety of vocations to help us grasp the reality of faith in the living God. David's experiences with God in storms, caves, and battles come to life in these sacred poems that assure us our God cares about our every need. From the very first psalm, in which the godly are compared to trees and the ungodly to chaff, the psalmists magnify the blessing of living in obedience to the Lord.

Since Psalm 1 begins with agricultural images, let's take that trail and see where it leads us. *Trees* and *chaff* illustrate the contrast between the useful and the useless, the living and the dead, the "weighty" and the trivial, the strong and the weak, the permanent and the transient. Jeremiah made a similar contrast (Jer. 11:5-8). The godly are like an olive tree (Ps. 52:8; and see Zech. 4) and a palm tree (Ps. 92:12-15), and their sons are like olive shoots (Ps. 128:3; and see 144:12). The wicked are like trees that appear to be flourishing, but soon are gone (Ps. 37:35-36; and see Job 5:3; Isa. 40:23-24; Ezek. 17:6-10). They are also like chaff that God blows away or burns (Pss. 35:5; 83:13-16).[10]

The image of *grass* depicts the transitoriness of life (Pss. 90:5-6; 103:15), especially the life of the wicked (Ps. 37:1-2). The wicked are compared to grass on the housetop that withers because it has no depth of earth (Ps. 129:6-7). Psalm 129 contrasts the godly and the wicked: the godly are "plowed up" because of their trials, but they at least produce fruit to the glory of God. The wicked don't amount to anything.

When we surveyed the images in the Pentateuch, we looked

at the significance of *fruit* and *water.* The "two ways" described in Psalm 1:1 and 6 make up a frequent theme in Scripture and one that our Lord used in the Sermon on the Mount (Matt. 7:13-14). Throughout Scripture, people are called upon to make a decision between walking God's way—the way of the Word—or man's way—the way of sin and death. There is no middle way and nobody can be neutral.

Life is a journey, and the destination we reach depends on the path we choose. This is a repeated theme in the Book of Proverbs (2:8-9; 4:17-18; 10:9; 11:5; 14:2, 12; 15:9, 19; 22:5; 28:10; etc.). The wicked woman leads the fool down the path to death, but Wisdom guides the obedient into life (2:16-19; 5:6-10; 9:1-18). The image of the Christian life as a "walk" is often used by both Paul and John (1 Cor. 3:3; 7:17; 2 Cor. 5:7; Gal. 5:25; 6:16; Eph. 2:10; 4:1, 17; 5:15; etc.).[11]

According to Psalm 2:3, the nations see the will of God as chains and fetters that rebels must break off if they are ever going to be free. But the Lord sees His will for us as "cords of human kindness . . . ties of love" (Hosea 11:4), and Jesus said that His Father's will was the food that nourished Him (John 4:34). If we resist His will, He may have to use a bit and bridle on us (Ps. 32:9); but He would rather guide us by His loving counsel, with His eye upon us (Ps. 32:8).

Stubborn sinners are like horses and mules (Ps. 32:9), but God's people should be like sheep who faithfully follow their shepherd (Pss. 23; 77:20; 78:52, 71-72; 79:13; 80:1; 95:7; 100:3; 119:176). The "shepherd" image is repeated in the prophets (Isa. 13:14, 20; 40:11; Jer. 31:10; Ezek. 34; Zech. 11; 13:7) and in the New Testament (Matt. 9:36; 25:32; Luke 12:32; John 10; Acts 20:28-29; 1 Cor. 9:7; Heb. 13:20; 1 Peter 2:25; 5:1-4; Rev. 7:17).[12] Like sheep, all of us have gone astray (Isa. 53:6), and all of us will one day perish (Ps. 49:14). While on the theme of creatures, "I am a worm" (Ps. 22:6) is a neglected I AM statement from the lips of our Lord. God calls the nation of Israel a worm in Isaiah 41:14 and promises in verse 15 to transform the little worm into a sharp threshing sledge!

The psalmists compared their enemies to snarling, prowling dogs (Pss. 22:16, 20; 59:6), bees (118:12), lions (7:2; 10:9-10;

22:13, 21), and bulls and wild oxen (22:12, 21). In Psalm 58, David saw the unjust rulers of his day as snakes (v. 4), lions (v. 6) and slugs (v. 8), as well as water that vanishes (v. 7) and stillborn children (v. 8). While they are cooking their food, a flash flood will come and sweep them away (v. 9).

The image in Psalm 2:9 of the king breaking pottery suggests that the proud rulers described in verses 1-3 are only clay pots! (See Rev. 2:27 and 19:15.) If the nations will submit to God, He can mold them after His will (Jer. 18); but if they rebel, He must shatter them (Jer. 19; and see Isa. 30:12-14).[13]

Since David was a soldier, and Israel maintained a large standing army, we would expect to find military images in the Book of Psalms. There are at least fifteen references to God as the believer's shield (Pss. 3:3; 7:10; 18:2, 30, 35; 28:7; 33:20; 59:11; 84:11; 91:4; 115:9-11; 119:114; 144:2), and Peter reminds us that believers are "shielded by God's power" (1 Peter 1:5). The same word (*phroureo*) is used in Philippians 4:7 to describe God's peace shielding the heart and mind.

There are two interesting images found in the Hebrew word *'arak*, which is translated "lay [my requests]" in Psalm 5:3. The word means "to arrange in order," as the priest arranged the wood and the pieces of the sacrifices on the altar. When we pray, we are like priests who bring acceptable sacrifices to God (Ps. 141:2); and there had better be some "fire" in our hearts to help "consume" our offering. There is also the suggestion here that our praying ought to be orderly and not helter-skelter. The second meaning is "to draw up for battle, to take up positions." Our time with God each morning is indeed a "morning watch" when, as His soldiers, we present ourselves for duty and hear the orders of the day. The priestly image speaks of worship while the military image speaks of warfare.

The sinner is "pregnant with evil and conceives trouble," but only "gives birth to disillusionment" (Ps. 7:14). This parallels Job 15:35, Isaiah 59:4 and 13, and James 1:15. False hope is like giving birth only to the wind (Isa. 26:17-18); and in the resurrection, the earth will "give birth to her dead" (Isa. 26:19). This reminds us of the image of "mother earth" that is suggested in Psalm 139:13-15. Job saw his burial as a return to his mother's womb (Job 1:21, NIV margin note).[14]

We find much bird imagery in the Psalms. At one time or another, all of us have probably felt like fleeing "like a bird" (Ps. 11:1) and escaping uncomfortable or difficult situations. "Oh, that I had the wings of a dove! I would fly away and be at rest" (Ps. 55:6).[15] Whoever wrote Psalm 102 felt like "an owl among the ruins. . . . like a bird alone on a roof" (vv. 6-7); and God's suffering people have often felt like hunted birds (Pss. 91:3; 124:7). David rejoiced that God could renew his youth like the eagle's (Ps. 103:5), most likely a reference to the freshness of the eagle after molting.

The psalmist in Psalm 11:3 sees the troubles of life as evidences that the very foundations of society are being destroyed (see Ps. 82:5). Isaiah saw a similar picture: "the foundations of the earth shake. . . . the earth reels like a drunkard" (Isa. 24:18, 20); and the prophet points to Jesus Christ as God's "sure foundation" (28:16; and see Rom. 9:33).

Psalm 12 contrasts the words of sinful men (vv. 1-4) with the Word of the Lord (vv. 5-6). The world depends on flattery, lies, and boasting; but God's Word is flawless, refined, and purified. The sinful person thinks he will triumph with his clever use of words, but it's God's Word that lasts and finally conquers. An alternate reading for verse 4 ("we own our lips") is "our lips are our plowshares" (NIV margin note). Sinners use their tongues as plows (see Ps. 129:3-4) and don't care who gets hurt.

Life is a *cup* and an *inheritance* according to Psalm 16:5, and it is God who prepares and assigns both. Jesus referred to His sufferings as the cup the Father gave Him to drink (Matt. 20:22-23; 26:36-46; John 18:11). The cup can also refer to the wrath of God which a sinful world cannot escape (Isa. 51:17-22; Jer. 25:15-28; Lam. 4:21; Ezek. 23:31-33; Hab. 2:16; Rev. 14:10; 16:19; 17:4; 18:6).

In Jewish society, it was important that each family's inheritance be protected so that the land, which actually belonged to God, would not be exploited by the wealthy. Originally, the land was assigned by lot (Josh. 14–21, and see Josh. 18:8-10), and it was forbidden to move the boundary stones that marked each parcel of ground (Deut. 19:14; 27:17; Prov. 22:28; 23:10). "The boundary lines have fallen for me in pleasant places; surely I have a delightful inheritance" was David's testimony (Ps. 16:6). The common phrase "It fell my lot" refers to the assigning of land by the casting of lots. Job asked, "For what is man's lot from God above, his heritage from the Almighty on high?" (Job 31:2) Solomon concluded, "So I saw that there is nothing better for a man than to enjoy his work, because that is his lot" (Ecc. 3:22; and see 5:18-19 and 9:9).

The tribe of Levi did not receive any inheritance in the land because the Lord was their inheritance (Num. 26:62; Deut. 10:9; Josh. 13:14, 33). As aliens and strangers in this world, we have no earthly inheritance; for the Lord is our inheritance now and forever. As far as our time on earth is concerned, "He chose our inheritance for us" (Ps. 47:4). The believer's eternal inheritance is mentioned in Ephesians 1:14 and 18, Colossians 1:12 and 3:24, and 1 Peter 1:4.

Psalm 19:4-6 compares the sunrise to a bridegroom coming out of the wedding pavilion and an athlete starting to run a race. Is David suggesting that we begin each day with devotion, like the bridegroom, and determination and discipline, like the athlete? This would certainly make for a balanced life.

Psalms with Multiple Images

It isn't possible in the small scope of a chapter to look at every image found in the Book of Psalms; but before we move on, I want you to get acquainted with some of the psalms that contain multiple images. For example, Psalm 38 presents several pictures of the consequences of sin in the life of the believer: receiving a father's chastening (vv. 1-2), experiencing sickness (vv. 3, 5-8, 10 [and see Ps. 32:3-4]), drowning (v. 4a), and bearing a burden (v. 4b, 6).

The swiftness and brevity of life are seen in the images in Psalm 39: a handbreadth (v. 5), a breath (vv. 5, 11), a phantom ("shadow," v. 6), an alien (v. 12). What we accumulate on this short journey disappears secretly and silently like a garment being eaten by a moth (v. 11; and see Job 13:28; Isa. 50:9;

51:8; Hosea 5:12; and our Lord's words in Matt. 6:19-20).

Psalm 49 warns against trusting in riches, for death is no respecter of bank accounts. The rich may have enough money to build elaborate tombs, but those tombs become their "houses" where their bodies lie (v. 11). "Their forms will decay in the grave, far from their princely mansions" (v. 14); and in those graves, they see no light (v. 19). If they leave God out of their lives, they die like animals (vv. 12, 14, 20). What a dismal picture!

In Psalm 55, David describes his difficult circumstances as a storm (vv. 6-8); pursuit by prowling animals (vv. 10-11); evil lodging near him like a neighbor (v. 15); a battle (vv. 18, 21); and deception from false friends (vv. 20-21). You find similar images in Psalm 57: the storm (v. 1), the beasts (v. 4), the traps (v. 6) and the burden (v. 6, "bowed down"). In Psalm 58, the focus is on people like creatures: snakes (v. 4), lions (v. 6), and slugs (v. 8). Psalm 59 compares David's enemies to snarling dogs (vv. 6, 14-15), and their "barking" to sharp swords (vv. 7, 12-13). The superscription connects this psalm to 1 Samuel 19:11-17.

David's prayer in Psalm 68 is that all his enemies will blow away like smoke and melt like wax (v. 2). They are but brute animals that God will rebuke (v. 30), like snow that He will scatter (v. 14). He asks God to make the land of the enemy a desert (v. 6), but to refresh His people with showers (v. 9). He sees the Lord coming to his rescue with thousands of chariots (v. 17), winning a great victory and leading off many captives (vv. 18, 24-27). Paul saw this as a picture of Christ's victory on the cross and His distribution of gifts to the victors (Eph. 4:7-12).

In Psalm 69, David is drowning (vv. 1-2, 14-15), a picture repeated in Psalms 18:4-6, 16-19; 32:6; 42:7; 88:7, 16-18; and 130:1.

The history of Israel recounted in Psalm 78 reveals a gracious God and a rebellious people. God opened the doors of heaven (v. 23; see Gen. 7:11; 2 Kings 7:2, 19; Mal. 3:10) and "rained down" bread and flesh (vv. 24, 27) to feed them; but they continued to disobey. His anger broke out like fire (v. 21), an image found frequently in Scripture (v. 49; Ex. 4:14; Num. 11:1, 33; 12:9; 24:10; 32:13; Josh. 7:1; Ps. 74:1; 79:5; 80:4; 89:46; etc.). He "ended their days in futility" (v. 33) or "like a passing breeze" (v. 39). According to Psalm 90, this refers to their years of wandering in the wilderness. He guided the nation like a flock (v. 52) and eventually gave them David to be their shepherd (v. 72). In spite of God's goodness to them, the new generation was "as unreliable as a faulty bow" (v. 57), an image repeated in Hosea 7:16.

In Psalm 83, Asaph wants to see his enemies treated like dung (vv. 9-10), blown away like tumbleweeds and chaff (v. 13), burned up like a forest in a storm (vv. 14-15).

Psalm 90 is the only psalm assigned to Moses, and it may have been written in connection with the judgment of God on Israel at Kadesh Barnea (Num. 13–14). The contrast is between the frailty of man and the eternality of God. God gave birth to the mountains (v. 2; see Job 15:7; 38:8), and He will endure forever; but frail human beings are swept away (v. 5; Ps. 58:9; 73:19; and see Gen. 19:15; Num. 16:26; Job 21:18) and wither like the grass that has but a day to live (vv. 5-6). Psalm 92 contrasts the fleeting life of the wicked ("like grass," v. 7, flourishing but frail) with the beauty and stability of the godly who are like trees (vv. 12-15; and see Ps. 1:3).

When he wrote Psalm 102, the psalmist was in an especially melancholy mood. His days vanish like smoke while his bones burn with some unnamed sickness (v. 3). His heart is weak and withered like grass (v. 4), and he sees himself as isolated as a lonely bird (vv. 6-7). When he does remember to eat, his diet is ashes and tears (vv. 4b, 9). God has "tossed him aside" like a useless piece of furniture (v. 10), and his days vanish like a shadow and like the grass (v. 11). Verse 23 sounds like the image of the loom used by King Hezekiah (Isa. 38:12). The heavens and earth may wear out like a garment and be discarded (vv. 25-26), but God will endure forever. The theme is similar to that expressed in Psalm 90.

"They defiled themselves by what they did," says Psalm 106:39; "by their deeds they prostituted themselves." As we have noted, idolatry is often pictured as prostitution, a violation of the "marriage covenant" with Jehovah (Ex. 34:15; Lev. 17:7; Deut. 31:16; Jud. 2:17; Jer. 3:2; Hosea 4:12). James 4:4-6 applies this image to the believer's relationship to the world; and see Isaiah 54:5, Jeremiah 3:20, and Hosea 2:2-5 and 3:1.

The writer of Psalm 119 compares the Word of God to riches (vv. 14, 72, 127, 162), food (v. 103), and light (vv. 105, 130; see Prov. 6:23; 2 Peter 1:19). The wicked are like dross (v. 119), but the suffering psalmist was "like a wineskin in the smoke" (v. 83).

When God delivered Israel from her enemies, as described in Psalm 124, He saved the nation from being swallowed alive, sinking in the waters, being torn by wild beasts, and being trapped like a bird. Psalm 126 probably describes Israel's sudden deliverance from Assyria (Isa. 36–37), which was "like a dream," like the waters filling the dry wadi, and like harvesters singing as they brought in the sheaves. Psalm 129 describes Israel's trials as the enemy plowing long furrows on their back; but then God cut the cords of the plow and set them free.

Note the emphasis in Psalm 132 on clothing: the priests clothed with righteousness and salvation (vv. 9, 16) and the enemy clothed with shame (v. 18). Unity among God's people, according to Psalm 133, is like oil and dew, both of which come down. One produces fragrance and the other produces fruitfulness. The mention of Aaron's beard (v. 2) suggests that the oil runs over the breastplate that hung over his heart; and thus the twelve stones, bearing the names of the twelve tribes of Israel, were bathed in the anointing oil.

David was not a priest and therefore couldn't minister in the tabernacle; but in Psalm 141, he saw that God accepted his prayer as incense and the lifting of his hands as a sacrifice. If his prayer was to be acceptable, he had to watch "the door of [his] lips" (v. 3). David saw the rebuke of a righteous man as a blessing, like oil on the head (v. 5; Prov. 9:8; 15:31; 19:25; 25:12; 27:5-6).

The Book of Proverbs[16]

The theme of Proverbs is the practical wisdom that comes from God and gives blessing to those who obey Him. The book itself states that the proverbs are "for attaining wisdom and discipline; for understanding words of insight" (Prov. 1:2). David Wyrtzen's paraphrase of this verse says it well: "to internalize the art of skillful living which comes through disciplined training; to discern the words of insight."[17] Wisdom is presented in several images: beautiful adornments (1:9; 3:22; 4:9); a gracious woman (1:20ff; 8:1-11); treasures (2:1-6; 3:16-18; 8:10-11); a feast (9:1-6); a path or "way" (2:8-22; 3:1-6, 23; 4:11, 14-15, 18-19; 15:10, 19, 24; etc.);[18] a light (6:23); a fountain (18:4); and a tree of life (3:18).[19]

The image of wisdom as a garland or chain (1:9) suggests that wisdom beautifies a person, as would a lei or a chain of gold. Wisdom is also like a crown that enables you to "reign in life" (4:9; 14:18, 24). Those who follow wisdom become like kings, while those who follow folly become slaves. The association of wisdom with one's father and mother (1:8-9) suggests that the best of the "family jewels" parents can give to their children is the wisdom that comes from the Word of God.

"Above all else, guard your heart, for it is the wellspring of life" (4:23). What flows out of our lives depends on what is found in our hearts. "The mouth of the righteous is a fountain of life" (10:11; 20:5) because it teaches wisdom (13:14; 18:4), the fear of the Lord (14:27), and understanding (16:22). The marriage relationship is compared to drinking at the pure fountain, while adultery is compared to water spilled in the gutters of the street (5:15-20; see 25:26).

Solomon has a great deal to say about eating and drinking, perhaps because entertainment was such an important part of his own life (1 Kings 4:20-28).[20] We've already noted that in Solomon's view, married love compares to drinking pure water (5:15-20); adultery is like drinking "stolen water" (9:17) and eating "honey" (5:3; but see 20:17). The adulteress "eats and wipes her mouth and says, 'I've done nothing wrong' " (30:20). She tells the sinner to "drink deep of love" (7:18), but it leads only to death.

Honey seems to be a major item on the menu in Proverbs. Pleasant words are like the honeycomb (16:24) because they impart wisdom, which is like honey (24:13-14). Fools feed on folly (15:14) and cheerful people have "a continual feast" (15:15). Honey also pictures honor and recognition from others (25:27); and if you eat too much of it, it will make you sick (25:16). In other words, don't go around looking for praise.

The Book of Proverbs has so much to say about the tongue and human speech that we can't begin to cite all the references. Words are like deep waters (18:4); reckless words are like a sword (12:18). Gossip is like "choice morsels" that are savored and swallowed (18:8; 26:22); the words of the wise nourish those who receive them (10:21; 12:14; 13:2; 18:20-21). Boastful words are like "clouds and wind without rain" (25:14; and see 2 Peter 2:17 and Jude 12). Apt words are valuable and beautiful, like "apples of gold in settings of silver" or beautiful jewelry (25:11-12; 10:20). The wise person knows what to say, when to say it, and how to say it. Wise words bring healing (12:18; 15:4; 16:24), but wicked words are like scorching fire (16:27; 26:20-21), and lying words are like dangerous weapons (25:18). Good news is like cold water to a weary person (25:25) and brings health to those who hear it (15:30).

Since he was a much-married man, Solomon included some interesting images of marriage and the home. A "quarrelsome wife is like a constant dripping" (27:15) and a disgraceful wife is like "decay in [the husband's] bones" (12:4). A godly wife is a crown (12:4), a fountain (5:18), and "a loving doe, a graceful deer" (5:19). A wayward wife is compared to "a narrow well" instead of a refreshing fountain, but the prostitute to a deep pit (23:27; and see 22:14). Of course, Proverbs 31 is the *locus classicus* in the Bible on the character of the ideal wife.

The sluggard does people more harm than good, like vinegar on teeth or smoke in the eyes (10:26); and he turns on his bed like a door on its hinges (26:14).

Proverbs 26 contains several images relating to the fool. Giving honor to a fool is like snow in summer or rain in harvest: it's out of place and will do more harm than good (v. 1). It's also like tying a stone in a sling (v. 8): it can't be used to accomplish anything. To send a message by a fool is like maiming yourself (v. 6); and to give him wisdom, such as a proverb, will get him nowhere (v. 7) or lead to him hurting others (v. 9).

131

Ecclesiastes

Life is a burden (1:13; 3:10) that "weighs heavily on men" (6:1) and leads to pain and grief (2:23). Trying to enjoy life is like chasing after the wind (1:14, 17; 2:11, 17, 26; 4:4, 6, 16; 5:16; 6:9). One reason for this widespread discontent is that our eyes have an appetite (2:10; 4:8; 5:11; 6:9) much bigger than life can satisfy.[21]

When Solomon writes that man's fate is like that of the animals, he's referring to death and decay, not destiny (Ecc. 3:18-21). Like the animals, we die and our bodies turn to dust.

The image in Ecclesiastes 5:3 suggests that as pleasant sleep indicates a sleeper who is a hard worker, many words indicate a person speaking who is a fool. Life as a fleeting shadow (Ecc. 6:12; and see 8:13) is a metaphor we have met before (1 Chron. 29:15; Job 8:9; 14:2; Ps. 102:11; 109:23; 144:4). Burning thorns make a lot of noise but don't produce much heat, and fools laugh but accomplish nothing worthwhile (7:6).

Ecclesiastes 12:1-7 is one of the greatest poetic descriptions of aging and death found anywhere in literature. Solomon compares the human body to a house (see Job 4:19; 2 Cor. 5:1-2; 2 Peter 1:13) and the process of aging to the decay of the house: the arms and hands shake; the back bends over; the teeth decay and fall out; eyesight and hearing begin to fail; the hair gets white; strength fails; appetite weakens; and the ultimate step is death.

In Ecclesiastes 12:11, the words of the Preacher are compared to *goads,* because they "prod" people into thinking, and to *nails,* because they give people something to "hang on to" as they try to live wisely, or something on which to "hang" truths as they learn. I'm tempted to suggest that the "goads" and "nails" may illustrate two aspects of preaching: the goads for the imagination, to stimulate interest and excitement; and the nails for the reason—the left brain, if you please—to give the logic of the message and the "points" that people can grasp and put into practice.

I've noticed that effective preachers use both goads and nails so that they present something for everybody. They will appeal to the imagination with images and illustrations, and then say, "Now, if you want this to work in your life, here are four simple steps you can follow." Then they pound in the nails, after which they move into the next image or illustration. The key to effective preaching and teaching is a balance between images (goads), and concepts (nails). "Images without concepts are blind," we've learned from Sallie McFague; "concepts without images are sterile."[22]

The Song of Songs[23]

The wealth of Oriental imagery in this neglected book is enough to challenge the most astute exegete, but the first question he or she must face is, "To what literary genre does the book belong?" Is it an allegory about Christ and the church, or Jehovah and Israel? Is it actual history that conveys a deeper spiritual meaning, with Solomon a type of Christ and his beloved a type of the church (or Jehovah and Israel)? Or is it a love poem or drama that extols marriage and the love of husband and wife? If a drama or poem, how many main characters are there, two or three? These aren't easy questions to answer, and good and godly scholars must be allowed to disagree. If we better understood the Eastern setting of this book, and the symbolism behind it, we would have an easier time interpreting it.

The flavor of food and drink, the fragrance of spices and the beauty of things in nature comprise the major images of the book. Solomon's love is more delightful than wine (1:2, 4; 4:10) and his fragrance more pleasing than perfume (1:3, 13-14). However, there are also references to "fragrance" that refer to the beloved rather than to her lover (1:12; 4:10-11, 16; 7:8). Note the extended use of images from nature whenever the lovers describe each other (2:1-3, 9, 14, 17; 4:1-5, 12-15; 5:10-16; 6:4-9; 7:1-9).

The phrase "his banner over me is love" (2:4) suggests that her lover openly reveals his love for her and glories in it, the way an army displays its banner. The military image is repeated in 6:4. For the New Testament believer, love is certainly the power that conquers; for "we are more than conquerors through him who loved us" (Rom. 8:37).

In 4:12–5:1, 6:2, and 8:13, we find the image of the garden, which speaks of the beauty and fruitfulness of the beloved. The phrase "a garden locked up" (4:12) suggests her purity and exclusive devotion to her lover. In the East, in ancient days, gardens were special places for joyful pleasure. If the Song of Songs teaches us anything, it's that married love is a beautiful and delightful thing because God made it that way.

"What a power of brain and imagination
belonged to these Old Testament prophets,
and with what decision they married it
to equally robust expression!
They were poets as well as prophets.
They had imagination as well as reason.
They had vision as well as sight."

—*John Henry Jowett*

"Civilization begins in the imagination.
The wild dream is the first step to reality."

—*Norman Cousins*

Chapter Twelve
Pictures in the Prophets

The prophets were seers as well as speakers, and what they spoke depended a great deal on what they saw. "What do you see, Jeremiah?" Jehovah asked the young priest, now called to be a prophet (Jer. 1:11). "What do you see, Amos?" He asked the farmer made prophet (Amos 7:8). "Formerly in Israel, if a man went to inquire of God, he would say, 'Come, let us go to the seer,' because the prophet of today used to be called a seer" (1 Sam. 9:9).

This is not to discount the importance of "the word of the Lord" coming to His servants, for prophets were hearers as well as seers. They had hearing ears and seeing eyes; and when they ministered the Word, they tried to help others see as they heard the Word of the Lord. The prophets often used picture language and even dramatic action to get their messages across. God's people were "ever hearing, but never understanding" and "ever seeing, but never perceiving" (Isa. 6:9; see Matt. 13:14-15); and the prophet had to shock them out of their blind lethargy.

Isaiah

The name Isaiah means "salvation of the Lord," and *salvation* (deliverance) is the major theme of the book. The prophet dealt with at least five different "deliverances":

(1) the deliverance of Judah from the Assyrians;

137

(2) the deliverance of Judah from Babylonian captivity;

(3) the future deliverance of the Jews from the Gentile nations;

(4) the future deliverance of the earth from bondage in the establishing of the kingdom; and

(5) the sinner's deliverance from sin and judgment through faith in God's Suffering Servant, Jesus Christ.

Among other things, Isaiah pictures salvation as cleansing (1:18; 4:4); sins blotted out (44:22; 43:25); a feast (25:6-12; 55:1-5; 12:3); a new exodus (11:15; 43:14-20; 51:9-11); healing (1:5; 6:10; 30:26; 33:24; 53:5; 57:18-19; 58:8); the dawn of a new day (61:1-3 [see Luke 1:78-79]); and a broken yoke (9:4). The image of the exodus connects with that of the *highway* (11:16; 19:23; 35:8; 40:3; 62:10). The prophet saw God's people leaving their bondage and walking on a "holy road" that leads to the Holy City.[1]

The imagery in the first chapter of Isaiah reveals the sad plight of Judah, for the nation was like rebellious children (vv. 1-4); a beaten and sick body, uncared for (vv. 5-6); a shack in a field (vv. 7-9); the wicked cities of Sodom and Gomorrah (v. 10); a harlot (v. 21); cheap dross and diluted wine (vv. 22, 25); and a fading oak and dying garden, about to be burned up (vv. 30-31).[2] Later, Isaiah used other pictures to reveal the sad condition of the nation: a fruitless vineyard (5:1-7); a bulging wall about to collapse (30:12-14); crushed grain on the threshing floor (21:10); and a sinking ship (33:23). Of course, the great tragedy was that the people were crowding the temple courts and bringing their prayers and sacrifices to God! It was a time of religious excitement, but it was not a time of spiritual power or true holiness.

Isaiah also wrote about the other nations. He pictured Assyria as a lion (5:29), bees (7:18), a razor (7:20), a swollen stream (8:5-8), God's weapon (10:5, 15, 24), and a tree to be cut down (10:33-34).[3] But Assyria would be trampled down like mud (10:6), and the nations would be gathered for judgment the way eggs are gathered by a farmer (10:14). Proud Moab would be pushed into the manure and have to swim through it! (25:10-12) And Egypt was a broken reed that nobody could confidently lean on (30:1-7; 31:1-3; 36:6).

God's call, "Come now, let us reason together" (1:18), was a summons for the people to appear in court; for the word translated "reason" (*yakah*) has definite judicial overtones (Isa. 2:4; 11:3-4; 41:1, 21; 43:26; 45:21; and see Gen. 31:36, 42; 1 Chron. 12:17; Ps. 50:8, 21; Hosea 4:4). Led by worldly priests and false prophets, the people of Judah were treading the temple courts; but God was about to call them into a court of judgment.

Along with the depressing images in Isaiah 1, the prophet also pictured sinners as worn-out garments (50:9; 51:7-8; and see 64:6); rejected branches (14:19); the tossing waves of the sea (57:20-21); tumbleweeds (17:13-14); and grass that withers and dies (15:6; 37:27; 40:6; 51:12; and see 1 Peter 1:24 and James 1:9-11).

Isaiah pictured the Lord as a purger of His people (1:25); a stone (8:14; 28:16); a crown (28:5); a potter (29:16; 45:9); a lion (31:4); hovering birds (31:5); a man of war (42:25; 49:24-26); a shepherd (40:11); a fortress (33:21); a tender mother (49:14-16; 66:13); and a husband (50:1-3).

Isaiah 22:15-25 records the dismissing of Shebna and the appointing of Eliakim because Shebna was using his office to get benefits for himself instead of to serve the nation. He would never use his beautiful tomb because God would roll Shebna up like a ball and hurl him away to Babylon (see Jer. 10:18; 22:26), where he would die in exile. What God says about Eliakim ought to be true of anybody in a place of leadership. He was a father who cared for people, not a robber who exploited them. He would use his key to open doors of opportunity for others, and he would be a peg on which they could hang responsibility. He would be a throne and exercise authority to the honor of the nation. But no human leader is in office forever, and the day would come when even faithful Eliakim would have his peg removed.[4]

Isaiah 28 presents a number of pictures of God's judgment of His people. They are but fading flowers cut down by a storm and trodden underfoot (vv. 1-4a, 17-19); a ripe fig swallowed (4b); drunks out of control, vomiting at a feast (vv. 7-8); a bed

139

without adequate covering (v. 20); a harvest to be threshed (vv. 23-29). While the leaders were making political alliances, hoping to save the nation, God was measuring them with His plumb line and laying a tested Stone for their refuge (vv. 14-19). The image of the stone or rock is found frequently in Isaiah (8:14; 17:10; 26:4;[5] 30:29; 44:8; 48:21; 51:1). God gave the nation a choice: rocks (2:10, 19, 21; 7:19) or the Rock.[6]

Isaiah 30:27-33 is a vivid description of judgment. God's anger will come like fire and smoke and His breath like a rushing torrent. The nations will be shaken in a sieve and then led away with bits in their mouths like animals. His anger will come like a storm and His breath like burning sulfur.

King Hezekiah's psalm commemorating his recovery from a near-fatal illness contains several striking pictures (Isa. 38). Hezekiah saw himself going through gates into the land of death[7] and being robbed of the years that belonged to him (v. 10). He saw his body as a shepherd's tent, about to be pulled down, and like a piece of weaving about to be cut off the loom (v. 12; see 2 Cor. 5:1-4; 2 Peter 1:13-14; Ps. 139:13-16). He felt like a helpless bird being attacked by a fierce lion (vv. 13-14).

Isaiah 40 introduces what the rabbis have called "The Book of Consolation." Looking ahead to the defeat of Babylon, the prophet announced that the exile was ended and that Judah had "served her term," a military phrase that means their years of conscripted service were ended. Job used it when referring to man's time of suffering on earth (Job 7:1; 14:14). Note the familiar themes of the highway (vv. 3-4; Matt. 3:1-3) and fragile human beings like the grass (vv. 6-8), as well as Jehovah as shepherd (v. 11; Gen. 48:15; 49:24; Ps. 23:1; 28:9; 80:1). The greatness of God as contrasted with the insignificance of the nations is seen in verses 12-26.

Babylon boasted that she was a queen (47:5, 7), but God would take her off the throne and put her in the dust (47:1). Instead of basking in glory, she would wade through the waters, her shame uncovered (47:3).

Many of the images in Isaiah 49–53 focus on God's Servant, Messiah, whom we know and worship as Jesus Christ our Lord. Messiah is compared to weapons in 49:2 and to a light in 49:6

(see Acts 13:47). God will care for His people like a mother (49:15) and treat them like ornaments for a bride (49:18). Isaiah 50:1 takes up the theme of Israel the bride of Jehovah, a theme developed further in Jeremiah and Hosea. According to Jewish law, once a wife was put away she could not return to her husband (Deut. 24:1-4), but the Lord pleaded with His people to return to Him.

Isaiah 52 should be contrasted with Isaiah 47, for the prophet sees the humiliated Jews now clothed with strength and seated on the throne (vv. 1-2), while Babylon has been pushed into the dust. Babylon had walked all over the exiles (Isa. 51:23), but now the tables are turned.

Looking ahead in chapter 54 to the glory of Israel in the promised kingdom, the prophet sees the barren woman giving birth (vv. 1-3), the widow happily married (vv. 4-6), the storm of judgment over (vv. 7-10), and the ruined city rebuilt and beautified with jewels (vv. 11-17).

God's description of the leaders of the nation in Isaiah 56 depicts them as blind watchmen, mute watchdogs, and selfish shepherds (56:9-12). In chapter 59, Isaiah explains why there is no justice in the land: the rulers "conceive trouble and give birth to evil" (v. 4; see James 1:14-15). Their plans are like vipers' eggs that hatch poisonous snakes; their works are like spiders' webs that have no strength and cannot cover them (vv. 4-6). The people are like the blind, groping in the light, and like animals and birds (vv. 10-11). Verse 14 describes a traffic jam: "truth has stumbled in the streets, honesty cannot enter." But the Lord will come like a mighty warrior (vv. 16-18) and a pent-up flood (vv. 19-20).

The coming kingdom is like the dawning of a new day (Isa. 60:1-3) and the people will return to their land and to the Lord, flying along like clouds and birds (60:8). The Gentile nations will become nursing mothers for Israel (60:16), and peace will be their governor and righteousness their ruler (v. 17). Isaiah 61:1-3 describes the great changes that will occur when the nation is restored to Jehovah's favor: from bondage to freedom, from sickness to health, from judgment to jubilee, from ashes on their heads to a crown of beauty, from mourning to gladness, and from despair to praise. They will go from a funeral to a wedding (v. 10).

Chapter 62 presents more pictures of the coming kingdom as the nations see Israel's righteousness like the dawn or like a blazing torch (v. 1) or a crown (v. 3). Israel will again be married to Jehovah and get a new name—Hephzibah, "My delight is in her." The land will be called Beulah—"married." Jehovah and His estranged wife will be united, and His grace and glory will be revealed to all the earth.

Before we leave Isaiah, we should note that along with his use of literary imagery, he also used more dramatic methods to get his message across. The names of his two sons were connected with his messages (Isa. 7–8); and Isaiah himself dressed like a prisoner of war for three years, a living reminder to the people that they should not trust Egypt. We shall see that some of the other prophets, especially Jeremiah, Ezekiel, and Hosea, had to "live" their message as well as preach it.

Jeremiah

The Prophet Jeremiah didn't have an easy time of it in his ministry, but God warned him in advance and then assured him of His presence and His help. The pictures of Jeremiah's ministry are: a destroyer, builder, and planter (1:10); a city, pillar, and wall (1:18); a guide at the crossroads (6:16; see 31:21); a watchman (6:17); a tester of metals (6:27); a physician (8:21-22); a sacrificial lamb (11:19); a runner (12:5); a shepherd (13:17, 20-21; and see 17:16, 23); a man of contention (15:10); and a tree (17:8).

What were the people like to whom Jeremiah ministered? The images presented in chapter 2 answer that question: an unfaithful spouse (vv. 1-8);[8] broken cisterns (vv. 9-13); drinkers at foreign rivers (vv. 14-19); a degenerate vine (vv. 20-22); camels and donkeys in heat (vv. 23-25; see 5:8; 31:18; Hosea 4:16; 10:11); and guilty thieves (vv. 26-28).

In chapter 6, the nation is described as: a delicate woman, unprepared for war (vv. 1-2); a defiled well (v. 7); a ruined vineyard (v. 9); a deceived patient (vv. 13-15); lost pilgrims (v.

16); deaf soldiers (v. 17); and cheap metal (vv. 27-30). It was Jeremiah's task, as it is the task of every faithful preacher, to expose their hearers' needs, reveal the perils they face, and call them back to the "old paths" of God's Word.

Jeremiah 3 develops the theme of "spiritual adultery," but it also presents the nation as suffering from the sickness of backsliding (v. 22).[9] Isaiah had touched upon this theme of healing the backslidden (Isa. 30:26; 57:18), and Hosea will also use it (Hosea 6:1; 14:4). The image of "healing" is often used by Jeremiah (8:15, 22; 14:19; 17:14; 30:12-13, 17; 33:6; 46:11; 51:8-9) and may hearken back to the promise in 2 Chronicles 7:14. The false prophets and worldly priests of Jeremiah's day were only counterfeit physicians who gave a false diagnosis and a useless remedy (8:11; 4:10), not unlike some "health and wealth" preachers today.

The theme of the *yoke* is important in Jeremiah's message. The nation had broken off their yoke by rebelling against God's Law (2:20; 5:5; and see Ps. 2:1-3). Jehovah had broken the yoke of Egyptian bondage (Lev. 26:13), but Israel wouldn't yield to the yoke of God's rule over them. The Prophet Jeremiah actually wore a yoke to get the attention of the people so they would listen to his plea that they submit to Babylon (Jer. 27). When the false prophet Hananiah broke the wooden yoke, God told Jeremiah it would be replaced with an iron yoke (Jer. 28); for when we resist the loving control of God, our bondage becomes only worse. If we submit to the yoke, then God can remove it and replace it with lighter "cords" of kindness and love (Hosea 11:4). Alas, Israel rebelled; and their very sins became the yoke that burdened them (Lam. 1:14; and see 3:27). God promised that He would eventually take off the yoke of Babylonian captivity (Jer. 30:8), even as He had done with the Assyrian threat (Isa. 10:24-27).

Jeremiah 4 spells out the remedy for the nation's sinful condition. They need to plow up their hard hearts (v. 3) and experience a true spiritual circumcision within (v. 4). They should take a bath (v. 14) and wash away their wickedness by confessing their sins. Instead of acting like foolish children (v. 22), they should "join the army" and act like mature men (vv. 5-6).

The Prophet Jeremiah is preeminently the prophet of the heart. The word "heart" is found more than sixty times in his book, and he repeatedly emphasizes the *inwardness* of religion. The false prophets and priests depended on the presence of the ark, but the day would come when the ark would not be needed (3:16-17). Even the temple would no longer be essential to their faith (7:4-11), and the sacrifices would be replaced by heart obedience (7:21-26) and the law, by a new covenant in the heart (31:30-34). God's people would experience a spiritual circumcision that would transform their lives (4:4; see 9:25).[10]

Jeremiah's greatest trouble came from the false prophets who were leading the people astray with their deceitful message of peace. These men were but wind (5:13), worthless physicians (6:13-15), selfish shepherds (23:1-8), wandering guides on slippery paths (23:9-12, 32; and see 6:16 and 18:15), and poor figs that were fit to be thrown away (29:17; chap. 24). Their words were but straw and would be burned up by God's Word (23:28-29); in fact, the prophets themselves were fuel for the fire (5:14). Instead of spreading holiness in the land, they were "toxic" and were spreading godlessness (23:15).

Known as "the weeping prophet," Jeremiah wanted a "spring of water" in his head so that he might be able to weep even more (9:1, 10, 18; 13:17; 14:17; Lam. 1:16; 2:11, 18; 3:48; and see Ps. 119:136; Isa. 22:4; and Rom. 9:1-2). In this, he was very much like Jesus Christ, the "man of sorrows" (John 11:35; Luke 19:41; Heb. 5:7-8; Isa. 53:3). No wonder the people thought that Jesus was Jeremiah the prophet (Matt. 16:14).

Death is personified in Jeremiah 9:21, and in 9:22 death is compared to a refuse collector and a reaper (see Job 5:26). Jezebel's body was treated like refuse (2 Kings 9:37), and see Psalm 83:10; Isaiah 5:25; Jeremiah 8:22; 16:4, 25:33; Zephaniah 1:17.

The prophet's treatment of the false gods in Jeremiah 10:1-16 reminds us of Isaiah 40:18-20 and 44:6-20. Jeremiah compared an idol to "a scarecrow in a melon patch"! (10:5)

Jeremiah's complaint against God in chapter 12 pictures the wicked as fruitful plants (vv. 1-2), but the prophet wants them dragged off and butchered like sheep (v. 3; see 11:19). God sees His people as a roaring lion, a speckled bird, and a wasted vineyard and field (vv. 8-13). In chapter 13, the nation is a flock destined for captivity (vv. 17, 20), a woman in travail (v. 21; and see 22:23), chaff driven by the wind (v. 24) and a shameless prostitute (vv. 22, 25-27).

Jeremiah's "eating" of God's Word (15:16) reminds us of Job 23:12, Deuteronomy 8:3 (quoted in Matt. 4:4), John 4:34, Ezekiel 2:8 and 3:3, and Revelation 10:10. We have already seen that the Word is compared to bread, meat, milk, and honey, and therefore it must be received within and digested.

The episodes involving the linen belt (chap. 13), the potter (chaps. 18–19), the yokes (chaps. 27–28), and the burial of the stones in Egypt (chap. 43) were in a sense "action sermons" for the communicating of abstract truth.[11] It's important to note that the Hebrew word translated "shaping" in 18:4 is translated "preparing" in 18:11. There was still time for the nation to repent, and God would change His plan. The smashed jar symbolized God's judgment on a people who could not "be repaired" (19:10-11; see 22:28; 25:34; 48:38; Isa. 30:14).

Jeremiah also used current events as "living texts" for his messages, such as the temporary release of the slaves (chap. 34), the opportunity to buy a field (chaps. 32–33), and the coming of the Recabites into Jerusalem (chap. 35). Of course, the constant threat of the Babylonian army outside Jerusalem's walls gave Jeremiah all the ammunition he needed!

"The cup of God's wrath" is a frequent symbol in Scripture and is used in Jeremiah 25:15, 17, 28; 49:12; 51:7; and see Lamentations 4:21; Psalm 75:8; Isaiah 51:17, 22; and Ezekiel 23:31-33. John picks up the image in Revelation 14:10, 16:19, 17:4, and 18:6. Four times Jeremiah pictures judgment in the image of the storm (11:16; 23:19; 25:32; 30:23; and see Isa. 30:30).

Jeremiah often compares the Jewish nation to a flock of sheep (10:21; 13:17, 20; 23:1-3; 25:34-36; 31:10; 49:20; 50:6, 17). More than any of the prophets, he uses a woman's birth pangs to describe people's response to judgment (4:31; 6:24; 13:21; 22:23; 30:6; 48:41; 49:22, 24; 50:43). The image is found in Psalm 48:6; Isaiah 13:8; 21:3; and 26:17-18;[12] Micah 4:9-10; and Hosea 13:13. Both Jesus (Matt. 24:8; Mark 13:8) and Paul (1 Thes. 5:3) used the image to describe tribulation at the end of the age. Paul also used birth pains to describe his struggles for his converts (Gal. 4:19) and the travail of creation under the bondage of sin (Rom. 8:22).

The judgment messages that close Jeremiah's prophecy (chaps. 46–51) contain some typical metaphorical images: the devouring sword (46:10, 14), trees being cut down (46:22-23), the flooding waters (47:2; 51:55), the swooping eagle (48:40), the travailing woman (48:41; 49:22-24; 50:43), the harvest (49:9; 51:2, 33), the cup (49:12; 51:7; see 25:15-16; Rev. 14:8-10), and the marauding lion (49:19; 50:44; 51:38).

Lamentations

One of the key images in Jeremiah's lament over the fall of Jerusalem is that of *swallowing.* The Lord swallowed up the dwellings of Jacob (2:2, 5, 8 ["destroying"]), but the enemy claimed that they did it (2:16). Of course, both were true; for the God who ordained the disciplining of His people also ordained Babylon to be the means of that discipline.

The city of Jerusalem had been a queen, but now it was a widow and a slave (1:1) and the crown had fallen (5:16; see Job 19:9; Ps. 89:39, 44). The gold is dull and the jewels are scattered, probably a reference to the cheapening effects of sin on the people (4:1-2, 7-8). What once was precious is now like a clay pot (4:2), and the nation is but "scum and refuse" (3:45). The wages of sin never increase a person's worth.

The people are caught in the net (1:13), wearing the yoke of their own sins (1:14) and being crushed in the winepress (1:15). The Lord's face no longer shines upon them (Num. 6:22-26) because there's a cloud between them and Jehovah (2:1) and their prayers can't break through (3:44). The fire of God's angry judgment is their portion (1:13; 2:3-4; 4:11). Zion, the beautiful garden, is now a waste (2:6).

The weeping prophet pours out his heart in anguish for his people (2:11), and he invites the people to pour out their hearts in prayer for God's help (2:19). He feels like a dead man in the darkness, walled in and weighed down (3:1-9). Jeremiah was given freedom by the Babylonians, but he felt worse than when he was imprisoned by his enemies in Jerusalem! God met him like a bear or a lion (3:10-11); his enemies in Judah hunted him like a bird and tried to drown him in a pit (3:52-54).

There is probably no book in the Bible that so vividly illustrates the wages of sin as the Book of Lamentations does; and in a day when God's people are weak on holy living, it's message is desperately needed.[13]

Ezekiel

Like Jeremiah, Ezekiel was a priest called to be a prophet; and, like both Isaiah and Jeremiah, he used vivid imagery and was himself a part of the message. "Ezekiel will be a sign to you" (24:24; and see 12:11 and Isa. 20:3).

As a sign, he was bound with ropes (3:24-27); he "played war" (4:1-17); he played barber (5:1-17); he clapped his hands and stamped his feet (6:11; see 21:14); he acted like he was going on a trip (12:1-16); he trembled as he ate (12:17-20) and groaned like a man in grief (21:6, 12); he played roadbuilder (21:18-23); he was not allowed to mourn his dead wife (24:15-27); and he made two sticks into one (37:15-17). Ezekiel also made use of parables (20:49; 24:3) and proverbs (11:3; 12:22; 16:44; 18:2-3).

The visions God gave him were very dramatic. His first vision was of a storm (see 13:13) that had fire "like glowing metal" at the heart of it and four cherubim within the fire (1:4-14), a picture of the holy judgment of God coming from the north (Jer. 1:14). The call of Moses (Ex. 3), of Isaiah (Isa. 6), and of Ezekiel all emphasized the holiness of God.

The next vision was of a throne on a firmament being moved about by intricate wheels within wheels (1:15-28), a manifestation of the sovereignty of God, His providential workings in the world, and the glory that it brings to Him. The vision was like that of a huge chariot surrounded by a rainbow and moving swiftly from place to place. Ezekiel began his ministry by seeing revelations of God's holy judgment and overruling providence.

The prophet would meet with resistance but God would make his forehead "like the hardest stone" (3:9; see Jer. 1:17-19).

In chapter 7, God's judgment would be unleashed like a beast (v. 3), awakened like a sleeping man (v. 5), and poured out like hot liquid (v. 8). The nation would feel the blow (v. 9); the seemingly dead stick had come to life and doom had blossomed (vv. 10-11). In the face of God's wrath, strong men will become like doves and strong knees will become "as weak as water" (vv. 16-17). God will come like a plunderer (v. 21), and even the rulers will be "clothed with despair" (v. 27).

The image of the "cooking pot" (11:3-15) is repeated in chapter 24. After the first deportation of exiles to Babylon (597 B.C.), the rulers left in Jerusalem considered themselves the "choice pieces of meat" while the exiles were the "leftovers." But God said that the innocent people of Jerusalem, people the rulers had killed, were the "choice meat" and the evil rulers were the "leftovers." When Nebuchadnezzar would begin his attack on Jerusalem, the city would indeed be a cooking pot, and the sinners would be destroyed.

Like Jeremiah in Jerusalem, Ezekiel in Babylon had to contend with false prophets (chap. 13). Instead of repairing the broken walls, these men were "like jackals among ruins," seeking for whatever dead bodies they could find (v. 4). Instead of giving the "bread of life" to the people, the false prophets lived like scavengers. Because they prophesied lies, they didn't repair the broken walls that made the nation so vulnerable; they only whitewashed the walls with a false peace. When the storm of God's wrath comes, the walls will collapse (vv. 10-16; see 22:28-31). Paul probably had this image in mind when he called the high priest a "whitewashed wall" (Acts 23:3).

According to chapter 15, the vine is good for either bearing fruit or being burned; you can't use it for building. If it stops bearing fruit, it becomes fuel. Of course, John 15 comes to mind. The vine image is repeated in chapter 17, a detailed allegory involving an eagle (v. 3, Nebuchadnezzar), a cedar tree (v. 3, David's royal line), the "topmost shoot" (vv. 3-4, King

Jehoiachin), a seed (vv. 5-6, Zedekiah), a second eagle (vv. 7-8, Egypt), the east wind (v. 10, Babylonian invasion), and a second shoot (vv. 22-24, Messiah). See Ezekiel 31 for another "tree" allegory.

Babylon is compared to a sword (21:1-5, 19) that will flash like lightning (vv. 9-10). Throughout Scripture, the sword is a consistent symbol of judgment and justice (see Ezek. 5–6; 30–33; Rom. 13:4). The word *sword* is used seventy-one times in Jeremiah and eighty-six times in Ezekiel.

Ezekiel names the sins of Jerusalem in 22:1-12 and pictures the nation as dross (vv. 17-22; see Jer. 6:27-30), the leaders as ravaging lions and wolves (vv. 23-27), and the prophets as liars whitewashing the tottering walls (vv. 28-31; see 13:10ff).

Ezekiel's funeral dirge for Tyre pictures the city as a great ship with a mighty crew, bearing tremendous wealth from port to port; but the "ship of state" would sink and be no more. You find a similar image in Isaiah 33:23 and Revelation 17–18.

Ezekiel 29–32 focuses on Egypt, the "great monster" that God will catch in His net (29:3; 32:1-8), the weak reed that the Jews must not trust (29:6; see 2 Kings 18:21; Isa. 36:6), the wages God will give Nebuchadnezzar for his work (29:17-20), and the mighty tree that God will hew down (chap. 31).

Ezekiel 37–48 deals primarily with the future of Israel. The Gentile nations are like graves and the Jews like dry bones in the graves, but God will give life to the bones and bring His people back to their land (33:1-14). The enemies of God will be offered like a sacrifice (39:17-20; see Isa. 34:6; Jer. 46:10; Zeph. 1:7; Rev. 19:17-21).

Ezekiel saw the glory of God depart from the temple and the city of Jerusalem (8:4; 9:3; 10:4, 18-19; 11:22-25), but he saw it return to the new temple and the new city (43:1-5).

Daniel

While the dreams and visions in the Book of Daniel are vivid in their imagery, and for the most part self-explained, there are not many similes and metaphors in the book. The man dressed in linen is described with references to fire, metals, jewels, and lightning (10:4-6; see Rev. 1:12-16). An empire will be uprooted (11:4; see Deut. 28:63; 29:28; 1 Kings 14:15; 2 Chron. 7:20; Ps. 52:5; Prov. 10:30; 12:3; Amos 9:15). Jeremiah makes considerable use of this image (1:10; 12:14-17; 18:7; 24:6; 31:28, 40; 42:10; 45:4.) See also Matthew 15:12-13.

Enemy invasion is pictured as a storm and a flood (Dan. 11:40); resurrection as awaking from sleep (12:2; see Matt. 9:24; John 11:11-14; Ps. 76:5; Acts 7:60; 13:36; 1 Cor. 11:30; 15:6, 18, 20; 1 Thes. 4:13-18); and rewards to the faithful like shining stars (12:3; Matt. 13:43; John 5:35; Phil. 2:15; Rev. 1:16, 20; 2:28; 8:10-12; 9:1; 12:1-4; 22:16).

Hosea

I have counted nearly eighty similes and metaphors in the Book of Hosea, which is certainly quite a record for a book of less than 200 verses. The overriding image, of course, is that of Jehovah's marriage covenant with His people, and the people's "prostitution" in worshiping foreign gods (4:10-18; 5:3-4; 6:10; 9:1). The theme is also dealt with in Jeremiah 3 and Ezekiel 16 and 23.

Hosea's message to the northern kingdom of Israel was illustrated in his own life (chaps. 1–3). Either he married a virgin and she became a prostitute, or he married a woman already a prostitute who returned to her old life. His wife fell so low that Hosea had to go to the slave market and buy her back. "Going back" and "returning" are key themes in the book (2:7; 3:5; 5:4; 6:1; 7:10; 12:6; 14:1). According to Jewish law, Gomer should have been stoned for her sin; but her husband forgave her and took her back.

Hosea used many images to describe the sinful people of the Northern Kingdom: stubborn heifers instead of meek lambs (4:16; 10:11); prostitutes (4:18; 5:1-7); adulterers "burning like an oven" (7:4-7); half-baked bread (7:8); senseless doves (7:11-12; see 11:11); faulty bows (7:16); wild donkeys (8:9); blighted plants (9:16) instead of a fruitful vine (10:1-2); unplowed soil (10:12); mist, dew, chaff, and smoke (13:3).

How will God judge Israel? He will make them like a desert

(2:3); a storm will sweep them away (4:19; 8:7); a flood will drown them (5:10); a moth will devour them (5:12); a lion will attack them (5:14; 13:7-8);[14] an eagle will swoop down (8:1); their glory will fly away like a bird (9:11); Samaria will float away like a twig on a river (10:7); they will reap a bitter harvest (10:13); they will have pains like a woman giving birth (13:13).

The emphasis of the book is on God's loving-kindness in forgiving His unfaithful people and welcoming back those who return to Him. When they return, the valley of Achor (trouble) will offer them a door of hope (2:15; see Josh. 7:24). When sinners return to the Lord, He heals them (6:1-2; 14:4) and brings life to them like the early and late rains (6:3). The withered plant (9:16) will grow and blossom from the dew of God's blessing and become like a cedar, an olive tree, a pine tree, and a fruitful vine (14:5-8).

Hosea 7:9 pictures the nation as getting old and weak but not realizing it (see Jud. 16:20). Their compromise with the godless Gentiles had cost them their strength.

Hosea 10:4 has a modern ring to it: "therefore lawsuits spring up like poisonous weeds in a plowed field." See Amos 6:12.

When God called His people at the beginning, they were like fresh fruit to Him (9:10). He took off their Egyptian yoke and bound them to Himself with kindness and love (11:4). But they turned to idols and began to feed on the wind and pursue vanity (12:1). Now they must offer the fruit of their lips, words of confession and repentance; and then He can heal them (14:1-2).

Joel

The overriding image here is that of a plague of locusts, insects invading the land like a conquering army (1:6; 2:2, 11, 25). They spread out like the dawning sun (2:2); they consumed the fields like crackling fire (2:5) and robbed houses like thieves (2:9). It was time for the people to repent, but not merely with outward demonstrations (2:13).

Joel saw in this devastating event a picture of the coming

"day of the Lord" when God would reap a harvest and judge the nations for their sins (3:13).

Amos

Since Amos was called from being a farmer, you can expect to find agricultural images used in his messages. God's Word is like the roar of a lion or a clap of thunder, and we had better listen (1:2). Damascus had treated her enemies like chaff (1:3). Sinful Israel will feel the weight of God's judgment like somebody run over by a cart full of grain (2:13). When the invading army is finished with Samaria, not much will be left, as when a lion catches a sheep (3:12). The kingdom would be overthrown even as Sodom and Gomorrah (4:11), like fire sweeping through a house (5:6).

Amos dared to call the leading women of the land "cows of Bashan" who would be led away to slaughter (4:1-3). The prophet saw the poor mistreated and exploited (5:7-13), and he cried out for justice to bring cleansing and healing to the land like a river and a stream (5:24). But until the people repent, God will send them a famine of His Word (8:11-12). He will shake the house of Israel "as grain is shaken in a sieve" (9:9; Luke 22:31; Isa. 30:28).

Amos closes his book on an encouraging note: The "house of David," now but a fallen tent, will one day be restored (9:11; Isa. 33:20; 54:2; Jer. 10:20), and Israel will enjoy God's blessings again. She will be planted, never to be uprooted again (9:15).

Obadiah

Edom was proud of its "nest among the stars" (v. 4) and sure of its security, but God would reach them and bring them down. Verses 5-6 parallel Jeremiah 49:9. One day, the Jews will be like fire and burn Edom like stubble (v. 18).

Jonah

Jesus said that Jonah's experience of death, burial, and resurrection was a "sign" and a picture of His own death, burial, and resurrection (Matt. 12:38-41). Jonah saw the depths as a prison that locked him in (2:6) as his life was "ebbing away" (2:7).

Micah

The Lord's coming in judgment is vividly described in 1:3-4, with the mountains melting like wax. (See Pss. 18:7ff; 144:5; Isa. 64:1.)

The prophet is so stirred he howls like a jackal and moans like an owl (1:8). Micah tries to find the godly, but it's like looking for fruit after the harvest is ended (7:1). He sees God's people dying from an incurable wound (1:9; Jer. 10:19; 14:17; 15:18; 30:12, 15; Lam. 2:13; Nahum 3:19; and see Isa. 1:5-6). The leaders of the nation are exploiting the people the way men butcher meat (3:1-3), and the judges are like thorns and briars (7:4).

The Lord summons His people to court (6:2) and warns that judgment is coming. The people will be trampled like mire in the street (7:10), but God will eventually judge Israel's enemies and make them lick the dust like snakes (7:17). God will forgive His people's sins, treading their sins underfoot and burying them in the depths of the sea (7:19). Israel will defeat their enemies and be like the dew and the rain (5:7), and a lion among the sheep (5:8). The Lord will give them horns of iron and hooves of bronze so they can thresh the nations (4:13). God will gather His people like sheep and bless them again (2:12).

Nahum

God's wrath is poured out like fire (1:6) and Nineveh will be burned up like stubble (1:10). The invading army is as fast as lightning (2:4). The slave girls moan like doves (2:7; Isa. 38:14; Ezek. 7:16). Nineveh is no longer a lions' den (2:11) but a pool that is leaking water and will soon be dry (2:8). Perhaps this is a picture of the people fleeing the city. The invaders will strip away everything, just like locusts (3:15-16).

Habakkuk

In the prophet's description of the invading Babylonian army, he compares the horses to leopards and wolves, and the soldiers to vultures. The army sweeps like the desert wind and picks up prisoners the way the wind picks up the sand (1:8-11). The army swallows people (1:13) and catches them like helpless fish in their nets (1:15).[15]

"Greedy as the grave" (2:5) reminds us that death "feeds" on people. (See Ps. 49:14; Prov. 27:20; 30:15-16; Isa. 5:14; 14:11.)

The promise of Habakkuk 2:14 echoes Isaiah 6:3, 11:9, and Psalm 72:19. The description in chapter 3 of God's coming down to earth compares His splendor to sunrise (v. 4) and His march to that of a conqueror in a chariot (vv. 8-9; and see Ps. 114). The mountains writhed in pain (v. 10) as God threshed the nations (v. 12) and trampled the sea (v. 15), another symbol of the nations.

The prophet's closing note is one of confidence: he has the feet of a deer and can climb higher! (v. 19)

Zephaniah

God's judgment of His people would be like a storm sweeping across the land (1:2-3; 2:2; Gen. 6:7) and a feast in connection with a sacrifice (1:7; Isa. 34:6; Jer. 46:10; Ezek. 39:17-20). The people, according to Zephaniah, would be like blind men (1:17) whose blood and entrails would be treated like dust and refuse.

Throughout Scripture, God's jealousy over His beloved people is often compared to fire (1:18; 3:8; Deut. 4:24; 6:15; Ps. 79:5; Zech. 8:2; see Ex. 20:5; 34:14). In His judgment, nations will be blown like chaff (2:2), uprooted (2:4), made like Sodom and Gomorrah (2:9), and made as dry and parched as a desert (2:13).

The prophet described the rapacious rulers as lions and wolves (3:3) to be devoured by His fire (3:8). These images are as frightening as they are powerful.

Haggai

The prophet used an object lesson based on the levitical laws of ritual uncleanness (2:10-13; Lev. 6:24-30; Num. 19:11-13; Ezek. 44:17-19; 46:20). God's people were defiled and therefore "toxic" and needed to be cleansed.

God made Zerubbabel, the governor, His "signet ring" (2:23), which was the seal a person used to "sign" documents. The governor was God's guarantee that the promised Messiah would indeed come and defeat Israel's enemies and establish the kingdom. Zerubbabel is named in the genealogy of Jesus Christ in Matthew 1:12-13. (On the spiritual implications of a seal or signet, see Song 8:6; Jer. 22:24-27; 2 Cor. 1:22; Eph. 1:13.)

Zechariah

The people tried to run away from God, but everything the prophets said caught up with them (1:6). Had they obeyed, God's blessings would have accompanied them (Deut. 28:2; "accompany" is the word "overtake"). God's Word runs swiftly to accomplish His purposes (Ps. 147:15; Isa. 55:11; 2 Thes. 3:1).

"The apple of his eye" (2:8) echoes Deuteronomy 32:10 and refers to the pupil. The word *apple* means "little man" because when you look into someone's eyes, you see yourself there in miniature. The pupil is a most sensitive and important part of the eye and must be guarded jealously. See Psalm 17:8 and Proverbs 7:2.

The image of the stick snatched from the fire (3:2) is also found in Amos 4:11 and Jude 23.

Zechariah 9:5 presents a withering dead hope, which is quite a contrast to the "living hope" that God's people have because of the resurrection of Jesus Christ (1 Peter 1:3).

The coming victory of God's people is pictured in Zechariah 9. God will use His people like weapons (v. 13) and their strength will be like that of men full of wine (v. 15). God will save them the way a shepherd saves his flock or a king his

155

jewels (v. 16). The sheep will be as strong as horses (10:3) and the people will pass safely through "the sea of trouble" (10:11-12), a reference to the exodus of Israel from Egypt.

Zechariah 12 deals with the defense of Jerusalem in the last days. God will use the city as a cup that will make the Gentile nations drunk so that they will attack and be defeated (v. 2; see Ps. 75:8; Isa. 51:17; Jer. 25:15). The city will be a rock (v. 3) that will injure those who attack. Judah will be a fire that will burn the enemy like firewood (v. 6). The nation will be refined like silver and gold (13:9; Job 23:10; Ps. 139:1-3; Mal. 3:2-4; 1 Peter 1:7; 4:12).

Malachi

"Opening the floodgates of heaven" (3:10) seems to be a proverbial phrase (2 Kings 7:2, 19; Ps. 78:23) that may be based on Genesis 7:11.

Israel as God's "treasured possession" (3:17) takes us back to Exodus 19:5 and also to God's special treatment of the Jews when they were in Egypt (Ex. 8:22; 9:4, 6, 26; 11:7; 12:13). See also Deuteronomy 4:20, 7:6, 14:2, 26:18, and Psalms 33:12, 135:4.

The closing images center around a day of judgment when God's fire will burn like a furnace (4:1) and destroy proud sinners who will become ashes (4:3). But the saints will rejoice like calves released from their stalls (4:2; Isa. 35:6). The sun that burns the wicked will bring healing to the righteous (4:2; Pss. 27:1; 118:27; Isa. 60:1, 19-20).

The English Old Testament ends with the warning that God will smite the earth with a curse. The New Testament closes with God promising that there will be no more curse (Rev. 22:3).

"He was often a healer, sometimes a worker of signs,
frequently a preacher, but always a teacher. . . .
Teaching was his chief business."

—*John A. Marquis*

"The common people are captivated more readily
by comparisons and examples
than by difficult and subtle disputations.
They would rather see a well-drawn picture
than a well-written book."

—*Martin Luther*

"Metaphors are much more tenacious
than facts."

—*Paul De Man*

Chapter Thirteen
Jesus, the Master Teacher/Preacher

Preaching has fallen low enough in our own church and country sometimes," said Alexander Whyte nearly a century ago, "but it has never sunk to such depths of imbecility as the preaching of the Scribes."[1]

James Stalker, Whyte's fellow minister in the Scottish Free Church, agreed with this evaluation when he wrote: "The scribes were their [the Jews'] accustomed teachers who harangued them week by week in the synagogues. No doubt there must have been differences among them; they cannot all have been equally bad; but, taken as a whole, they were probably the most barren and unspiritual set of men who have ever held sway over the mind of a nation."[2]

As you study the Gospel records, you learn that the scribes and Pharisees opposed Jesus not only because of what He said but also because of the way He said it. It has often been said that the scribes spoke *from authorities,* while Jesus spoke *with authority;* and the common people recognized the difference. "When Jesus had finished saying these things, the crowds were amazed at his teaching, because he taught as one who had authority, and not as their teachers of the law" (Matt. 7:28-29).

"Even if Jesus had no other claim to be remembered," wrote William Barclay, "he would be remembered as one of the world's masters of the technique of teaching."[3] He was able to attract and instruct all kinds of people in all kinds of situations, and He did it without the aid of the "gimmicks" that we think are so necessary for ministry today. There was a vitality to our Lord's messages that arrested the minds and hearts of His listeners. To quote Stalker again: "The Bible can be converted into a prison in which God is confined, or a museum in which the spiritual life is preserved as an antiquarian curiosity. But those who came to hear Jesus felt that he was in direct contact with the spiritual world and brought to them news of what He had Himself seen and felt."[4]

One of the obvious characteristics of our Lord's ministry is His effective use of imagination. He used similes, metaphors, epigrams, parables, and paradoxes as He transformed everyday objects and experiences into messages from heaven. Jesus did supremely what Hushai and Nathan and we preachers today do rather haltingly: He turned His listeners' ears into eyes so they could see the truth and respond to it.

A Philosophy of Preaching

I think that our Lord's "philosophy of preaching," if I may be permitted to use that phrase, is revealed in these statements.

> This is why I speak to them in parables: "Though seeing, they do not see; though hearing, they do not hear or understand." In them is fulfilled the prophecy of Isaiah: "You will be ever hearing but never understanding; you will be ever seeing but never perceiving. For this people's heart has become calloused; they hardly hear with their ears, and they have closed their eyes. Otherwise they might see with their eyes, hear with their ears, understand with their hearts and turn, and I would heal them." Therefore every teacher of the law who has been instructed about the kingdom of heaven is like the owner of a house who brings out of his storeroom new treasures as well as old. (Matt. 13:13-15, 52)

When asked why He taught the crowds in parables, Jesus gave a human reason in the verses quoted above, and Matthew, true to the purpose of his book, added a divine reason by

160

quoting Psalm 78:2 and applying it to Jesus (Matt. 13:34-35).[5] Jesus taught in parables because of the commission of the Lord and the condition of the people. The stultifying influence of dull religious leaders, combined with the sinful tendencies of human nature, helped to make the people blind and deaf to spiritual truth. The people needed to be awakened, and Jesus knew how to do it.

Jesus didn't "hide the truth" in order to condemn people who were already condemned. He "hid the truth" in parables and pictures so that the people might have their curiosity aroused and become interested enough to open their eyes and ears and start to understand the truth. "For whatever is hidden is meant to be disclosed, and whatever is concealed is meant to be brought out into the open. If anyone has ears to hear, let him hear" (Mark 4:22-23).

The Jewish people of that day had grown blind looking at God's creation and not perceiving the messages it conveyed. They didn't think of God's Word when they sowed seed, or the new birth when they felt the wind, or faith when they gathered the tiny mustard seed; but Jesus did. Because they were blind to God's message in the world around them, they had grown deaf to the messages in the Scriptures that they heard. In His teaching, the Lord Jesus united the truth around them in creation with the truth before them in the Scriptures, and in this way He was able to open their eyes and ears and penetrate their calloused hearts. The progression from sermon to salvation is clear: hear—see—understand—turn—be forgiven!

The neglected parable in Matthew 13:52 gives us another aspect of our Lord's "philosophy of preaching." I prefer the translation in *The New Testament in the Language of the People:* "Every scribe who has become a disciple in the kingdom of heaven is like a householder who can bring out of his storeroom new furnishings as well as old" (WMS).[6] There's a definite sequence here: the *scribe* becomes a *disciple,* and then the disciple becomes a *householder* with treasures new and old to share with others.

The scribe is one who *studies* the Word, the disciple is one who *practices* the Word,[7] and the *householder* is one who shares the treasures of the truth with others. Scribes *discover* the truth and become disciples who *do* the truth and house-holders who *dispense* the truth; and it takes all three to have an effective and balanced ministry.

Scribes who learn the truth but never live it will have nothing vital to share. In fact, those people are really hypocrites (Matt. 23:1-4). People who try to live what they have not really learned are going to face difficult struggles, but those who keep the truth to themselves and fail to share it will also suffer. God wants us to be channels and not reservoirs; in fact, we only really keep that which we give away. Ezra is a perfect example of the kind of balance Jesus is asking for in our ministries: "For Ezra had devoted himself to the study [the scribe] and obser-vance [the disciple] of the Law of the Lord, and to teaching its decrees and laws in Israel [the householder]" (Ezra 7:10).[8]

The householder brings out of his storeroom things new and old. "Do not think that I have come to abolish the Law or the Prophets," said Jesus; "I have not come to abolish them but to fulfill them" (Matt. 5:17). The scribes embalmed the old teach-ings, but Jesus fulfilled them by explaining the principles in them that are always new and applicable to every age.

Jesus compared the Word of God to seed (Luke 8:11), and there are three ways to destroy a seed: (1) you can guard it but never plant it; (2) you can pound it to bits with a rock or hammer; or (3) you can plant the seed and let it fulfill itself by producing more seed. Today, people like the scribes take the first approach and become devoted keepers of religious muse-ums. Those who worship novelty and make "contemporary" their buzz word, take the second approach; but in their quest for the new, they ignore the old, forgetting that the new always grows out of the old. After all, the Word is like seed; and the purpose of the seed is the perpetuation of successive harvests.[9]

Our Lord took the third approach. He planted the seed (the old) and cultivated it in such a way that it bore a harvest (the new). He reached back into the Old Testament and took famil-iar figures like wind, leaven, thieves, harvests, salt, sheep, gates, roads, all of which were a part of the everyday life of the peo-ple, and He "planted" these seeds in such an imaginative way

162

that they were rescued from the scribal museums and bore fruit.

This is what preaching with imagination is all about. We're not inventing new things; we're discovering new things in the old things and new applications of old principles. We're seeing with new eyes and hearing with new ears. We're following the example of our Lord as expressed by E.P. Boys-Smith: "His thoughts were always concrete, not abstract; His intellectual processes were *intuitive*, not argumentative; His views were ever *positive*, not negative."[10]

This summary of our Lord's approach to preaching reminds me of the first three principles of preaching espoused by F.W. Robertson.

> First. The establishment of positive truth, instead of the negative destruction of error. Secondly. That truth is made up of two opposite propositions, and not found in a *via media* between the two. Thirdly. That spiritual truth is discerned by the spirit, instead of intellectually in propositions; and, therefore, truth should be taught suggestively, not dogmatically.[11]

The first principle certainly doesn't rule out the necessity for exposing error and engaging in apologetics. All it's saying is that nobody knows where he or she is going if the street signs read "This road does not go to Boston" or "This freeway does not lead to Los Angeles." Drivers want to know where the route *is* taking them; and once they know where they're going, they'll be glad to discuss alternate routes with you. Knowing positive truth is the best way to detect error.

The second principle, that truth is made up of two opposite propositions, doesn't deny absolutes (after all, the statement itself is an absolute), but it warns the preacher against the sin of one-sidedness. It's possible to so emphasize human responsibility that we end up weakening or denying divine sovereignty, and vice versa. In spite of what our tidy analytical minds may crave, there are doctrinal paradoxes in Christian theology; and the mature response of faith is to accept both sides. God is both transcendent and immanent; Jesus Christ is both God and man; the Bible is an inspired book expressing divine truth in human language; believers are imperfect people with a perfect standing before God.[12]

Robertson's third proposition, that truth is taught suggestively and discerned intuitively, is not a rejection of propositional truth but a recognition of the poetical side of human intelligence, the right brain, if you please. Nicodemus wanted Jesus to explain everything to him, but our Lord instead only gave him pictures: birth, wind, the brazen serpent, light and darkness. Twentieth-century homiletics has so emphasized analysis and explanation that we've forgotten synthesis and illustration. Thomas Carlyle wrote, "It is the heart always that sees, before the head can see." It's unfortunate that the computer has become a metaphor for the human mind, because this image, if followed to its conclusion, could lead to more "mental mechanization" and, therefore, a possible diminution of human creativity. Science writer Isaac Asimov reminds us that "if insight, intuition, creativity, the ability to view a problem as a whole and guess the answer by a 'feel' of the situation, is a measure of intelligence, computers are very unintelligent indeed."[13]

Lewis Mumford wrote, "One of the functions of intelligence is to take account of the dangers that come from trusting solely in the intelligence." Jesus didn't bypass or insult the intelligence of His hearers, but neither did He present His message only to the intelligence. He reached into the heart, the intuition, and used the key of images to unlock the imagination and reach to the will.

Parables[14]

At least one-third of our Lord's teaching as recorded in the Synoptics is comprised of parables. "At its simplest," wrote C.H. Dodd, "the parable is a metaphor or simile drawn from nature or common life, arresting the hearer by its vividness or strangeness, and leaving the mind in sufficient doubt about its precise application to tease it into active thought."[15] I like to think of a parable as a *picture* that becomes a *mirror* and then a *window.*

164

A parable starts out as a picture of something in life, something recognizable that at the same time contains something different and, to use Dodd's phrasing, "arresting." The owner of the vineyard hires workers all day long (So what?) but pays all his workers the same wage for their day's work and starts with those last hired. *(How strange!)* The crooked steward gives his master's customers big discounts and his master commends him for it. *(That's unusual!)* The owner of the vineyard sends his only son to get payment from the tenants even after they had beaten and killed the other agents. *(Why did he do that?)*

The longer we look at the "parable picture," the more it becomes a mirror *and we start to see ourselves.* When the chief priests and Pharisees heard our Lord's Parable of the Tenants, they saw themselves in it and wanted to arrest Him (Matt. 21:33-46). Jesus didn't simply use parables as "illustrations," the way preachers tell stories to explain their points, but as *illumination,* the kind of light that pierced the very hearts and minds of the listeners and made them aware of their own needs. Parables are not entertainment; they're powerful shock therapy.

But that isn't the end: the mirror must then become a window *so that the listeners see God and His truth and receive the message by faith.* Our Lord's enemies never got to this third stage. Having seen themselves reflected, they then tried to break the mirror by resisting the truth. The "shock of recognition" was too much for them. But the purpose of parables is to reveal some truth about God and His kingdom that will help us know Him better and do His will.

In thinking through the stages, we might present them as follows:

The picture	The mirror	The window
We see life	We see ourselves	We see God
Sight	Insight	Vision
Information	Intimidation	Invitation
Somebody else	Me!	God and I
I'm interested	I'm shattered	I'm healed

Pictures in the Synoptics

It isn't necessary for us to go through the four Gospels and list every simile, metaphor, and parable, since most of them are rather obvious and there are excellent volumes available that do this.[16] Many of the images used have already been commented on from Old Testament texts. What I want to do is mention some of the less obvious pictorial images that have special value for the expositor.

Matthew

2:6 — "who will be the shepherd of my people Israel"

3:3 — The preacher as a roadbuilder. See 2 Timothy 2:15 where the phrase "correctly handles" (*orthotomeo*) means "to cut a straight path."

3:7 — "brood of vipers" connects with the serpent in Genesis 3; and see Matthew 12:34, 23:33, John 8:44, the Parable of the Weeds, and Revelation 12.

4:19 — "Fishers of men" was not a new phrase coined by Jesus. It had been used by philosophers to describe their "catching" of disciples by casting out the net of truth.[17]

6:22 — Outlook determines outcome. A single eye (Matt. 6:23) brings in light, but double vision brings in darkness. The tragedy is, double-visioned people think they're receiving light when it's really darkness!

7:7 — Open doors generally speak of service for the Lord. See Acts 14:27, Revelation 3:8.

9:9-17 — Jesus used three illustrations to answer His critics: the physician, the bridegroom, and the wine merchant. He came to heal sinners, not praise the righteous; He came to bring joy, not sorrow; He came to give newness and wholeness and not merely to patch up the old.

11:16 — The people were childish but not childlike. See 11:25-26.

12:20 — The verse seems to refer to Christ's enemies rather than to the weak and needy to whom He ministered. His enemies were weak and about to be extinguished, but He would be gracious to them and give them opportunity to repent. See Isaiah 7:4.

15:13-14 — The plants probably refer to the Pharisees rather than to their teachings. See Isaiah 60:21.

16:18 — The city gate was the place where the leaders met and exercised civil power. The phrase stands for "the authority of Hades" and suggests that the church is on the offensive.

16:24 — The phrase "take up his cross" is obviously not literal since Christians don't carry crosses the way people do once a year in Holy Week processions. Discipleship and cross-bearing are images of the Christian life, speaking of devotion and denial. Crucifixion is a form of death that people can't perform on themselves; they must yield to another. There is a once-for-all surrender and then a daily death to self.

23:32 — The measuring of gradually increasing sin; see Genesis 15:16, 1 Thessalonians 2:16.

Mark

9:49 — Salt was important in the sacrifices the Jews brought to the Lord (Lev. 2:13; Num. 18:19; 2 Chron. 13:5; Ezek. 43:24).

Luke

1:78 — Our Lord's coming to earth meant the dawning of a new day. See Luke 2:32, Malachi 4:2, Matthew 4:15-16.

7:24 — John was not a weak reed easily swayed by people or circumstances. See Ephesians 4:14, James 1:6, Jude 12.

10:3 — "Lambs among wolves" is a proverbial saying. See Acts 20:29, Jeremiah 11:19.

12:32 — This sentence appears to be a terribly mixed metaphor involving a flock, a family, and a kingdom. But in the light of the Eastern way of life, where a sheik would be a king, a father, and a shepherd, the sentence glows with imagery.

12:50 — Our Lord's baptism of suffering on the cross was prefigured by His baptism in the Jordan. "All your waves and breakers have swept over me" (Ps. 42:7; Ps. 69:2; Jonah 2:3). Jonah is a type of Christ in His death, burial, and resurrection.

Pictures in John's Gospel

John is the "poet" among the Gospel writers and in his selection and presentation of the material he makes creative use of symbolism. In both his Gospel and his epistles, John contrasts darkness and light as well as life and death, and he makes much of the figure of spiritual birth. The phrase "born of God" is used eight times in his first epistle. Wine, water, bread, marriage, the temple, the lamb, sheep and shepherds, the vine, wind, and seed are among the images used in John's Gospel.

It's significant that most of the images John uses are universal in their meaning. Except for the temple of His body (2:19), shepherds (John 10), and the vine (John 15), the images John uses can be understood in most cultures. This goes along with John's purpose in writing a Gospel for the whole world.

John does refer to some Old Testament images: Jacob's ladder (stairway) at Bethel (1:51; Gen. 28); the brazen serpent (3:14; Num. 21); the manna (chap. 6; Ex. 16); and the vine (15:1-8; Isa. 5). But it would appear that he is presenting life in Christ as God's "new creation" in contrast to Moses and the Law (1:17). The seven days marked out in chapters 1–2 suggest the seven days of Genesis 1.

Jesus is the new temple (2:19) and He gives a new birth that doesn't depend on one's parents (1:12-13; 3:1-16). The two Sabbath miracles (chaps. 5 and 9) indicate that He is ushering in a new Sabbath of rest, and the sermon in chapter 6 presents Christ as the life-giving manna. Israel was God's flock, but now there is a new flock led by the Good Shepherd (chap. 10). God gave Israel water from the rock, but Jesus gives living water (chap. 4; 7:37-39). He gave new meaning to Passover and also to the vine. The image of "eating flesh and drinking blood" in chapter 6 must not be taken literally, as the Jews took it, or even sacramentally. It's difficult to understand why Jesus would discuss a sacrament with a group of rebellious, unbelieving Jews. The manna came down from heaven and Jesus came down from heaven, sent by the Father. The manna sustained life for the Jews, but Jesus gives life to the whole world, a life that triumphs over death. Just as they had to receive the manna within, so we must receive Christ within by faith as we receive His Word. "The Spirit gives life," said Jesus; "the flesh counts for nothing. The words I have spoken to you are spirit and they are life" (6:63). In receiving the Word, we receive the Word that was made flesh (1:14).

John selected five images of the death of Jesus Christ: the sacrifice of the lamb (1:29); the destruction of the temple (2:19); the lifting up of the serpent (3:14); the volunteer death of the shepherd for the sheep (10:11-18); and the planting of the seed (12:20-25). In all but two of these images — the lamb and the serpent — His resurrection is incipient in the figure.

Pictures of the Church

In the record of the four Gospels, our Lord uses the word *church* only twice, once in the universal sense (Matt. 16:18) and once with a local reference (Matt. 18:17). The Greeks recognized *ekklesia* as the lawful assembly of citizens in a free city, called together to transact civic affairs. There was no such thing as "the *ekklesia*" in a universal sense, as we today speak of "the church." The *ekklesia* was local and autonomous, and it didn't think of itself as belonging to a "larger" *ekklesia*.

In the New Testament, most of the references to an *ekklesia* are local. Paul writes to "the *ekklesia* of God which is at Corinth" or some other city. However, Peter wrote to believers in five different provinces (1 Peter 1:1) and yet gave them titles that were singular and not plural: "a chosen people, a royal priesthood, a holy nation, a people belonging to God" (1 Peter 2:9). The saints in each province assembled in a local *ekklesia*, but they all were a part of a larger *ekklesia* that included all of God's people everywhere. Passages like Ephesians 1:22, 3:10 and 21, 5:23-32, Colossians 1:18 and 24, and Hebrews 12:23 seem to speak of something bigger than a local assembly.

The statement "I will build my church" pictures the church as a temple, and the reference to "the gates of Hades" suggests conflict. Our Lord's statement to Peter presents the church as an assembly, a building, and an army; and all three metaphors are expanded in the epistles.

169

In the Sermon on the Mount, Jesus compared His disciples to salt, light, and a city set on a hill (Matt. 5:13-16); and we usually apply these images to the church collectively.

We have already considered the image of the *flock* and will have occasion to notice it again when we survey Acts and the epistles. Jesus referred to "the lost sheep of Israel" (Matt. 10:6; 15:24) as well as the "one flock" and "one shepherd" (John 10:16; see 11:52). Christ's commission to Peter in John 21 uses the metaphor of the flock.

The word translated "disciple" (*mathetes*) is used over 260 times in the Gospels and Acts, but never in the epistles; and the record shows that our Lord used it sparingly (Matt. 10:2; 28:19; Mark 14:14; Luke 14:26-27, 33; 22:11; John 8:31; 13:35; 15:8). The verb *manthano* is used twenty-five times but doesn't always refer to learning as a disciple. Believers were often called "disciples," but there is no indication that the title was used in a universal sense as was *ekklesia*. The church was composed of disciples, but the church was not a "discipleship" or a "discipledom."

The church as the bride is suggested in John 3:29, Matthew 9:14-15, Mark 2:18-20, and Luke 5:33-35.

In John 15, Jesus used the image of the church as *branches in the vine*, a figure we touched upon when we considered Ezekiel 15. Israel was God's choice vine (Isa. 5), but it produced "wild grapes." Today, God's people are branches in the true vine; and as we abide in Christ, we produce fruit for His glory. But there's a third vine, "the vine of the earth" (Rev. 14:14-20), which seems to represent society ripening for judgment.

"You must hear the bird's song without attempting to render it into nouns and verbs."

—*Ralph Waldo Emerson*

"What is experience but a wealth of parallels upon which our imagination can draw?"

—*Alex Osborn*

"The creation of a thousand forests is in one acorn."

—*Ralph Waldo Emerson*

Chapter Fourteen
Pictures in the Book of Acts

Dr. Luke wrote two travel books. In his Gospel, he described our Lord's journey from Bethlehem to Jerusalem (Luke 9:51); and in the Book of Acts, he told how the Gospel traveled from Jerusalem to Rome. A reader completing the Gospel of John and turning immediately to the Epistle to the Romans would wonder what happened to Peter, who Paul was, and how the church got from Jerusalem to Rome. The Book of Acts answers those questions.

2:1 — That the church was "born" on the Day of Pentecost suggests that we look at Leviticus 23:15-21 and see what this Jewish feast might teach us.[1] Pentecost was a harvest festival, and the Book of Acts records the progress of the spiritual harvest as believers shared the Gospel. On the Feast of Firstfruits, the priest waved sheaves; but on the Feast of Pentecost, he waved two loaves of bread. It was on Pentecost that the believers were united by the Spirit into one body, first the Jews and then the Gentiles (Acts 10).[2] The presence of the forbidden leaven in the two loaves (Lev. 23:17; 2:11) suggests that sin is in the church even though the believers are accepted before God. Of course, the blood of the sacrifices offered that day would cover the sins of priest and people.

2:2-13 — Three images stand out: the sound of wind, the tongues of fire, and wine, with its accompanying accusation of drunkenness. Each of these images is connected with the Holy Spirit. The words "wind" or "breath" are the same as "spirit"

173

or "Spirit" in the Hebrew and Greek (*ruah, pneuma*), and passages like Ezekiel 37 and John 3:8 and 20:22 connect the Spirit with wind and breath. Fire is also a symbol of the Spirit as "a spirit of judgment and a spirit of fire" (Isa. 4:4; the NIV margin note gives "Spirit"). The seven burning lamps before God's throne are called "the seven spirits of God" (Rev. 4:5; the NIV margin note reads "the sevenfold Spirit"). The combination of a rushing wind and fire would certainly make for a mighty blaze![3]

The enthusiastic praises of the assembled believers gave the spectators the impression that Peter and his friends were drunk.[4] This reminds us of Paul's admonition, "Do not get drunk on wine, which leads to debauchery. Instead, be filled with the Spirit" (Eph. 5:18). Paul wasn't suggesting that when believers are filled with the Spirit they will act like drunks. For the most part, he is *contrasting* the two experiences. The drunkard is exuberant because alcohol is a sedative that robs him of the full control of his faculties. But "the fruit of the Spirit is . . . self-control" (Gal. 5:22-23), not loss of control. The Spirit-filled Christian's expressions of praise and worship are voluntary and deliberate, motivated and energized by the Spirit of God. But like the drunk, the Spirit-filled believer is happy and not ashamed to show it.[5]

4:30 — The familiar anthropomorphic description of God "stretching out His hand" is found again in 11:21 and 13:11. It is frequently found in Scripture to express the power of God working in and through His servants. See Ezra 7:6, 9, 14, 28; 8:18, 22, 31; and note the use of the phrase in Nehemiah and in the Book of Psalms.

6:15 — We aren't told specifically how Stephen's face was like that of an angel, but we assume it means a supernatural radiance that all could see (Matt. 28:1-3; Dan. 10:6; Rev. 10:1). This radiance was the perfect preparation for Stephen's opening statement, "The God of glory appeared to our father Abraham" (7:2). It was also a foretaste of the glory he would see and soon enter (7:55-56).

When you find an arresting image like this one, begin to search your Bible for other examples. Is it recorded anywhere else in Scripture that anyone had a shining face? Moses did (Ex. 34:29-35, and see 2 Cor. 3), and so did Jesus on the Mount of Transfiguration (Matt. 17:1-8). The word translated "transfigured" in Matthew 17:2 is used in Romans 12:2 ("transformed") and 2 Corinthians 3:18 ("transformed"). Paul shares the amazing truth that all believers can have their own personal "transfiguration" and experience heaven's glory shining through them, not just once but constantly.

8:4 — We have already noted that "scattered" carried the image of the sowing of the seed (see 11:19). Satan's scattering of the saints only resulted in a bigger harvest! God expects us to "bloom where we're planted"! Ministry is like sowing (1 Cor. 9:11; 2 Cor. 9:10), and giving is like sowing (2 Cor. 9:6; Gal. 6:7-9). See also Proverbs 11:18 and 22:8.

9:1 — The phrase "breathing out murderous threats" reminds us of a wild animal snorting and charging in anger, and the Lord's words to Saul about "kicking against the goads" parallel this image (Acts 26:14). David's enemies were "breathing out violence" (Ps. 27:12), and Isaiah said that "the breath of the ruthless is like a storm driving against a wall" (Isa. 25:4). But the raging rabbi was led away as meek as a lamb, and the grace of God completely transformed him.

20:17-35 — Paul's farewell message to the Ephesian elders helps us better understand the work of the ministry. Verse 24 presents a number of images of ministry. Paul saw himself as an *accountant* ("I consider") who evaluated his life and decided he would give all to Christ.[6] He saw himself as a *runner* ("finish the race"), a parallel to Philippians 3:12-14 and 2 Timothy 4:7. The same image is applied to John the Baptist in Acts 13:25, literally "as John completed his course." God saw the ministry of Jeremiah as the running of a race (Jer. 12:5), and Hebrews 12:1-2 relates the image to Jesus. Paul was also a *steward*, seeking to be faithful in the ministry he received from the Lord; and he was a *witness*, called to testify on behalf of the Gospel of God's grace.

Verse 25 presents Paul as a *herald*, for the word translated "preaching" (*kerysso*) means "to deliver a message as the herald of a king." Heralds don't invent their messages; they are called and commissioned to deliver the messages entrusted to them. Paul saw himself as a *watchman* (v. 26) who had been faithful to warn all of his listeners, and therefore he was free from their blood (Ezek. 3:17-21; 33:1-9). The image of the flock and the shepherd (20:28-31) reminds us of Matthew 7:15 and 10:16, Luke 10:3, John 10:12, and Ezekiel 34.

"God thinks metaphorically.
The Bible is full striking metaphors,
but we've become too familiar with them
to realize how vivid they are."

—Luci Shaw

"The great instrument of moral good
is the imagination."

—Percy Bysshe Shelley

"The Christian church does not need
more popular preaching,
but more unpopular preaching."

—Walter Russell Bowie

Chapter Fifteen
Pictures of the Church[1]

Charles Haddon Spurgeon was a great and godly man, a gifted preacher whose sermons I read and study with appreciation and edification. He was indeed "a preacher's preacher." I quote Spurgeon frequently in my preaching and writing because he has the gift of saying wise things in a creative way, but the following quotation isn't one of his best.

> It is noticeable that after the Holy Ghost had been given, fewer parables were used, and the saints were more plainly taught of God. When Paul spoke or wrote to the churches in his epistles he employed few parables, because he addressed those who were advanced in grace and willing to learn. As Christian minds made progress the style of their teachers became less figurative, and more plainly doctrinal.[2]

I'm unworthy to carry Spurgeon's shoes, but I must humbly disagree with him. It's my conviction that just the opposite is true: God often used metaphorical language *especially for mature Christians* knowing that they knew how to interpret and apply it.[3] The New Testament epistles are exploding with exciting images that help us better understand our relationship to Christ and His church.

As for Spurgeon's dichotomy between the "figurative" and the "more plainly doctrinal," it just doesn't hold water. Some

179

of the most important doctrinal truths in Scripture are presented in the epistles in metaphorical language, because that was
the best way for the writers to present them. When he wanted
to refute the stupid ideas some Greeks held about the resurrection of the human body, Paul wrote about seeds and stars
(1 Cor. 15:35-49). Peter reached into political life when he
called God's people "aliens and strangers" (1 Peter 1:17; 2:11),
and he reached back into Jewish religious life when he called
the saints "a holy priesthood," "a royal priesthood," and "living stones" in God's temple (1 Peter 2:5, 9). This imagery isn't
a picture book for babes, although they can learn from it; it's a
picture gallery, a Louvre, if you please, for the more mature.

Paul's favorite images seem to be architecture, agriculture,
the army, and anatomy. But he often borrowed from Old Testament Jewish life and used images like leaven and bread, tents,
sheep, the priesthood, and the annual Jewish feasts. In his book
Images of the Church in the New Testament, Paul Minear lists
nearly 100 different analogies of the believer or the church,
most of them found in the Pauline epistles.

In this incomplete survey of images in the epistles, I will first
summarize the major pictures of the church (and the believer),
and then mention some of the other important images that
relate to the Christian life.

The Army

Living as they did in a military state, the writers of the New
Testament epistles would be expected to use military figures
that would be familiar to their readers. Ephesians 6:10-18 describes both the enemy that opposes us and the equipment we
must use to defeat him. See also Romans 13:11-13 and 1 Thessalonians 5:5-8 (Isa. 59:17). Ephesians 4:8 refers to "prisoners
of war," and the verb *methistemi* in Colossians 1:13 can refer
to the deporting of prisoners. See also Luke 4:18. The three
images Paul uses in 1 Corinthians 9:7 can all be applied to the
church, and see also 2 Corinthians 6:7 and 10:2-6. Paul called
his associate Epaphroditus a "fellow soldier" (Phil. 2:25).

The image of the "Roman triumph" in 2 Corinthians 2:14-17

reminds us that Jesus Christ has won the victory and we follow in His train.[4] The fragrance of the incense offered to the gods would mean life and honor to the victorious soldiers, but death to the captives in the procession. Colossians 2:15 is a parallel passage.

The verb *parangello* carries the idea of a military command given by a superior officer, as does the noun *parangellia;* and both are used by Paul in writing to the Thessalonians and to Timothy. See 1 Thessalonians 4:2, 11 and 2 Thessalonians 3:4, 6, 10, 12. God gave these orders to the Apostle Paul, who in turn passed them on to the church; and God expected His people to obey.

Paul reminded Timothy of his calling as a soldier (2 Tim. 2:3-4), and he ordered him (*parangello*) to stay on duty (1 Tim. 1:3), fight the battle (1 Tim. 1:18), obey the orders given to him (1 Tim. 6:13-14), and guard what had been committed to his care (1 Tim. 6:20; see 2 Tim. 1:14). Timothy was also to "command" the church to obey what Paul had written in his letters (1 Tim. 4:11; 5:7; 6:17). As soldiers of the Lord, God's people aren't given the privilege of "picking and choosing" what order they will obey.[5]

Athletics

Things athletic were almost as pervasive in the Empire as things military, and the people didn't lack for gymnasiums, coliseums, and opportunities to compete in official games, both national and local. Not unlike many "sports fans" today, the Romans were spectators who considered sports primarily as entertainment, while the Greeks stressed participation for the glory of one's city or nation. Amateur sports today is more like the Greek approach, while professional sports follows the Roman pattern of athletics.

Greek boys were enrolled in the gymnasium at an early age, and the goal of their education was the developing of "a sound mind in a sound body." Boxing, wrestling, running, swimming, rowing, discus throwing, and weight lifting were among the activities they had to master. In the official games, the Greeks

181

counted first place only, which adds light to Paul's statement in 1 Corinthians 9:24 that *all* of God's "athletes" may win a crown.

We have already seen that ministry is compared to running a race and finishing a course (Acts 13:25; 20:24; Gal. 2:2; Phil. 2:16; and see Jer. 12:5). The Christian life is a race (Gal. 5:7; Phil. 3:12-14; Heb. 12:1), and success demands discipline and obedience to the rules (1 Cor. 9:24-27; 2 Tim. 2:5; see also Heb. 10:32 and 12:4-13). Successful Christian living also demands determination. The Greek words *agon* and *agonizomai* (cf. our English word "agony") relate to athletics and are translated variously: fight, strive, race, struggle, wrestle, compete. Paul's familiar statement in 2 Timothy 4:7 ("I have fought the good fight") has nothing to do with war; it's a description of the foot race. Paul was about to finish the race and he wanted to finish triumphantly.[6]

The good athlete knows how to practice teamwork. Paul uses *sunathleo* ("striving together") in Philippians 1:27 and 4:3. Euodia and Syntyche had been "teammates" with Paul in Philippi, and it pained him to see them disagreeing and causing division on the "team."

First Corinthians 4:9 certainly refers to the Roman gladiatorial entertainments in the arena, when the prisoners fought wild beasts and the crowds cried for blood. Usually the weakest prisoners, who couldn't provide much entertainment, were brought in at the end of the show; and that's where Paul put himself and the other apostles. The "super-apostles" that had taken over in Corinth (2 Cor. 11) would have been champions in the arena, but Paul was just God's weakling.

The significant references to "crowns" are: 1 Corinthians 9:25; Philippians 4:1; 1 Thessalonians 2:19; 2 Timothy 4:8; and 1 Peter 5:4. Colossians 2:18 warns the believer not to let false teachers "declare [them] unworthy of a prize." The "rich welcome into the eternal kingdom" (2 Peter 1:11) has athletic overtones. Those who won prizes at the national games were welcomed royally by their townspeople and led through a special gate or flowered arch. Often a statue of the winner was dedicated in his honor.

Agriculture

"You are God's field" (1 Cor. 3:9)[7] applies to the local church. In the Parable of the Sower, the soil represents human hearts receiving the seed of the Word; and in the Parable of the Weeds, "the field is the world," and the seed represents children of the kingdom planted where the Lord of the Harvest wants them.

Paul "planted" the church in Corinth by sowing the seed of the Word of the Gospel (1 Cor. 2; see Col. 1:6), Apollos continued the work, and "God made it grow" (1 Cor. 3:6-7). God desires that His "field" increase and produce a harvest, and to do this, He assigns different workers to different tasks. There is no competition in the work because all of us are serving the Lord and seeking a harvest (John 4:34-38). Whether we plow (Luke 9:62), sow, water, or harvest, we are all working for one Master and seeking to achieve one purpose; and the Master will see to it that each worker receives the right reward.

The Apostle Paul longed to go to Rome that he might "have a harvest" among the people there (Rom. 1:13). He prayed that the Philippian saints might be "filled with the fruit of righteousness" (Phil. 1:11; see Gal. 5:22-23) and that the Colossian believers might bear "fruit in every good work" (Col. 1:10). Believers are God's "firstfruits" (Rom. 16:5; James 1:18; and see 1 Cor. 15:20-23 and Rom. 8:22-23).

It's interesting to see how often Paul related Christian giving to the metaphor of sowing and reaping (1 Cor. 9:1-12; 2 Cor. 9:6-11; Gal. 6:6-9), and he specifically applied it to the paying of the pastor (2 Tim. 2:6; see 1 Tim. 5:17-18). The special offering for the Jewish believers in Judea was "fruit" and not something Paul had extorted from the churches (Rom. 15:28). Christian worship and praise are fruit from the lips of grateful people (Heb. 13:15; see Hosea 14:2).

In the area of practical godliness, Paul warned the Ephesian believers against "the fruitless deeds of darkness" (Eph. 5:1-14). If the church wants to bear fruit to the glory of God, the saints must walk in the light and yield themselves to God. This is emphasized in Romans 6:21-23 where Paul contrasts the painful harvest of the old life with the holy harvest of the new life.

The Body

There was a solidarity in the nation of Israel, so that the sin of one person brought guilt to the whole nation (Josh. 7:1, 11); but the concept of God's people being members of a spiritual body is not found in the Old Testament. Three key passages are involved here[8] — Romans 12, 1 Corinthians 12–14, and Ephesians 4:1-16 — and they follow a similar pattern.

Romans 12	*1 Corinthians 12–14*	*Ephesians 4:1-16*
Unity 12:4-5	Unity 12:1-13	Unity 4:1-6
Diversity 12:6-8	Diversity 12:14-31	Diversity 4:7-13
Maturity 12:9-21	Maturity chapters 13–14	Maturity 4:14-16

All of the passages emphasize the unity of the church under one Head, Jesus Christ, through the baptism of the Spirit of God (1 Cor. 12:13). But unity without diversity is uniformity, and a body can't function if the whole body is an eye or an ear. At the same time, a body can't function if the individual members "do their own thing" and fail to minister together. Unity without diversity is uniformity, but diversity without unity is anarchy; and both are destructive.

The thing that keeps unity and diversity from destroying each other (and the functioning of the body) is *maturity*. As the body matures to be more like Jesus Christ, and as each member functions in the Spirit, there is harmony in the body and growth that glorifies God. The believers in Corinth were so anxious to practice their individual gifts for personal recognition that diversity was creating disunity, and it all stemmed from the spiritual immaturity of the believers (1 Cor. 3:1-4; 13:11; 14:20). In our churches today, we read 1 Corinthians 13 at weddings when we should also read it at business meetings!

Several of the New Testament images of the church include the elements of unity and diversity. For example, an army is made up of diverse elements (infantry, signal corps, intelligence, etc.), and yet there is a unity that comes from the individuals and the various units fighting the same enemy and obeying the same orders. The family, marriage, a building, a farm, and the priesthood all illustrate diversity within unity and a unity that makes diversity possible. The key, of course, is maturity, whether in marriage, the family, or the church. The church grows through nutrition, not just "addition."

There is so much division today among churches and within churches that we fail to appreciate the impact that was made upon pagan society in the first century when the church burst upon the scene. There was no other assembly in society where rich and poor, free people and slaves, men and women, officials and social outcasts, Jews and Gentiles, educated people and barbarians could meet as one without comparison or competition, for no other purpose than to worship and glorify God. That we have moved away from this miracle is a scandal in the church.

Bread

First Corinthians 5:6-8 and 10:16-17 associate the local church with the loaf of unleavened bread used in the eucharist. We have already noted that leaven in Scripture is consistently an image of corruption, whether personal sin or doctrinal heresy. The sin that the Corinthians permitted in their assembly had turned unleavened bread into leavened bread, and God couldn't accept it.

The preacher may be tempted to go beyond the basic truths that Paul was teaching. He was concerned primarily about unity (one loaf) and purity (an unleavened loaf). A loaf of bread begins with many individual heads of grain that must be ground, united, and put through the fire. While there may be spiritual applications to the grinding and baking, Paul ignores these two processes; and perhaps we should too.

The Bride

Paul saw Christ and His church illustrated by the relationship between husband and wife (Eph. 5:22-31; Gen. 2:24). The emphasis in the passage is on the loving care of the husband and the willing submission of the wife. The Old Testament prophets pictured Israel as the unfaithful wife who had gone into idolatrous prostitution, but this image isn't used of the church collectively in the New Testament. The contrast in the Book of Revelation is between the prostitute (Rev. 17–18) and the pure bride of the Lamb (19:1-9; 21:9ff).[9]

While the church collectively is a bride, the local church also is pictured this way (2 Cor. 11:1-3). Like a concerned father, Paul wanted to keep the church at Corinth faithful to the Lord so that she would be ready for her wedding day. I'll have more to say about this image when we consider the local church as a family. Some expositors would interpret and apply the Song of Songs to the relationship between Christ and His church.

The Building

The first mention of the church in the New Testament involves the metaphor of *building*: "I will build my church" (Matt. 16:18); and Paul's frequent use of "edify" (*oikodomeo*) echoes this metaphor. God's people are built up through the Word (Acts 20:32; 1 Cor. 14:4, 17), love (1 Cor. 8:1 and 10:23; Rom. 14:19), fellowship (1 Thes. 5:11), exercising gifts in the local church (1 Cor. 14:1-12; Eph. 4:12, 16), caring for one another (Rom. 15:1-3), submission to authority (2 Cor. 12:19; 13:10), and godly conversation (Eph. 4:29).

The spiritual temple of God is both universal (Eph. 2:19-22) and local (1 Cor. 3:9b-17). The foundation of the church universal was laid by the apostles and prophets, and Jesus Christ is the chief cornerstone (Eph. 2:20); but the foundation of the local church is Jesus Christ, and that foundation is laid when the Gospel is proclaimed (1 Cor. 2:1-5). *Anything in the local assembly that cannot be built on Christ will not survive the judgment of God.*[10]

It's unfortunate that 1 Corinthians 3:9b-17 is so often preached with an emphasis on "building your life" instead of building the local church. While there is certainly a personal application in the passage, the basic interpretation has to do with the local assembly.[11] Some of the Corinthian believers thought they could build the church by following philosophy

186

and human wisdom and imitating the world, but this approach actually destroys the church (3:18-22). To build with man's wisdom and methods is to use perishable materials, but to follow God's wisdom is to build with that which is beautiful and permanent (Prov. 2:1-10; 3:13-15; 8:8-11), that which would endure the fires of divine judgment.

God's people are "living stones" in the temple He is building, and Jesus is also a "living stone," chosen and precious (1 Peter 2:4-9). We must not forget that Peter was originally named Simon, and that "Peter" means "a rock." The reference to Matthew 16:13-20 is clear.

The Family

The frequent use of "brother" and "brothers" in the epistles reminds us that the church is a family made up of sinners who were born again into the family of God.[12] Along with "disciples," "brothers" is the title most frequently used for God's people in the Book of Acts. The church as "God's household" or "family" is mentioned in Galatians 6:10, Ephesians 2:19, 1 Timothy 3:15 (and see 2 Tim. 2:20), and 1 Peter 4:17 (with reference to Ezek. 9).

When writing to the Corinthians, Paul referred to himself as a "spiritual father" who had "begotten them" through the Gospel (1 Cor. 4:14-15; and see 1 Peter 1:23–2:3). Jesus cautioned His disciples not to follow the example of the rabbis and covet titles (Matt. 23:8-12), but the function of "spiritual father" is certainly included in ministry. Not only does the father beget the children, but he feeds them (1 Cor. 3:1-2; see Heb. 5:11-14), encourages them (1 Thes. 2:9-12), instructs them (1 Cor. 4:14-17), and disciplines them if necessary (1 Cor. 4:21). He protects the church from seduction the way a father protects a daughter engaged to be married (2 Cor. 11:1-5).

But Paul also compared himself to a loving "nursing mother." He would gladly have imparted his own life for the sake of the children he loved (1 Thes. 2:7-8). Paul travailed to bring spiritual children into the family, and he travailed again to see them mature in the Lord (Gal. 4:19; see Col. 1:28). See Numbers 11:12-14 for Moses' burdens as a "father" to Israel, and note also Isaiah 40:11.

Paul uniformly used the word *teknon* when referring to spiritual children, except in Galatians 4:19, where he used John's favorite word, *teknion* — "little children" in the KJV, "dear children" in the NIV. In John 13:33, Jesus used this diminutive of *teknon* as a term of endearment, and John uses it seven times (1 John 2:1, 12, 28; 3:7, 18; 4:4; 5:21). John also uses the phrase "born of God" eight times (1 John 2:29; 3:9 [twice]; 4:7; 5:1, 4, 18 [twice]). Of course, all of this refers back to Christ's teaching on "the new birth" recorded in John 3.

The church is a nursery where children are born into God's family and helped to mature. Paul the evangelist was the obstetrician, and Paul the pastor was the pediatrician; but he was also a "spiritual father and mother" to his converts. The people in the church family are at all stages of life and growth (1 John 2:12-14), and those who minister must keep this in mind. As spiritual parents, we reproduce ourselves, *but we don't duplicate ourselves.* Each new child of God born into the family is unique and must be allowed to develop according to the plan God has for that individual. As believers become more like Christ (Eph. 4:13, 15), they become "more like themselves" and produce in their own unique way the good works God has prepared for them (Eph. 2:10).

The Priesthood

The key references are 1 Peter 2:5 and 9, and Revelation 1:6 and 5:10. We are a holy priesthood because we serve a holy God. We are a royal priesthood because we minister through Jesus Christ, a High Priest after the order of Melchizedek, who ministers as both King and Priest (Heb. 7). Under the Old Covenant, God's people *had* a priesthood; but under the New Covenant, God's people *are* a priesthood. Lesslie Newbigin explains why:

We are not made ministers in order that the rest of the Church may be excused from serving; we are made ministers in order to help the whole Church to be a serving church and to lead it in this service. Just so, we are made priests in order that the whole Church may be trained to be a truly priestly body, fulfilling in its whole life the great High Priesthood of Jesus.[13]

Clustered around the concept of priestly ministry are the Greek words *leitourgeo, leitourgia,* and *leitourgos,* which give us our English word "liturgy." While the original words meant "to give public service to the State at one's own expense," they are used in the LXX (Septuagint) for the ministry of the Jewish priests and Levites. (See also Luke 1:23 and Heb. 8:2, 6.) As New Testament priests, our sacrifice and service to God are acceptable only through the Lord Jesus Christ (1 Peter 2:5).

Paul and Barnabas were offering priestly service to God in worship when He called them to leave Antioch and carry the Gospel abroad (Acts 13:2). Believers are to present their bodies as living sacrifices to God (Rom. 12:1-2; see Phil. 2:17). Our praise to the Lord (Heb. 13:15) and our works for the Lord (Heb. 13:16) should be presented as sacrifices to God. Paul considered the winning of lost souls to Christ as the offering up of a sacrifice (Rom. 15:16), and likewise the sharing of money to meet the needs of God's people (Rom. 15:27; see 2 Cor. 9:12; Phil. 2:25 and 4:18). Whatever we are doing for God as believers, we must do as priests who are seeking to glorify Him.

The Flock[14]

We've had occasion to deal with this image as used in the Old Testament, the Gospels, and the Book of Acts. The word "pastor" in Ephesians 4:11 is "shepherd." Jesus Christ is the Shepherd (1 Peter 2:25), the Great Shepherd (Heb. 13:20), and the Chief Shepherd (1 Peter 5:4). All who serve the church in pastoral roles are under-shepherds who must answer to Him. Peter calls the church "the flock" (1 Peter 5:2-3), certainly an allusion to our Lord's words to him in John 21. Paul used the shepherd as an illustration of ministers of the Gospel being supported by the people they serve (1 Cor. 9:7).

Even though many great men in Scripture were shepherds—Abel, Abraham, Isaac, Jacob, Moses, and David, for example—in New Testament days, shepherds were at the bottom of the social ladder. Their work not only prevented them from attending temple and synagogue services, but it rendered them almost constantly ceremonially unclean. Shepherds were generally despised by the people, even though their work was essential to the entire worship system of the nation. By His life, death, and present ministry, our Lord certainly elevated the position of the shepherd.

The verb *poimaino*, "to shepherd, to tend a flock," is also used of civil rulers and can mean "to govern." See Matthew 2:6 and Revelation 2:27, 12:5, 19:15. Even in heaven, Jesus the Lamb will minister as the Shepherd (Rev. 7:17).

The People of God

According to Acts 15:14, God is today calling out "a people for himself." For centuries, Israel was identified as "the people" or "his people," that is, the people of God. (See Matt. 1:21; 2:6; 4:16; Luke 1:77; 2:32; 7:16; John 18:14.) But as the church moved across the Roman Empire, the followers of Jesus Christ came to be identified as "the people of God" (John 11:49-52; 2 Cor. 6:16; Titus 2:14; 1 Peter 2:9-10; Rev. 18:4; 21:3). The fact that God had His people in Corinth was an encouragement for Paul to stay there in spite of great opposition (Acts 18:1-11).[15]

This "new people" is the "one new man" (Eph. 2:12ff) that God has created out of believing Jews and Gentiles.[16] That there is continuity between God's Old Testament people and His New Covenant people is seen in the way Old Testament passages are quoted and applied to the church (Heb. 8:7-13 [Jer. 31:31-34]; Heb. 10:30 [Deut. 32:35]; 1 Peter 2:9-10 [Ex. 19:1-6]; Gal. 4:21-31). That continuity does not mean identity is seen in the fact that Jesus and the New Testament writers seem to see a distinction between the future of national Israel and the future of the church.[17]

God's people today are seen as *citizens of another country* (Eph. 2:12, 19; Phil. 1:27 [*politeuo,* "conduct yourselves as citizens"]; Phil. 3:17-20 [*politeuma*, "citizenship"]). Paul uses *politeuo* in his testimony in Acts 23:1, translated in the NIV as "fulfilled my duty." Perhaps there's the suggestion here that Paul considered himself a good Roman citizen as well as a good citizen of heaven.

As the people of God, we are *aliens, sojourners, pilgrims,* and *strangers* (1 Peter 1:1; 2:11; Heb. 11:9, 13). Someone has well said that a vagabond has no home, a stranger is away from home, but a pilgrim is headed home and is motivated by that hope. Abraham lived in a tent and looked for a city; his nephew Lot looked at a city and abandoned his tent (Gen. 13). The words *paroikos* and *parepidemos* describe people who are "resident aliens in a foreign land" (see Gen. 17:8; 23:4; 1 Chron. 29:15; Ps. 39:12; 119:19).

This metaphor introduces the subject of the church's relationship to the world and its responsibilities in the world.[18] Israel was warned not to mingle with the nations or imitate their practices, but to live as a "separated people" to the glory of God (Deut. 4, 7, 11). Abraham the sojourner was able to do business with the natives of the land (Gen. 23), and even enlist them to fight a war, but he didn't compromise his testimony (Gen. 14). His descendants, however, didn't follow his good example but frequently turned for help to the idols of the nations and had to be warned by the prophets. Solomon used religious compromise as a political expedient, a practice that eventually brought the judgment of God on the nation. Paul used several Old Testament images to exhort the Corinthians to live separated lives (2 Cor. 6:14-18).[19]

The Circumcision

The references are Galatians 6:12-16, Philippians 3:2-3, and Colossians 2:11. As we have seen, this important Jewish initiation rite was meant to symbolize an *inner change* (Deut. 10:16; 30:6; Jer. 4:4; 6:10; Ezek. 44:7; Rom. 2:26-29). The "Judaizers" who hounded Paul and tried to capture his converts ("Watch out for those dogs!") were practicing "mutilation of the flesh" and not true circumcision. The true circumcision is performed by the Spirit, not men, and it brings glory to Jesus Christ, not to preachers or converts. Paul boasted in the cross because that's where Christ performed the work necessary for him to become a part of the true "Israel of God."

There are other pictures of the church in the epistles, but this survey will give you some idea of the opportunities the preacher has to present imaginatively the nature and ministry of the church in today's world.

One question remains: Why did the writers of the New Testament epistles use so many pictures of the church? Why not just settle for one major image, or perhaps a few? *Because the church of Jesus Christ is so great, and our Lord's relationship to His church is so rich and varied, that no one image can tell us all we need to know.*

How the church sees itself will determine what the church does and the way it does it. If we see the church only as an army, then our ministry will become aggressively militant. If we see only the image of the body, then we might become "ingrown" as we seek to discover our gifts and minister to each other. An overemphasis on the image of the bride could make us mystical and so wrapped up in devotion that we forget duty. If we are only priests, then worship becomes the most important thing. If we are only witnesses, then proclamation takes the forefront.

As we minister the Word of God, we must maintain a balanced view of the church, lest both preacher and people start limping instead of walking. "Body life" is a good thing; so is "Evangelism Explosion." The one doesn't cancel the other. A spiritually healthy body ought to reach out to a lost world, and faithful witnesses ought to contribute to worship as well as world evangelism. But being the kind of creatures we are, it's difficult to keep in balance.

There are times when the church must be reminded that it's an army and that there's an enemy to fight. At other times, God's people need to be told that they are priests at the altar and that God delights in their worship. Wise is the householder who knows when to bring out of the treasury just the truths that the people need to keep them rightly related to their Lord (Matt. 13:52).

"Are we aware of this living, powerful character of God's Word? Does it deal with us like a sharp, two-edged sword? Or do we handle it as though it were just one more book to be studied and analyzed?"

—*Watchman Nee*

"Logicians may reason about abstractions. But the great mass of men must have images."

—*Thomas Babington Macaulay*

Chapter Sixteen
Pictures in the Apocalypse[1]

The revelation that God gave to John was "signified" by His angel (Rev. 1:1). The text uses *semaino* which means "to give a sign" (*semeion*) or "to signify."[2] How much weight we can put on this one verb is debatable, but one thing is sure: the Apocalypse is a book of signs, images, symbols, and not a few enigmas. "The Greek verb carries the idea of figurative representation," writes Robert H. Mounce. "Strictly speaking, it means to make known by some sort of sign. . . . Thus it is admirably suited to the symbolic character of the book. This should warn the reader not to expect a literal presentation of future history, but a symbolic portrayal of that which must yet come to pass."[3]

1:9-16 — The "voice like a trumpet" (1:10; 4:1) reminds us of the trumpets in Numbers 10. It appears that Jesus Christ is trying to wake up His church and get them ready![4] The Apocalypse is "the revelation of Jesus Christ," so the Christology of the book is very important. *If we don't see Christ in this book, we have missed the main message.*

The symbolic description of the exalted Lord Jesus should be compared with Daniel 7:9-13; Exodus 28:4; Ezekiel 1:13, 24, 27 and 43:2; and Matthew 17:2. On the candlesticks, see Exodus 25:31ff and Zechariah 4. It's important to note that some part of this description is referred to in each of the letters to the seven churches in chapters 2 and 3.

The Apocalypse begins with the glorified Christ on earth,

investigating His people; but it continues with the glorified Christ in heaven, receiving the praises of His creatures (chaps. 4–5). Wonder, worship, warfare, and witness seem to be the main emphases of the book as the scenes shift from earth to heaven and then back to earth again.[5]

Chapter 4—We discussed in chapter 6 of this book the symbolism of the rainbow. See also Revelation 10:1. Note that the throne room of heaven is similar in arrangement to the design of the tabernacle. The throne[6] takes the place of the ark of the covenant, which was the throne of God (Ps. 80:1; 99:1; see Rev. 11:19); the seven lamps represent the seven-branched lampstand; and the sea of glass resembles the laver. The creatures embroidered on the tabernacle veil (Ex. 36:35; and see Ezek. 1:5) are seen worshiping God before the throne. There is a brazen altar (6:9) and a golden altar of incense (8:1-5). Instead of twenty-four courses of priests (1 Chron. 24), we have twenty-four elders, probably representing the people of God (1:6).

Chapters 5 and 6—This is not only the book of the throne, but it is also the book of the Lamb. Christ is mentioned as the Lamb twenty-eight times, and the word used is *arnion*, "a little lamb." This immediately ties the vision to Passover (Ex. 12), the Suffering Servant (Isa. 53:7), the ministry of John the Baptist (John 1:29), and the witness of the early church (Acts 8:32; see 1 Peter 1:19).

But the meek lamb is also "the Lion of the tribe of Judah" (Rev. 5:5; Gen. 49:9), and "the wrath of the Lamb" will make Him like a lion when He judges the earth (Rev. 6:16).

Prayer as incense takes us back to the tabernacle and temple (Ex. 30:1-10; see Luke 1:5-23; Ps. 141:2; and Rev. 8:3-4).

Exegetes differ as to the meaning of the scroll (5:1), but Revelation 10:7 suggests that it has something to do with the accomplishing of "the mystery of God" on earth. Whether we see the scroll as "the title deed to creation" or "a will" by which Jesus Christ inherits all things, it amounts to just about the same thing. Because of His victory on the cross, Jesus Christ alone has the right to consummate God's great plan, defeat His enemies, and claim His inheritance.

7:17—Not only is the Lamb a lion (5:5-6), but He is also a shepherd on a throne!

10:9—See Jeremiah 15:16 and Ezekiel 2:8–3:3. Eating the Word of God is a familiar figure: Job 23:12; Psalm 119:103; Matthew 4:4; 1 Peter 2:2; Hebrews 5:12-14.

11:4—The obvious reference is to Zechariah 4.

Chapter 12—The description of the woman relates so closely to Joseph's dream in Genesis 37:9 that we're encouraged to see her as a symbol of Israel, through whom God brought the Savior into the world; but not everyone would agree with this interpretation. If the woman symbolizes Mary, the mother of Jesus, then it's difficult to know when the events occurred that are symbolized in this chapter.

The dragon is mentioned fourteen times in the Apocalypse, and except for 13:11, the reference is to Satan. The dragon's access to heaven doesn't surprise us (Job 1–2; Zech. 3), nor does his bitter enmity against the people of God.

14:10—We have met with the symbol of "the cup of wrath" before (Isa. 51:17; Jer. 25:15 and 51:7; and see Rev. 16:19 and 18:6).

14:14-20—We have already noted the three vines in Scripture: the nation of Israel (Isa. 5), the church in union with Christ (John 15), and civilization ripening for judgment (here). Some see this vision in the evangelistic sense of John 4:34-38, but the image of the winepress in Revelation 14:19-20 suggests that judgment is the theme. The winepress is an Old Testament symbol of judgment (Rev. 19:15 and see Isa. 63:1-6; Lam. 1:15; Joel 3:13).

16:13—The only other reference to frogs in Scripture is in Exodus 8 (Pss. 78:45; 105:30) when God sent frogs to plague Egypt. Most people think of a frog as an ugly, loathsome creature, and that's probably what the figure implies. The three satanic spirits prepare the way for the judgment of the nations.

16:15—Coming "like a thief" is a proverbial image that implies unpreparedness (Matt. 24:43; Luke 12:39; 1 Thes. 5:2, 4; 2 Peter 3:10; Rev. 3:3). It is a call for alertness. The image of clothing suggests that God's people must be ready and acceptable when their Lord returns. See Revelation 3:18 and 19:6-8.

Chapters 17 and 18—The "great prostitute" is presented in contrast to the bride of the Lamb, and Babylon is contrasted with the heavenly Jerusalem, which is also identified with the bride (21:2). The prostitute is a religious system, Babylon is a commercial system, and they work together to control the world and oppose the people of God. The two images of drunkenness and adultery are here (18:3; 19:2), and the whole thing is demonic (18:2).

19:17-21—The image of a battle as a feast is found in Isaiah 34, Jeremiah 46, and Ezekiel 39:17-20.

Chapters 21 and 22—Many of the things described in the heavenly city are found initially in the Book of Genesis, such as the garden, the river, the tree of life, and the bride. Some things are also missing in the heavenly city: the light of the sun, night, the curse, and tears.

22:16—Christ is the "Root of David" in that He brought David and his royal line into existence; He is the "Offspring of David" because He was born into this world through David's line (Matt. 1:1; Isa. 11:1; Rom. 1:1-5).

The Book of Revelation is a prophecy (1:3; 22:7, 10, 18-19), so we must not consider it a "theological poem" that deals with "spiritual ideals" wrapped in symbolism. John does have something to tell the church about the future; how detailed we make his prophecy depends on our hermeneutical approach.

At the same time, we must recognize the fact that John uses symbolic language to convey his message. Metaphorical language speaks to all of God's people in every age, and therefore the book that encouraged the suffering church in John's day can also encourage us in our day. In every age, the church has had to face a Jezebel, a Babylon, the dragon, and the prostitute; and in every age, the church has had to struggle to maintain devotion to Jesus Christ and be ready for His coming. Regardless of our eschatological position, we can claim the abiding message of the book and encourage and warn the people of God.

Part Three
Imagination
and Biblical Preaching

"But I wish to remind you that if
fancy is active and imagination vigorous,
the walls will not merely be pierced with occasional windows—
the walls themselves will be transparent,
the light will come through everywhere."

—Robert W. Dale

"It is a fallacy to think that
one's world view consists only of ideas.
It is a world picture as well as a set of ideas."

—Leland Ryken

Chapter Seventeen
If You Don't Talk to Your Bible,
Your Bible Might Not Talk to You

When the Lord commanded Joshua, "Do not let this Book of the Law depart from your mouth," He was encouraging him to meditate on the Word. The Hebrew word translated "meditate" in Joshua 1:8 means "to mutter"; for in their study of the Law, the Jews would read the Scriptures aloud and talk to themselves as they meditated (see Acts 8:26-31). In daily conversation, they would talk *among* themselves as they discussed the Holy Word (Deut. 6:4-9). "The reading of all good books," wrote Descartes, "is like conversation with the finest men of past centuries"; and that especially applies to the reading of the Word of God.

If you happen to be present in my study or library when I'm at work on a message, you'll hear me talking to the Lord, to myself, to my emerging message, and especially to my Bible. (Occasionally you'll hear me talking rather stridently to my computer, but that's another matter.) I've learned that if I don't talk to my Bible, my Bible isn't likely to talk to me. God's Word is supposed to be a companion that speaks to me, not just a "textbook" that I study (Prov. 6:20-22). When we read the Word of God, we must *hear* it and respond to it as we would to a friend who is conversing with us.

But *conversation* isn't the only picture of Bible study in the Scriptures. Studying the Bible is like going on *a pilgrimage,* with the Word as a lamp that leads us from one truth to another (Ps. 119:105). Bible study is also like *mining treasures* (Prov.

2:1-8; see Ps. 119:14, 72, 127) and *discovering rich spoils* after the battle (Ps. 119:162).[1] Passages such as Matthew 4:4, 1 Corinthians 3:1-3, Hebrews 5:12-14, and 1 Peter 2:2 remind us that Bible study means getting nourishment from the Word and *preparing a "spiritual meal"* for others. Too many of our sermons share the recipe, or the menu, but not the meal; and our people go away hungry.

"Giving birth to a sermon" is an organic process that grows out of the life of the minister in contact with the life of the Word. Sermons that are "born" don't ignore content and organization, but they allow the "baby" to decide what it will look like and how it will be dressed.

It isn't enough simply to exegete a passage, find a theme, and then develop an outline on that theme, based on the truths in the passage. This process is usually called "building a sermon," and the resultant outline is usually preachable and the Spirit of God can use it to help people. *But sermons are not only "built," they're also "born."* The preacher's imagination is impregnated with a "truth-in-metaphor," and the message grows like a baby in the womb, coming to birth when it's ready. This is why the preacher or teacher must devote adequate time to message preparation; otherwise, the "baby" might be aborted or stillborn.

"Building a sermon" is too often a mechanical process that focuses so much on analysis, content, and organization that it minimizes synthesis, intent, and motivation. "Giving birth to a sermon" is an organic process that grows out of the life of the minister in contact with the life of the Word. Sermons that are "born" don't ignore content and organization, but they allow the "baby" to decide what it will look like and how it will be dressed. Two tables, constructed by carpenters following the same blueprints, will be similar if not identical; but two babies, conceived in the same time-honored fashion, will be similar and yet vastly different. Tables are built; babies are conceived and born.

"The problem in Art," wrote Anne Morrow Lindbergh, "is

that of extreme freedom encased in extreme discipline."[2] No matter how creative we are, if freedom isn't disciplined, what we do isn't likely to succeed. The river that ignores its banks becomes a swamp. It's this tension between *form* and *function, craftsman* and *artist, priest* and *prophet* that helps make people creative. That's why I suggest you ask yourself these seven questions as you prepare your messages. They'll help you keep the river of creativity in its banks without robbing the river of either power or depth.

1. What does the text *say?*
2. *How* does the text say it?
3. What *did* the text mean to the original hearers?
4. What *does* the text mean to the church today?
5. What does the text mean to *me?*
6. What does the text mean to *the congregation?*
7. How can I make the text meaningful to *my hearers?*

Keep in mind that these questions are only guides to help us stay on track in our preparation. They don't guarantee results. Apart from the enlightening ministry of the Holy Spirit, nobody can understand and assimilate the truths of the Word of God and make them meaningful to others. The ability to use the tools of Bible study and to apply the principles of biblical hermeneutics is invaluable and indispensable; but it is still the Spirit who guides us into all the truth, and we must depend on Him. We need to ponder the words of Thomas Merton: "If we are merely speculative students of Scripture, breaking the words of God up into scientific fragments and deafening our spirit with the noise of human argument—which is too often the noise of human 'flesh' with its spirit of factions and divisions—then we cannot hear the word who speaks to us silently in the words of God."[3]

One more piece of counsel: I think the questions are listed in logical sequence, but that doesn't mean you must "complete" one question before you move to the next one. Preparing a sermon isn't like baking a cake, an enterprise that requires sequential actions. (I'd hate to have to add two eggs after the batter is in the oven.) My experience tells me that, once you get past the first three questions, you'll be considering all of them simultaneously as you study and ideas come to you. When the "art" and "science" of sermon preparation start to blend, then the discipline of the science will help to release the creativity of the art; and you'll become like the jet pilot or the surgeon, naturally doing the right thing, sequence or no sequence.

1. What Does the Text Say?

One summer Sunday evening, while on holiday, Campbell Morgan worshiped in a nearby town and subsequently recorded in his diary: "Heard a capital sermon with which I did not at all agree on a text which had no relation to the subject. Text, Proverbs 9:5. Subject, 'Holy Communion.' "[4] The village preacher had used a pretext and not a text, for Proverbs 9:5 says, "Come, eat my food and drink the wine I have mixed." The only connection with Holy Communion is the mention of bread and wine, but the context relates the verse to the getting of wisdom.

Sermonic pretexts are heard even in famous pulpits. George W. Truett preached a sermon entitled "Life's Middle Time," and based it tangentially on the phrase from Psalm 91:6, "the plague that destroys at midday."[5] James S. Stewart used Acts 27:29 to preach about the "four anchors" that sustain the believer in the storms of life: hope, duty, prayer, and the cross of Christ.[6] Willard L. Sperry preached at Harvard on "Larger Ideas of God," and his text was Isaiah 28:20, "The bed is too short to stretch out on, the blanket too narrow to wrap around you."[7] Frank Boreham based his sermon "William Knibb's Text" on Jeremiah 3:4, "My father, thou art the guide of my youth" (KJV), and described how God had directed the heroic missionary. But the text has to do, not with guidance, but with Israel's marriage to Jehovah and her unfaithfulness to the "guide of her youth," i.e., her husband.[8] Even the great Charles Haddon Spurgeon occasionally ignored the context and "spiritualized" his text, such as the time he preached from Judges 16:20-21 and held Samson up as a picture of the "consecrated man."[9]

All who preach and teach the Word have as their first responsibility learning what the biblical text actually says, not what they want it to say. "To interpret and apply his text in accordance with its real meaning, is one of the preacher's most sacred duties," wrote the dean of American homileticians, John A. Broadus.[10] He went on to warn that the preacher "is verily guilty before God if he does not honestly strive to understand that which he interprets, and give forth its real meaning and no other."[11]

Early in our ministry, perhaps all of us go through an adolescent phase during which we try to display our abilities by preaching from obscure texts or about obscure truths from familiar texts, things that nobody has ever heard before or cares to hear again. But the more we mature in ministry, the more we desire to preach the great truths of the Bible *and permit the texts to speak for themselves.*

The best way to find out what the text is saying is simply to read it repeatedly and meditatively, using different translations and studying the original text.[12] Ask yourself the basic questions that help to unlock the passage:

(1) Who is speaking or writing?
(2) To whom was the passage addressed and why?
(3) Where and when did it all take place?
(4) What message was the writer or speaker trying to convey?
(5) Are there any parallel passages elsewhere in Scripture that can help me understand the passage?
(6) Do I understand the context?
(7) Are there any repeated words or phrases that indicate the major theme?
(8) What pictures are found in the text?

Homileticians call this body of material "the factual data," and it's important that we gather it and understand it. For one thing, we want to be accurate in our understanding of the passage; and the first step toward accuracy is knowing the facts.[13]

Misunderstanding the words and ignoring the context are two of the chief obstacles to discovering what a passage is really saying. A third obstacle is raised when we bring to our studies *our own preconceived notions about the text*. Unfortunately, floating around in every preacher's mind is an assortment of homiletical and theological flotsam and jetsam that has accumulated over the years and is difficult to get rid of. This nebulous, subjective "body of divinity" can get in the way of our objective study and sometimes hinder us from really understanding the text.[14] This doesn't mean we abandon our personal convictions about doctrine; it only means we try not to squeeze every text into our own preconceived mold and so rob it of its unique impact. While it's difficult to look at a text as though we'd never seen it before, that ought to be our goal.

As we read the text and seek its message, we must beware of going off on homiletical detours every time we get an idea. If a striking thought or exciting insight comes your way, write it down; but stick with your reading and meditating, and save the possible development of that idea until later. The idea may turn out to be the truth that "impregnates" your imagination and leads to the birth of the sermon. But if that's true, the longer you read and think, the more obvious it will become, and the healthier the baby will be when it's born.

By the time you've finished answering this first question (What does the text say?), you ought to have a body of material to work with, plus an idea of what the passage says. No doubt you're developing a "feeling" for the passage, and you've probably written down several ideas that could become propositional statements for a message. But don't get in a hurry; there's still much work to be done.

2. How Does the Text Say It?

Here we enter the field of literary theory, sometimes foggy, sometimes frightening, often frustrating, but always essential to the task of understanding the text; for if we ignore the literary genre of the text, our interpretation is sure to be suspect. Is the text a parable or an allegory, a proverb or a narrative? And if it's a narrative, is it fiction, history, myth, or a combination of all three? What are the figures of speech employed—hyperbole, apostrophe, simile, metaphor?[15] The careful student has to deal with these matters honestly and with spiritual perception.

You don't address the arguments of the Epistle to the Romans in the same way you approach the poetry of the Psalms or the imagery of the Apocalypse. People who affirm that "they take the Bible literally" need to face the fact that there are things in the Bible that obviously can't be taken literally, such as John's description of Christ in Revelation 1:12-16 or the account in Psalm 114 of Israel's exodus from Egypt.[16] These two descriptions refer to real (literal) entities; but the authors didn't write in literal terms, because they had something to express that could be better conveyed by the use of symbols.

The old adage is still valid: when the plain sense of Scripture makes good sense, seek no other sense. However, we must be sensitive to the fact that more than one literary genre might be found in a given passage of Scripture, and this could modify the "plain sense" that seems obvious to us.[17]

It's here that the preacher must be alert to the "pictures" in the text. Sometimes they're obvious, but often they're hidden in a Greek or Hebrew word or in an idiomatic expression. Having found the pictures, the next step is to identify the "semantic domains" to which they belong—agriculture, building, jurisprudence, and such.[18] By using your concordances and lexicons, and by tracing cross-references, you can locate other passages containing material belonging to that same domain; and you can relate the passages and perhaps generate something new and exciting. Remember the "rainbow sermon" in chapter 6.

Paul's admonition to the Galatians to reject the legalistic doctrines of the Judaizers (Gal. 5:1-12) is teeming with pictures: the yoke, slavery, and freedom (v. 1); profit, loss, and debts (v. 2); falling (vv. 3-4); running (vv. 7-8); baking (v. 9); stirring things up, causing a riot (v. 10); surgery (vv. 11-12).

3. What Did the Text Mean to the Original Hearers?[19]

"What *did* it mean?" must precede "What does it mean?" because the biblical revelation is progressive and cumulative. To read into an Old Testament text truths that weren't revealed until centuries later is to rob that text of the message it had for the original writers, speakers, or hearers. At the same time, to ignore the Old Testament context of a New Testament truth is equally damaging to our studies. From the messianic promise to the doctrine of the resurrection of the human body, the truths of Scripture were revealed gradually and progressively; and as we study the Word, it's important that we know where we are on the road of revelation.

For example, when David prayed, "Do not cast me from your presence or take your Holy Spirit from me" (Ps. 51:11), he wasn't reflecting on eternal security so much as remembering the terrible judgment that God sent to his predecessor, King Saul (1 Sam. 16:13-14). Nor was he contradicting John 14:16, because he had never heard John 14:16. But when the disciples heard the Lord's words in the Upper Room, they must have been thrilled; for they knew that, in the old dispensation, the Holy Spirit's constant and certain presence wasn't guaranteed to His servants. Imagine having God's Spirit abiding with you forever!

A respect for biblical theology is essential for accurate inter-pretation of the Word of God. What does Genesis say about man? What does Leviticus say about sin? What do the Psalms reveal about creation? What does the Gospel of John tell us about divine sovereignty and human responsibility? It's exciting to discover the unfolding of divine revelation in the Bible and to see unity come out of diversity in the revelation of God and His works.[20]

4. What Does the Text Mean to the Church Today?

Here we enter the field of historical theology.[21] The doctrines treasured by the Christian church were, for the most part, won on the field of battle as the church defended its faith against the paganism around it and the heresy within it. It's good to know what the church believes, but it's also good to know *how the church came to believe it* and what battles were involved in defending "the faith that was once for all entrusted to the saints" (Jude 3).

We have nearly twenty centuries of church history behind us; and even though the historians give us an unsettling and sometimes conflicting record of disagreements, disputes, and divisions, as well as concordats and compromises, the careful preacher is helped by gaining this historical perspective. As the philosopher George Santayana said, "Those who cannot remember the past are condemned to repeat it." I like to balance that quotation with one from Alfred North Whitehead: "How the past perishes is how the future becomes."[22]

But when we speak about "the church," which "church" do we mean? I suppose we mean "the church of Christian church history." While different communions disagree on some of the finer points of doctrine, there's a body of truth that belongs to all of us who claim to follow Jesus Christ. It does us good to find out where and why we disagree and to discover that God blesses people we disagree with! "He who knows only his own position doesn't even know that." I don't recall who said that, but it's true.

Historical theology forces us to move Bible doctrine out of the serene ivory tower into the noisy battlefield. It also forces us to learn the hard way how dependable our own personal doctrinal weapons are and whether or not we're able to wield them skillfully. The First Council of Nicea and the Diet of Worms may seem light years away from the pastoral problems you face in your church today, but they're not. Human nature is the same, spiritual needs are the same, and the better we know God and obey His will, the better the church will be.

Harry Emerson Fosdick used to remind his listeners that astronomers and systems of astronomy come and go, but the stars remain.[23] I don't agree with Fosdick's theology, but I think that here he makes a valid point. We study church history in order to see the stars. But as we read church history, we'd better interview the astronomers and check their equipment to see if they have the authority to describe the stars to anybody. Church history records lies as well as truths, and we need discernment.

Someone has described historians as "people who catch up with the past." But some preachers have never caught up with the past. After graduating from seminary, they gleefully sell their textbooks and get busy running from seminar to seminar, learning how to duplicate the latest religious fads. Having scuttled the past, they become like boats without rudders or compasses, adrift on a sea of pragmatism, always hoping to land on the nebulous Island of Success.

There's not a heresy or religious novelty today that hasn't appeared in some form or another somewhere on the stage of church history. Historical theology and systematic theology work hand-in-hand to assist the preacher in the interpretation of the text. Theologians need to be preachers to keep doctrine personal and practical, and preachers need to be theologians to keep doctrine accurate and authoritative.[24]

Reading historical theology can be depressing when we see religious leaders attacking each other in the name of Christ and acting very unlike the Christ they claim to defend. But even that's a part of life, including the life of the church today. "The divisions of Christendom," wrote Philip Schaff, "bring to light the various aspects and phases of revealed truth, and will be overruled at last for a deeper and richer harmony, of which Christ is the keynote. In him and by him all problems of theology and history will be solved. The nearer believers of different creeds approach the Christological center, the better they will understand and love each other."[25]

5. What Does the Text Mean to Me?[26]

Biblical preaching must be *witness* as well as *proclamation,* and the congregation has a right to believe that something good happened when their pastor confronted the text, wrestled with it, wooed it, and received from the encounter spiritual nourishment for their hearts. (I apologize for the mixed metaphors, but that's what's involved in preparing a sermon.) "Truth through Personality is our description of real preaching," said Phillips Brooks in his famous Yale lectures;[27] and that oft-quoted definition is a valid one. If the truth of the Word bypasses the personality of the preacher, then the sermon may become a lecture, and the preacher may become a hypocrite. If the text isn't real to me, I'll have a hard time making it real to others.

It's often been said that what we get out of an experience largely depends on what we bring to it. That may not apply to every area of life, but it certainly applies to preaching. As we study the text, we bring to it a mixed bag of beliefs, hopes, fears, desires, failures, joys, and other experiences that help to keep us human. The preacher who isn't vulnerable isn't likely to be accepted as credible, although there's no place in the pulpit for turning God's truth into "true confession." Do your serious confessing in the secret chamber, but by all means tell your people what God has done for your soul.

Somewhere Luther says that "prayer, meditation, and temptation make a preacher." We have little difficulty with "prayer" and "meditation," but the "temptation" part we'd rather escape. One reason why God allows preachers to suffer is that they might have opportunities to grow spiritually and therefore to preach better. Even our Lord had to go through suffering to prepare Him for His heavenly ministry (Heb. 2:14-18), so why should we escape? "The true preacher can be known by this," said Emerson, "that he deals out to the people his life—life passed through the fire of thought."[28]

The preacher's study is a sacred place, not just because of the person who works there or the work that's done there, but because of what happens there. We meet the Lord as we study His Word, and in meeting Him, we find the message He wants us to share. We also meet ourselves, and that can be a painful experience. However, it's the only way we can receive from the Lord what He wants us to declare when we meet His people in the place of divine worship.[29]

I like what Andrew Bonar wrote about Robert Murray M'Cheyne.

From the first he fed others by what he himself was feeding upon. His preaching was in a manner the development of his soul's experience. It was a giving out of the inward life. He loved to come up from the pastures wherein the Chief Shepherd had met him—to lead the flock entrusted to his care to the spots where he found nourishment. . . . His heart was filled, and his lips then spoke what he felt within his heart. He gave out not merely living water, but living water drawn at the springs that he had himself drunk of; and is not this a true gospel ministry?"[30]

Sermon preparation ought to be an exciting personal adventure, with God teaching us the truth for which He has prepared us by His providence. There is a difference between preaching because you have to say something and preaching because you have something to say. Congregations can usually tell the difference, and they will eventually let you know.

> **One of the best ways to make sure you confront the text personally is to turn it into prayer. Pray as a sinner needing forgiveness, as a worshiper expressing praise, as a servant accepting the Master's will, as a pilgrim seeking companionship and guidance, as a disciple asking for truth.**

One of the best ways to make sure you confront the text personally is to turn it into a matter of prayer. Pray as a sinner needing forgiveness, as a worshiper expressing praise, as a servant accepting the Master's will, as a pilgrim seeking companionship and guidance, and as a disciple asking for truth. In other words, *make the text your own* until, as happened to the Emmaus disciples, your heart burns within you. Then you will hardly be able to wait to tell somebody that you have walked with the Lord Jesus and He has opened to you the Scriptures and changed your life (Luke 24:13-35). It will transform your preaching.

The preacher must be concerned with feelings as well as facts, experiencing the text as well as examining the text and letting the text examine him. What Thoreau wrote in his journal about writing can be applied to preaching: "The forcible writer stands boldly behind his words with his experience. He does not make books out of books, but he has been *there* in person."[31]

6. What Does the Text Mean to the Congregation?

It's here that the pastor and the preacher meet; for if you don't know your people, how can you successfully apply the Word to their needs? Granted, human nature is pretty much the same from church to church; but happy is that congregation whose pastor, like the Jewish high priest, carries the members collectively on his shoulders and individually over his heart (Ex. 39:1-21).[32]

In your mind's eye, survey your congregation and try to imagine how various people will respond to the teachings in the text. What does the passage say to the abused child, the struggling teenager, the out-of-work breadwinner, the retired businessman, the lonely widower, the weary housewife, the new believer, the young bride and groom? We never take intimate confidences into the pulpit, no matter how we disguise them; but we do bring these confidences into the light of the Word to see what kind of medicine the Great Physician would have us apply.

Each congregation has a "preaching history"; and if you remain on the field long enough, you'll learn what it is. Perhaps one former pastor so emphasized missions that everybody felt intimidated for not applying for a visa and heading overseas. Another pastor walked with Moses, while his successor preached the grace of God with such zeal that he almost became an antinomian. Even if your predecessor was on the field a long time, giving a consistent ministry of the Word, you will still find people in the church family who misunderstood some things he said or, perhaps, objected to the way he said them.

I'm not suggesting that we become ecclesiastical dilettantes who tiptoe through the theological tulips and try to keep from stepping on anybody's corns. We must be "as shrewd as snakes and as innocent as doves" (Matt. 10:16), especially when we tell our people things they may not want to hear. It's not so much *what we say* as *how we say it*. If we know what our people are thinking, we can deal with their objections in a fair and loving way and accomplish much more with the sermon.

But something more is involved. The people who sit in the

pews have been exposed, consciously or unconsciously, to the numerous "myths"[33] that influence the thinking of society; and our preaching somehow has to break through those barriers and introduce people to truth.

The "American myth" that excited the Pilgrim fathers was that they were the "new Israel" establishing a "new Canaan" in the new world. They were "a city set on a hill." When it turned out that their accomplishments didn't quite measure up to those of Joshua in the Promised Land, they altered the myth and began to expand the frontier westward. The new "American myth" defined the United States as God's chosen "messiah nation" to lead the world and deliver other nations from bondage.[34] Both myths are still with us, along with several new ones that especially excite the younger generation, not the least of which is the age-old "New Age" myth that says, "You shall be as God!"

No matter how much counseling and visiting we do, our best opportunity for pastoral work is from the pulpit.[35] After all, we don't preach to congregations; we preach to individuals. God's Word is "boundless" (Ps. 119:96) and meets the needs of people in ways that would amaze us if we knew all about them. It's impossible for us to prepare messages that deal with every problem in every life; but if we are true to the Word and point to Jesus Christ, the Holy Spirit will apply the truth and help God's people. If this were not true, I would have quit preaching a long time ago.

7. How Can I Make the Text Meaningful to My Hearers?

At this point, your sanctified imagination must pull everything together and help you in several areas.[36] To begin with, your imagination must help you move your thinking *from the particular to the general.* What happened to David or Jeremiah is past history, but their experiences have relevance to our lives today as we see the principles behind the events. The factual data that we've collected would be useful for a Bible lecture; but unless we see the spiritual truths behind those facts, we'll never grow ourselves a message that will magnify the Lord and help His people.

For example, David's experience at Ziklag, recorded in 1 Samuel 30, shows us how God can help us when we're going through severe trials. We can give up (v. 4); we can look for somebody to blame (v. 6); or we can get our encouragement from the Lord (vv. 6-8). David sought God's will, depended on God's guidance, relied on God's strength, and glorified God in the victory. While we don't have an ephod to consult, we do have an interceding High Priest to whom we can pray and the inspired Word of God with all its precepts and promises.

The sermon is based on historic facts, but it points to spiritual truths and principles that transcend history. Unless we move from the particular to the general, we'll not be preaching a sermon; we'll simply be telling a Bible story and making some "practical applications" at the conclusion, hoping that somebody is still listening.

Imagination also helps us move our thinking *from the past to the present.* This doesn't mean we "modernize" the text and describe the Prodigal Son speeding out of town in a souped-up Jaguar, heading for Las Vegas. The Bible doesn't need to be "made relevant"; it already is relevant. People can see themselves in Aaron, making excuses for the golden calf; in Elijah, nursing his wounded pride and looking for sympathy; in Abraham, giving to God what was dearest to his heart; in David, covering up his sins and then confessing them with a broken heart; and in Peter, going out to weep bitterly. The people and the events recorded on the pages of the Bible are contemporary, except when we make them religious history instead of present reality.

Imagination helps us to move *from the impersonal to the personal.* I read about a photographer who was taking nature pictures in a park where several children were playing. The children watched him for several minutes, and then one of them called out, "Mister, when are you gonna get *us* in the picture?" The people to whom we preach would probably like to interrupt us as we preach and ask us the same question. But if our people aren't "in the picture" as we prepare, they'll never get there while we preach.

If the preacher has honestly answered the other six questions, especially questions four through six, there shouldn't be any problem getting the people into the picture. Remember that the purpose of preaching is to achieve an object, not explain a subject. We want something to happen in our hearts and in the hearts of our people. We want the Spirit of God to use the truth to make Jesus Christ real *and to transform us to become like Him.*

This is a good place to say something about introductions and conclusions, because these two parts of the sermon must be very personal. The shorter the introduction, the better, especially when you're preaching to your own congregation. They're expecting you to preach and they want to listen, so why delay? After all, the main purposes of the introduction are to declare the text (which should have been read earlier in the service) and to tell the people why they ought to listen to what God has to say in the text. It shouldn't take ten minutes to do that! In this day of fast food and five-minute oil changes, people don't have the patience to listen to the traditional sermon introduction that explains the context, gives the background, and deals with all the problems in the text. If you take too long aiming your rifle, the game may disappear.

If I were to introduce a sermon about David at Ziklag, I might say something like this:

You're driving home from work, looking forward to seeing the family and enjoying a good dinner. You imagine yourself sitting in your lounge chair, reading the paper, and listening to good music. But then you hear sirens screaming, and as you turn the corner, you discover that your street is blocked off and that the police are in charge. "Sorry, pal; you can't get through!" a policeman shouts. "A house is burning down!" Then you discover that the house is yours. *How do you respond in the crises of life?*

Of course, the crisis may not be a fire. It might be a death in the family, or losing your job, or having your grandson tell you he's got AIDS, or having the doctor explain that you have cancer. But the question still has to be answered: *How do we respond in the crises of life?*

216

It's an easy transition into the three responses found in the text, and you can work in the necessary background material as you develop the message. Please note also that the pronoun changed from the first stating of the proposition ("How do *you* respond?") to the second ("How do *we* respond?"). The preacher isn't a lecturer on a pedestal, shaking his finger and telling his people what to do. He's a fellow pilgrim, going through the same valley with them, sharing what God has helped him to learn and to do.

Most books on classic homiletics list numerous ways for us to bring the sermon to a close, but they all say to do one thing for sure: make an application. I used to interpret that to mean, "Tell them what to do!" But I've changed my mind.

The English word *apply* comes from a Latin word that means "to fold," hence, "to bring together." When you apply paint, you bring a brush and a surface together. When you apply truth, you bring people and truth together. To "apply" a sermon doesn't mean to review all the points and "hammer them home." It means *to bring together* God's truth and God's people in such a way that the people's hearts feel the truth, their minds understand the truth, and their wills want to act on what they've heard from the Word. The "application" is their opportunity to experience personal changes within as they are "folded together" with God's truth and ministered to by God's Spirit.

The application, then, is an opportunity, a situation in which the Spirit of God can work. It might be created by a few minutes of silent meditation and prayer, or the singing of a song, or the corporate reading of a litany. The giving of an opportunity to come forward and pray, though perhaps overdone in some churches, is still a valid way to apply the Word. Some of the saints will want to confess; others will rejoice; still others will affirm their love for Christ and vow to obey what He's told them to do. And some will trust Christ for salvation for the first time.

One afternoon, when I should have been studying, I was looking around in the basement stacks of the seminary library. I came across a bound set of old magazines devoted to Bible study. While paging through one volume, I found this gem:

A sermon isn't a picture on the wall, hanging there for folks to admire. It isn't even a window in the wall, giving people a glimpse of a beautiful life that's beyond their reach. The sermon is a door that opens onto a path that leads the pilgrim into new steps of growth and service to the glory of God.

All Scripture is given by inspiration of God and is profitable for:

> *doctrine* — what is right
> *reproof* — what is not right
> *correction* — how to get right
> *instruction in righteousness* —
>   how to stay right

Isn't that what preaching is all about? A sermon isn't a picture on the wall, hanging there for folks to admire. It isn't even a window in the wall, giving people a glimpse of a beautiful life that's beyond their reach. The sermon is a door that opens onto a path that leads the pilgrim into new steps of growth and service to the glory of God. What a privilege we have to be called to preach the Word! Now let's think about the mechanics of "imagineering" a sermon.

"Where there is an original sound in the world,
it makes a hundred echoes."

—John A. Shedd

"Creativity is a by-product of hard work."

—Andrew Rooney

"In the creative state a man is taken out of himself.
He lets down as it were a bucket into his subconscious,
and draws up something which is normally beyond his reach.
He mixes this thing which his normal experiences
and out of the mixture he makes a work of art.

—E.M. Forster

Chapter Eighteen
Taking Things Apart and Putting Things Together

As important as outlines are to preaching, we must remember that an outline isn't necessarily a sermon. Of course, I can't criticize outlining too much because I've published outlines on every chapter in the New Testament, as well as most of the chapters in the Old Testament.[1] I'm grateful for the excellent instruction I received in seminary on how to analyze and exegete a text and then develop an outline. But now I realize that a message doesn't result just because I've outlined a text, added an introduction and conclusion, and given the whole thing a clever title. I'm sure somebody told me this when I was a student; but for some reason, I didn't grab it or it didn't grab me. Exegesis and analysis are important preliminary steps in the process of giving birth to a sermon. Bypass them and you have nothing worth saying; depend only on them and you won't know how to say it effectively. Exegesis and analysis are launching pads, not parking lots; and it's imagination that fuels the rocket.

Preachers who depend on outlines to change people's lives need to face several arresting facts.

1. *The Bible wasn't written that way.* Some parts of the Bible, such as Romans, Galatians, and Ephesians, are an outliner's delight. But what about Ecclesiastes, with its seemingly meandering observations on life? Or Proverbs, with its many changing topics? Or 1 John, with its cyclical development of

several repeated themes?[2] The Lord does all things decently and in order, but there's no evidence that the Holy Spirit gave the biblical writers outlines to follow as they wrote the inspired Scriptures.[3]

Nor is there evidence that the sermons recorded in the Bible all fit a common inspired homiletical pattern. Five preachers analyzing Peter's sermon at Pentecost would probably produce five different outlines. If preaching is "truth through personality," then the same truths will be "packaged" differently by different preachers. Jeremiah doesn't preach like Isaiah, nor Paul like Peter; and no preacher in Scripture presents the truth exactly the way Jesus did.[4]

I fear that the current profusion of "study Bibles" may give people two erroneous ideas: first, that God can't speak to us from His Word unless we get "professional help"; and second, that the most important thing you can do with the Scripture is to outline it. While marginal notes and textual outlines may help us grasp some of the basic facts of Scripture and thus better understand them, there is more to studying the Bible than amassing facts. T.S. Eliot reminded us "that a study of anatomy will not teach you how to make a hen lay eggs."[5] Exegesis *empties* language and enriches us with facts; but imagination *fills* language and yields nourishing truths. If we're going to preach effectively, it isn't enough to take things apart; we must also put them back together with meaning and creativity. Analysis and exegesis are important, and good outlines can be very useful; but we must beware lest (to use Wordsworth's phrase) we "murder to dissect." We must also beware lest we impose upon the text our own artificial design that imprisons the truth instead of liberates it. Finally, we must remember that our people's understanding of an outline is no guarantee that they have grasped the spiritual truth of the Word or been changed by the Spirit of God.[6] I discussed this in the first section of this book, so there's no reason to go over the territory again.

2. *Truth isn't always discovered that way.* "Homiletics is the science, of which preaching is the art, of which the sermon

is the product." I heard Dr. Lloyd M. Perry make that statement often in his homiletics classes in seminary, and I agree with it. As with most skills, preaching is both a *science* and an *art*; and woe unto the preacher who forgets this fact! It takes both information and imagination, analysis and synthesis, logic and intuition, to discover God's truth and give birth to a message.

It comes as a surprise to some people to learn that the scientist depends on intuition and imagination as well as on experimental investigation. "To try to deal with all matters by logico-scientific language is as self-defeating as to try to capture water in a net, or a breeze in a bag," wrote Philip Wheelwright.[7] On Sept. 5, 1851, Thoreau wrote in his journal: "All perception of truth is the detection of an analogy; we reason from our hands to our head."[8] Investigation amasses the factual data, but imagination and intuition discover the pattern that gives meaning to the data. Walt Whitman's "learn'd astronomer" forgot this truth and lost at least one listener.

> When I heard the learn'd astronomer,
> When the proofs, the figures, were ranged in columns
>   before me,
> When I was shown the charts and diagrams, to add,
>   divide, and measure them,
> When I sitting heard the astronomer where he lectured
>   with much applause in the lecture-room,
> How soon unaccountable I became tired and sick,
> Till rising and gliding out I wander'd off by myself,
> In the mystical moist night-air, and from time to time,
> Look'd up in perfect silence at the stars.[9]

I must confess that I have occasionally been tempted to steal out of the sanctuary-turned-lecture-room, where the greatness and glory of God were being concealed by biblical facts that had become blinders instead of lenses.[10] "The highest truths are not reached by analysis," said Hugh Black. "The deepest appeal is not made to logic but to imagination, not to intellect but to heart. . . . When science has done its best, or its worst, we need the poet, the prophet, the seer to interpret nature to us, not by analysis but by constructive imagination."[11]

Again, let me assure you that I'm not suggesting we abandon exegesis and analysis, but only that we stop preaching our learned notes and logical outlines and stop calling them sermons. People can get very hungry while we're reading them the list of ingredients on the cereal box or the recipes in the cookbook.

Professor and poet Marvin Bell, in giving advice to writers, also gives some good advice to preachers: "The difficulty of writing [substitute "preaching"] lies in turning from our reasonable, pragmatic selves long enough to idle our way into the imagination."[12] Also true of some sermons is what novelist and short-story writer Nancy Hale wrote about novels: "The dead hand of research lies heavy on too many novels. The part most alive in them comes out of imagination."[13]

It's not a question of investigation vs. imagination, as though these two approaches to discovering truth were adversaries. *All honest investigation includes imagination, including the investigations now going on in scientific laboratories.* The creative scientist uses "models" to help him manipulate abstract concepts and discover things that might otherwise elude him. "These models," writes Eva Feder Kittay, "must be understood as extended metaphors—not literally true, but useful representations of the phenomena which often lead to fruitful theoretic conceptions and new empirical discoveries."[14]

I've touched on two difficulties connected with limiting messages to "logical outlines": the Bible wasn't written that way, and truth isn't always discovered that way. There's a third difficulty:

3. *Life is rarely lived that way.* In the November 1884 issue of *Longman's Magazine*, Robert Louis Stevenson wrote: "Life is monstrous, infinite, illogical, abrupt and poignant; a work of art, in comparison, is neat, finite, self-contained, rational, flowing and emasculated."[15] In contrasting "real life" with a work of art, Stevenson may have exaggerated a bit to make his point, but the point is well-taken. The drama of life is difficult, and we don't always get to choose the scenery or write the script.

When our people assemble to worship, they move out of the confusion, ugliness, and disarray of everyday life into the order and beauty of liturgy, which includes a sermon, carefully organized and outlined. But for too many people, the experience of worship is an *escape* from reality instead of an *encounter* with reality, an encounter that might give them a deeper understanding of God and His will for their lives. You'll recall that I suggested earlier in this book that fantasy *escapes* reality in an alternate world, while imagination *penetrates* reality and helps us better understand God, ourselves, and the world around us. Worship that is built on fantasy is only *religious entertainment* and provides only temporary escape from the world we live in. Worship built on the sanctified imagination is *enrichment* and leads to changed lives that can cope with today's world.

Certainly our sermons must be organized, for God is not the author of confusion. But if we fabricate every text into a tidy homiletical package, *even if the passage isn't that tidy*, we may end up giving our people a false impression about the life of faith. They may start believing that the people who wrote the Bible, or who lived what's written in the Bible, experienced life as "a work of art" and somehow escaped the "illogical, abrupt and poignant" experiences that people face today.

"The strange thing about Scripture is that it does not aim to make us understand doctrines in a systematic way," wrote Watchman Nee. "Perhaps it would have been better if Paul and the others had got together to provide a detailed handbook of Christian doctrines. But God did not permit this. How easily He could have settled some of our theological arguments, but it seems He loves to confuse those who only approach the Bible intellectually. He wants to prevent men from merely getting hold of doctrines. He wants truth to get hold of them."[16]

Life is filled with contradictions, paradoxes, and ambiguities; and an intellectual and analytical approach to preaching simply won't meet the needs of the people. This is where metaphor comes in. People feel isolated when we deal with abstract concepts, but they feel right at home when we paint pictures and they find themselves in those pictures. Terence Hawkes explains it this way:

Classical art is concerned to point out the balanced harmony existing in a well-ordered nature. Its basic principle is one of decorum, whereby elements are fitted to their proper classes and types, which are carefully distinguished. . . . The Romantic concern is the depiction of a unity that lies underneath surface distinctions, and which ignores clear-cut boundaries.[17]

Like life itself, metaphors aren't tidy or logical; but they help us grasp that "underlying unity" that helps give meaning to life. "As for metaphor," writes Northrop Frye, "where you're really saying 'this is that,' you're turning your back on logic and reason completely, because logically two things can never be the same thing and still remain two things."[18]

So, when we use biblical metaphors in our preaching, we're admitting that life isn't always orderly and logical, obedient to "clear-cut boundaries." But we're also telling people that there's an underlying unity revealed by the metaphor, and that they can "put themselves into the picture" and receive God's help.

Our Lord saw the people of His day "harassed and helpless, like sheep without a shepherd" (Matt. 9:36); and He presented Himself to them as "the good shepherd" who would love them to the extent of dying for them (John 10). The people who identified with the "sheep metaphor" were able to identify also with the "shepherd metaphor" and thus trust the Lord for salvation and security. "Metaphor uses the language of sense experience to lead us into the world of the unseen: faith, guilt, mind, God," says Eugene Peterson. "The visible and invisible, put asunder by sin, are joined by metaphor."[19]

When I was pastoring in Chicago, I received a phone call one evening from a young lady who was threatening to commit suicide. She kept saying, "I did everything he told me to do and it didn't work!" After much patient listening, I finally discovered that she had attended a seminar on Christian living where she had learned some "sure-fire formulas" for solving life's problems. She put the formulas into practice, but nothing came out right; so she concluded that the trouble lay with her and that nothing would ever go right for her. The logical thing to do was to end it all. We who minister to broken people sometimes wish that life were a tidy little package and that life's problems could all be solved with our neat little "sermon formulas," but such desires are only a mirage. In our preaching, we must give our people something more than well-groomed outlines that suggest that life is simple and we have the answers. "The mind craves nothing so much as a closed system," wrote John Peale Bishop, "and the writer's [preacher's] mind is no exception; and yet he should, at whatever cost of violence, constantly set against any system . . . the spontaneity and variety of life."[20]

4. Communication rarely works that way. It takes a great deal of naivete for us to believe that what we say always conveys what we mean, or that our listeners receive our words whole and undamaged, like newly minted coins. Words are not coins. Words are not even arbitrary signs that never change their meaning or value. "[Words] are animals, alive and with a will of their own," wrote Guy Davenport. "Put together, they are invariably less or more than their sum . . . asked to be neutral, they display allegiances and stubborn propensities. They assume the color of their new surroundings, like chameleons; they perversely develop echoes."[21]

Apart from the ministry of the Holy Spirit in the preacher and the listener, there can be no valid communication of spiritual truth from the Word. When the Spirit is at work, there is an imperceptible bond between speaker and listener that makes for powerful communication and changed lives. In outlining the message, we must be careful not to grieve the Spirit by handling the text in a manner that makes us the author of truth instead of the interpreter of truth.

In other words, language is dynamic; and therefore, language is sometimes ambiguous. Apart from the ministry of the Holy Spirit in the preacher and the listener, there can be no valid communication of spiritual truth from the Word.[22] When the Spirit is at work, there is an imperceptible bond between speaker and listener that makes for powerful communication and changed lives. In outlining the message, we must be careful not to grieve the Spirit by handling the text in a manner that makes us the author of truth instead of the interpreter of truth.

In preparing a message, we need two different kinds of outlines: the homiletical/hermeneutical analysis, and the poetical/imaginative synthesis. The first is "left brain" and informational, closely following the development of the passage; while the second is "right brain" and intuitive, arranging spiritual truths in imaginative ways. For example, look at Matthew 14:22-33:

    I. Jesus
        A. made the disciples get into the boat (22)
        B. sent them to the other side (He would join them later) (22)
        C. dismissed the crowd (22; cf. John 6 — they wanted to make Him king)
        D. went into the hills alone to pray (23)
        E. time passed — it was evening (23)
        F. saw the plight of the Twelve (Mark 6:48)
        G. came to the men on the water (25)

    II. The disciples
        A. obeyed His will — ran into a severe storm (24)
        B. saw a figure approaching — cried out in fear (26)
        C. heard His words of assurance (27)
    III. Peter
        A. asked permission to walk on the water (28)
        B. received permission (29) — one word, "Come."
        C. walked on the water (29)
        D. became frightened by the circumstances (30)
        E. started to sink (30)
        F. cried out to Jesus (30)
        G. was saved from drowning by Jesus (31)
        H. was rebuked for his little faith (31)
        I. returned with Jesus to the boat (32)

IV. The disciples
   A. received Jesus and Peter into the boat (32)
   B. saw the storm die down and end (32)
   C. arrived at their destination (John 6:21)
   D. worshiped Jesus (33)
   E. confessed that He is the Son of God (33)

But preaching is more than a recitation of facts, no matter how dramatically we might present them to our people. Preaching involves the *interpretation* of the facts and the *investigation* and *application* of the truths that grow out of the facts. Without much effort, the unimaginative minister could make the above analysis into a preachable outline:

I. Jesus commands our lives: obey Him
II. Jesus controls our circumstances: trust Him
III. Jesus calms our fears: worship Him

But isn't there much more in the passage than three alliterated platitudes? This is where your sanctified imagination goes to work. Imagination searches for relationships, because relationships produce patterns, and patterns reveal new truths for us to share. Apart from imagination, the text is only past history and not present reality.

Let's start with the storm, a metaphor that speaks of trials and testings in life. "The storms of life" is a familiar phrase, and Longfellow reminded us that "Into each life some rain must fall." As we allow our imagination to "play over" the Scriptures, we jot down ideas that come to us:

Jonah was in a storm because of disobedience; the disciples, because of obedience.

Obeying God's will is no guarantee the way will be easy.

The last time they were in a storm, Jesus was with them in the ship (Matt. 8:23-27). Now He was absent.

Storms don't hinder Jesus from coming to help us.

Storms must obey His will.

Storms can teach us important lessons about ourselves and about Jesus.

Storms are a test of faith and an opportunity to grow.

Now, let's change our perspective and look at Peter. It's significant that Peter had three "boat experiences" with Jesus: the great catch of fish (Luke 5:1-11), the first stilling of the storm (Matt. 8:23-27), and the second stilling of the storm (our text).[23] What is the connection here? Is there a pattern that will reveal spiritual truths to us?

It appears that Jesus was giving Peter and the other disciples lessons on how to exercise faith. The first lesson took place in calm water in the morning, with Jesus in the ship (Luke 5:1-11). The second occurred in stormy weather at night *with Jesus asleep in the ship* (Matt. 8:23-27). The third experience was at night, in stormy weather, *with Jesus not in the ship!* Each new test required more faith on their part: Jesus present, Jesus asleep, Jesus absent. Our Lord's purpose was to encourage the disciples to trust Him whether or not He was in the ship or whether or not they were in the ship! It must have delighted His heart when He saw that Peter had the faith to walk on the water.[24]

But my imagination tells me that something else is involved; for as I review Peter's life, I note that this wasn't the first time Peter took his "eyes of faith" off of Jesus (Heb. 12:1-2), nor would it be the last. In Luke 5:8, he got his eyes on *himself*; and in John 21:20-22, he got his eyes on *another believer,* in this case, the Apostle John. Maybe we can work this into our message, or perhaps it should be a message all its own. We could preach on "the distractions of life" that lead to defeat in our walk of faith: looking at *self,* looking at *circumstances,* and looking at *other people.*

But, back to Matthew 14:22-33. Perhaps we can take this approach:

A faith that can't be tested can't be trusted. Whether we like it or not, our faith in Jesus Christ *will* be tested in the storms of life. How do you respond to these storms?

From the experience of the apostles, let's work out a "statement of faith for the storms of life." When you find yourself in a storm, turn to these affirmations of faith and remind yourself:

I. He brought me here
II. He sees my circumstances
III. He is praying for me
IV. He will speak to me by His Word
V. He will help me grow in my faith
VI. He will see me through

The analytical outline is *past tense* and records what Jesus did for the disciples; but the homiletical outline is *present tense* and explains what Jesus does for all His people today, if they will trust Him. Each of the above "affirmations of faith" can be documented from the text and substantiated from other passages of Scripture.

But this isn't the only approach. We can see in this episode our Lord teaching His disciples some of "the lessons of life": a lesson in *love*, for He sent them into the storm because it was good for them; a lesson in *faith*, for they learned to trust Him; and a lesson in *hope*, for when their plight was at its worst, Jesus came to rescue them. The whole event illustrates our situation today as we wait for our Lord to come to take us out of the storms of life. This second approach is of a more devotional nature and doesn't offer as much opportunity for expository fullness as the first approach does.

So, as the example demonstrates, after you've done your exegetical homework, and you have the analytical outline and the factual data before you, don't immediately write an outline that "fits" the passage.[25] *First, decide on the overriding metaphor that will control the development of the message.* Will it be the storms of life, or life as a school in which we learn the lessons of faith? Maybe we should emphasize the distractions of life? Will our focus be on the disciples or on Jesus, what He did for them or what they did with Him? Will we examine the process or the results of the process? Once you've settled on the metaphor and the approach, then you can sift through your notes and select the material that fits.[26] The resulting outline won't be something you manufacture for the occasion by organizing a stack of notes, like writing a term paper or doing your income tax. The outline will "grow" out of the passage in a way that "fits," and you'll know intuitively which items of factual data belong in the message.

Preparing a message is something like engaging in an athletic contest or playing a musical instrument: you have to work at it; some of the things you do will come from habit or native intuition; and the more you do it, the better you'll understand what "works." *But you have to know the rules.* Every celebrated concert pianist got his or her start like every other pianist, by practicing the scales. *You are free to break the rules once the rules have broken you.* "I believe in rules," said Leo Durocher. "If there weren't any rules, how could you break them?"

> **Preparing a message is something like engaging in an athletic contest or playing a musical instrument: you have to work at it; some of the things you do will come from habit or native intuition; and the more you do it, the better you'll understand what "works."**

When I was teaching homiletics, I would occasionally meet students who resisted submitting to the "basic training" that's involved in preaching. "That's not the way Dr. Ironside did it," they would argue, "or Campbell Morgan or Charles Spurgeon." Then they'd remind me that not one of those three homiletical heroes ever studied in a Bible school or seminary!

My response was: "If any of you is a Spurgeon, a Campbell Morgan, or a Harry Ironside, we'll soon find it out. And please remember that Spurgeon founded a school for training pastors, and Morgan and Ironside each sat on faculties in schools that trained Christian workers. Now, about last week's assignment. . . !"

This, then, is the conclusion of the whole matter: fear God and do your homework. But after you've done your homework, put your imagination to work by asking yourself: (1) How does this text relate to other passages that involve the same semantic domains (storms, boats, Peter, etc.)? (2) What patterns do I see? (3) What truths emerge from these patterns? (4) What pictures (metaphors) are in the text? (5) What metaphor will best convey the message of this passage?[27] (6) As the people hear the development of the outline, *will they see something?*

Let's try another illustration. I once preached from Romans 5:1-11 and took this approach:

> Let me run some names past you; see how many you can recognize: Junias — Julia — Rufus — Olympus — Phoebe — Urbanus.
>
> Recognize them? Well, they were all friends of the Apostle Paul, and you'll find him greeting them, along with several other friends, in the last chapter of his Letter to the Romans. They were ordinary people, not theologians or scholars, because Paul wrote Romans for everyday garden-variety Christians like you and me.
>
> Just imagine how thrilled these Christians in Rome must have been when they heard read in their Lord's Day assembly the words we identify as Romans 5:1-11. We take these verses for granted, but what Paul wrote here is doctrinal dynamite. In these verses, Paul explains what really happens when the sinner trusts Jesus Christ and receives the gift of salvation.

My outline for the passage in the sermon follows:
   I. The court case is settled — justified! (1a)
   II. The war is ended — peace with God! (1b)
   III. The treasury is opened — the grace of God! (2)
   IV. The transformation begins — godly character! (2–5)

Working from such a suggested outline, our task is to weave in all the doctrine our congregation can assimilate from one message, but to do this in a pictorial way that transforms a theological lecture into a warm-hearted message that will make listeners want to praise God and share the Gospel with others.

It isn't enough for us to write an outline that "takes things apart." We must go a step further and develop from this analysis an outline that "puts things together" so that our listeners can see the truth. Most biblical passages have an inherent metaphor (or perhaps several metaphors) that can be used to help us picture the truth. When things start to come together in the text, and you begin to get excited about the patterns you see, then you'll know you've discovered the picture(s) you can use to make the truth alive in your message. Your outline then becomes the "frame" for the picture(s). One word of caution: be sure the "frame" doesn't detract from the picture(s) or your message won't get through. Samuel Johnson advised young writers, "Read over your compositions, and wherever you meet with a passage which you think is particularly fine, strike it out."[28] The outline of the message should be so simple and clear that the worshiper might say to himself or herself, "Why, what's so difficult about preaching? I could have said the same thing!"

I once listened to a church pianist generate brilliant keyboard pyrotechnics during the offering, after which the congregation applauded enthusiastically; but somehow I felt cheated. His "performance" only called attention to his skill and distracted from the meaning of the offering and the glory due to God alone. A sensitive hymn interpretation instead would have added to our worship experience. We must remind ourselves that the preacher often makes the same mistake in his preaching.

Donald Coggan relates the story of a bishop who gave a masterful oration that drew the ecstatic applause of the people when he finished. He then noticed that Francis de Sales was in the congregation, and he asked the spiritual leader what he thought of the sermon. After a long silence, St. Francis replied, "You pleased all but One."[29]

Some preachers are gifted wordsmiths. With the help of a thesaurus and a dictionary of synonyms, they can construct outlines that are so verbally ingenious you find yourself admiring the menu instead of eating the meal, if there is a meal to eat. Their particular homiletical sin is an overdose of alliteration.

Now, if a simple alliterative outline grows naturally out of the text, the preacher may be wise to use it; but he is unwise to waste precious hours searching through the dictionary for another word that starts with *M* and means "confidence." Some preachers alliterate every main point and sub-point until you find yourself second-guessing them and predicting what the next point will be. Excessive alliteration can lead to obliteration and wipe out the message. People get distracted from the sermon itself, and anything that distracts from God's truth is suspect if not sinful. "Apt Alliteration's artful aid" is what Charles Churchill wrote in his 1763 satire *Prophecy of Famine,* and there may be times when alliteration helps people grasp and remember some statement of truth. But the warning spoken by one of my professors keeps echoing in the homiletical lobe of my brain: "Gentlemen, alliteration will sell you short every time."[30]

I manufactured the following outline to illustrate the oppressive extent to which alliteration can kill a text. As they say in the detective novels, any resemblance between this outline and outlines preached by any other preacher is purely coincidental. The text is Psalm 23. If you get desperate some day and actually preach this outline, please don't mention my name.

I. A relationship that is precious ("my shepherd")
II. A resource that is plentiful ("I shall not want")
III. A rest that is pleasant ("pastures . . . waters")
IV. A restoration that is perfect
V. A righteousness that is practical
VI. A reassurance that is personal ("You are with me")
VII. A repast that is peaceful ("a table before me")
VIII. A recovery that is powerful ("oil . . . cup")
IX. A realization that is phenomenal ("follow me")
X. A regularity that is positive ("all the days . . . ")
XI. A reward that is perennial ("house of the Lord")

I confess that this is a caricature of a sermon outline, and I apologize. But at least it illustrates some of the major weaknesses of using overly alliterated outlines: distracting the preacher from the main message; using words without precise definition;[31] straining to impress instead of express; and disregarding the "flow" of the text. To say the least, it's artificial; and sermons are supposed to be authentic and alive. They are born, not manufactured.

"Imagination is the eye of the soul."

—Joseph Joubert

"When one discovers a living truth,
one has great difficulty in putting it into words.
Every artist suffers from the contrast
between his finished work and the infinitely
more complex reality which he first experienced
in his inner being."

—Paul Tournier

Chapter Nineteen
Imagination and Biographical Preaching

According to Harry Farra, the biographical sermon rates highest in effectiveness on the "homiletical grid," combining the strengths of both biblical exposition and "life-situation" preaching.[1] People like to hear about people, including "Bible people"; and sometimes they're shocked to discover that Bible people are very much like people today. When you preach about Bible characters, you have the opportunity of making abstract truth concrete and universal principles very personal.[2] The Word becomes flesh and blood, here and now.

The Bible tells the stories of heroes and heroines of the faith who, in spite of their blemishes and blunders, got something done for God. We live in a world in which real heroes are scarce and we have to settle for substitute heroes, such as overrated movie stars and overpaid athletes and rock singers, people who are famous only for being famous and, of course, for being rich.[3] Even some of our favorite heroes of history have been reclassified by revisionist historians so that their achievements don't shine as gloriously as they once did. So, whether you're reading a history textbook, a new biography, or *Time*, you're probably finding it more and more difficult to discover somebody worthy of admiration, somebody you can call a hero or a heroine.[4]

"Great men make small men aware of their smallness," writes historian Arthur M. Schlesinger, Jr., in a perceptive essay originally published in *The Saturday Evening Post*. He quotes

Emerson's statement, "We feed on genius. Great men exist that there may be greater men."[5] In this essay, Schlesinger laments the decline of the hero in society; and he explains why he thinks there's a scarcity of heroes.

It's important that preachers hold before their people the unvarnished lives of Bible heroes and heroines and challenge the church to emulate the best that these men and women have to offer. By preaching Bible biography, we have the opportunity of teaching theology, history, and practical godly living all at one time, with the Bible as the textbook. As these ancient characters come alive in each message, our people can learn about themselves, the Bible, and the Lord; and perhaps this will encourage them to take some important steps of faith that will help to make them heroes or heroines in their own personal world.

What are some of the essentials for successful biographical preaching?

Honesty. Too many of us have a tendency to categorize Bible characters as "godly" and "ungodly" and leave it at that. We forget that most of the "godly" people occasionally acted like sinners and that some of the "ungodly" accomplished some good things, although the Lord certainly didn't agree with their sins.[6] The first essential for effective biographical preaching is to set aside our pious prejudices and homiletical halos, without abandoning our spiritual perceptivity, and to try to see the actors and actresses in the biblical drama as real people. At least, let's be as honest about them as the Bible is.[7]

Of course, when we examine Bible personalities, we really end up examining *ourselves.* Perhaps our hesitation at being honest about *them* suggests that we may not want to be honest about *ourselves.*[8] Biographical preaching involves both the biography of the preacher's subject *and the autobiography of the subject's preacher.* Columnist Russell Baker wrote, "The biographer's problem is that he never knows enough. The autobiographer's problem is that he knows much too much."[9] When you prepare biographical sermons, you're looking *back* at the record of somebody's life and looking *within* at your own heart; and this might be a painful experience for some of us.

What we need is the right "spiritual mind-set" as we study the biblical accounts of God's people. After all, we're not investigative reporters, looking for some new scandal to expose; nor are we revisionist historians, debunking the past and promoting our novelties. We're ambassadors of the King, walking through His inspired picture gallery and getting to know some of His choicest subjects, people whose sandals we're not worthy to carry. We want to get to know these people because they knew God and can teach us a great deal about Him.

Thorough investigation. In her delightful book *Biography: The Craft and the Calling,* Catherine Drinker Bowen suggests that as researchers do their investigating, they maintain a special file folder labeled "What the reader must know" to remind themselves that what may be clear to the researcher might well be a mystery to others. Into this folder go those extra facts that must be included if the reader (or listener) is to understand what's going on.[10] In this day of biblical as well as historical illiteracy, the suggestion is a good one. No longer can we assume that everybody in the congregation understands that Abraham came before Moses, or why the Jewish kingdom divided into Israel and Judah, or how Paul got from Jerusalem to Rome.

The need, then, is for thorough investigation so that we not only know the person's career, as outlined in Scripture, but we also know the historical, political, and cultural context of that career. Of course, we first exhaust the biblical data;[11] but we don't stop there. Preachers of effective biographical sermons read widely, because they never know what discoveries they will make that will shed new light on an old subject. It isn't enough just to gather "devotional thoughts" as we study, as important as every spiritual truth might be to our sermon. We must have the facts at our command so that we're preaching about real people in a real world.

One of the handiest tools for biographical preaching is the copying machine. Some years ago, before preparing a series of radio messages on John the Baptist, I copied out of a harmony of the Gospels all the passages that related to my subject. I then arranged them in chronological order and put them in a binder, with blank pages interleaved. (It would be difficult to do this for every Bible character—Moses or Paul, for instance—but most of the Bible personalities we preach about don't take up that much space.) This collection of texts was a helpful tool and a great time-saver as I did my research.

What facts are we looking for as we study the life of a Bible personality? Here's a checklist that might prove helpful.

Suggested Study Guide for Biographical Sermons

    I. Chronology of the person's life
        A. Family background; important relatives
        B. Birth—anything special about it?
        C. Name—any special meaning?
        D. Influences: family, nation, enemies, events
        E. Calling and service; vocational changes
        F. Offices and titles
        G. Crises: victories, disappointments, failures
        H. Children—family activities
        I. Death and burial
        J. Accomplishments: immediate; ultimate
    II. Setting of the life
        A. Historical (Bible history; secular history)
        B. Geographical
        C. Cultural
        D. Religious
   III. Significant references
        A. Old Testament
        B. New Testament
        C. Secular history
        D. Current opinions
   IV. Character
        A. Virtues
        B. Vices
        C. Experiences with God
        D. Influence on others
    V. Practical application
        A. What major lessons does the person teach us?

    B. How would he/she fit into society today?

    C. What contributions did he/she make to salvation history?

    D. What doctrines are illustrated in his/her life?

    E. What metaphors help to describe his/her life?

    F. Is there one Bible verse that is a summary of the person's life?

    G. What has God said to me as I have studied this life?

As you develop your skills in biographical preaching, you will no doubt add other items to the list; but this will at least get you started.

Insight. Biographical preaching is not the mere recitation of historical facts, with a few "practical applications" dropped in along the way.[12] As we've noted before, information must lead to interpretation and illumination. The sanctified imagination looks for relationships among the facts, because relationships reveal patterns; and new patterns help us to discover new truths.

While preparing a series of messages on the life of King Saul, I was struck with the fact that Saul's spear was often mentioned in the text (1 Sam. 18:10; 19:9-10; 20:33; 22:6; 26:7, 11-12, 16, 22; 2 Sam. 1:6). Apparently he used his spear as his royal scepter; it was a reminder to those around him that Saul was in charge. But the spear didn't offer him much protection—on at least two occasions, David and his men could have killed the king. Saul couldn't kill David with the spear; and in the end, it was that same spear that killed Saul! God asks each of us, as He asked Moses, "What is that in your hand?" (Ex. 4:2) All David had was a sling and a stone in his hand when he faced the giant. Shamgar had only an oxgoad (Jud. 3:31), and Gideon and his men had only pitchers and torches; but God gave all of them great victories. *It's not the weapon in your hand, but the integrity of your heart that God honors and uses.*[13]

I noticed something else about Saul: his career as king began in the morning, at the dawning of a new day (1 Sam. 9:25 – 10:1), but it gradually moved into the darkness, both spiritually and literally. Before his death on the battlefield, Saul visited the home of a witch at night and sought for help from the spirit world. I thought of Proverbs 4:18-19 — "The path of the righteous is like the first gleam of dawn, shining ever brighter till the full light of day. But the way of the wicked is like deep darkness; they do not know what makes them stumble."

As you study the factual data, ask the Lord to give you insight into the spiritual truths that lie behind the facts. One area that is especially important in biographical studies has to do with *names*. Pay close attention to the meaning of names, the changing of names, or the giving of a nickname.[14] Not every name in the Bible is significant, but many of them carry meanings that are very important.

The name "Judas" comes from "Judah," which means "praise." Jesus nicknamed him "the son of perdition" (John 17:12, KJV), and the word translated "perdition" (*apoleia*) means "waste." Compare this with Matthew 26:8, where Judas and the other disciples ask, "Why this waste?" *It was Judas, not Mary, who was the waster.* Judas wasted every spiritual opportunity Jesus gave him, and he defiled everything he touched, including his name. Who today would name a son Judas?

The name Samson means "sunny" or "little sun," and yet he too ended up in the darkness because spiritually he "walked" in the darkness. For that matter, Judas also ended up in the dark: "As soon as Judas had taken the bread, he went out. And it was night" (John 13:30). Saul, Samson, and Judas: three men who ended up in the dark. Is there a pattern here? Nicodemus is identified as "the man who came to Jesus by night" (John 3:2; 7:50), but he ended up at Calvary, identifying himself with Jesus in broad daylight! Is there a lesson here? (John 3:20-21)

We all know that Abram's name was changed to Abraham, Sarai's to Sarah, and Simon's to Peter, or Cephas, "a rock" (John 1:42). But rabbi Saul's name became Paul, from the Latin *paulus* meaning "little, small." The Old Testament Saul stood head and shoulders above his peers, but the New Testament Saul/Paul wasn't that imposing a figure (2 Cor. 10:10). King Saul ended up a defeated suicide, and the Apostle Paul, a victorious martyr.

Ben-Oni ("son of my sorrow") was wisely changed by Jacob into Benjamin ("son of my right hand" — Gen. 35:16-18). Esau became Edom ("red"), and Jesus nicknamed James and John "the sons of thunder." Joses received the nickname "Barnabas, the encourager." What's in a name? It all depends on whose name it is!

The interpreter must be on the alert for even the smallest clue that might help open up a rich vein of spiritual wealth. It might be an object (Saul's spear), or a name ("Barnabas — the encourager"), or the time of day ("And it was night"), or a statement ("Why this waste?"), or an action (Peter pulling out his sword in the garden). Put yourself in the actor's place and ask, "Would I have said that or done that? If so, why? If not, why not? Why did he/she do it or say it?"

It's also valuable to trace *growth and decline* in a person's life. King Saul started out a humble man, refusing to speak to his family about his kingship and spurning the suggestion that his opponents in Israel be slain. But then he changed, and pride began to rule his life. Pride is the number one sin on God's hate list (Prov. 6:16-19), and that list describes the sins that are spawned by pride, all of which occurred in Saul's career. Instead of following heavenly wisdom, Saul listened to the wisdom of this world (James 3:13–4:10).

The references to Proverbs and James that I cited above remind us that a person's life can sometimes be summarized in a key passage of Scripture. Proverbs 28:13 certainly applies to certain aspects of David's life: "He who conceals his sins does not prosper, but whoever confesses and renounces them finds mercy." We must be careful, however, not to make human nature so simple that we think we can summarize a person's whole life in sixteen words or less. The

We must remind ourselves that we're preaching the biographical sermon in order to help our people personally, not just to better acquaint them with some Bible character. The message isn't a Bible lecture with the emphasis on *content*; it's a word from the Lord with the emphasis on *intent*.

eminent American historian Charles A. Beard refused to write any biographies. "I cannot be sure enough about human character and human motives to write the life of anyone," he said.[15]

Focus. We must remind ourselves that we're preaching the biographical sermon in order to help our people personally, not just to better acquaint them with some Bible character. The message isn't a Bible lecture with the emphasis on *content;* it's a word from the Lord with the emphasis on *intent.* There's a point we want to get across, and we've decided that the best way to do it is to preach about a person. But through whose eyes do we look at this person?

Do we look at Judas from our Lord's point of view and list all the things Jesus said and did, even up to the Last Supper, to try to rescue him?[16] Or do we look at Judas from Satan's point of view and watch the man's moral and spiritual decline? In Matthew 10:4, Judas is paired up with Simon the Zealot; and we assume they went out and ministered together. How would Simon tell the story of Judas?[17] Perhaps we should take the "If-I-had-been-there" point of view and interpret his life from our own perspective. This is an important decision, because it determines the way we select and fashion the material.

The sermon must be focused not only in viewpoint but also in theme. Is Judas a warning against covetousness, or hypocrisy? Do we refer the people to 1 Timothy 6:10, and trace the roots and fruits of Judas' love of money; or do we quote Matthew 7:21-23 and point out how close hypocrites can come to the kingdom and still be shut out?[18] Perhaps there's too much territory for us to cover in one message and we should do a brief series of two or three sermons and deal with several aspects of the person's life. This leads to a fourth essential.

Time. Serious biographers invest years of hard work researching their subjects. They read letters, journals, and books, interview all kinds of people, listen to tapes, watch videos, visit sites important to the subject, and gather as much information as they can from every source available. Obviously, we can't devote that much time and energy to every biographical sermon, but we do need to give ourselves adequate time for preparation.

For one thing, we have to get to know the people we're preaching about; and that takes time. I thought I knew John the Baptist until I started working on that series of sermons, and I discovered I didn't even know what I thought I knew!

Isaiah compared John to a roadbuilder and a herald of the king (Isa. 40:1-5). The Angel Gabriel said that John's ministry would be like that of Elijah the prophet (Luke 1:11-17). Zechariah saw his son as an evangelist who would rescue sinners and bring to Israel the dawning of a new day (Luke 1:76-79).

But in the life of John the Baptist, the focus is always on the Lord and not on John. Jesus is the bridegroom; John was but the best man at the wedding (John 3:29). Jesus is the Light, but John was only a lamp (John 5:33-35) and a witness to the Light (John 1:6-9). Jesus is the Word, but John was a voice proclaiming God's message (John 1:23).

Joy seems to be a recurring theme in John's life. The angel promised that John would bring joy to many, starting with his parents (Luke 1:14). The unborn prophet leaped for joy when he heard Mary's voice (Luke 1:39-45); and during his adult ministry, John's greatest joy was to magnify Christ (John 3:27-31).

It takes time to assimilate all this material and to penetrate to the heart of it. It also takes time to discover how it applies to life today. What does John's birth have to say about answered prayer? What does the infant John say about babies in general and parents in particular? Does God still send us people who live "in the wilderness" and emerge to deliver apocalyptic messages? How would society today respond to a John the Baptist? In what ways do preachers today build roads and prepare the way of the Lord? We need time, not only to find the right answers, but even more, to discover the right questions.

Participation. We dare not make ourselves spectators who merely watch the biblical drama from a distance. As much as possible, we need to enter into the narrative as participants, using our imagination and all our senses to seek to understand what happened. This means feeling the joys and the pains, sensing the confusion, being aware of the conflicts, perceiving the motives, and responding to the decisions. Suppose this plot were occurring today? Who do we know that would be in it? Why would they be in it? If our family or church were involved in a situation like this, what would they do? What would I do? What would God want us to do?[19]

Again, we must be careful not to simply "tell a story" and leave it at that. Granted, there is a way of telling a story that could carry more power than the preaching of a sermon; but some of us don't have the story-telling gifts of Garrison Keillor, Frederick Buechner, Robert Fulghum, or Walter Wangerin, Jr.[20] It is important that we see the plot in the narrative and deal with it accordingly.

Is the plot a tragedy, in which the good becomes evil? Or is it a comedy, in which failure turns into success?[21] Are the bad people punished and the good people rewarded, or do the good people suffer because of the bad? Do any bad people become good? Are there any heroes in the plot? Do they triumph or are they defeated? All of these questions and more help us understand narrative literature and its message.

Simple narrative is the reporting of an event and is usually chronological, while narrative with a plot is more complex because it involves causes and people with motives and personal aims. Novelist E.M. Forster said that "The king died and the queen died" is a story, but "The king died and then the queen died of grief" is a plot.[22]

Bible people are involved in "life stories" that include other people with desires, motives, and good or bad purposes they want to fulfill. Some Bible people seem to be in control of what's happening, while others must "roll with the punches" and adjust as well as they can to their circumstances. And above all these people and events, in complete control, sits Almighty God on His throne, working out purposes that the actors in the drama may know nothing about. Even when they rebel against Him, the actors and actresses in the biblical drama still end up playing by the script, whether they realize it or not. What a challenge to the preacher's imagination! Following is a checklist helpful for narrative and biographical sermon preparation.

A Suggested Guide for Narrative Bible Study

I. The text
 A. Its place in the total message of the book
 B. Its place in that section of the book

II. People
 A. Their previous history and significance
    to the narrative
 B. Relationship to each other
 C. Future history: what happened to them? Why?
 D. Are they mentioned elsewhere in Scripture?

III. Places
 A. Importance in the biblical narrative
 B. Significance of names; name changes
 C. Importance in secular history
 D. Significant archaeological data

IV. Events
 A. List the events in chronological order
 B. Determine the time frame in history
 C. Any parallel events in secular history?
 D. Motives behind the actions of people
 E. Consequences of actions
 F. Look at events from the viewpoint
    of each individual
 G. Events referred to elsewhere in Scripture?

V. Speakers
 A. Who speaks? To whom? Why? How?
 B. What do the words reveal about the speakers?
 C. What are the consequences of each speech?
 D. Are there silences? What is left unsaid?
 E. Are there repeated words and phrases?
    Are there changes?
 F. Are there words/phrases with special meanings?

VI. Doctrines
   A. What does the narrative say about God?
   B. What does it say about man?
   C. What does it say about creation and providence?
   D. How does it fit into salvation history?
   E. Is there a messianic message?
   F. What does it say about the people of God?

VII. Symbols
   A. Are there symbolic objects, persons, events/actions, words?
   B. Is there any clear typology?

VIII. Special problems in the text
   A. Translation problems
   B. Theological problems
   C. Historical problems (chronology)

IX. Practical application
   A. Promises and encouragements
   B. Warnings and commands
   C. Spiritual principles
   D. Parallels to current events
   E. OT illustration; NT interpretation

"Even the most unlearned of men
knows that the truly important matters of life
are those for which we have no words."

—Chaim Potok

"True creativity often starts where language ends."

—Arthur Koestler

"How vain it is to sit down to write
when you have not stood up to live."

—Henry David Thoreau

Chapter Twenty
Imagination and Comfort

Early in my ministry, I was encouraged to buy and read *The Funeral: A Source Book for Ministers* by Andrew W. Blackwood. I'm grateful that I had sense enough to heed the admonition. That one book gave me the right start on how to prepare the kind of funeral messages that would do more than fill up time and carry on tradition. If Dr. Blackwood were writing his book today, he would no doubt make some changes because of the changes in society; but I think his basic philosophy would remain unchanged. It's a philosophy I heartily recommend.

"The appeal should be mainly to the imagination," says Blackwood about the message. "In a few minutes there is time for only a single truth. It should be luminous. . . . Since the time is short, there should be little exegesis, and no argument."[1]

Most of the mourners at a funeral aren't capable of following a doctrinal argument, complete with Greek and Hebrew vocabulary. Of course, every message must be doctrinally sound; but the best way to communicate God's comforting Word to broken hearts is not with an argument but with a picture. The effective funeral message calls for sanctified imagination.[2]

The funeral message is not like any other message that the minister proclaims. It must be biblical, and it must be organized; but it must not "sound like a sermon," either in organization or presentation. The message must present one truth, in a vivid manner, so that the listeners may understand it and appropriate it for themselves.[3]

A pastor friend of mine shared a funeral service with a minister who used 2 Corinthians 5:1-5 as the text, but apparently hadn't done his homework. Instead of seeing the "eternal house in heaven" as the Christian's glorified body, the minister related the text to John 14:1-6; and the result was a grotesque picture of Jesus and the deceased, climbing up and down ladders and building a heavenly mansion. That's the kind of homiletical fantasy we can do without at funerals—or anywhere else.

When we surveyed the images found in Scripture, you undoubtedly noticed how many images there are in the Bible of both life and death. Some of these images emphasize the hopelessness of the unbeliever without God, but others are radiant with hope for all who have trusted Jesus Christ. It's the job of the sensitive pastor to find the biblical metaphor that best fits the situation and use it to meet the needs of the people.

While attending a funeral, my wife and I patiently endured a thirty-minute academic doctrinal discourse on the Christian view of the resurrection of the human body as explained in 1 Corinthians 15. Instead of trying to expound the whole chapter, the preacher could have focused on one of Paul's telling metaphors in that passage: death as sleep (vv. 6, 18, 51), Christ as the firstfruits (vv. 20, 23), burial as sowing and resurrection as the harvest (vv. 35-44), and glorification as the changing of clothing (vv. 50-55). Our minds just weren't in the right mood for logic, but our hearts would have responded quickly to pictures.

Some Biblical Pictures of Death

Death as *sleep* is one of the repeated images used in Scripture (Deut. 31:16; Job 14:12; Pss. 13:3 and 17:15; Jer. 51:39; Dan. 12:2; Matt. 9:24; John 11:11-14; Acts 7:59-60; 13:36; 1 Cor. 15:6; 1 Thes. 4:13-18). The image speaks, of course, of the sleep of the body which is no longer functioning because the spirit has departed (James 2:26). For the believer, to be away from the body means to be present with the Lord (2 Cor. 5:6-8) while the body is sleeping in the dust.

Both death and sleep are universal experiences and therefore the image of sleep has universal significance and appeal. From the baby in the nursery to the senior citizen in the nursing home, all people need sleep; and when the body is weary, that sleep is eagerly sought. We don't fear sleep; we welcome it and anticipate awakening to a new day. For the Christian, the parallels between death and sleep are clear and comforting.

When Jesus told His disciples that Lazarus was sleeping, they misunderstood Him (as they often did) and thought He was describing symptoms of recovery (John 11:11-14). To Jesus, the death of believers is like sleep, and the resurrection of believers is like awakening people from sleep. Paul agreed with this metaphor and used it. The one great difference, of course, between us and Lazarus is that our "resurrection awakening" will mean a new and glorified body, a change of clothes![4] "When I awake, I will be satisfied with seeing your likeness" (Ps. 17:15). Not only shall we see Him, but "we shall be like Him"! (1 John 3:2)

Jesus compared His own death to an "exodus" (Luke 9:31), and Peter borrowed this metaphor (2 Peter 1:14-15). The word "exodus" reminds us of the experience of the people of Israel when they left Egypt, an experience of mingled joy and fear, triumph and trepidation, but one that ultimately led to victory. Death is an

253

enemy (1 Cor. 15:26) that would like to conquer us and hold us forever, but Christ leads His people victoriously from bondage to freedom (Heb. 2:14-15). What most of us fear isn't death itself but the mysterious experience of death, and the Word assures us that the believer's death is an "exodus" of victory.

In his "psalm of recovery after illness" (Isa. 38:9-20), King Hezekiah used three striking images of death: walking through gates (v. 10), taking down a tent (v. 12), and cutting a weaving from the loom (v. 12). The phrase "the gates of death" is found in Psalms 9:13 and 107:18 and is an image that suggests walking into a city. The word "death" is *Sheol* in the Hebrew, the realm of the dead; and in the Old Testament, *Sheol* is pictured for the most part as a gloomy place of shadows where hopelessness abounds. If this were the only image we had of death, we would have every reason to be discouraged. But the gates of Sheol cannot prevail against Jesus Christ! (Matt. 16:18) He has "destroyed death and has brought life and immortality to light through the gospel" (2 Tim. 1:10).

Death is also like taking down a tent. Like a tent, the body is but a temporary dwelling place; and one day we shall have our glorified permanent dwelling place (2 Cor. 5:1-8). The Greek word *analusis,* translated "departure" in 2 Timothy 4:6, carries the meaning of "a sailor loosing a ship to set sail" or "a soldier taking down a tent and breaking camp." (See also *analuo* in Phil. 1:23.)

Hezekiah also pictured death as cutting a weaving from the loom. In our discussion of the images in Isaiah 38, I have shown how this image relates to Psalm 139. Life is a weaving (see Job 7:6), and only God knows the pattern on the loom of life and when it will be completed. We see the underside of the weaving, which doesn't always make sense; but one day we shall see the picture that the Lord was making, and then all shall be well. All of this would be pure fancy if we didn't have a biblical image to back it up.

The image of the loom is a helpful one to use when mystery surrounds the death of the person, and people are asking, "Why should this happen? What is God doing?" After all, we don't see the pattern from God's point of view; and we must trust Him to do what is best. On the other hand, the weaving image is also a good image to use at the funerals of those whose lives have been "completed" and were ready for "display in heaven" (Eph. 1:12-14). How we thank God for the devoted "senior saints" who have allowed the Lord to weave their lives into something beautiful for eternity![5]

Psalm 23 is probably the favorite psalm for funerals. I see it quoted on the memorial folders I pick up when I sign in at the funeral home, and many people request the use of Psalm 23 when they discuss funeral plans for their deceased loved one. It was the first psalm I memorized in childhood and it has "grown up" with me all these years. The image of Jesus the Shepherd, believers as His sheep, and life as a journey to the Father's house, comforts and encourages us, no matter what the circumstances may be.[6]

However, the emphasis in the psalm is not death but instead what the Shepherd does for us "all the days of [our] life" (Ps. 23:6).[7] No matter what our circumstances, the Shepherd is adequate to handle them and see us through. Only when I get to the Father's house[8] will I be able to look back and see fully that God's goodness and love have indeed followed me all the days of my life. Until that time comes, I'll have to walk by faith in the Good Shepherd and believe Romans 8:28.[9]

F. Crossley Morgan sees in the psalm the ministry of the Shepherd to His own from childhood to old age. More than one commentator points out that the various "Jehovah" names of God are found in Psalm 23: "I shall lack nothing"—Jehovah-Jireh, "the Lord will provide"; "he leads me beside quiet waters"—Jehovah-Shalom, "the Lord our peace"; "he restores my soul"—Jehovah-Rapha, "the Lord who heals."[10] You probably don't want to use this kind of material in a funeral message because it's too esoteric for the average congregation, but it does show what imagination can do when applied to a familiar text.

I suggest that you make a notebook of the biblical images that strike you as ones having a message for broken hearts. As you meditate on them from time to time, study them and pray over them, the Lord will give you thoughts that you must write down and later develop into funeral messages. Very few funerals are scheduled; most of them come as interruptions. The pastor who captures ideas when they come is the one who is best prepared.

Consider the images hidden in a text such as Psalm 90:12 — "Teach us to number our days aright, that we may gain a heart of wisdom." In our review of the images in the Psalms, I suggested that Israel's experience at Kadesh Barnea is the background for this psalm (Num. 13–14). The days indeed were numbered for the older generation in Israel as they embarked on history's longest funeral march!

Yet, for each person born on earth, life is a funeral march. Even we believers will die unless the Lord returns in our lifetime and takes us to glory. But when we trusted Jesus Christ, He invited us to leave the funeral march and come to the wedding (Matt. 9:14-15); and that changed everything! Now we're waiting for the Bridegroom to appear so we can go to the wedding supper!

Most people don't really number their days "aright" because we count our *years* and not our days. We live a year at a time when everything else in the universe lives a day at a time. Too many people are like the successful businessmen that James wrote about, making grandiose plans and paying no attention to the authority of God's will or the reality of death (James 4:13-17). In preparing for one funeral service, I took time to calculate how many days the deceased person had lived; and when I mentioned this number in the message, it sounded like a terribly short time. If you want your days to count, then count your days.

Life is a school ("teach us") in which we must learn arithmetic ("to number our days aright") and practical wisdom ("gain a heart of wisdom"). "Above all else, guard your heart, for it is the wellspring of life" (Prov. 4:23). "My son, give me your heart" (Prov. 23:26). What a text to preach at the memorial service of an educator or a faithful Sunday School teacher! What an opportunity for the preaching of the Gospel!

Sometimes the vocation or even the hobby of the deceased can give us a hint for the message. At the funeral of an amateur gardener, I spoke about the three gardens in the Bible: the garden where sin entered (Eden); the garden where sin was defeated (Calvary; John 19:41); the garden where sin shall never enter (Rev. 21–22).[11] The memorial service for a carpenter focused on Jesus the carpenter who is building a home for His own in glory.[12] With so many luminous texts available in the Scriptures, we shouldn't be tempted to turn verses into mottoes by wresting them from their contexts. As you read and study the Word, texts will jump out at you; and you must add them to your notebook. By diligently cultivating what Blackwood called "the sermonic seed plot," you will always have a word in season for those who need encouragement.

"Though the view from my door was still more contracted,
I did not feel crowded or confined in the least.
There was pasture enough for my imagination."
—*Henry David Thoreau*

"Reason respects the differences,
and imagination the similitudes of things."
—*Percy Bysshe Shelley*

"The sky is the daily bread of the eyes."
—*Ralph Waldo Emerson*

"My imagination takes its strength
and guides its direction
from what I see and hear and learn
and feel and remember of my living world."
—*Eudora Welty*

Chapter Twenty-one
Messages for Special Days

S hortly before Thanksgiving, I asked a pastor friend what he planned to preach during Advent; and his reply was, "I haven't decided yet." My heart went out to his congregation.

It isn't enough for preachers to keep their eyes on the clock as they preach; they must also keep their eyes on the calendar as they plan and prepare to preach. We know that these special days are coming—they come every year—and we ought to be ready for them. This includes the calendar not only for the Christian church as a whole but also for the local church that you pastor.[1] I don't think that pastors and churches necessarily fall from grace if they commemorate special days as long as they focus on Jesus Christ and seek to honor Him. These celebrations are not essential to our salvation; and, if others prefer not to celebrate, so be it. There is room for loving disagreement even among the most devoted believers (Gal. 4:10; Rom. 14:1ff). I think it does a church good to review "salvation history" each year and to rejoice at what the Lord has done for His people.

I always planned an Advent series to celebrate our Lord's birth, and we recognized Epiphany as well. There was usually a Lenten series and, of course, I preached messages to commemorate Good Friday and Easter Sunday. I also felt that Pentecost, Trinity Sunday, and Reformation Sunday were important to the church. When you add to this list the important national holidays and special local church events, you soon end up with a full calendar. But if you plan ahead, you can usually work some of these special days into the regular course of your preaching; and you won't have to keep interrupting your expository series.[2]

Advent Preaching[3]

The first rule for Advent preaching is to resist every temptation to say something new and clever about Christmas. Instead, try to say the old truths in a fresh way and wrap each series in an exciting new package. In one of the churches I pastored, the staff decided to use some of the newer Christmas music in the worship services during Advent ("newer" meaning something written in the last half of the twentieth century), and the reaction of the congregation was shocking. We even received nasty notes from visitors! It was obvious that the people wanted to sing the familiar Christmas songs, although they were grudgingly willing to accept "newer music" from the choir.

One of my favorite Christmas series was called "Some Christmas Questions," and I tried to answer four of them: (1) "Why Bethlehem?" (2) "Why Shepherds?" (3) "Why a Manger?" (4) "Why a Savior?" It aroused interest and gained a respectful hearing.

The four songs of Christmas make an excellent series: the songs of Elizabeth (Luke 1:39-45), Mary (Luke 1:46-56), Zechariah (Luke 1:67-80), and the angels (Luke 2:13-14). For an after-Christmas message, you could add the song of Simeon (Luke 2:25-35). I once gave a series based entirely on Mary's song, and I called it "Mary's Christmas."[4]

Since Christmas has to do with the birth of a baby, we ought to consider some of the "birth announcements" that were involved. God gave the first announcement to our first parents in Genesis 3:15; Isaiah gave one to the Jewish nation in Isaiah 7:14; Gabriel gave one to Mary (Luke 1:26-38); and the angels gave one to the shepherds (Luke 2:1-20). This series gives you opportunity to deal with some of the broader aspects of biblical teaching about the coming of the Savior.

"Christmas is for children!" is the usual adult disclaimer of those in the family who really enjoy Christmas but don't want to admit it (or go shopping). Indeed, Christmas is for children; so let's preach about the two wonderful babies, John the Baptist and Jesus. (John rejoiced about Christmas even before he was born!) But Christmas is also for young people, the greatest example of which is Mary, the mother of our Lord. It's likely that she was a teenager when she gave birth to Jesus. Christmas is for busy adults, like shepherds and magi; and Christmas is also for older people like Zechariah, Elizabeth, Simeon, and Anna. If Christmas does nothing else, it helps to close the so-called generation gap!

When Prince William of England was only sixteen months old, he accidentally pushed the "panic button" at Balmoral Castle and sounded an alarm at the Aberdeen police headquarters. Of course, all of this gave the security agents a royal scare until they discovered what had happened. When I read that item in the newspaper, I thought of Christmas. We usually associate the birth of Christ with the angel's "fear not," and rightly so; but in sending His Son, God was also "pushing the panic button" and giving the world some warnings. Here is one poet's view:

I saw a stable low and very bare,
    A little child in a manger.

The oxen knew Him, had Him in their care,
    To men He was a stranger.
The safety of the world was lying there,
    And the world's danger.[5]

Christ's birth was a warning to Satan that the ancient prophecy was fulfilled (Gen. 3:15). The Parable of the Strong Man is a vivid description of what happened because Jesus was born (Luke 11:14-28). Satan, beware! But Christ's coming to earth was also a warning to proud, ruthless people that things were going to change. King Herod comes to mind (Matt. 2), and also Mary's words about those who are proud in her song of praise.

The birth of Jesus gave a warning to the proud leaders of Israel that God was reaching out to a whole world. Israel had been called to be the "servant of Jehovah" to witness to the Gentiles, but they had failed in their mission. Now God's Suffering Servant would come to die for the sins of the whole world, and the kingdom would be taken from Israel. "The Father has sent his Son to be the Savior of the world" (1 John 4:14).

There's also a warning to people today who haven't bowed the knee to Jesus Christ. There's danger ahead! Our Lord's words in John 15:18-25 are pertinent, and note especially His statement "If I had not come . . . " (v. 22). People who give a passing glance at Jesus Christ during Christmas, but who will not trust Him, don't hear the alarm ringing.

I probably wouldn't do it, but I'd be tempted to call a message series on these themes, "Danger! Christmas Is Coming!"

Lenten Preaching

The seven weeks preceding Good Friday and Easter Sunday have traditionally been set aside for believers to prepare themselves for "the fellowship of His sufferings" and the glory of His resurrection. Whether we devote all the Sundays to Lenten preaching is not important, but it is important that we use the opportunity to get our people ready for standing at the cross and visiting the empty tomb. Sunday worship attendance usually increases at this time of the year, affording us a splendid opportunity for evangelism.

Since biographical preaching can be very effective, why not consider preaching about some of the people involved in the passion narrative? The choices are many: Pilate, Herod, Annas and Caiaphas, Mary of Bethany, Nicodemus and Joseph of Arimathea, Simon of Cyrene and Judas.[6] You might also consider some of the personalities that we don't usually associate with the cross, but that have every right to be considered: Abraham and Isaac; Moses (the Passover lamb; the uplifted serpent); Ruth and Boaz (the kinsman redeemer); David (Christ's sufferings recorded in the psalms); Isaiah (the evangelical prophet); and the Apostle Paul.

In fact, you might want to bring together Old Testament and New Testament people and have them "meet at Calvary." Abraham could meet Mary, because both of them sacrificed a son. Moses could meet Nicodemus, whom Jesus told about the uplifted serpent (John 3:14); or Moses could meet John the Baptist and discuss the Passover lamb. Isaiah could meet Paul, who quoted frequently from Isaiah's prophecy and so magnified God's Suffering Servant. Annas and Caiaphas could meet Aaron the high priest and learn the real meaning of the Jewish sacrificial system. And don't forget Moses and Elijah talking about the cross with Jesus on the Mount of Transfiguration.

But how shall we imaginatively "package" such a series? We could borrow an idea from Clovis Chappell and call the series "The Cross Before Calvary."[7] Another possible title for the series is, "They Were There When They Crucified Our Lord — But Nobody Saw Them." Or, "Unseen People at the Cross."

The cross was not only a place for reconciliation, but it was also a place of substitution. Simon of Cyrene took the place of Simon Peter who boasted he would go with Jesus even to death. Jesus took the place of Barabbas, and He also took the place of every lost sinner. Nicodemus and Joseph of Arimathea took the place of the disciples who should have buried their Lord. (Of course, Isa. 53:9 had something to say about that.) The Apostle John took the place of Jesus when he "adopted" Mary as his own mother.

More than any of the Gospel writers, the Apostle John emphasizes the pictures of the death of Christ: the sacrificial lamb (1:29); the destroyed temple (2:13-25); the uplifted serpent (3:14); the willing shepherd (10:11-18); the fruitful seed (12:20-25). Note too that John records three instances when Jesus used the phrase "lifted up" (3:14; 8:28; 12:32).[8] We could do a series on the cross from John's Gospel alone.

My esteemed instructor in homiletics, Dr. Charles W. Koller, preached a powerful message on "The Living Plus Sign" that focused on the reconciling work of Christ on the cross.[9] Paul deals with the theology of this especially in Romans 4, 2 Corinthians 5, and Ephesians 2. On the cross, God reconciled love and justice, Jew and Gentile, and sinners and God. Today, the cross is still the means of reconciliation; and the word of the cross is the message of reconciliation that the church must herald abroad (2 Cor. 5:11-21).

What did the various actors in the Good Friday drama think about the cross? The Jewish religious leaders saw it as the solution to their problem of how to get rid of Jesus. Mary of Bethany saw His crucifixion as the fulfillment of God's will, and she prepared Jesus for His burial. Peter, you will remember, opposed the cross (Matt. 16:21-28) and in the garden used his sword to defend Jesus. Carrying the cross for Jesus was the depth of humiliation for Simon of Cyrene, yet the experience transformed his life (Mark 15:21). To Pilate, the cross was the only way to make the Jewish people happy, even though this weak politician tried to deliver Jesus from their hands. To Jesus, the cross was the Father's will; and He accepted it, endured it, and ultimately triumphed through it.

What was on the cross of Jesus? Well, to begin with, a sacrifice was there—the Lamb of God giving His life for the sins of the world. But Pilate's declaration was there (Matt. 27:37; Mark 15:26; Luke 23:38; John 19:19-22) and so was the "written code . . . that was against us" (Col. 2:14). And, amazingly, *every believer was there;* when Jesus died, we died with Him (Rom. 6).

Let's remind God's people of the profound theological aspects of the death of Christ. Because of the work of Christ on the cross, the world and the flesh are robbed of their power (Gal. 5:24; 6:12-18); and Satan has been defeated (John 12:31; Col. 2:15). These three enemies once controlled us (Eph. 2:1-3), but now they are disarmed.

It has been traditional in some churches during the Lenten season to focus on the seven statements of Christ from the cross or on the seven penitential psalms (Pss. 6, 32, 38, 51, 102, 130, 143). Either of these themes would be suitable if your church schedules a special weeknight service during Lent.

National Holidays

So many special days are marked on the calendar that the preacher sometimes wonders what to do with them: Mother's

Day, Father's Day,[10] Children's Day, Labor Day Sunday, Thanksgiving Sunday, Brotherhood Sunday, Independence Day, Human Rights Day, Armed Forces Day, Veteran's Day, President's Day, and on it goes. If you belong to a denomination that plans ahead, you may be expected to honor (each on its special day): home missions, foreign missions, retired missionaries, retired pastors, hospitals, children's homes, literature, and a host of ministries and projects that are worthy of attention and support.

What is the burdened expositor to do? I've already suggested that you can plan ahead and work the special emphasis into the regular course of your preaching. I did that once on Mother's Day, and a visiting mother accosted me after the service, telling me she'd never again set foot in our church. "Imagine not preaching a special message for mothers on Mother's Day!" Not everybody approves of this approach. If I had to do it over, I'd take time earlier in the service and honor the mothers present in a special way; and that way they'd get a double dose of recognition.

But there's another and more imaginative way to solve the problem. Stay with your text, *but look at it through the eyes of several mothers.* These can be biblical mothers, mothers from history, or mothers you have actually known.[11] The same approach can be used for your Father's Day message. Granted, not every text can be preached this way, but give it a try. Prepare the basic outline as though you were planning for a regular Sunday, and then "imagineer" the outline into a message that conveys the special emphasis.

One of the problems with Mother's Day, Father's Day, and Children's Day messages is that we're tempted to get sentimental and ignore the spiritual. The sermon then consists primarily of platitudes and poems, all loosely tied together with selected Scripture texts. Older preachers sometimes use the occasion for lamenting the good old days when mothers worked at home, fathers laid down the law, and children were seen and not heard. Younger preachers might be tempted to give thanks for the freedom that has come to the home, along with the new awareness of society to the hidden dangers that can lurk there.

Historians tell us that the good old days weren't really that good, and honest statisticians tell us that the horrors of the modern home aren't that frightening. Yes, there are abused wives and battered children; but there are also many happy families that enjoy each other and bring joy to others. Keep in mind that there are also single parents who carry many burdens, married couples who can't have children, and divorced people who sometimes feel lonely and unwanted in the average church. What shall we say to them? As always, the best approach is to emphasize the great truths of the Christian faith, truths that all our people should hear no matter what the day or what their marital status. And we must package these truths so that nobody feels left out of the picture.

In Scripture, children are pictured in several ways: as God's gracious gift (Gen. 33:4-5); as a heritage and as arrows (Ps. 127:3-5); as clusters of grapes and olive plants (Ps. 128:3); and as plants and cornerstones (Ps. 144:12). Alas, in some parts of society today, children are considered liabilities, not a heritage; and we dispose of them before they have a chance to pay us any dividends! But were it not for each new generation, how would we protect and transmit moral, spiritual, and cultural values? Children aren't the future of the church; they're the future *in the church right now.* Paul had this in mind when he wrote 2 Timothy 2:2.

The social world of women and children was different in Bible days, but the enduring spiritual values that make any home worthwhile are the same today as in Abraham's day: truth, love, discipline, worship, loyalty, sacrifice.[12] We don't have the fruits today because we lack the roots. We need to see our children as beautiful plants that need cultivation, treasures that must be protected, arrows that must be made straight and strong, cornerstones that will be ready for the building of homes yet to come. The imagery is certainly compelling!

Thanksgiving Sunday

Most pastors have little trouble preparing messages for Thanksgiving Sunday because there are scores of texts in Scripture that deal with praise and thanksgiving. However, sameness leads to tameness; and we ought to occasionally catch our people by surprise.

We usually remind the flock to be grateful for the blessings God has given, but have you ever considered the obligation of being thankful for things that God *hasn't done?* For example, have you ever been thankful for unanswered prayer? "So he gave them what they asked for, but sent a wasting disease upon them" (Ps. 106:15). Sometimes we think we're asking for bread when all the while we're asking for a stone, and the Father is too loving to give us what we ask. For other statements of things God hasn't done, for which we should be thankful, see Psalm 103:10, 1 Kings 8:56, 1 Thessalonians 5:9, and 2 Timothy 1:7. There are more, but these will get you started.

Have you ever preached on the theme "When God Gives Thanks"? Here are some texts that describe our Lord's thanksgivings when He was ministering on earth: John 6:11, 23; Luke 10:21 (Matt. 11:25-30); John 11:41; Matthew 26:26-27. Use your imagination and see what patterns can be found as you survey these passages.

"Political" Holidays

When it comes to Independence Day and the other "political holidays," pastors find themselves walking a knife's edge. Revisionist history has made some of our national heroes into rogues and their feats of valor into questionable activities at best. The older generation may revere them, the younger generation may reject them, and the preacher had better stay with the Bible and leave politics and history to the experts.

The major question, of course, is this: Can we apply to our own nation warnings and promises that were originally given only to the covenant nation of Israel? Is our native land in the same covenant relationship to the Lord as was Israel from the calling of Abraham to the coming of the Messiah? How you answer these questions will determine how you apply your selected texts. If basic principles of morality don't apply to all nations, then Amos 1–2 and Romans 1:18-32 are all wrong.

The great danger to avoid is preaching about a "nation" and forgetting that we're addressing only individuals. The nation isn't listening to us; and even if it were, changes in nations begin with changes within individuals, starting with God's people. We are the salt of the earth and the light of the world. If our nation is going to ruin, it's because sinners are acting like sinners (which you expect) and believers aren't acting like Christians (which you don't expect).[13] In a speech at Plymouth, Massachusetts, Dec. 22, 1820, Daniel Webster said, "Whatever makes men good Christians makes them good citizens." Keep that in mind when you prepare sermons that focus on national celebrations.[14]

David's pouring out the water in the cave (1 Chron. 11:15-19) is to me a perfect text for any anniversary that honors those who died for freedom. Each new generation is handed the cup of freedom. Do we use it for ourselves or do we give it to God in gratitude for the price others paid for us? Of course, it's but a short step from David's cup of water to our Lord's cup in the upper room and in the garden.

The next time you read the Book of Joshua, make a note of the various "memorials" that were raised, some bearing witness to great victories and others to tragic defeats. (See Josh. 4:9, 20-24; 7:26; 8:29-30, 32; 10:27; 22:10ff; 24:26-28.) Joshua's farewell speeches in chapters 23 and 24, and the memorial that he raised, offer the expositor many opportunities for preaching about the importance of individual commitment to God if the nation is to prosper. What a contrast between the monument to disobedient Achan (7:26) and the monument Joshua erected to the faithfulness of God and the promise of the people to obey Him! (24:26-28)

Church Anniversaries

I think that church anniversaries are important and ought to be celebrated annually. Each anniversary is an opportunity for the church family to "raise their Ebenezer" and joyfully confess, "Thus far has the Lord helped us" (1 Sam. 7:12).[15] The older generation enjoys recalling the past and the new generation needs to learn what happened before they arrived on the scene with their computers and credit cards. The focus must not be simply on past history but on the God of the past, the God of our fathers who has been our refuge and help all these years.

My predecessor at the Moody Church in Chicago, Dr. George Sweeting, started a new tradition there when he and the church established "Founder's Day," a day to honor Dwight Lyman Moody and the Lord who used him so mightily. Sometimes we brought in guest speakers, but they were always cautioned to relate their message in some way to the heritage of Moody Church. One year I preached from Mr. Moody's life text, 1 John 2:17; and another year I used Mr. Moody's favorite psalm, Psalm 91. It was challenging to study his life and discover those texts that meant the most to him.

> **An anniversary message should both remind us of God's goodness in the past and challenge us to the task He has assigned for us for the future.**

Some anniversary messages can be related to people who were a part of the church; other messages can be tied to events. If you've done your research and know the key events in the life of the church, then you can find the messages in those events and "raise your Ebenezer."[16]

An anniversary message should both remind us of God's goodness in the past and challenge us to the task He has assigned for us for the future. An effective anniversary celebration must always say "Hats off to the past—coats off to the future!" Otherwise, the church may find itself looking in a rearview mirror and plowing crooked furrows.

Some of the images of the church offer rich possibilities for anniversary preaching. The church is a bride, and every married couple knows what it means to celebrate one anniversary after another, to grow in devotion to each other, and to plan for the future. As a bride, does the church still rejoice at hearing the bridegroom's voice? (John 3:29) Are we still enjoying "honeymoon love" with our Lord? (Jer. 2:1-2; Rev. 2:1-4) Are we true to Him so we'll be ready to meet Him when He comes? (2 Cor. 11:1-6)

Sometimes *change* is the thing to emphasize in an anniversary message, particularly if the church has quietly been resisting change. Paul's three pictures of the church in 1 Corinthians 9:7 offer some tempting ideas on this theme. Vineyards and flocks have been around for centuries, and what they do hasn't changed. If you want grapes, you have to cultivate vines; if you want wool and milk and meat, you have to tend a flock. Some things don't change.

But today's armies aren't using bows and arrows or slings and stones. Military leaders make use of the latest technology as they seek to keep our nation free. Some things do change. The famous prayer of Reinhold Niebuhr certainly applies here: "O God, give us serenity to accept what cannot be changed, courage to change what should be changed, and wisdom to distinguish the one from the other."[17]

"The difference between the right word
and the nearly right word
is the same as that between lightning
and the lightning bug."
—*Mark Twain*

"Originality is simply a pair of fresh eyes."
—*T.W. Higginson*

"A life lived without fantasy and day-dreams
is a seriously impoverished one."
—*Eugene Raudsepp*

Chapter Twenty-two
Imagination, Humor, and Preaching

araphrasing William Wordsworth's famous definition of poetry,[1] James Thurber defined humor as "emotional chaos remembered in tranquility."[2] The contrast between "chaos" and "tranquility" suggests that humor and paradox go together, and we've already learned that paradox usually involves metaphor and imagination. A humorist has been described as "a person who can see more than one thing at a time," and this also can be said of those who do the laughing. Eva Feder Kittay claims that "metaphor results in the placing of an object in two perspectives simultaneously."[3] Conclusion: humor depends largely on imagination.

For example, if during a rainstorm you saw a truck splash mud on a poor aged woman waiting for a bus, you'd be sympathetic and would probably hurry over to help her. But if the same thing happened to a pompous aristocrat, cane in hand and nose in the air, waiting for his limousine, you'd probably laugh first and afterward offer to help him. The contrast between his elegant clothing and a mud bath, and his pompous attitude and the humbling accident, would create in your imagination that simultaneous "placing of an object in two perspectives" that Kittay wrote about; and this would make the situation comical.[4]

From clowns and stand-up comedians to the most erudite wits, humorists depend on *unexpected contrast* to make us laugh.[5] I've seen Victor Borge, both on video and in person, pull a seat belt out of his piano bench; and each time I've seen it, I've laughed. Even now, just thinking about it makes me smile. But humorous contrasts can be *verbal* as well as *visual,* and most funny stories depend on listeners (or readers) "viewing" the story in their imagination. When somebody says, "I don't see what's so funny about that," the statement may say more about the listener's lack of imagination than about the speaker's lack of ability to tell a funny story. Appreciating humor depends on our ability to "see" contrasts and paradoxes in the imagination.[6]

I especially enjoy traditional rabbinical humor. A rabbi was awakened one night by a sound in the house and asked, "Who's there?" A voice from the shadows replied, "A burglar." "What are you looking for?" asked the rabbi, and the voice replied, "Money." The rabbi said, "Wait, I'll get up and help you!"

That isn't the reply we expected, but that's what makes the story funny. "My wife spent four hours at the beauty parlor today," says the comedian, "and that was just for the estimate." We laugh. Why? Because you don't go to a beauty parlor for an estimate, and the woman who does so must be in need of a major makeover. You take a wrecked car to a garage to get an estimate on the repairs, and an ugly wife and a wrecked car are two different things. But that's what humor is all about: the ability to see more than one thing at a time. "Humor confronts us with the incongruous in our lives," writes Philip S. Keane,[7] and the ability to see the incongruous and even laugh at it is a mark of emotional maturity.

But enough of this. "Humor can be dissected, as a frog can," wrote E.B. White, "but the thing dies in the process and the innards are discouraging to any but the pure scientific mind."[8] If you have a sense of humor, you know what I'm talking about; and if you don't have a sense of humor, what I say isn't likely to change you.[9]

What does all of this have to do with preaching? It appears to me that a good sense of humor is often the mark of a creative person whose imagination is functioning in a healthy way. People with a sense of humor take God's work seriously, but they don't take themselves seriously; and they've learned to laugh at their achievements as well as their mistakes. The Bible is not a joke book, but there's humor in the Bible, and the interpreter had better be able to identify it and discover why it's there.[10]

Often biblical humor takes the form of irony or satire, such as Isaiah's descriptions of the manufacturing of idols (Isa. 40:18-20; 41:5-7; and especially 44:9-20) or our Lord's exposé of the Pharisees (Matt. 23). Paul used a similar approach when writing about the "super-apostles" (2 Cor. 11) and the legalists (Phil. 3:1-2), and the Lord God took this approach when speaking to Job (Job 38).[11]

> **People with a sense of humor take God's work seriously, but they don't take themselves seriously; and they've learned to laugh at their achievements as well as their mistakes.**

If the Holy Spirit saw fit to write humor into the Scriptures, does this give us the freedom to use it in our preaching? *If humor is natural to the preacher, then it should be used in preaching; but one must never "import" jokes just to make the congregation laugh.* "Humor involves the perception of the true proportions of life," said Phillips Brooks. "It is one of the most helpful qualities that the preacher can possess."[12] The preacher is not a comedian, but if the use of true humor will help him get his message across, then he's wise to make use of his talent.

"When Spurgeon was cheerful and humorous in the pulpit," wrote Helmut Thielicke, "he was putting himself into his preaching; he was entering into the sermon with his whole nature. He who wants the interest of his hearers and wants them to be 'in it' must first be in it himself. . . . A church is in a bad way when it banishes laughter from the sanctuary and leaves it to the cabaret, the night club, and the toastmasters."[13]

The whole person must be in the pulpit, sanctified and empowered by the Spirit of God. If the preacher has a sense of humor, then it must be given to God as well. "The humor of one preacher may be as reverent as the solemnity of another," said William Jewett Tucker.[14] But we must be careful to exercise discernment, especially when "something funny" enters our mind. More than one preacher has been embarrassed by the frigid silence of a congregation that was supposed to be laughing.

The whole person must be in the pulpit, sanctified and empowered by the Spirit of God. If the preacher has a sense of humor, then it must be given to God as well.

If in your devotional reading you've used *My Utmost for His Highest* by Oswald Chambers, you may be surprised to learn that Chambers had a marvelous sense of humor and used it in his preaching. One man called Chambers "the most irreverent Reverend" he had ever met. But Oswald Chambers wasn't a clown. He used humor to prepare the way for the reception of the Word. One listener said to him, "Ah, I see! Your jokes and lightheartedness plough the land, then you put in the seed."[15] To change the image, the Word of God is the arrowhead; but humor can be the feathers on the shaft that help the arrow reach its target.

Humor, then, can help us better understand the message of the Bible; and the right kind of humor in our preaching can make it easier for our listeners to receive that message. A sense of humor enables us to face life with courage because we see things in perspective, and this can give balance to our messages. Instead of always radiating inflexible, sunny optimism which is far from biblical faith, or exhibiting constant pessimism and gloom, our messages will reflect the healthy balance of the believer who is a realist, who sees God on the throne even when truth seems to be dangling from the gallows.

If you still doubt that serious theology and a sense of humor can be allies in the battle for truth, take time to read C.S. Lewis' *The Screwtape Letters*. "Humor involves a sense of proportion and a power of seeing yourself from the outside," Lewis wrote in his preface to that classic book. We need to take those words seriously.

"The task of the artist is to sense more keenly
than others the harmony of the world,
the beauty and the outrage of what man has done to it,
and poignantly, to let people know."

—*Alexander Solzhenitsyn*

"Imagination is more important than knowledge."

—*Albert Einstein*

Chapter Twenty-three
Imagination and Evangelistic Preaching

A ll preaching should be evangelistic. No matter what the content of the sermon, the intent must be to magnify Christ and tell people what He did for them on the cross. Regardless of our text or theme, we must preach Jesus Christ. When you read Paul's epistles, you soon discover that he was able to relate the cross of Christ to the most practical matters of life: giving (2 Cor. 8:9), forgiving (Eph. 4:32), citizenship (Titus 3:1-8), brotherly love (Eph. 5:2), and the love of husbands and wives (Eph. 5:25). The message of the cross is both good news for lost sinners outside the church and good spiritual motivation for saved sinners inside the church. We never outgrow our need for the story of the cross.

Some of God's people have the gift of evangelism (Eph. 4:11), but all of us in ministry should "do the work of an evangelist" (2 Tim. 4:5). The Spirit wants to empower all of us to be witnesses to and for Jesus Christ (Acts 1:8), for it is Jesus Christ that sinners need to know.[1]

The images of the evangelist in Scripture help us understand the plight of the sinner and the ministry of the believer. According to Proverbs 11:30, Christians are to be hunters who "win souls." The Hebrew word translated "wins" (*laqah*) is used nearly a thousand times in the Old Testament and primarily means "to take, to seize, to snatch," like a hunter capturing game. It's used to describe Absalom "stealing the hearts" of the Jewish people (2 Sam. 15:6) and the harlot "capturing" her prey with her alluring eyes (Prov. 6:25). Proverbs 11:30 isn't suggesting that we use violence to win lost souls but rather that we exercise skill and practical wisdom, just as a hunter does in catching game. We must use the right bait if we hope to catch our prey.

When Jesus said to Saul of Tarsus, "It is hard for you to kick against the goads" (Acts 26:14), He may have been suggesting that Saul was like a raging animal as he persecuted the church, "breathing out murderous threats" (Acts 9:1). We noticed the spiritual significance of animals when we surveyed Psalms 22 and 32 (chap. 11), and it's worth noting that Paul described himself as "a violent man" in his unconverted days (1 Tim. 1:13).

Along with the image of the *hunter* is that of the *fisherman,* an image that we discussed in chapter 13 when we looked at the familiar phrase "fishers of men" (Mark 1:17). Satan "baits the hook" with attractive temptations (James 1:14, where "enticed" [*deleazo*] carries the image of "luring with bait"), and we must be wise to find the right approach when "catching" the lost. However, we must take care not to present the Gospel in such a way that we resort to trickery and flattery (1 Thes. 2:1-6). There are presentations of the Gospel that are unworthy of the Gospel, and we must avoid them. Witnessing is not the same as "Christian salesmanship."

The evangelist is like a *shepherd* who searches for a lost sheep (Luke 15:1-7; Matt. 18:11-14), or a *woman* who searches for a lost coin (Luke 15:8-10). The sheep was lost because of heedlessness, for sheep are stupid creatures who easily go astray; but the coin was lost because of somebody's carelessness. "Lostness" for the sheep meant being away from the flock, away from the place of safety and care; but for the coin, "lostness" meant being "out of circulation" and therefore without value. When we're apart from Christ, life is wasted; but when we belong to Christ, life is invested.

It's worth noting in Luke 15 that, though the shepherd searched for the lost sheep and the woman for the lost coin, *the father didn't go looking for his wayward son.* He stayed home and waited; and when the boy returned, he ran and welcomed him (Luke 15:11ff).[2] The son was lost because of selfishness and willfulness, and the father waited for him to "come to his senses." The parables in Luke 15 seem to balance divine sovereignty and human responsibility: God searches for the lost sinner (Luke 19:10), but the sinner must also say, "I will arise and go!" The imaginative evangelist, meditating on Luke 15, can discover many truths about what it means to be lost, what it means to be found, and why being found brings so much joy.

The image of the *harvester* is found frequently in Scripture and we've noted many of these references in our survey. The Parable of the Sower and the Parable of the Weeds in Matthew 13 are foundational texts for an understanding of the "harvest" image. If the human heart is like soil, then it must be prepared for the seed. If the Word of God is like seed, then it must be planted before it can bear fruit. Jesus makes it clear that when the Word is received and understood, then the heart is changed and starts to produce fruit. The harvest image also reminds us that the laborers must work together (John 4:34-35; 1 Cor. 3:5-9). There's no competition among people who have a burden to reach lost sinners. God assigns the work, God gives the increase, and God gets the glory.

Zechariah 3:2 and Jude 23 combine to picture the evangelist as *one who pulls people out of the fire.*[3] In order to succeed, the hunter and fisherman must exercise wisdom and skill, the shepherd must have courage and determination, and the farmer must be patient and wait for the harvest; but the "fireman" must sense the urgency of the situation and take risks in order to save lives. Lost sinners are already condemned (John 3:18), but God in His mercy has postponed the executing of the sentence.

Images of Heaven and Hell

One of the questions troubling the church today is whether or not a God of love would condemn lost sinners to an eternity of punishment. The images Jesus used of hell included fire, worms, darkness, separation, and pain (Matt. 5:22; 13:42, 49-50; 18:8-9; 22:13; 25:30, 41; Mark 9:42-50; Luke 16:19-31), images that are found in the prophets (e.g., Isa. 66:24) and the writings of the apostles (2 Thes. 1:8-9; Rev. 20:10). The word "Gehenna" that Jesus used referred to the garbage dump outside Jerusalem in the valley that had once been used for the sacrifice of little children to pagan gods. *Hell is an eternal garbage dump where the waste of the universe is deposited.*[4]

Now, this awful fact of eternal judgment shouldn't make God's people happy, because it doesn't make God happy (Ezek. 18:23, 32; 33:11). Rather, the reality of hell should motivate us to examine our own hearts to be sure of our relationship to God;[5] the fact of hell should make us want to share the Gospel with as many lost people as possible. No matter how unattractive they may be to the world, saved people are "God's workmanship" (Eph. 2:10) and will never be thrown on the trash heap. No matter how attractive and successful lost people may be in this world, they will be eternally rejected like common rubbish.

But how does the concerned preacher address the subject of hell from the pulpit today? Does the vast unsaved public take hell seriously?[6] Perhaps not, and for several reasons. For one thing, theological liberalism and religious illiteracy have so diluted both the seriousness of sin and the reality of divine wrath that the man or woman on the street, untaught and unconcerned, prefers not to worry too much about hell. They agree with the immigrant who wrote on a wall at Ellis Island, "Why should I fear the fires of Hell? I have been through Ellis Island!" This caricature of Satan and hell is prevalent in the media today, and things caricatured aren't usually taken seriously. A popular comedian was sure of laughs every time he said, "The devil made me do it!"

Another factor in the modern rejection of hell is the injustice that people witness in their world. Good people suffer and evil people prosper, and the legal loopholes are large enough to provide escape hatches for the biggest offenders. "Truth forever on the scaffold, wrong forever on the throne." If God isn't exercising His holy justice in *this* world, why should we worry about justice in the *next* world?[7]

There's a sense in which modern science has contributed to

the modern abandonment of a belief in the existence of hell. The psychiatrist may tell us that we're basically victims of our upbringing and not responsible for what we do. Therefore, we're not subject to judgment. We're only bundles of hidden desires, woven by our parents and teachers and other influential people in our lives; and if anybody's to blame, they are. Then the evolutionist tells us that we're basically animals and that only the "fit" survive; so if we do "evil" and still survive, it must be good. Personal responsibility, accountability, and morality end up on the scaffold in the name of scientific progress.

Some people have abandoned the idea of eternal judgment because of the way they've heard it preached. While fear is certainly a legitimate tool of learning, it must be balanced with love. Parents warn their children about the dangers of busy streets, fire, poisons, and electricity; and they give these warnings to their children because they love them. Furthermore, parents will do everything they can to encourage their children to obey. God's warnings of judgment certainly come from a heart of love; but if that love is rejected, He has no other alternative but to punish. Let us never preach about hell as though we're glad people are going there!

Whenever in a sermon we deal with eternal judgment, we must imaginatively anticipate the objections that will arise in the minds of our listeners.

Furthermore, let's not preach about hell in such a melodramatic fashion that we go beyond the simple statements of Scripture, which are vivid enough without our embellishment.[8] The liberals have accused the orthodox of majoring on "the temperature of hell and the furniture of heaven"; and for some preachers, the accusation may be true. But the images of eternal punishment used in Scripture speak of realities so terrible that every sane person would want to avoid them, and the images of eternal blessing describe joys so gloriously magnificent that every sane person would want to experience them. Every major doctrine in Scripture impinges in some way on the facts of heaven and hell, so the doctrines can't honestly be avoided and certainly shouldn't be diluted.

283

Whenever in a sermon we deal with eternal judgment, we must imaginatively anticipate the objections that will arise in the minds of our listeners. "What about God's love?" (His love is a holy love.) "Surely judgment won't last forever!" (Do you want heaven to be temporary?) "If I were God, I wouldn't allow hell to exist!" (Would you want justice to exist? And are you sure you see sin the way God sees it?) "But what about the Cross?" (The Cross shows that God loves sinners but also that God hates sin. The Cross reveals the sinfulness of sin.) "The existence of hell seems to say that God is defeated." (No, the existence of hell shows His omnipotence; for only an all-powerful God could give human beings the responsibility of choice and still accomplish His great purposes.) In *The Problem of Pain,* C.S. Lewis reminds us that "the doors of hell are locked on the *inside.*"[9]

Images of Salvation

The pictures of salvation in Scripture are many and varied, and they offer the preacher numerous opportunities to present Christ to lost sinners. To cite but a few, trusting Jesus Christ is like: walking through a gate (Matt. 7:13-14) or a door (John 10:9); enjoying a bountiful feast (Luke 14:16-23); coming home to love and plenty (Luke 15:11ff); taking a drink of water (John 4:13-14; 7:37-39); receiving a gift (Rom. 6:23); taking a bath (1 Cor. 6:9-11); depositing money in a bank (2 Tim. 1:12);[10] or putting on a change of clothes (Luke 5:36; Isa. 61:10). Each of these pictures, and many more that I didn't cite, can easily be related to life today to help the unbeliever see the reality and simplicity of salvation.

Let's take the image of the strait gate and the narrow road that Jesus used in the Sermon on the Mount (Matt. 7:13-14).[11] Except to people in rural congregations, the picture isn't a familiar one; for very few city dwellers use footpaths through the fields. But the message is clear even if the image isn't familiar: you can't go to heaven on your own terms. When you trust Jesus Christ, you must leave behind all the baggage that you've been carrying, because it won't fit through the gate. This fact implies both joy and pain: joy, because we can get rid of the sins that have burdened us; pain, because we must repent and forsake the things that we think we enjoy and need.

The question that Jesus doesn't answer is, "Where is the narrow road located with respect to the broad road that leads to destruction?" Are the two roads parallel so that, as we "march to Zion," we see people going in the opposite direction and we try to win them? Or does the narrow road run right down the middle of the broad road, so that believers have both opposition and opportunity as they travel toward heaven? I opt for the second interpretation. I can't prove it by exegeting the passage, but it seems to agree with what the Bible teaches about the believer's relationship to the world. "We must go through many hardships to enter the kingdom of God" (Acts 14:22).

It doesn't take a great deal of imagination to picture the two roads in contemporary terms. What would happen on a modern superhighway if a driver decided to cross the median and start driving in the opposite direction against the traffic? Or suppose this driver entered the highway on the exit ramp and refused to pull over or turn around? I've read about confused or inebriated persons who have done just that and have caused fatal accidents. Jesus tells us, however, that on this road going against the traffic is the way to save your life!

Most of us resent the person who runs up the down escalator or tries to go to the rear of the airplane while the passengers are trying to get out. Going the wrong way on a one-way street is not an unpardonable sin, but it comes close to qualifying. As we walk down the middle of the broad road, we meet lost people face to face; and our task as witnesses is to warn them that the map they're using is all wrong and the destination they're heading for is named Destruction.

> **"Imagineering" a text means trying to see it in a contemporary setting and identifying in it images that speak to people today.**

"Imagineering" a text means trying to see it in a contemporary setting and identifying in it images that speak to people

285

today. We must take care, though, in presenting this contemporary image (i.e., the superhighway), that we don't abandon the original image or alter it to suit our purposes, because we're preaching God's Word and not our own ideas. The modern equivalent is the point of contact for the text and never a substitute for the text.

Take, for example, the image of receiving a gift (Rom. 6:23; Eph. 2:8; Rev. 22:17). Most people are acquainted with offers of "valuable free gifts" through mail and media promotion, and most people are suspicious of them. Why? Because by the time you do everything the promoters ask you to do, you end up with a "gift" that's cheap in value but expensive in cost. Is God's offer of salvation that kind of a scam? If eternal life is a free gift, who paid for it? What must I do to receive it? Will God ever ask me to give it back? Only rooting our discussion in God's Word disposes of these problems.

There's nothing wrong with presenting the good news of the Gospel in pictures. After all, the first announcement of the Gospel involved a good deal of imagery: "And I will put enmity between you and the woman, and between your offspring and hers; he will crush your head, and you will strike his heel" (Gen. 3:15). Here we see pictured two enemies, two families, and two wounds, images that are repeated frequently in the Bible and climax in the Book of Revelation.

The theological vocabulary of the Bible abounds in pictures. *Justification* takes us into the law court where the criminal is declared righteous. *Redemption* belongs to the slave market where the helpless chattel is purchased and set free. Atonement, adoption, imputation, ransom, reconciliation, and remission can all be identified with everyday images in the Bible world. Our task is to help our listeners see these images, understand them, and then apply to their own situation the spiritual truths that the pictures reveal.

In seeking to win the lost, our Lord used imaginative approaches that took advantage of circumstances (John 4), criticisms (Luke 5:27-39), interruptions (Luke 12:13-21; 14:15-24), and even national observances (John 7:37-39). The creative preacher and witness can do the same.

"The Possible's slow fuse is lit by the Imagination."
—*Emily Dickinson*

"We have all become so scientific
that there is but little room left for imagination.
This, to me, is most regrettable,
because imagination in preaching is most important
and most helpful. I am very ready to agree
that it can be dangerous; but imagination,
let us not forget, is a gift of God."
—*D. Martyn Lloyd-Jones*

"If you would learn to write,
'tis in the street you must learn it. . . .
The people, and not the college, is the writer's home."
—*Ralph Waldo Emerson*

Chapter Twenty-four
Imagination and Creativity

A t the beginning of our quest, we met Hushai and Ahithophel and learned from them something about words and the "picture gallery" of the human mind. Now, as we near the end of our quest, we need to get acquainted with Bezalel and Oholiab and listen to what they have to teach us about creativity in the service of the Lord.

In case you've forgotten, Bezalel and Oholiab were the two craftsmen God chose to supervise and implement the artistic work involved in the building of the tabernacle (Ex. 35:30-35). Because they were filled with the Spirit of God, they had the required "skill, ability, and knowledge" for following God's plans and making the tabernacle the way He wanted it. These two men encourage me because they remind me that the Holy Spirit is able to help us use our abilities to work creatively for the glory of God. *Imagination and creativity should be a normal part of the Spirit-filled life.*

At this point, you probably want to raise two objections.

Objection #1—"But Bezalel and Oholiab had a God-given pattern to follow, and the Israelites brought them more than enough material to work with. When we prepare sermons, we have to find our own material and develop our own pattern. What kind of encouragement is that?"

Never minimize the power of the Holy Spirit in your life! He is "able to do immeasurably more than all we ask or imagine, according to his power that is at work within us" (Eph. 3:20).

Some of us need to "fan into flame the gift of God" (2 Tim. 1:6) and trust the Spirit to use our training, skills, and studies in creative ways to the glory of the Lord. After all, if the Holy Spirit enabled Bezalel and Oholiab to make a *material* building for ministry to His people, shouldn't He be able to help us prepare messages that will help edify the saints and build the *spiritual* temple? (Eph. 2:19-22)

Objection #2—"I'm just not the creative type. I don't have much of an imagination."

Who told you that?

"Imagination grows by exercise and contrary to common belief is more powerful in the mature than in the young," wrote novelist W. Somerset Maugham in *The Summing Up;* and I agree with him. If you and I are created in the image of God, and if God is infinitely original, then surely He can help us be creative too. If the mind He put within us is a picture gallery that responds to the world He put around us, then we must have the ability needed to think and act creatively. The problem isn't that we lack imagination but that we haven't exercised it as we should.

"Are You Creative?" is the title of the cover story of *Business Week* for September 30, 1985; the subtitle reads, "Research Shows That Creativity Can Be Taught—and Companies Are Listening." The article describes the work of three "gurus" who are preaching "the gospel of creativity," including Roger von Oech, "The Creativity Consultant of Silicon Valley" and author of *A Whack on the Side of the Head,* a best-selling primer on creative thinking. "By the age of 40," says the article, "most adults are about 2% as creative as they were at 5"; and the blame is put on modern education that "stresses logic [and] seems to squelch creativity."[1]

So, the first step toward a more creative ministry is to thank the Lord for giving you an imagination and to ask Him to help you exercise that imagination so that it will be used by the Spirit as a powerful creative force in your life. Each morning, in my own personal devotional time, I yield my body, mind, will, heart, and imagination to the Lord (Rom. 12:1-2) and ask Him to use me to be a transformer, not a conformer, and a creator, not a destroyer. Whether I'm studying, preaching, writing, counseling, or chatting with friends, I want my imagination to enrich me and help me have the insights I need to minister at my best.

Granted, some people have greater gifts in this area than do others; but all of us can still do a better job of using what we have for the glory of God. If that 2 percent imagination were increased to only 10 percent, we'd have five times the creativity we used to have; and that's a giant step forward!

"I've read several articles on creativity and I just don't think I qualify," somebody protests. "I don't have the marks of a creative person."[2]

I've read some of those articles. However, I rate most of them as helpful as those Sunday supplement tests—"Are You Fit to Own a Parrot?" or "Are You a Closet Kleptomaniac?" Applying "pop" psychology to the challenges of life is something like trying to nail shadows to the wall, and I wouldn't worry about it too much if I were you. Rest assured that you have an imagination, you can learn to exercise it more effectively, and the Lord will help you do it.

How do we as preachers and teachers of God's Word develop the imagination and use it to serve the Lord? Let me answer that question by suggesting these ideas:

1. Creativity is a way of life and not just a series of techniques applied to a specific challenge. In their desire to be creative, too many people look for guaranteed formulas and quick shortcuts instead of following the disciplines that make for a creative life. Whether you're learning to swim, to speak Swedish, or to bake a cake, you start by obeying certain time-tested rules that everybody follows; *and you don't break the rules until first the rules have broken you.*

Once such principles become a part of your inner person, they will liberate you and enable you to practice them creatively in your own way. People who are *dominated* by rules become imitators; people who are *liberated* by rules become innovators. Rules have to be digested and become "second nature" to us before they can do us much good. Once the rules

291

are digested, they help us develop a creative lifestyle that seems to ignore the rules but actually never forsakes them.

Creativity is the result of the imagination bringing together both science and art and allowing them to interact.[3] Creativity is both left-brain and right-brain, both analysis and synthesis. Analysis deals primarily with facts and concepts, synthesis with truths and pictures. The scientist in you takes the text apart (exegesis) and the poet in you puts it back together (homiletics) so that concepts become pictures and information becomes motivation.

> **Creativity is the result of the imagination bringing together both science and art and allowing them to interact. Creativity is both left-brain and right-brain, both analysis and synthesis.**

So, you do your homework, exegete the text, and gather all the information you can. You "brood over it" and look for pictures and relationships that help explain and apply the text. Then you step aside for a time of "incubation" when your inner faculties, guided by God's Spirit, are free to "process" the information you've studied. Often during this "incubation period," ideas and insights will come unbidden, and these, of course, must be tested by the truth of Scripture. There are times, however, when gestation and delivery are slow and painful. Be patient and prayerful at these times, and avoid panic. Pressure smothers creativity, so be sure to give yourself enough time for sermon preparation.

I repeat: creativity is a way of life, and only you know the best schedule to make for accomplishing the work God has given you to do. When you find yourself pressured by the calendar and sense that the creative juices are drying up, evaluate your schedule and see if you don't need to start saying no to some invitations and opportunities. In my own ministry, I've found that the regular preparation of weekly messages for the church family was the best thermometer for testing my spiritual life and my daily schedule. When preparing messages started to become a secondary burden instead of a joyful priority, I knew something was wrong with the schedule; and I had to start saying no. *If you want to be a creative preacher of the Word, you and the Lord must control your schedule; and there will always be a price to pay.* We don't choose merely between the good and the bad; we choose between the better and the best.

2. The creative lifestyle is balanced. The eccentric "mad professor" or "oddball poet" is often a pose or a caricature; for while there may be exceptions, truly creative people are normal and balanced. However, most of them do have certain traits in common.

For one thing, they're alert and pay attention to life around them. They use their eyes and ears and other senses to "take in" the people and circumstances around them and learn all they can. They "breathe" experience the way mammals breathe air. Short-story writer Eudora Welty said, "My imagination takes its strength and guides its direction from what I see and hear and learn and feel and remember of my living world."[4] To paraphrase poet John Ciardi, "The preacher's task is not to talk about experience, but to make it happen."[5] But the preacher who steers himself against the experiences of life will have a difficult time making the Christian experience described in the Bible real to others. To the creative person, no experience is a wasted experience.[6]

Creative people get the most out of life's experiences, both happy and tragic, because they pay attention; they look and listen; they "drop their guard" and, like little children, wonder and marvel unashamed. They aren't afraid to use their senses or to express their feelings.[7] While other people are aiming cameras or camcorders, making records to look at later, creative people are first *living the scene* and imbibing its elements with all their senses. Only after they've done that will they get the cameras out of the car and take pictures; and when they view the pictures later, it's mainly to recreate experiences and not to remember places.[8]

I said before that the lifestyle of creative people is balanced. Creative people work hard, but they also know when to get away from their work and devote time to play and relaxation.[9] In fact, play and rest are a part of the creative process. When we're relaxing after the mind has been hard at work, the imagination often starts to produce exactly what we were looking for. It isn't enough that we gather information and study it. We must also take time for incubation, when the inner person can digest the material and give the imagination opportunity to make something out of it.[10] Creative people never consider relaxation a waste of time.

The busy schedule of the "pastoral CEO" can be the greatest enemy of creativity in ministry, no matter how successful the pastor's work may appear to the watching church. If you don't have margins to your life, you have no room for growth; and without growth, there can be little or no creativity. The worker can be pressured, but the creative artist demands leisure.[11] When I was in the pastorate, I usually took Thursday as a day off. I found that the change of pace helped to accelerate the creative juices, and often I would awaken on Friday morning with the outline of the Sunday message nicely developed in my mind. After hours of intense study and concentration, that brief incubation period gave my imagination just the margin it needed to do something creative.

The minister's annual vacation should be a time of re-creation as well as recreation. (Too often the annual holiday gets so demanding it becomes wreck-reation!) Body, mind, and spirit need refreshing and renewal, but at the same time the relaxing minister must be alert to capture ideas that will start to appear. During vacation, I usually carried a 3 x 5 card in my pocket so I could write down the ideas that came to me while my body was resting but my imagination was still at work, not only sermon ideas but ideas for whole series of messages. Once you develop a creative lifestyle, ideas will come to you at unexpected moments; and you'd better be able to hold on to them.

No two people are identical when it comes to work habits, and only you can determine when you are at your creative best. I happen to be a morning person and can get more work done between 6 A.M. and noon than at any other time of the day, but some of my creative friends burn the midnight oil. The British writer and critic Samuel Johnson could write a masterful essay thirty minutes before the printer needed it, and Charles

Spurgeon prepared his Sunday evening message on Sunday afternoon after his nap. You must dare to be yourself—your *best* self—and plan to do your creative work when you function best.

There are times when the preacher just needs to get away for mental and emotional "ventilation." Blessed are those churches that give their pastors occasional mini-sabbaticals and full sabbaticals, because they're investing not only in the welfare of the pastor and his family, but also in the welfare of the entire congregation. We "get away," not to escape, but to be able to come back with new perspective. Many a weary pastor, drained of his creative juices, would have been saved from a premature resignation if he had only taken time off for re-creation.

3. *Creative people are readers.* Like any other human faculty, the imagination must be "fed" if it's to be healthy and strong. If the imagination isn't nourished with the best, it will turn to the worst; and the worst will defile it and debilitate it. Creative ministers feed their imagination by what they hear, see, read, and ponder; and reading is a particularly important source of nourishment.

You'll recall that one of the functions of imagination is the building of bridges, the relating of things to each other that seemingly have no relationship at all. Because of this, it's important that we read widely and not focus only on authors we agree with or books that relate specifically to our work. Cer-

When I read a book, I often use a 3 x 5 card for a bookmark so I'll have something to write on when ideas spring out of my reading. I usually keep a dozen or so books "working" on my reading shelf, and I read them as I feel motivated, depending on my mood and the time available. I don't feel compelled to complete a book in any given amount of time; in fact, I might not complete the book at all. I've learned that books are tools, and a tool that helps one worker may not help another.

295

tainly the expositor must specialize in biblical studies; but if that's the only diet we get, our imagination may find itself painfully undernourished. I've discovered that even the comics can give my imagination something to chew on![12] When you develop a creative lifestyle, you find yourself discovering insights and ideas in the most unexpected places.

When I read a book, I often use a 3 x 5 card for a bookmark so I'll have something to write on when ideas spring out of my reading. I usually keep a dozen or so books "working" on my reading shelf, and I read them as I feel motivated, depending on my mood and the time available. I don't feel compelled to complete a book in any given amount of time; in fact, I might not complete the book at all.[13] I've learned that books are tools, and a tool that helps one worker may not help another.

There are the "books of the hour" and the "books of the ages," and the creative reader is careful to keep a balance. I've never found it necessary to read all the bestsellers, secular or religious, or all the classics that my professors told me I couldn't live without.[14] It's impossible for the average person to read even 10 percent of the books being published today, so make up your mind that you'll have to be selective and occasionally a bit abusive when some well-meaning member of a book club wants to assault you with a new volume.[15]

The remarkable thing is this: as you read contemporary and classic writings in many fields—fiction and nonfiction, history and biography, poetry and prose, science and the arts—you start to see "patterns of truth" as your imagination puts things together. You discover firsthand that "all truth is God's truth" and all truth intersects. Your mind is enriched from many sources and your imagination shows you how all of these things relate to the eternal truths in God's Word.[16] "The imagination must be fed," wrote English critic John Ruskin. "The most imaginative men always study the hardest and are the most thirsty for knowledge." The imagination doesn't work well in a vacuum; you have to give it something to digest.

I must emphasize again that creative people don't neglect the developing of their technical skills. Painters study the works of other artists, classic and contemporary, and seek to perfect their own techniques; and musicians and writers do the same. Likewise, creative preachers listen to other ministers preach; they read and study printed sermons[17] and expose themselves to the best in homiletical thought and communications theory; and then they trust the Lord to help them use all of this information imaginatively in the proclamation of the Gospel of Jesus Christ.

If we are to be creative preachers, we must effectively keep in touch with four different worlds: the world of creation and humanity around us, the world of feelings and insights within us, the world of ideas in the arts and sciences, and the unchanging world of the Bible which is the basis for our ministry. Like the Holy Spirit described in Genesis 1:2, the imagination hovers over this mass of material and brings order out of chaos.

Before leaving the subject of creative reading, I want to say something about poetry. Yes, real men read poetry and aren't ashamed to admit it! Reading good poetry is one of the best ways to challenge your intellect and stretch your imagination, provided you *experience what you read.*[18]

Poetry has been defined as "distilled emotion." The fact that God reveals Himself in the Bible through poetry ought to assure us that there's nothing wrong with the *genre* itself.[19] The problem with most of us is that we were introduced to poetry at a time when we didn't know how to approach it or appreciate it and, like a vaccination, we got just enough not to be able to "catch" the real thing.

When in January 1965, *Time* magazine reported the death of T.S. Eliot, I wondered why a poet should get that much attention; so I decided to see what he had to say. That launched me on an exciting and enriching journey into the vast and expanding universe of poetry, a journey that I wish I had started sooner. I now enjoy browsing through poetry anthologies to discover new poems and poets and new experiences. Carl Sandburg described poetry as "the journal of a sea animal living on land, wanting to fly in the air." He said poetry was "the synthesis of hyacinths and biscuits."[20] No wonder poetry can nourish the imagination!

4. Creative people build their vocabulary. Words are lamps that help us see, tools that help us build, handles that help us grasp, and sometimes weapons that help us fight. Philosopher Ludwig Wittgenstein said, "The limits of one's language are the limits of one's world"; so, when your vocabulary grows, your world gets bigger.

The best way to increase your vocabulary is to use a good dictionary when you read and to be diligent to "digest" each new word you meet. "Digesting" a word means much more than simply discovering its meaning and learning how to use it. It also means knowing where the word came from and what pictures might be hidden in its background. Sometimes a new word will introduce you to a whole new family of words and you can have a great time getting acquainted with all the cousins! We don't drop these new words into every sermon just to display our erudition,[21] but we do add new words to our bag of tools—or verbal arsenal—so we can use them when needed. Remember what Proverbs 12:27 says about the lazy hunter.

Along with a current college-level dictionary, your library ought to contain a dictionary of synonyms; and don't settle for a thesaurus or "synonym book," as helpful as they are. A dictionary of synonyms will tell you how one word differs in meaning from another, and this is important to good communication. I get considerable help from consulting my *Oxford Dictionary of English Etymology,* edited by C.T. Onions (Oxford: The Clarendon Press, 1991) and also my ancient *Concise Etymological Dictionary of the English Language* by Walter W. Skeat (Oxford: The Clarendon Press, 1901). *Origins: A Short Etymological Dictionary of Modern English,* by Eric Partridge (New York: Greenwich House, 1983) is helpful, as is *Cassell's Latin Dictionary,* edited by D.P. Simpson (New York: Macmillan, 1968).[22]

All this counsel may seem light years away from the burden you carry of preaching the Word week by week and shepherding God's people, but it really isn't. Words are very important to ministry; if you doubt that, read the Book of Proverbs and see how much it says about human speech. The Holy Spirit has chosen to reveal God's truth in *words* (1 Cor. 2:13), and He has called us to use *words* to convey that truth to others. Just as the carpenter and mechanic take care of their tools, add to them regularly, and use the right tool for the right job, so the preacher must protect his "toolbox" of words, add to it steadily, and learn which tools will best accomplish what he wants to do.

5. *Creative people aren't afraid to do new things.* Innovation always involves risk, but creative people are willing to take reasonable chances and are not afraid to make mistakes. Ministers who are comfortable with the ecclesiastical routine and satisfied with their homiletical skills may be in great danger and not know it. What started out as a trench on the battlefield may have become a grave in the cemetery.

"The curse of our calling, brethren, is professionalism," writes Bishop Gerald Kennedy. "It makes us more desirous of protecting our status than saving souls. We would rather die in rigid respectability than risk being caught with our dignity down."[23]

I'm not suggesting that we become careless and rash in our quest for creativity—that approach to ministry might frighten the flock and leave the shepherd alone to ponder his clever new ideas. Perhaps you heard about the teenager who decided to be different by parting his hair from ear to ear instead of in the usual manner. The experiment wasn't at all successful: he got attention, but people kept whispering in his nose. Unfortunately, some people can't distinguish between being *odd* and being *different.*

Spurgeon warned his pastoral students that "suddenness leads to shallowness," so let's be sure that we've prayed and pondered before we engineer important changes. Let's also be sure that we know the difference between *creativity* and *novelty.* But when the wind of the Spirit is blowing in new directions, and we're sure God is at work, let's not be afraid to set our sails and move, even if the breeze takes us to parts unknown. We need to meet new people, read new authors, meditate on new passages of Scripture that we've long neglected, face new challenges, consider new procedures, and take the risk of acquiring some new wineskins. This doesn't mean we abandon the foundation of our faith, but it does mean we're not afraid to rearrange the furniture and even occasionally throw away some dusty bric-a-brac.

As we move along the road of life, *comfort* and *competence* become the enemies of creativity. The Lord has a way of sending thorns to disturb our comfort; and if we're honest with ourselves, we'll admit that we still have a lot to learn no matter how competent we may think we are in our technical skills. Always be content with the Lord's will, but never be satisfied with yourself. We need to take to heart the words of Russian composer Dmitri Shostakovich: "A creative artist works on his next composition because he was not satisfied with his previous one."

> **As we move along the road of life, *comfort* and *competence* become the enemies of creativity.**

In our ministry, you and I probably won't say anything that hasn't been said before, but let's at least try to say it in a fresh way that will capture the imagination of our listeners. Originality in the *product* may be heresy; what we need is originality in the *packaging* and the *delivery*. Allow the Holy Spirit to use your imagination and you will be pleasantly surprised to find new principles in familiar truths and new applications for old ideas. That's what the church is waiting for.

"Preaching is truth through personality."
— *Phillips Brooks*

"The imagination can express truth in its own unique way for the glory of God and the edification of people."
— *Leland Ryken*

"We would do well to labor with [Jonathan] Edwards to find images and analogies that produce impressions in our people comparable to reality."
— *John Piper*

Chapter Twenty-five
Preaching the Bible Biblically

A las! alas! I have not the recollection of one strong moment. A cold mechanical preparation for a delivery as
decorous—fine things, pretty things, wise things—but
no arrows, no axes, no nectar, no growling, no transpiercing,
no loving, no enchantment."[1]
Maybe you've occasionally felt that way about some of your
sermons: "no arrows, no axes, no nectar." Ralph Waldo Emerson wrote those words when he evaluated a series of lectures
he delivered in Boston between 4 December and 12 February
1840. Note that he blamed his "decorous delivery" on "cold
mechanical preparation," something that occasionally occurs in
ministers' studies today. "A burning heart will soon find for
itself a flaming tongue," Spurgeon told his students; and he
warned them against being the kind of people who "gathered
fuel, but lost the fire which is to kindle it."[2]
Dr. D. Martyn Lloyd-Jones defined preaching as "logic on
fire . . . theology coming through a man who is on fire."[3]
Trained as a physician, his approach to preaching was definitely
that of the logical diagnostician, stethoscope in hand. Whether
the focus of his sermon was the hopeless sinner, the careless
saint, the powerless church, or the godless society, Dr. Lloyd-
Jones was always the compassionate physician examining sick
patients and prescribing biblical cures.
His definition of preaching is a good one, and the Doctor
exemplified it marvelously in his ministry, especially when he

was expounding Romans and Ephesians, two of Paul's most logically arranged letters. But the Doctor's definition of preaching has one flaw: not all of Scripture is what we would call a "logical" presentation of God's revelation. As we've seen in this quest, Scripture also contains images and metaphors that picture God's truth in many different ways. In fact, even Lloyd-Jones' phrase "logic on fire" isn't strictly logical; it's metaphorical. Who ever saw logic "on fire" or, for that matter, a preacher "on fire"? Yet we know exactly what Spurgeon and Lloyd-Jones were talking about because we know that metaphors have a logic of their own.

James Boswell once asked his learned friend Samuel Johnson what poetry was, and Johnson replied, "Why, Sir, it is much easier to say what it is not. We all *know* what light is; but it is not easy to *tell* what it is."[4] However, in his essay on John Milton, Johnson gave an excellent definition of poetry: "the art of uniting pleasure with truth, by calling imagination to the help of reason."[5]

Pleasure, truth, imagination, and reason are the four elements that Johnson identified in poetry; and I have a feeling that these same four elements are also involved in biblical preaching. While preaching is not a form of entertainment, we certainly experience intellectual and emotional pleasure in hearing a good sermon: the mind enjoys grasping the truth presented reasonably and the heart enjoys responding to the truth presented imaginatively. Without the truth of the Word, explained and applied, there could be no true ministry; and without the imagination, even the most faithful ministry would be stale and boring.

> **A biblical sermon is a form of human verbal communication that involves the organized explanation and application of biblical truth, presented in a manner that is reasonable, imaginative, and intrinsic to the text.**

For a tentative definition of biblical preaching, let's start with this: a biblical sermon is a form of human verbal communication that involves the organized explanation and application of biblical truth, presented in a manner that is reasonable, imaginative, and intrinsic to the text.[6]

Nobody needs to defend the assertion that a biblical sermon must be based on the truth found in the Bible, a truth stated in what we call "a text." It's the preacher's task to explain and apply the truth of that text to those who hear or read the sermon. The preacher may use visual effects to illustrate the message, but the primary form of communication is verbal. God uses human instruments to convey His truth, what Phillips Brooks called "truth through personality." Preachers are both heralds and witnesses. We announce what the King tells us to announce, but we also announce what the message means to us personally. Heralds come with the authority and urgency of their calling; witnesses come with the reality of personal experience to back up the proclamation.

A biblical sermon must both *explain* and *apply* God's truth. If you want explanations without applications, you attend a theological lecture. On the other hand, applications that aren't based on doctrinal explanations are merely moralistic exhortations. The preacher must appeal to both the mind and the heart in an attempt to capture the will.

What the preacher has to say must be put together and presented in an organized manner. I don't know of any Scripture that tells us how a sermon should be organized; and we all realize that no two preachers preach alike. The biblical record and church history testify to that. But no matter what approach we take in arranging our exposition of the Word, what we say must be organized. We must know where we're going and why we're going there, and we must not go on detours. One of my homiletics professors used to warn us, "When you hear a preacher say 'Today, I just want to talk to you out of my heart,' you can be sure he's not prepared." Preaching that's organized (reasonable) can permanently impact and instruct the mind.

The phrase in my definition "intrinsic to the text" was a tough one to come up with, and maybe it isn't the best way to say it. What I mean is this: our treatment of the text must not violate the nature of the text itself. If the text is a psalm, we must deal with it as poetry and not as if it were a doctrinal argument from a Pauline epistle. In our desire to come up with a neat outline, with every point snugly in place, we must beware lest we rape the text rather than woo it. Perhaps there sometimes shouldn't even be what the homileticians would call a "formal outline" with main points and sub-points. I'm not suggesting that the sermon lack order and progress, because then you'd have confusion in both the pulpit and the pews, and God is not the author of confusion. All I'm suggesting is that the organization of the message must respect the literary *genre* of the text. We must honor the way the biblical writers and speakers communicated the truth to us.[7]

Imagination is the tool that helps us make the "connections" needed to bring sinners and the Savior together. Those who proclaim the Word are *ambassadors* who must know the language and mind-set of the people to whom they're sent if they hope to be understood (2 Cor. 5:20).

If we don't muzzle biblical images with our rigid and sterile approaches, they can speak to our generation with just as much vigor and excitement as they spoke to generations in ages past. In our scientific computer age, people are accustomed to learning new vocabularies and the significance of symbols; if they don't fully grasp a biblical image the first time, let's keep instructing them until they do understand. Even the 12 Apostles, who lived in the presence of Jesus, didn't always understand what the Master Teacher was talking about.[8] Rather than dilute the Word of God to bring it down to the level of the learner, let's seek to lift the learner up to the level of the unadulterated Word of God.[9]

Imagination is the tool that helps us make the "connections" needed to bring sinners and the Savior together. Those who proclaim the Word are *ambassadors* who must know the language and mind-set of the people to whom they're sent if they hope to be understood (2 Cor. 5:20). We're *roadbuilders* who must connect the city of Man-Soul with the City of God (2 Tim. 2:15; *orthotomeo*, "to cut straight, as a road"). We're *fathers and mothers* (1 Thes. 2:7-12) who must be able to identify with the needs of God's children and show them how Christ can meet those needs.

We must never lose faith in the power of the Word of God. Our listeners are like those six empty waterpots at the wedding feast Christ attended in Cana (John 2:1-11). As we preach the Word, we pour the water into their minds and hearts; and one day, the miracle will take place and the water will turn to wine. When you proclaim the Word in a way that "connects" with human minds and hearts, you're sending out the light (2 Cor. 4:6; Ps. 119:130), planting the seed (Luke 8:1-15), giving the medicine (Ps. 107:20), wielding the sword (Heb. 4:12; Eph. 6:17), serving the food (Matt. 4:4; 1 Peter 2:2; Jer. 15:16), applying the water (John 15:3; Eph. 5:25-27), and holding up the mirror so that people can see Christ and be transformed into His image (2 Cor. 3:17-18). What a privilege! What a responsibility!

Phillips Brooks encouraged the ministerial students of his day to "seize the human side of all divinity [and] the divine side of all humanity."[10] In other words, find the place where human life and divine truth meet and there grow your sermon.

Biblical preaching requires a preacher whose life witnesses that it is lived under the authority of the Word. Emerson said some ridiculous things, but when he made this statement in his famous "Divinity School Address," he was right on target: "The true preacher can be known by this, that he deals out to the people his life—life passed through the fire of thought."[11] We might add "life passed through the power of prayer, the awe of worship, the joy of obedience."

To summarize: for our preaching to be biblical, the message must be based on the truth of the Word of God, presented by a messenger who lives under the authority of that Word, organized in a manner that instructs the mind and moves the heart and captures the will, and interpreted and applied in a way that is true (intrinsic) to the text. That's enough to challenge any preacher!

Our quest has been a long and complex one, and we've not yet reached our destination. As I said in the Preface, my purpose has been to try to open some neglected paths on the homiletical landscape; but when it comes to the ministry of preaching, the quest never ends. There will always be more land to be possessed.

In his excellent book *Stewards of Grace*, Donald Coggan quotes F.W. Dillistone, whose words beautifully summarize what I've been trying to say in this book:

> The preacher is the man whose calling it is to create forms out of the most precious material which this world provides. His material is the everlasting Gospel, his tools are his full powers of thought and imagination, his object is to create a form which shall be the best possible to convey to other minds and imaginations the glory and beauty of that which he is seeking to portray.[12]

The great teacher is the one who turns listeners' ears into eyes so they can see the truth.

Appendix A
Questions Preachers and Teachers Ask

1. Do you really think that anybody can develop the kind of imagination that can lead to creative preaching and teaching?

Of course! Otherwise, I wouldn't have written this book!

You and I were made in the image of God to have dominion over His creation. In Adam, we lost that dominion; but in Christ, we can begin to experience a "renewing of the mind" that enables us to "reign in life" (Rom. 5:17). I believe this "renewing" includes the creative work of the imagination.

The important thing to remember is that creativity in Christian ministry isn't especially the result of formulas or techniques. It's the result of disciplined communion with the Lord that allows the Holy Spirit to work in our minds and hearts.

2. Where do I begin?

I suggest you take two or three of your favorite sermons and "imagineer" them by studying the texts again and looking for the pictures. Remember that sometimes the pictures are hidden in the words and not always stated in the text.

Recently I looked at an outline I'd prepared on Hebrews 6 and was appalled by its dullness. As I read the chapter again, I realized that there was an emphasis in the text on patience (v. 11—*diligence*; vv. 12, 15—*patience*). Then I noted the pictures that help to convey the image of patience and diligence: a child maturing (v. 1), a harvest (vv. 7-8), an inheritance (vv. 12, 17), an anchor (v. 19). It takes time for a child to mature, for seed to produce a harvest, for an inheritance to be received. What keeps us diligently waiting? We're anchored heavenward!

To be sure, there are some knotty theological problems to deal with in the text; but the main emphasis seems to be "Be patient and don't quit!" Let people see the pictures, and they'll have an easier time understanding your doctrinal explanations.

3. Must all of my main points always be pictures?

Not always. Point out the pictures, but be sure to explain what they signify. Going back to the example from Hebrews 6, my sermon proposition might be, "God encourages us to keep on trusting Him in spite of the trials of life." How does He encourage us? Simply by showing us some everyday pictures of perseverance. Parents are patient as their children mature. Farmers are patient as they wait for the harvest. Relatives are patient as they wait for their promised inheritance. The fact that we are "anchored heavenward" gives us the stability we need. This is the only anchor that enables us to *move forward!* The essential doctrinal material can easily be worked into the various sections of the message. The pictures must never take the place of the major message of the passage. The pictures only help us make the doctrinal themes easier to understand and apply.

4. But won't there be a sameness to our preaching if all we do is point out the pictures in the text?

Yes, there will be a sameness—if that's the way you preach! But I don't advise you to do it that way. In the Hebrews 6 example, you don't have to major on the pictures. Your key word might be *encouragements,* and the message could be developed like this:

Many people avoid Hebrews 6 because they've heard it contains some frightening theology. But this chapter is right at the heart of the book and we can't ignore it. In fact, the major theme of the chapter is encouragement, not fear; and if we understand what it teaches and put it into practice, it can bring stability and maturity to our Christian walk.

The writer gives us four encouragements to keep us trusting and obeying even when the going is tough.
1. You were born for maturity (the child)
    Food and exercise (Heb. 5:11-14)
2. It takes time for maturity (the harvest)
3. The promise of maturity is sure (the heir)
    We are written into His will
4. Christ holds you fast (the anchor)

Let your sanctified imagination "hover over" the images in the text and reveal the possibilities for homiletical development. If you do your homework, you won't wander off into fanciful ideas, because the doctrines in the text will keep you steady.

As another example, you might want to build your message around verse 9, "things that accompany salvation." The question isn't so much "Will I lose my salvation?" as "Is there evidence of real salvation in my life?" What are the "things that accompany salvation"? Maturity (the child), fruitfulness (the farmer), spiritual wealth (the inheritance), stability (the anchor). Once you discover the images in the text, there are many ways you can develop them in your sermon.

5. It's much easier to find pictures in a longer passage, such as a chapter; but what about individual verses?

Not every verse is a picture gallery, but you'd be surprised what you'd discover if you checked the original Hebrew and Greek. Colossians 2:5-7 contains the images of an *army* (v. 5, "how orderly you are"), a *pilgrim* (v. 6, "continue to live [walk] in him"), a *tree* (v. 7a, "rooted"), a *building* (v. 7b, "built up in him"), and a *river* (7c, "overflowing"). You ought to be able to make something out of that.

6. What about the left-brain people in the congregation? They may not want a diet of pictures.

Nobody wants a *diet* of pictures! Let me emphasize that your approach must be *balanced*. After you've fed their imagination with pictures, shift into the practical left-brain material that tells your people how to make the truth work in their lives. The left-brain people wait for the "firstly . . . secondly . . . thirdly" points because that's the way they think. Both kinds of material are needed.

For instance, after you've presented the image of the child maturing, you might say, "But you're probably wondering how we go about maturing in the Lord Jesus Christ. The biblical writer actually discusses that matter in the previous chapter, and it comes down to two essentials: spiritual food and spiritual exercise." Even though "food" and "exercise" are still images, you can develop them in a concrete way as you apply the truth. What is the food? How do we digest it? What is the exercise? Why are both necessary?

7. You claim that the imagination plays a big part in personal morality and Christian obedience. Please explain further.

I fear that our "cerebral preaching" has created a church composed of people who have big heads but small hearts. The sanctuary has become a lecture hall and too many people are more concerned with filling their notebooks with outlines than filling their hearts with God's love. How many believers have said to me, "Our pastor preaches the truth, but his sermons lack something. There's nothing in it for our hearts."

All I'm pleading for is a return to the biblical way of presenting God's truth in a balanced way for both the mind and the imagination.

As I hear the Word of God, unless a "connection" takes place between my mind and heart, I won't grow in a balanced way. I can know the truth and yet not obey it! That's the tragedy of ministry that leaves out the emotions and the imagination. What people love and delight in is what motivates their lives, so our job is to excite them with the Word so that they have new appetites and motivations.

All I'm pleading for is a return to the biblical way of presenting God's truth in a balanced way for both the mind and the imagination.

8. Are you crusading for a homiletical "Romantic Movement"?

The Romantic Movement was a reaction against the "scientism" of that day and called people back to imagination and emotions. However, in their zeal to restore the human element to fine arts and liberate life from the laboratory, some of the Romanticists went too far and jettisoned things intellectual.

I think we need to restore imagination and human emotions to preaching *without neglecting the intellectual.* Keep in mind the words of Sallie McFague: "Images without concepts are blind; concepts without images are sterile." Pictures without exposition won't teach very much, but exposition without pictures won't be easy to listen to or obey. Again, the key word is *balance.*

9. You say that biblical preaching "preaches the Bible the way the Bible preaches it," or words to that effect. You used the phrase "intrinsic to the text." Please explain.

That phrase can be improved upon, but it's the best I can do right now. Let me illustrate what I mean. One of the funniest plots for a comedy is to have a couple go to a masquerade party dressed in outlandish costumes, only to discover that they read the calendar wrong and have walked in on a formal dinner. Now, if I deal with Psalm 103 the same way as Ephesians 1, I'm wearing a costume to a formal dinner. It covers me up, but it just doesn't seem to fit the occasion. What I say may be doctrinally sound and even helpful to my congregation, but the sermon won't be "dressed right" and will not "fit" the worship situation.

Biblical poetry can't always be analyzed and outlined as neatly as some of Paul's doctrinal passages, nor should it be. There's an "atmosphere" to each biblical text that helps to determine how we're going to handle it. When you preach Romans, you lead your people into a law court where Paul's invincible logic defends justification by faith. When you preach Psalm 103, however, you're praising the Lord in the temple. The joys expressed in Psalm 24 would be out of place in a sermon on Genesis 22, yet in both passages people are seen going up a mountain.

In too many churches, the "atmosphere" is didactic Sunday after Sunday, and it gives people the impression that the Bible is primarily a textbook that the saints study so they can be smart. Certainly the saints need to study the Bible, but they also need to "feel" the Bible in their hearts and "see" the Bible in their imaginations. "Cerebral" Christianity can be proud, brittle, divisive, sterile, and cultic. "Heart" Christianity can be shallow, unstable, ignorant, and undependable. It's not a case of either/or but both/and. Again, I'm pleading for balance.

10. You claim that preaching a sermon should be "an act of worship." Please amplify that.

Our first obligation is to serve the Lord, not the Lord's people, and to bring joy to His heart. If I've worked hard on a message and done the best I can, I want to present that message first of all to God as a "living sacrifice" to His glory. If I don't present it to Him, then the message may bring glory to me instead of to the Lord, and it may not help His people. When preaching is an act of worship, we'll do our best in both the preparation and the presentation of the message. I suppose I'm pleading for an attitude of heart on the part of the preacher that lifts preaching to a higher level.

11. Why are you so critical of our using sermon outlines?

I'm not! I use outlines all the time, but I try not to let the outline get in the way of the sermon. When it comes to outlines, there are two dangers that preachers must avoid: first, dissecting Scripture for the facts but ignoring the truths revealed in biblical images, and second, thinking that an outline is a message. "When we murder to dissect," then display the corpse and talk about it, preaching is not an act of worship; it's an autopsy.

Not every preacher in church history outlined the passage and "walked" the congregation through it point by point. Some preachers, like Joseph Parker, took one luminous truth from a text and held it up as a jewel to be studied from all sides. Others, like F.W. Robertson, showed two sides of a truth and then applied the "higher truth" of both to human life.

314

What we do depends on our own gifts, the nature of the text, and the way the Spirit leads us.

By all means organize the message so you know where you're going and how to get there. But don't preach the outline. Use it as a means of conveying God's truth to the minds and hearts of the listeners. The "points" of an outline should be like "pegs" on which people can hang God's truth, or, to change the analogy, like "picture frames" into which they can put the images that reveal God's truth. An outline lets us maintain order, progress, and purpose in the message; but an outline isn't a message.

I get the impression from hearing some preachers that they want me to notice the outline rather than the message, the "package" rather than the contents of the package. They're proud of the outline and keep referring to it. "Look at my great outline! Notice especially my clever alliteration!" But this only distracts from the message itself. Preaching isn't reading a road map; it's taking people on a journey.

12. Who is your favorite preacher and why?

I don't know that I have a "favorite preacher," because I read different preachers for different reasons. I suppose Charles Spurgeon, G. Campbell Morgan, and George H. Morrison have been my closest "homiletical friends" and have influenced me the most, but I read sermons by preachers as diverse as John Henry Newman and George W. Truett.

When I read a sermon, I first read it as a sinner who needs to hear God's voice and receive God's grace. I imagine myself seated in church, hearing the voice of the preacher. After I've gotten the blessing from the Word, then I read the sermon a second time as a preacher seeking to develop his skills. How does the sermon show imagination? Why did the preacher develop the text as he did? Was the message true to the text? These are some of the questions I ask. Most preachers have their "homiletical heroes," and this is a good thing; but we must take care not to develop tunnel vision and see only our "favorite preacher." If we do, we'll get out of balance; because no preacher can teach us all we need to know.

Appendix B
A Short History of the Imagination[1]

Not all peoples in history have valued the imagination as we do today. In fact, some of them feared what the imagination might do to their view of reality or their practice of the spiritual life.

Greece

Plato was an Idealist who saw reality as a copy of absolutes or universals. The artist who made a statue or painted a picture was only copying the copies, so art was "twice removed" from reality and therefore false. This explains why Plato expelled artists from his ideal state, for he felt they were dangerous.[2]

To begin with, artists were ignorant for making copies of the copies. Since what we see in nature isn't the reality itself but only a copy, what the artists make can't teach us anything about reality itself. They're dealing only with appearances, and true philosophers seek for reality.

When we stop living by reason and start living only for appearances, we have a tendency to emphasize the lower desires at the expense of human reason; and this can make us less than human. Conclusion: art is dangerous. The fact that it can also lead to idolatry is another inherent weakness. (Paul would agree at this point; see Rom. 1:18ff.)

Not being an Idealist but a Nominalist, Aristotle encouraged the imagination as an important "link" with reality. Art imitates truth and helps us to "see" the universals. Aristotle believed that there were two aspects to the imagination, the rational and the sensible. The rational built the "bridge" from the inner person (the reason) to the world of reality. Aristotle taught that we think in images and these images are provided by the imagination. Here he would agree with Emerson. But he also believed that the imagination affects the feelings and helps to produce internal emotions and desires. Here he would agree with the Romanticists.

Both Plato and Aristotle saw the imagination as *reproductive* and not *productive*. Art imitates, it doesn't create. The emphasis in Plato's philosophy was on synthesis, putting things together; while in Aristotle's philosophy, the emphasis was on taking things apart, analysis.

Israel[3]

Since the greatest sin the Jewish people could commit was idolatry, they saw the imagination as something basically evil, something that could lead people to create things that were contrary to God's will. The Hebrew word translated "imagination" in many English texts (*yasar/yeser*) carries the idea of "forming, fashioning, desiring, inclining."[4] Most Old Testament references to the imagination carry an overtone of evil (Gen. 6:5; 8:21; Ezek. 13:2, 17).

> The Jewish people saw nature as a manifestation of God's power and glory, a "window" through which they could see God.

The Jewish people saw nature as a manifestation of God's power and glory, a "window" through which they could see God. Their pagan neighbors worshiped the powers of nature and tempted Israel to imitate them; and when Israel did, God had to chasten them.

Nature was also a "treasury" provided by God, and His people were stewards of His bounties. Adam and Eve were given dominion over creation and served as God's "managers" in the garden.

In the building of the tabernacle and the temple, God gave His people the design. The art in these structures imitated reality and copied the things that God had created. Their art was imitation, not creation. Jewish crafts were utilitarian, not decorative. They were careful not to appear to make anything that might be conceived as an image, and thus sin against God.

Medieval Life

Augustine appears to be the first religious writer to use the Latin word *imaginatio* ("imagination") consistently. Like Plato, he saw the imagination as the power to reproduce but not to create; and like the Jews, he saw the imagination as a possible source of trouble. Roman Catholic theologians were fearful lest the imagination take the worshiper's mind away from the holy things of the Lord.

However, some of the fathers and teachers thought the imagination could be a "handmaid" of the intellect if allowed to be controlled by the Lord. Aquinas held a view similar to that of Aristotle, that the imagination was a "storehouse of images" that "mediated" between the mind and the real world. Of itself, the imagination was not any more wicked than any other human faculty; but it could be a source of sin if the images it created were not holy.

Renaissance Thought (mid-14th to 16th centuries)

Renaissance scholars interpreted Christian thought in the light of the classics and built the bridge from the medieval to the modern world. There was a new humanism abroad as man became the measure of all things. Also a new individualism appeared that was contrary to the "group think" mentality of medieval Europe. It was during this era that the foundations were laid for modern science.

The imagination was no longer seen merely as a mirror that *reflected* light (imitation), but as a lamp that *radiated* light (creation). People could investigate the world and discover truths by using their intellect and their imagination, both of which could glorify God. However, this new scientific approach to life led to the 18th-century Age of Enlightenment, or Age of Reason, when science began to replace revealed religion and the gospel of the perfectibility of man and the progress of society replaced the Gospel of Jesus Christ. From now on, it was "glory to Man in the highest" and salvation through the achievements of science.

The Puritans (1550–1660)

While the Renaissance was exalting humanism, the Puritans were seeking to exalt God alone. In doctrine and conduct, the Puritans exemplify for many people the quintessence of the Christian life. It's unfortunate that the word Puritan has become a synonym for a person who is gloomy and opposed to pleasure. The caustic American editor H.L. Mencken defined "Puritanism" as "the haunting fear that someone, somewhere, may be happy." They were indeed a people who lived austere lives, but they loved God, sought to love one another, and tried with God's help to enjoy the sinless pleasures of life He had granted to them. The family as we know it is the product of the Puritan way of life, based on the Scripture.

The Puritans were a simple people who refused to give in to the artificial embellishments of life. In their dress, their houses, and their social habits, they avoided anything that called attention to itself. Even in their preaching, they avoided the kind of oratory or decoration that would exalt the preacher and not the Savior. They preached the Scriptures line upon line, precept upon precept, seeking to extract spiritual nourishment from every word and phrase. When John Bunyan published *The Pilgrim's Progress,* he had to introduce it with a defense ("apology") because he had written in the form of an allegory, a kind of literature that the Puritans didn't readily approve. Bunyan pointed out that hunters and fishermen used "bait" to catch their prey, and his allegory was "bait" to catch the reader. The Lord used types, symbols, metaphors, and allegories in the Scriptures, so the precedent had already been set.

It's unfortunate that many modern editions of *The Pilgrim's Progress* omit "The Author's Apology for His Book," because it is a striking defense of the ministry of the Christian imagination. Bunyan closes his "apology" with: "And lay my book, thy head, and heart together." He realized that you can't teach effectively unless you address both the head and the heart, the intellect and the emotions. No wonder *The Pilgrim's Progress,* written by an untrained humble tinker, has been a bestseller for centuries. Had Bunyan chosen any other approach instead of an allegory, his book might have been forgotten.

The Puritans have left us a wealth of expository sermons and commentaries, but I must confess that many of their books are difficult to read. I wish they had followed Bunyan's example and used their imagination in packaging their spiritual treasures. They thought that the imaginative was something special that we did with language; they didn't realize that imagination is the way language works no matter what we do with it.

Plain living and plain preaching were important elements in the Puritans' lives; and even though they were suspicious of the power of the imagination, the Puritans were for the most part exemplary people who sought to glorify God in all things.

The Romantic Era (1760–1870)

Plato said that the imagination destroyed reality and the Jews said it *threatened* reality. The medieval church warned that the imagination could *distract* the devoted mind from reality; and the Renaissance Man learned that the imagination could help to *create* reality, thus ushering in the Age of Science. It was inevitable that a reaction would set it, and it did with the emerging of the Romantic Era, a protest against the mechanism and scientism of Locke, Hume, Voltaire, Kant, and Newton. The basic approach of the Romantics (Wordsworth, Coleridge, Tennyson, Schiller, Goethe, Emerson, Thoreau) was that the imagination helps us to experience reality.

The Romantic emphasis was on the sensory (not the sensual) and the fact that truth could be known "intuitively" as well as scientifically. Romanticism was an appeal for humankind to "return to nature" and experience something besides the artificiality of the new "scientific industrial complex." Reality isn't just something cerebral. The world around us must be experienced as well as explained, and there are many things in life that even the scientists can't measure and explain. William Wordsworth's poem "The Tables Turned," quoted in chapter 3, is an expression of the Romantic philosophy.

The Enlightenment Man and the Romantic Man weren't really enemies. They just didn't see that *both* views of reality were necessary for an accurate assessment of the world. The scientist could take things apart and give us the facts, but it took the poet and philosopher to put things together and give us the truths. Fortunately, what started out as competition eventually became cooperation. Science today realizes how dependent it is upon imagination as well as investigation.[5]

The Western Contemporary World

If asked what the role of the imagination is in today's world, the average scientist would probably reply, "Imagination helps us to *interpret* reality." Scientists admit that the often nebulous images in their minds, the "models of reality" that they create, play an important part in discovering and defining what reality is and how it works. Imagination is not just an imitator; it is an interpreter, and therefore a co-creator. This helps to explain the great number of books that have appeared on creativity and innovation.

The Eastern World

If the Western contemporary world says that imagination helps us understand and interpret reality, the Eastern world claims that imagination *is* reality.[6] Because imagination "links" matter and spirit, it helps us perceive things as they are and not merely as they appear in the "accidentals" measured by science. While this approach is probably too subjective for most people, it does remind us that humans are more than bodies and minds and that the human psyche isn't satisfied merely with facts and formulas.

Appendix C
Imagination and Myth

If you devote any time to the further study of imagination, and I hope you will, sooner or later you'll run across the concept of "myth" and the name of Joseph Campbell (1904–1987). Campbell's interviews with Bill Moyers, "The Power of Myth," were telecast in 1988 and became one of the most popular series in Public Broadcasting history, a series that brought Campbell posthumous fame. Though no longer among the living, Campbell still reigns as the high priest of a "mythology cult" whose ideas have become the philosophy, if not the religion, of thousands.[1]

The English word *myth* comes from the Greek *muthos* which means both "speech or conversation" and "a story, a narrative." The Latin equivalent is *fabula* which also means "talk, conversation" as well as "a fable, a story." In later Greek, however, *muthos* came to mean "a fictional narrative" as opposed to *logos* "a true narrative." According to Tom McArthur, *muthos* eventually became identified with poetry and emotion, while *logos* was identified with "prose, reason and analytical thought."[2] Even the ancient Greeks grasped the idea of left-brain and right-brain and saw the need for narratives that would satisfy the emotional needs of the people in a way *logos* could never do.

In the ancient Greek and Roman world, "myths" were tales about the gods and goddesses that explained where things came from and why things happened as they did.[3] Paul warned Timothy and Titus about the danger of myths (1 Tim. 1:4; 4:7; 2 Tim. 4:4; Titus 1:14), and Peter echoed the warning (2 Peter

1:16). Whether these dangerous myths that invaded the early church were the ancient Greek and Roman stories allegorized to give them "Christian" meanings, or simply Jewish and Gnostic fables, we have no way of knowing. Stahlin writes, "The firm rejection of myth is one of the decisions characteristic of the NT. Myth is a pagan category."[4] In his *Dictionary of Literary Terms and Literary Theory,* J.A. Cuddon defines a myth as "a fiction which conveys a psychological truth."[5]

We write history to record what happened, but we devise myths to explain what happened and what the happening means to us. Perplexed people have to try to make sense out of their world or their world will destroy them. Says psychiatrist Rollo May, "Myths are like the beams in a house: not exposed to outside view, they are the structure which holds the house together so people can live in it."

The human mind may be content with *logos,* but the inner person must have *muthos.* The heart and imagination must be fed. The Swiss psychiatrist Carl Jung built his approach to therapy on a theory of "the racial unconscious" and the "archetypes" that are found in the ancient Greek and Roman myths.[6] Jung taught that in everybody's "unconscious" lies the "collective unconscious" of the entire human race, as expressed in mythology. Our dreams, fantasies, and emotional problems can be identified with these "archetypical patterns" and thus understood and treated.[7]

Northrop Frye was perhaps the leading literary critic to espouse a "mythological" theory of literature.[8] In *The Great Code: The Bible and Literature,*[9] Frye discusses myth and metaphor and defends his theory that the basic symbols and metaphors found in the Bible parallel what we find in classical mythology. He maintains that because English literature is saturated with allusions to mythology, students would not understand what they were reading if they didn't have a working knowledge of the Bible.

Malcolm Muggeridge writes, "Men can live without history, but not without myths. In this sense everything that happens is a parable rather than an event, or series of events; seen through, rather than with, the eye, the message is clear."[10]

We write history to record what happened, but we devise myths to explain what happened and what the happening means to us. Perplexed people have to try to make sense out of their world or their world will destroy them. Says psychiatrist Rollo May, "Myths are like the beams in a house: not exposed to outside view, they are the structure which holds the house together so people can live in it."[11]

Nobody in his right mind would accept the classical myths as true, but they do illustrate basic instincts and conflicts of human life. Just as you can meet yourself in the Bible, you can meet yourself somewhere in mythology, because great literature has a way of mirroring human life and, if we're honest, helping us discover ourselves.

The preacher will not want to invite the cast of Hesiod's *Theogeny* into the pulpit with him, for at least two reasons. To begin with, if you want to illustrate a human characteristic, there are better examples in the Bible than in mythology. And, if you did use an example from mythology, chances are few people in your congregation would recognize it or understand it. You'd have to spend so much time explaining the illustration that the story would be out of steam by the time you got around to applying it.

The people who listen to us preach may not sit in the pews thinking about the image of Narcissus or the labors of Hercules or Arachne and her loom. *But they bring with them myths of their own that they have inherited, invented, or borrowed.* Some of these myths they can "support" from Scripture ("If you obey God, He'll make you healthy and wealthy"), and others they defend from what they've seen or read (the Horatio Alger myth or the Cinderella myth). By clinging to these myths, people consciously or unconsciously reject or resist the truth; and the preaching of the Word does them no good.

Psychiatrists tell us that healing can begin when patients recognize the metaphor or metaphors that control their lives.

There's a sense in which a myth is a dramatized extended metaphor. It's the story (*muthos*) that keeps people going when they feel like giving up. But if the story is a fable, then the climax will be a catastrophe instead of "and they lived happily ever after." Biblical preaching involves replacing in the imaginations of our people the make-believe of *muthos* with the reality of *logos,* a reality that satisfies both the heart and the mind. "Once upon a time" must become "In the beginning God" before people can live authentic lives that are rooted in reality.

So, when we prepare our messages, we must discover how the text attacks and destroys the myths people live by, myths that are robbing them of reality. The weapons God has given us "have divine power to demolish strongholds. . . . arguments and every pretension that sets itself up against the knowledge of God" (2 Cor. 10:4-5). Because myths explain the past and give hope for the future, they enable people to face the present with all of its problems and perplexities. But the Word of God does it so much better!

Just like the Greeks and Romans, we North Americans have our myths, and we can defend them if necessary. The USA is "a city set on a hill," commissioned by God to redeem the world. The "log cabin to White House" myth, the "Lone Ranger" rugged individualism myth, the "American dream" myth, and the "Horatio Alger" myth are all a part of the storybook called The American Way of Life. Some of these myths have even been canonized and made a part of the rubric of some churches, especially those associated with the Religious Right.

C.S. Lewis believed that the classic myths found their fulfillment in the Christian drama of redemption. If the gods came down to visit men and women, our God came down in the person of His Son and tabernacled among us. If the gods annually died and came to life again, our Redeemer died for us once and for all and rose again to take the throne. "The heart of Christianity is a myth which is also a fact."[12]

Whether Lewis is right or wrong in seeing "redemptive analogies" in classical mythology, this much is true: the truth of the message of the Gospel so transcends any other message, is so rooted in history and reality, and displays its power so evidently, that the preacher need not tremble before the gods of the heathen.

In a commencement address at Yale University on 11 June 1962, President John F. Kennedy said, "The great enemy of the truth is very often not the lie—deliberate, contrived and dishonest—but the myth—persistent, persuasive and unrealistic." When Paul contemplated his visit to Rome, he wrote, "I am not ashamed of the gospel, because it is the power of God for the salvation of everyone who believes: first for the Jew, then for the Gentile" (Rom. 1:16).

Notes

One

1. Norman Cousins, *Human Options* (New York: W.W. Norton and Co., 1981), 100.
2. This is not to say that there isn't logic involved in the writing of a song or imagination in the conducting of a scientific experiment. Creative activity depends on both sides of the brain, and the more we can build a bridge between the two, the more creative we can be.
3. If you have read the best detective fiction at all, you probably know that a change took place between the earlier Sherlock Holmes and the more recent Hercule Poirot. While Holmes often mentioned the need for imagination in detective work, he majored on facts and not feelings. More than once, he infuriated Dr. Watson who thought his friend acted like an impersonal calculating machine. Agatha Christie's Poirot is a psychologist who sees meanings in how people speak, what they say and don't say, and how they react to questions. His "little gray cells" investigate the suspects' right brains as well as their left brains.
4. Michael J. Reddy, "The Conduit Metaphor—A Case of Frame Conflict in Our Language about Language," in *Metaphor and Thought*, ed. Andrew Ortony (Cambridge: Cambridge Univ. Press, 1979), 284–324.

Two

1. Blaise Pascal, *Pensees and Provincial Letters* (New York: Modern Library, 1941), 95. This is number 177 of the *Pensees* and is quite a confession from a man who was primarily a mathematician and scientist.
2. Quoted in John R.W. Stott *Between Two Worlds* (Grand Rapids: Eerdmans, 1982), 238–39.
3. Halford Luccock, in *the Minister's Workshop* (New York: Abingdon, 1944), 112. Luccock's chapter on imagination, though brief, is one of the best I've read on imagination and preaching.
4. See Clyde S. Kilby, *Christianity and Aesthetics* (Chicago: InterVarsity, 1961), and his essay "Christian Imagination," in *The Christian Imagination*, ed. Leland Ryken (Grand Rapids: Baker, 1981), 37–46.
5. Dwight E. Stevenson, in *the Biblical Preacher's Workshop* (Nashville: Abingdon, 1967), 86.

6. Ryken, *Christian Imagination,* 37.

7. Charles Darwin, *The Descent of Man,* vol. 49 of *The Great Books of the Western World* (Chicago: Encyclopaedia Britannica, 1952), 292.

8. Alexander Whyte confronts this fear in his sermon on the Apostle John: "Do not be afraid at the word 'imagination,' my brethren. It has been sadly ill-used, both name and thing. But it is a noble name and a noble thing. There is nothing so noble in all that is within us. Our outward eye is the noblest of all our outward organs, and our inward eye is the noblest of all our inward organs. And its noblest use is to be filled full of Jesus Christ." *Bible Characters from the Old and New Testaments* (Grand Rapids: Kregel, 1990), 481.

9. This is not to suggest that fancy can't teach us anything about the "real world." You can't read *Gulliver's Travels* or *Animal Farm* or *1984* without learning something about the foibles of society today. C.S. Lewis' *Narnia* series enlightens while it entertains. Perhaps the closest things we have to "fancy" in Scripture are Jotham's story (fable?) in Judges 9 and King Jehoash's story (fable?) in 2 Kings 14:8-10, where we find talking trees and bushes. Our Lord's parables dealt with a real world; and even though some of the people in His parables did unusual things, what they did was believable.

10. James Boswell, *The Life of Samuel Johnson,* 2 vols. (London: James M. Dent and Son, 1906), 1:499.

11. Colin Duriez, *A C.S. Lewis Handbook* (Grand Rapids: Baker, 1990), 127.

12. Quoted in George Morrison, *The Wind on the Heath* (London: Hodder and Stoughton, 1931), 282. George Morrison is one of my favorite preachers, a man who combined imagination with solid biblical truth and always exalted Christ and His Gospel. I once had an interesting discussion with Dr. D. Martyn Lloyd-Jones about Morrison's sermons. The Doctor thought they were "nothing but poetry" and lacked doctrinal substance, but he didn't change my mind. I still read Morrison's sermons and profit from them.

13. Quoted in *The Harper Religious and Inspirational Companion,* ed. and comp. Margaret Pepper (New York: Harper and Row, 1989), 249.

14. William Temple, *Readings in St. John's Gospel* (London: Macmillan and Co., 1939), 1:68. Italics in the quoted passage are mine.

15. Kilby, *Christianity and Aesthetics,* 19.

16. Note that Jesus made it clear to His disciples in v. 63 that He wasn't speaking in literal terms. We feed on Jesus Christ as we feed on His Word.

17. R.W. Dale, *Nine Lectures on Preaching* (London: Hodder and Stoughton, 1887), 52. Dale's treatment of the imagination in his second lecture is quite good. I especially like his statement that "every word that stands for a spiritual idea was at first a picture and a poem" (p. 47).

18. Luccock, *Minister's Workshop,* 116.

19. I recall another chat with Dr. Lloyd-Jones about this very subject. He told me he had been preaching in the Gospel of John and that some people said he wouldn't be able to handle it well because he was too accustomed to the analytical mind-set of Paul in the Epistle to the Romans. "But I sought to enter into the mind of John," said the Doctor, "and in spite of what they said, *I did it!*"

20. A.J. Gossip, *In Christ's Stead* (London: Hodder and Stoughton, 1925), 200.

21. Henry Ward Beecher, *Yale Lectures on Preaching: First, Second and Third Series* (New York: Fords, Howard and Hulbert, 1881), 109.

22. Though I disagree with his theology, I must confess that to me the master of "homiletical anticipation" was Harry Emerson Fosdick. I will be reading one of his sermons and starting to disagree, and when I turn the page, I find Fosdick saying, "But at this point, somebody is thinking—"; and then he reads my mind and heads me off at the pass! He may not convince me, but at least he does me the service of acknowledging that I am thinking.

Three

1. John Calvin, *Commentaries* (Grand Rapids: Baker, 1981), 1:80.

2. John Calvin, *Institutes of the Christian Religion* (Philadelphia: Westminster, 1960), 1:61, 72, 341.

3. Ralph Waldo Emerson, *Nature* (Boston: Beacon, 1985), 41. This is a facsimile edition of this important work which was first published in 1836. The introductory essay by Jaroslav Pelikan is an excellent summary and interpretation of Emerson's "natural philosophy." The Christian theologian may not agree with everything Emerson wrote, but his emphasis is needed today.

4. *The Complete Essays and Other Writings of Ralph Waldo Emerson*, ed. Brooks Atkinson (New York: Modern Library, 1950), 76–77. Oddly enough, the name of the preacher who paled against the snowstorm was Barzillai Frost, about whom Emerson wrote in his journal four months later, "Here is friend B.F. [He] grinds and grinds in the mill of a truism and nothing comes out but what was put in." (See Emerson, *Journal*, vol. 5, 481.) On hearing the church bells ring on Sunday morning, Jan. 3, 1853, Emerson's friend Henry David Thoreau wrote in his journal: "The bells are particularly sweet this morning. I hear more, methinks, than ever before. How much more religion in their sound, than they ever call men together to! Men obey their call and go to the stove-warmed church, though God exhibits himself to the walker in a frosted bush today, as much as in a burning one to Moses of old" (*The Journal of Henry David Thoreau*, vol. 1, ed. Bradford Torrey and Francis H. Allen [New York: Dover, 1962], 511).

5. G. Campbell Morgan, *Westminster Pulpit* (London: Pickering and Inglis, n.d.), 3:27.

6. Charles H. Spurgeon, *The New Park Street Pulpit* (London: Alabaster and Passmore, 1859), 4:330.

7. Joseph Parker, *The People's Bible* (London: Hazell, Watson and Viney, 1900), 16:176.

8. A.W. Tozer, *Born after Midnight* (Harrisburg, Pa: Christian Publications, 1959), 92–95.

9. Luccock, *Minister's Workshop*, 112.

10. For a perceptive essay on Blake and imagination, from which I have

borrowed several ideas, see Northrop Frye, "Blake's Bible" in *Myth and Metaphor*, ed. Robert D. Denham (Charlottesville: Univ. Press of Virginia, 1990), 270–86. The late Northrop Frye was trained for the ministry but moved into education and became a well-known literary critic and teacher of literature. It was Frye's belief that a knowledge of the Bible and the Greek and Roman myths was basic to an understanding of great literature. I will have occasion to mention him often in this book.

Four

1. David Buttrick, *Homiletic: Moves and Structures* (Philadelphia: Fortress, 1987), 113.
2. H. Grady Davis, *Design for Preaching* (Philadelphia: Fortress, 1958). Both Buttrick and Davis were bold enough to abandon some of the classical homiletical armor and face the giant of sermon preparation using equipment meaningful to preachers ministering in the atomic age. Davis dared to develop a new vocabulary for homileticians, and Buttrick enlisted the aid of current communications theory. I can't conceive of a serious preacher of the Gospel ignoring these books.
3. Buttrick, *Homiletic*, 132.
4. Sallie McFague, *Metaphorical Theology* (London: SCM, 1983), 26. McFague presents an excellent discussion of both metaphors and models, and her documentary notes and bibliography are especially helpful.
5. Emerson, *Nature* 32. I quote Emerson's examples even though I'm aware of James Barr's warning that "the etymology of a word is not a statement about its meaning but about its history." *The Semantics of Biblical Language* (London: SCM, 1983), 09. The fact that some people carry "word studies" too far certainly doesn't mean we should discard them completely.
6. Eva Feder Kittay, *Metaphor: Its Cognitive Force and Linguistic Structure* (Oxford: Clarendon, 1987), 39.
7. Janet Martin Soskice, *Metaphor and Religious Language* (Oxford: Clarendon, 1985), 15.
8. Cited in Leland Ryken, *The Liberated Imagination* (Wheaton, Ill.: Harold Shaw, 1989), 137. Conrad wrote this in the preface to his novel *The Nigger of the Narcissus*.
9. In the play, M. Jourdain asks his philosophy teacher: "What? when I say: 'Nicole, bring me my slippers, and give me my night-cap,' is that prose?" His teacher replies, "Yes, sir." Then M. Jourdain exclaims, "Good heavens! For more than forty years I have been speaking prose without knowing it." Moliere, *Le Bourgeois Gentilhomme*, act 2, sc. 4.
10. George Lakoff and Mark Johnson, *Metaphors We Live By* (Chicago: Univ. of Chicago Press, 1980). Though the book was written primarily to defend a semantic theory that the authors espouse, it is still one of the best introductions to the study of the place of metaphor in everyday life. Their second book, *More Than Cool Reason: A Field Guide to Poetic Metaphor* (Univ. of

Chicago Press, 1989), explains how metaphor works in poetry and helps us understand what a poem means. *Women, Fire, and Dangerous Things*, by Lakoff (Univ. of Chicago Press, 1987), deals with metaphor, semantics, and psychology and is, I must confess, beyond me. (Now there's the conduit metaphor!) For a simple introduction to metaphor, see Terence Hawkes, *Metaphor* (London: Methuen, 1972).

11. Kittay, *Metaphor*, 5.

12. Aristotle, *Poetics*, in *The Works of Aristotle* in *The Great Books of the Western World*, vol. 9, p. 694 (Chicago: Encyclopedia Britannica, 1952).

13. It's worth noting that the word translated "captivated" in vv. 19-20 (NIV) can also mean "intoxicated." The water has turned into wine! Is there some connection here with our Lord's first miracle at a marriage feast (John 2)?

14. Paul makes the same point in 1 Thes. 4:6, where "take advantage" (NIV) also means "to defraud." There are two ways to get money out of a bank. You can rob the bank, creating a whole new set of problems for youself; or you can become a depositor, commit yourself to the bank, and have the privilege of making use of its assets. Sex outside of marriage is like robbing the bank. Marriage is the commitment that enriches life as husband and wife live together in the will of God.

15. Cited in McFague, *Metaphorical Theology*, 201. Lewis could write not only stimulating theological essays and novels but also captivating children's stories, the mark of a person with a healthy imagination.

16. H. Richard Niebuhr, *The Responsible Self* (San Francisco: Harper & Row, 1963), 151–52.

17. McFague, *Metaphorical Theology*, 17.

18. Bible students will recognize a reference to Ezekiel 34, where the prophet denounces the political leaders (shepherds) of the nation, who exploited the people and were blind to their needs.

19. See Kittay, *Metaphor*, 316ff. Sometimes it takes a metaphor to explain a metaphor.

20. Quoted in Eugene H. Peterson, *Answering God* (San Francisco: Harper & Row, 1989), 69.

21. See Aristotle *Rhetoric* 3.10.

22. The story is told about two farmers who met at the market one Monday morning. One asked, "What did your minister preach about yesterday?" The other replied, "Oh, the same old thing—ding-dong, ding-dong, ding-dong!" The first farmer smiled and said, "You're fortunate! All we ever get is ding - ding - ding - ding!"

23. See Mark 5:25-34.

Five

1. Whyte, *Bible Characters*, 244.

2. McFague, *Metaphorical Theology*, 26.

3. Walter Brueggemann, *Finally Comes the Poet: Daring Speech for Procla-*

mation (Minneapolis: Fortress, 1989), 85. This book explodes with so many exciting concepts that one reading will never do. Brueggemann explains the relationship between poetry and proclamation, between information and imagination, in a way that is itself imaginative and creative.

Six

1. Northrop Frye, *The Educated Imagination* (Bloomington, Ind.: Indiana Univ. Press, 1964), 135.
2. Ellen Y. Siegelman, *Metaphor and Meaning in Psychotherapy* (New York: Guildford, 1990), 42.
3. Philip Keane, *Christian Ethics and Imagination* (New York: Paulist, 1984), 63.
4. Cynthia Ozick, "The Moral Necessity of Metaphor" *Harper's*, May 1986, 62–68.
5. Harvey Cox, *Religion in the Secular City* (New York: Simon and Schuster, 1984), 204. See also H. Richard Niebuhr, *The Responsible Self* (New York: Harper and Row, 1963), 149–60. This appendix, entitled, "Metaphors and Morals," shows the important place that symbols play in both language and faith.
6. Luccock, *Minister's Workshop*, 112.
7. Brueggemann, *Finally Comes the Poet*, 84.
8. Ibid., 109–10.

Seven

1. Robert N. Bellah, *The Broken Covenant* (New York: Seabury, 1975), 71.
2. Ibid., 72.
3. I dealt with this in chapter 3. Blake saw Bacon, Newton, and Locke as enemies of true humanness because they so emphasized what was scientific and "real" and minimized the imaginative and the poetic. Bellah adds: "When we remember that Jefferson's three intellectual heroes were Bacon and Newton and Locke, and that Jefferson was, like most of the Founding Fathers, a once-born man, we will begin to understand the growing prevalence of single vision in the early decades of the republic."
4. Oswald Chambers, *My Utmost for His Highest* (New York: Dodd, Mead and Company, 1965), 41. Chambers defines imagination as "the power God gives a saint to posit himself out of himself into relationships he never was in."
5. Jerry Mander, *Four Arguments for the Elimination of Television* (New York: Quill, 1978), 131.
6. Quoted in Rollo May, *The Cry for Myth* (New York: W.W. Norton, 1991), 57.
7. "The Place of Pornography," *Harper's*, November 1984, 33. Her statement that pornography is "sex . . . without consequences" doesn't suggest

that people who violate God's standards of purity don't reap what they sow. Rather, it means that there is a spirit of lawlessness in those who defy these standards, but they never think about the consequences. Along with Decter, the symposium for the article included the editor of *Harper's*, Lewis H. Lapham; Al Goldstein, publisher of a popular sex-oriented magazine; novelist Erica Jong; Susan Brownmiller, founder of Women Against Pornography; Jean Bethke Elshtain, professor of political science at the University of Massachusetts; and civil liberties leader Aryeh Neier. The fact that pornography is a 7 billion dollar *plus* business in the United States alone says something about its strength.

8. Mark Schorer, "The Necessity of Myth" in *Myth and Mythmaking*, ed. Henry A. Murray (Boston: Beacon, 1968), 357.

9. Siegelman, *Metaphor and Meaning*, 9. For helpful information on the important role of imagination in education, see Kieran Egan and Dan Nadaner, eds., *Imagination and Education* (New York: Teachers College Press, 1988), and Kieran Egan, *Imagination in Teaching and Learning* (Chicago: Univ. of Chicago Press, 1992). See also the research paper by Howard Gardner and Ellen Winner in *On Metaphor*, ed. Sheldon Sacks (Chicago: Univ. of Chicago Press, 1979), 121–39. Gardner and Winner note "the puzzling appearance, during middle childhood, of a penchant for literalness" (p. 134).

10. Clifton Fadiman, *The Little, Brown Book of Anecdotes* (Boston: Little, Brown, 1985), 452.

11. Egan, *Imagination in Teaching*, 4.

12. For an interesting discussion of television from the secular point of view, see "Television Looks at Itself," *Harper's* March 1985. Eight leaders in the television industry—producers, writers, executives—give us the "insider's" perspective on what television is and how it ought to work.

13. Mander, *Four Arguments*, 132.

14. Ibid., 200.

15. Neil Postman, *Amusing Ourselves to Death* (New York: Viking, 1985), 31. In the third act of his play *Man and Superman*, George Bernard Shaw has the statue say, "Hell, in short, is a place where you have nothing to do but amuse yourself."

16. Quoted in Malcolm Muggeridge, *Christ and the Media* (Grand Rapids: Eerdmans, 1977), 67.

17. Postman, *Amusing Ourselves*, 111.

18. Quoted in John Fiske and John Hartley, *Reading Television* (London: Methuen, 1978), 190.

19. Muggeridge, *Christ and the Media*, 81.

20. Ibid., 92. For a fascinating discussion of the importance of words in the Christian faith, see Jacques Ellul, *The Humiliation of the Word* (Grand Rapids: Eerdmans, 1985). Ellul's examination of the media, from a philosophical and theological point of view, is penetrating and disturbing.

21. Ibid., 88.

22. *USA Today,* 16 March 1992, p. 1D.

23. Neil Postman, *U.S. News and World Report,* 19 January 1981, 43.

24. I don't like it when gifted *communicators* are put on television and turned into *actors.* The old Bob Newhart "telephone routines" are priceless because they give us the freedom to build our own images, but, to me, Newhart is not that funny on television. Likewise with Bill Cosby, one of the best monologue comedians of our generation. When Garrison Keillor is on television, I enjoy it more *with my eyes closed.* "The pictures are clearer."

25. Andrew A. Bonar, *Memoir and Remains of Robert Murray M'Cheyne* (London: Banner of Truth, 1966), 29.

26. On the place of imagination in ethical behavior, see Mark Johnson, *Moral Imagination* (Chicago: Univ. of Chicago Press, 1963). Using the insights of "cognitive science," Johnson explains the function of imagination in making moral decisions. As evangelical Christians, we would question Johnson's position concerning moral absolutes, but this should not hinder us from learning from him. At least he emphasizes the importance of the imagination in making enlightened moral decisions.

Eight

1. Quoted in Eugene Peterson, *Answering God* (San Francisco: Harper and Row, 1989), 69. This is an excellent book on the Psalms as vehicles for personal prayer. The chapter on "metaphor" is especially good.

2. Siegelman, *Metaphor and Meaning,* 67.

3. Ibid., 65.

4. G.K. Chesterton, "A Defense of Nonsense," in *Great Essays,* ed. Houston Peterson (New York: Washington Square, 1950), 318.

5. His essay of that title is found in *Of God and Man* (Harrisburg, Pa: Christian Publications, 1960), 116–18.

6. McFague, *Metaphorical Theology,* 17.

7. Quoted in Siegelman, *Metaphor and Meaning,* 55.

8. Siegelman, *Metaphor and Meaning,* 44.

9. Alfred North Whitehead, *The Aims of Education* (New York: Macmillan, 1929), 139.

10. Ibid., 140.

11. Phillips Brooks, *The Joy of Preaching* (Grand Rapids: Kregel, 1989), 54. This is a new edition of Brooks's *Lectures on Preaching,* delivered at Yale University in 1877 as a part of the annual Lyman Beecher Lectures series. In my opinion, almost everything written in America on homiletics and pastoral work since then is a footnote to what Brooks says in these lectures. While Brooks' statement is a valid one, he confessed that he didn't always practice it. He told Dr. George A. Gordon, "When I am interesting I am vague; when I am definite I am dull." See Edgar DeWitt Jones, *The Royalty of the Pulpit* (New York: Harper and Row, 1951), 20.

12. I'm aware of the hermeneutical dangers that exist when we try to

squeeze more out of a Hebrew or Greek word than is really there. But many Bible words contain imagery that ought to be liberated and put to work making God's truth vivid and exciting. It's true that "the etymology of a word is not a statement about its meaning but about its history"; but don't let James Barr's warning make you so timid in your exegesis that you become paralyzed. See James Barr, *The Semantics of Biblical Language* (London: SCM, 1983), 109.

13. Benjamin Keach's *Tropologia: A Key to Open Scripture Metaphors* was first published in London in 1855 and has been reprinted by Kregel (1972) with the title *Preaching from the Types and Metaphors of the Bible*. The book is worth studying but please don't adopt Keach's approach to metaphor. Spurgeon said it best in his *Commenting and Commentaries*, "Although our honored predecessor makes metaphors run on as many legs as a centipede, he has been useful to thousands. His work is old-fashioned, but it is not to be sneered at" (London: Banner of Truth, 1969), 155. Benjamin Keach was the second pastor of the church that eventually became the Metropolitan Tabernacle. He served for thirty-six years, from 1668 to 1704.

14. Quoted in Conrad Cherry, *Nature and Religious Imagination* (Philadelphia: Fortress, 1980), 5. Cherry agrees with Bellah that "religious imagination" declined in America after Jonathan Edwards, but he feels that it was revived under Bushnell. He calls Bushnell's approach to theology "religious romanticism." Cherry's book is an excellent survey of the place of imagination in theology and preaching in America from Edwards to Bushnell, a period of about 150 years.

Nine

1. For an interesting enumeration of the things in Genesis that find their fulfillment in the Book of Revelation, see *The Companion Bible* (London: Lamp Press, n.d.), Appendix 3, 5.

2. That the word "taste" here means much more than "sample" is indicated by its application to the death of Jesus: " . . . so that by the grace of God he might taste death for everyone" (Heb. 2:9). To taste something is to experience it.

3. I have not been able to discover when the Jews added wine to the Passover menu. It's not included in the original instructions (Ex. 12) or anywhere else in the Mosaic Law.

4. The Book of Exodus abounds with typology and symbolism, all of which have been adequately dealt with in available commentaries both critical and devotional. The expositor must take care not to spiritualize the text so that it loses its meaning in the "application." Scriptures such as Romans 15:4 and 1 Corinthians 10:1-13 give us the authority to make spiritual applications from the Old Testament Scriptures, but they don't give us license to make everything in the Old Testament a type or an analogy. I'm reminded of the lady who said to a guest preacher, "I just love to hear you preach! You find so

many wonderful things in the Bible that aren't even there!"

5. The chapter on "redemption" in Leon Morris, *The Apostolic Preaching of the Cross* (Grand Rapids: Eerdmans, 1956) remains one of the best treatments of this important subject. See also Morris' *The Cross in the New Testament* (Eerdmans, 1965) and John R.W. Stott, *The Cross of Christ* (Downers Grove, Ill.: InterVarsity, 1986).

6. See J. Sidlow Baxter, *The Master Theme of the Bible* (Wheaton, Ill.: Tyndale, 1973), and the articles on "Lamb of God" in the revised *International Standard Bible Encyclopedia* (Grand Rapids: Eerdmans, 1986) and *The Dictionary of Jesus and the Gospels* (InterVarsity, 1992).

7. Note that v. 2 is repeated in Psalm 118:14 and Isaiah 12:2, and that Revelation 15:3 records a song of Moses sung at a heavenly sea. There is rich material here for the creative preacher!

8. Israel's being "planted" in the land (2 Sam. 7:10; Ps. 44:2) relates to the image of the nation as God's choice vine (Ps. 80:8, 15; Isa. 5:2; 60:21; Jer. 2:21; 11:17; 24:6; Amos 9:15). Our Lord used this image in His Parable of the Tenants (Matt. 21:33-46; Luke 20:9-19).

9. Whenever the going got tough, the Jews expressed a desire to return to Egypt where they had security and food (see Ex. 16:1-4; 17:1-7; Num. 14:1-4; 20:1-5). Instead of wanting to go forward to their promised inheritance, they wanted to go back to the old life. This fact parallels one of the themes of the Epistle to the Hebrews, "Therefore let us leave the elementary teachings about Christ and go on to maturity" (Heb. 6:1). There is no standing still in the Christian life: we either go forward by faith or go backward in unbelief.

10. Too often we want to fly away from the storm like frightened doves (Ps. 55:6), when we ought to rise above the storm like soaring eagles!

11. Premillennialists will interpret this passage as describing God's special care for the Jewish remnant during the reign of the Beast. Amillennialists will apply it to God's providential care for His people during their time of tribulation and persecution. See William Hendriksen, *More Than Conquerors* (Grand Rapids: Baker, 1940), 141–42. But the image is the same: when His people are in trouble, God can lift them out or give them the "wings" they need to fly out.

12. The use of an Old Testament image by a New Testament writer affirms *continuity* of spiritual truth from one age to another, but it doesn't necessarily prove *identity* of persons. Peter didn't allude to Exodus 19 to prove that the church was a "continuation" of Israel, but to encourage his readers to live up to all that they had in Jesus Christ. We would expect the people of God who today live under the New Covenant to have similarities with the people of God who lived under the Old Covenant. Totally apart from matters hermeneutical and theological, the images convey the messages the writers wanted to convey.

13. On the basis of this "treasured inheritance" image, dispensationalists interpret our Lord's Parable of the Hidden Treasure (Matt. 13:44) as applying to Israel. Christ came to His own people, but was rejected by them; so He

"hid" them back in the world ("the field is the world" [Matt. 13:38]), but purchased the whole field that He might possess them.

14. The *NIV Study Bible* has an especially good cross-reference system which is also found in most of the NIV reference Bibles. The *NIV Exhaustive Concordance,* comp. by Goodrick and Kohlenberger (Grand Rapids: Zondervan, 1990) is also a very helpful tool. For many years, I've used *The Treasury of Scriptural Knowledge,* a book of half a million cross references, covering the entire Bible. It was compiled by George Wigram, who also gave us *The Englishman's Greek Concordance* and *The Englishman's Hebrew Concordance,* and was originally published in the United States by Fleming H. Revell. The revised and improved edition was edited by Jerome H. Smith and was published by Thomas Nelson in 1992. It follows the *Authorized Version* but this does not necessarily limit the book's usefulness if you use another translation.

Ten

1. Werner Foerster, *Theological Dictionary of the New Testament,* ed. Gerhard Kittel (Grand Rapids: Eerdmans, 1964), s.v. "axios."
2. This image reminds me of the words of saintly Robert Murray M'Cheyne, written to a missionary: "How diligently the calvary officer keeps his sabre clean and sharp; every stain he rubs off with the greatest care. Remember you are God's sword—His instrument—I trust a chosen vessel unto Him to bear His name. In great measure, according to the purity and perfections of the instrument, will be the success. It is not great talents God blesses so much as great likeness to Jesus. A holy minister is an awful [awesome] weapon in the hand of God" from Andrew A. Bonar, *Memoirs and Remains of Robert Murray M'Cheyne* (London: Banner of Truth, 1966), 282. See also the entry "Sword of the Spirit" in *A Dictionary of Biblical Tradition in English Literature,* ed. David Lyle Jeffrey (Grand Rapids: Eerdmans, 1992).
3. In Scripture, death is pictured as God putting out a light and leaving the person in darkness. See Job 3:1-5; 5:14; 18:5-6, 18; 21:17; Prov. 13:9; 20:20; 24:20.
4. Of course, God selected Solomon to be the next king, to keep the lamp of David burning in Israel.
5. The fact that in Scripture human beings are often compared to grass doesn't minimize their importance at all. The image reminds us that human beings are weak and transitory, but not useless. There are between six and ten thousand varieties of grasses in the world, including cereal grains, and they play an important part in the balancing of nature, the protecting of land and the feeding of both people and animals.

Eleven

1. James Boswell, *The Life of Dr. Johnson* (London: J.M. Dent and Sons, 1973), 2:27.

2. Samuel Johnson, *Lives of the English Poets* (London: Oxford Univ. Press, 1977), 1:117.

3. C. Hassell Bullock, *An Introduction to the Old Testament Poet Books* (Chicago: Moody, 1988) is an excellent volume for the student who wants to dig deeper.

4.) For some excellent studies on the literary qualities of the Book of Job, see Roy Zuck, ed. *Sitting With Job* (Grand Rapids: Baker, 1992). This excellent anthology contains scholarly material from a variety of sources and helps the serious student get a broad perspective on the fascinating but difficult Book of Job.

5. The term "daysman" used in Job 9:33 in the KJV is a fifteenth century word for the man who told the defendants the days they were scheduled to appear in court. The word "day" was once a verb, and "to day" meant "to appoint a day." Christian theologians see Jesus Christ as the "umpire" who brings sinners and God together because of His incarnation and sacrifice on the cross. For a popular treatment of the theme, see G. Campbell Morgan, "The Cry for a Daysman," in *The Answers of Jesus to Job* (Old Tappan, N.J.: Revell, 1964).

6. Some commentators see this as a euphemism for Job's inability to beget more children. Speaking of his earlier days of prosperity, Job had said, "My glory will remain fresh in me, the bow ever new in my hand" (29:20), a description of his masculine vigor.

7. King Hezekiah used the same image in his lament: "Like a weaver I have rolled up my life, and he has cut me off from the loom" (Isa. 38:12). Psalm 139:15 states that the unborn child is being "woven together" by the Lord. Those who die too soon have had their days "cut short" by the Lord (Pss. 89:45; 102:23). The image opens up many possibilities for imaginative preaching. In Job 10:8-12, Job describes the same prenatal process as the molding of clay and the making of cheese.

8. The English poet Francis Thompson in his poem "The Poppy" compared time to a reaper: "The goodly grain and the sun-flushed sleeper/The reaper reaps, and Time is the reaper." The American poet Henry Wadsworth Longfellow saw death as the reaper in his poem "The Reaper and the Flowers": "There is a Reaper whose name is Death/And with his sickle keen/He reaps the bearded grain at a breath/And the flowers that grow between." Paul compared the burial of the dead body to the planting of a seed and the resurrection to a glorious harvest, of which Jesus Christ is the firstfruits (1 Cor. 15:35-49).

9. Eugene Peterson, *Answering God: The Psalms as Tools for Prayer* (New York: Harper and Row, 1989), 77. This is an excellent volume not only on the devotional use of the Psalms, but also on the theology of the Psalms. The chapter on metaphor is especially insightful.

10. The chaff comes from the threshing floor, which is often an image of chastening or judgment (Jer. 51:33; Dan. 2:35; Matt. 3:12; Luke 3:17). Sometimes God sees His people Israel as His threshing instrument to judge the

godless nations (Isa. 41:15-16; Micah 4:13).

11. When *peripateo* and *stoicheo* are used by Paul in a figurative sense to describe the Christian life, the NIV usually translates them as "to live" rather than "to walk." In the Epistles of John, the word "walk" is preferred by the NIV translators (1 John 1:6-7; 2:6; 2 John 1:6; 3 John 3).

12. It should be noted that in the Old Testament, "shepherd" applies to leaders in general, including kings, priests, and prophets, as Ezekiel 34 makes clear. Our common word for a spiritual leader is "pastor," used only once in the English New Testament (Eph. 4:11). With reference to spiritual leadership, the verb *poimaino* ("to act as shepherd") is found in John 21:15, Acts 20:28, 1 Corinthians 9:7, 1 Peter 5:2, and Revelation 7:17. The Lord Jesus shall "rule" (*poimaino*) the nations with a rod of iron (Matt. 2:6; Rev. 2:27; 12:5; 19:15; see Ps. 2:9).

13. One of the most useful books on biblical imagery is Othmar Keel, *The Symbols of the Biblical World* (New York: Seabury, 1978). He relates biblical images to the findings of the archaeologists and to the myths of the Eastern nations. It seems that Eastern kings smashed vases with their scepters to guarantee victory over their enemies. See Keel, pp. 266–67.

14. Greek mythology refers to "the earth mother" and explains the origin of all things from the marriage of the earth and the sky (Uranus). "Rain falls from the bridegroom Heaven and makes Earth pregnant," wrote the Greek dramatist Aeschylus. The Greeks called her Gaia (Ge, Gaea) and believed she was born out of Chaos. See the references to "earth-mother" and Gaia in Robert Graves, *The Greek Myths* (Mt. Kisco, N.Y.: Moyer Bell, 1988); John Ferguson, *Greek and Roman Religion, A Source Book* (Park Ridge, N.J.: Noyes, 1980); and David Adams Leeming, *The World of Myth* (New York: Oxford Univ. Press, 1990). The name "Gaia," referring to "Mother Earth," is today a part of the "pop mythology" used by people promoting the proper care of the earth.

15. God wants to give us "wings like eagles" (Isa. 40:31), so that we can face the storm and rise above it.

16. One of the best topical summaries of the Book of Proverbs is Ronald M. Sailler and David Wyrtzen, *The Practice of Wisdom* (Chicago: Moody, 1992). The editors are alert to the Hebrew text and not just the topics as expressed in the English Bible.

17. Sailler and Wyrtzen, *Practice of Wisdom*, 151.

18. Consult your concordance and you will see that there are dozens of references to wisdom as a path or way on which we are to walk if we want the blessing of God. Wisdom calls people to the path of life while Folly (the harlot) calls them to the path that leads to death.

19. For the "tree of life" image in the Book of Proverbs, see 11:30, 13:12, 15:4; and for other agricultural images, see 10:30, 11:28, and 12:3 and 12.

20. The section on "nutrition" in Sailler and Wyrtzen is especially insightful.

21. This reminds us of the Apostle John's statement that worldliness involves "the lust of the eyes" (1 John 2:16, KJV), that is, the sensuous enjoyment of

the things that we see, acquire and accomplish. "The lust of the eyes" can contribute to the "lust of the flesh" and also promote "the pride of life." This is illustrated by King Nebuchadnezzar's words, "Is not this the great Babylon I have built as the royal residence, by my mighty power and for the glory of my majesty?" (Dan. 4:30)

22. See note 4, chapter 4.

23. For an excellent introduction to the Song of Songs, see Bullock, *An Introduction to the Old Testament Poetic Books.*

Twelve

1. The *exodus* theme in the New Testament is found in Luke 1:68; 2:38; 9:30-31; Romans 3:24; Ephesians 1:14; Colossians 1:13; 1 Peter 1:13, 19.

2. It isn't difficult to apply these images to the church today. We're God's children, but do we obey Him? We're the body of Christ, but are we keeping the body healthy? We're the temple of God, but we look like a cheap shack. We're the bride of Christ, but we have become harlots by our compromise with the world. Our treasures are cheapened and our beauty has faded. No wonder judgment begins at the house of the Lord (1 Peter 4:17)

3. The felling of trees is often used in Scripture as a picture of the destruction of a nation or an empire that stands in proud defiance against God. See Isaiah 2:12-18; 10:33-34; Ezekiel 17:24; 31:1ff; Daniel 4. Note in Isaiah 10:33–11:1 the contrast between the proud tree cut down and the humble tender shoot coming forth from the stump of Jesse.

4. On the basis of Revelation 3:7 and Zechariah 10:4, some see in Eliakim an illustration of the Messiah. See Isaiah 36 for Eliakim's role in the Assyrian negotiations.

5. Isaiah 26:4 is the basis for the familiar hymn, "Rock of Ages," by Augustus Toplady. The KJV reads "for in the Lord God is everlasting strength," but the margin reads "the rock of ages." The NIV reads "the Rock eternal."

6. The image of Christ the Stone is mentioned in Psalm 118:22-23; Daniel 2:34; Zechariah 4:7; Matthew 21:42-44 (and parallels); 1 Corinthians 10:4; Ephesians 2:20; and Romans 9:32-33.

7. Job wondered if his hope would go with him "down to the gates of death" (Job 17:16). The word translated "death" is *sheol*, the realm of the dead, the same word Hezekiah used in Isaiah 38:10. See also Psalms 9:13 and 107:18, as well as our Lord's words in Matthew 16:18.

8. The image of idolatry as adultery and prostitution surfaces frequently in Scripture: Exodus 34:15; Leviticus 17:7; Jeremiah 3; Ezekiel 23:3; 1 Corinthians 10:20; James 4:4-5; Revelation 18:1-3. God's people are a covenant people, and when they give their devotion to that which is not God, they prostitute themselves. We will see this image developed further in Hosea.

9. The KJV uses the word "backsliding" twelve times in Jeremiah (2:19; 3:6, 8, 11-12, 14, 22; 5:6; 8:5; 14:7; 31:22; 49:4). It's a translation of a word (*shobab, shobeb*) from the Hebrew root *shub*, which means "to return." The

NIV prefers "faithless," although it uses "backsliding" in 2:19, 3:22, 5:6, 14:7, and 15:6. The word means "to turn away, to apostasize."

10. The Jews, like many pious people today, were prone to put their faith in the externals of religion, particularly circumcision, rather than in the Lord and His Word. From the beginning, circumcision was a *sign* of God's covenant (Gen. 17; Rom. 4:11) and not the *means* of obtaining salvation (Rom. 2:25-29). Moses urged the people to circumcise their hearts and not depend on external rites (Deut. 10:16; 30:6), and the New Testament echoes this admonition (Matt. 3:7-12; Acts 15:1-35; Rom. 4; 2 Cor. 3; Gal. 1–6; Col. 2:11).

11. We aren't told whether anybody actually saw Jeremiah bury the linen belt and then take it out of the rock again, but the fact that the incident and its interpretation were recorded in his book proves that the message was meant for public consumption. It was one way of showing people what is meant by the word "useless."

12. Isaiah 66:7 uses the image differently. Before the mother's pains begin, she gives birth to the child! So shall the "birth" of the nation of Israel be in the day when God restores His people. See also Isaiah 54:1 (Gal. 4:27).

13. For an excellent introduction and commentary that is sensitive to both the theological and homiletical values of the book, see Walter C. Kaiser, Jr., *A Biblical Approach to Personal Suffering* (Chicago: Moody, 1982).

14. The moth and the rot eat things away silently and nobody knows it. The flood can sometimes be anticipated, but the lion strikes without warning. The nation was decaying long before the Assyrian "lion" attacked. Like the moth and the rot, sin works quietly and brings its own judgment.

15. The net seems to symbolize the military power of Babylon, which the Babylonians themselves revered as one would worship a god. Your god is the thing that you trust, and Babylon trusted in its army.

Thirteen

1. Alexander Whyte, *The Walk, Conversation and Character of Jesus Christ Our Lord* (Grand Rapids: Baker, 1975), 134.

2. James Stalker, *Imago Christi* (New York: A.C. Armstrong & Son, 1890), 246.

3. William Barclay, *The Mind of Jesus* (New York: Harper and Row, 1976), 89.

4. Stalker, *Imago Christi,* 247.

5. Matthew uses the word "fulfilled" fifteen times in his Gospel. One of his purposes is to show his readers that Jesus of Nazareth is indeed the Messiah who fulfilled what was written in the Old Testament Scriptures. This applies not only to what He said and did, but also to the way He ministered.

6. Charles B. Williams, *The New Testament in the Language of the People* (Chicago: Moody, 1966), 40.

7. We think of disciples as learners, and this is true; but the important thing is that *disciples learn by doing* and not just by listening to lectures or reading

books. Perhaps the best contemporary equivalent is *apprentice.* Jesus would teach the Twelve and then send them out to put into practice what they thought they had learned.

8. I noticed one day in my devotional reading that Psalm 1 somewhat parallels the three responsibilities we have to the truth of God's Word. We must learn the truth (Ps. 1:2), live the truth (Ps. 1:1) and share the truth with others (Ps. 1:3). The tree doesn't eat the fruit it produces but makes it available to hungry people. It's only as we live the truth of the Word that we can effectively minister to others.

9. Dr. H.A. Ironside often quoted the adage, "If it's new, it's not true; if it's true, it's not new." He probably had Ecclesiastes 1:9 in mind. The Pulitzer-Prize-winning American historian Richard Hofstadter wrote insightfully about America's love affair with novelty: "We have learned so well how to absorb novelty that receptivity itself has turned into a kind of tradition — 'the tradition of the new.' Yesterday's avant-garde experiment is today's chic and tomorrow's cliche." *Anti-intellectualism in American Life* (New York: Alfred A. Knopf, 1974), 418.

10. E.P. Boys-Smith, in the article "Mental Characteristics," in *Dictionary of Christ and the Gospels,* ed. James Hastings (Grand Rapids: Baker, 1973), 2:164.

11. Stopford A. Brooke, *Life and Letters of the Rev. Frederick W. Robertson* (London: Smith, Elder & Co., 1866), 2:160–61. Various editions of Robertson's sermons are available but must be purchased second-hand. If Robertson is a new name to you, I suggest you get acquainted with him by reading *The Preaching of F.W. Robertson,* ed. Gilbert E. Doan, Jr., and published by Fortress Press in their "Preacher's Paperback Library" (1964). The editor's introductory essay provides an excellent introduction to Robertson's life and interpretation of his philosophy of preaching. The ten sermons included in the book should make you hungry for more. In his day, Robertson was too liberal for the doctrinaire evangelicals of the Anglican church, but too evangelical for the liberals with their nebulous theology.

12. More attention needs to be given to the paradoxes in Scripture. In one sense, the Incarnation is itself a paradox; and many of our Lord's most memorable sayings were couched in paradoxical terms. For examples of how the paradoxes may be made practical in our preaching, see: Charles W.F. Smith, *The Paradox of Jesus in the Gospels* (Philadelphia: Westminster, 1969); Gerald Kennedy, *The Lion and the Lamb* (New York: Abingdon, 1960); Ralph W. Sockman, *The Paradoxes of Jesus* (New York: Abingdon, 1936); Albert D. Belden, *The Paradoxes of Jesus* (London: Independent Press, 1962); and Henry Clay Trumbull, *Practical Paradoxes* (Philadelphia: John D. Wattles, 1889).

13. The statement is found in the book *Machines That Think,* published in 1983. I found it in *The New York Public Library Book of 20th Century American Quotations* (New York: Warner, 1992), 374–75.

14. Many of the classic studies on the parables, while helpful for sermon

ideas, are inadequate for serious study in the light of recent research. I'm referring to those by Campbell Morgan, Marcus Dodds, Ada Habershon, William Taylor and Arthur Pink. Bernard Brandon Scott, *Hear Then the Parable* (Minneapolis: Fortress, 1990) is an excellent study of the parables and has a splendid bibliography. See also: Craig Blomberg, *Interpreting the Parables* (Downers Grove, Ill.: InterVarsity, 1990); Norman Perrin, *Jesus and the Language of the Kingdom* (Philadelphia: Fortress, 1976); Jan Lambrecht, *Once More Astonished* (New York: Crossroad, 1981); David Wenham, *The Parables of Jesus: Pictures of Revolution* (London: Hodder and Stoughton, 1989); Joachim Jeremias, *The Parables of Jesus* (London: SCM, 1963) and *Rediscovering the Parables* (New York: Scribners, 1967); Archibald Hunter, *The Parables Then and Now* (Philadelphia: Westminster, 1972); Robert H. Stein, *An Introduction to the Parables of Jesus* (Philadelphia: Westminster, 1981); Martin H. Scharlemann, *Proclaiming the Parables* (St. Louis: Concordia, 1963); Dan Otto Via, Jr., *The Parables* (Philadelphia: Fortress, 1967); Madeleine I. Boucher, *The Parables* (Wilmington, Del.: Michael Glazier, 1981); Herman Hendrickx, *The Parables of Jesus* (San Francisco: Harper and Row, 1986); and Robert McAfee Brown, *Unexpected News* (Philadelphia: Westminster, 1984). I especially recommend the books by Kenneth E. Bailey, a recognized expert in Eastern culture and language: *Through Peasant Eyes* (Grand Rapids: Eerdmans, 1980), *Poet and Peasant* (Grand Rapids: Eerdmans, 1976), and *The Cross and the Prodigal* (St. Louis: Concordia, 1973). Helmut Thielicke's sermons on the parables are insightful: *The Waiting Father* (New York: Harper and Row, 1959) and *Christ and the Meaning of Life* (New York: Harper, 1962). Three books of sermons by Robert F. Capon are also stimulating: *The Parables of Grace, The Parables of Judgment*, and *The Parables of the Kingdom* (Grand Rapids: Eerdmans, 1988 and 1989). On the Parable of the Prodgal Son, see: J. Wallace Hamilton, *Horns and Halos in Human Nature* (Westwood, N.J.: Revell, 1954), R.H. Ward, *The Prodigal Son* (London: Gollancz, 1968), and Henri J.M. Nouwen, *The Return of the Prodigal Son* (New York: Doubleday, 1992).

15. C.H. Dodd, *The Parables of the Kingdom* (Glasgow: William Collins Sons, 1978), 16.

16. See W. Graham Scroggie, *A Guide To the Gospels* (London: Pickering and Inglis, 1952); and Roy B. Zuck, *Basic Bible Interpretation* (Wheaton, Ill: Victor, 1992), especially chapter 9.

17. See Wilhelm H. Wuellner, *The Meaning of "Fishers of Men"* (Philadelphia: Westminster, 1967).

Fourteen

1. It's possible to carry to extremes teaching from the types, but it's also possible to rob ourselves of nourishing truth if we neglect the types. With reference to the feasts of Jehovah listed in Leviticus 23, see: Roy L. Gustafson, *Feasting on the Feasts* (Grand Rapids: Dunham, 1958); H.K. Downie, *Harvest*

Festivals (New York: Loizeaux, 1951); G.C. Willis, *The Seven Feasts of Jehovah* (Hong Kong: Christian Book Room, 1957); Lehman Strauss, *God's Prophetic Calendar* (Neptune, N.J.: Loizeaux, 1987); John Ritchie, *Feasts of Jehovah* (Grand Rapids: Kregel, 1982); and Richard Booker, *Jesus in the Feasts of Israel* (South Plainfield, N.J.: Bridge, 1987). The classic text is Patrick Fairbairn, *The Typology of Scripture*, 2 vols. (New York: Funk and Wagnalls, 1900). On the hermeneutics of typological study, see chapter 8 of Roy B. Zuck, *Basic Bible Interpretation* (Wheaton, Ill.: Victor, 1992), and chapter 11 of A. Berkeley Mickelsen, *Interpreting the Bible* (Grand Rapids: Eerdmans, 1963). For a critique of Fairbairn's hermeneutic, see chapter 14 of Earl D. Radmacher and Robert D. Preus eds., *Hermeneutics, Inerrancy and the Bible* (Grand Rapids: Zondervan/Academie Books, 1984).

2. Gentiles were present at Pentecost *but as Jewish proselytes* (Acts 2:11). From Acts 1–9, the message is ministered "to the Jew first" (see Acts 13:46; Rom. 1:16).

3. For a rich devotional and practical study of Acts 2, see G. Campbell Morgan *The Birth of the Church* (Old Tappan, N.J.: Revell, 1968). His approach to the symbolism is insightful.

4. "Peter was not a popular preacher drawing a crowd. The crowd was drawn by the Church. . . . The Spirit-filled Church always presents to the world supernatural phenomena, producing amazement, perplexity, criticism. No church is doing its work unless it is doing something supernatural that cannot be done anywhere else." Morgan, *Birth of the Church*, 65–66.

5. In his commentary on Ephesians 5:18–6:9, *Life in the Spirit* (Grand Rapids: Baker, 1975), D. Martyn Lloyd-Jones devotes five messages to Ephesians 5:18-21; and I recommend them to you. As a physician and gifted expositor, Dr. Lloyd-Jones was eminently qualified to deal with this text.

6. Luke didn't use *logizomai* as Paul did in Philippians 3:1-10, but the meaning is the same.

Fifteen

1. Paul S. Minear's *Images of the Church in the New Testament* (Philadelphia: Westminster, 1977) is a basic text that concisely covers a great deal of territory. In the volume on ecclesiology in his *Systematic Theology* (Dallas: Dallas Seminary Press, 1948) Lewis Sperry Chafer discusses seven key images of the church from the dispensationalist's point of view. Earl D. Radmacher, *What the Church Is All About* (Chicago: Moody, 1972) discusses six pictures of the church. John S. Howson, *The Metaphors of St. Paul* (London: Hodder and Stoughton, 1883) contains valuable material on four images used frequently by Paul and shows their relationship to the Christian life: the Roman army, architecture, agriculture and the Greek games. Herbert M. Gale explains and applies many of Paul's metaphors in *The Use of Analogy in the Letters of Paul* (Philadelphia: Westminster, 1964); however, he deals with only seven epistles. Harriet Crabtree, *The Christian Life* (Minneapolis: For-

tress, 1991) focuses on seven images of the Christian life and gives a satisfying introduction to the place of metaphor in theology. Francis Lyall, *Slaves, Citizens, Sons* (Grand Rapids: Zondervan/Academie Books, 1984) is subtitled *Legal Metaphors in the Epistles* and gives an excellent summary of the Roman legal system of Paul's day and his use of it in his letters. Douglas John Hall, *The Steward: A Biblical Symbol Come of Age* (Grand Rapids: Eerdmans, 1990), explains this important biblical metaphor and applies it to economic and ecological problems confronting today's world. Dwight E. Stevenson, *Faith Takes a Name* is a book of sermons on twelve images of the believer, (New York: Harper, 1954). On the devotional side, Guy H. King, *Brought In* (London: Marshall, Morgan and Scott, 1953) contains nineteen excellent devotional studies on the believer's position "in Christ," such as, "In the Family," "In the Army," "In the Building," etc. The author brings together a great deal of Scripture and applies it in a practical way. See also pages 687–94 of Walter Elwell's *Topical Analysis of the Bible* (Grand Rapids: Baker, 1991). The student will also want to read the relevant articles in the Bible encyclopedias and dictionaries as well as in the volumes on Greek and Roman life. I have found the following to be helpful: The National Geographic Society's *Greece and Rome: Builders of Our World* (1968); T.G. Tucker, *Life in Ancient Athens* (London: Macmillan, 1918); Jerome Carcopino, *Daily Life in Ancient Rome* (New Haven: Yale University Press, 1940); T.G. Tucker, *Life in the Roman World of Nero and St. Paul* (London: Macmillan, 1910); G.R. Watson, *The Roman Soldier* (Ithaca, N.Y.: Cornell Univ. Press, 1969); H.A. Harris, *Sport in Greece and Rome* (London: Thames and Hudson, 1972); C.E. Robinson, *Everyday Life in Ancient Greece* (Oxford: Clarendon, 1933); Paul Veyne, ed., *A History of Private Life, From Pagan Rome to Byzantium*, vol. 1 of (Cambridge, Mass: Harvard Univ. Press, 1987). The five volumes in this series cover almost every aspect of "private life" from the time of the Roman Empire to our present day and are valuable additions to your library.

2. Charles H. Spurgeon, *Lectures to My Students* (London: Marshall, Morgan and Scott, 1954), 354.

3. Let Solomon settle the matter. "Like a lame man's legs that hang limp is a proverb in the mouth of a fool" (Prov. 26:7). "Like a thornbush in a drunkard's hand is a proverb in the mouth of a fool" (Prov. 26:9). The word translated "proverb" (*masal*) refers to any wise saying, parable, or oracle that conveys truth, sometimes stated in paradox or symbolism. The fool understands and explains this kind of statement as effectively as the lame man can walk. Like the drunk wielding the thornbush, he does more harm than good, both to himself and to others.

4. See Robert Payne, *The Roman Triumph* (London: Abelard-Schuman, 1962).

5. For an imaginative approach to the church as an army gone AWOL, see Halford Luccock's *Like a Mighty Army* (New York: Oxford Univ. Press, 1954), 3–5. Luccock's "Simeon Stylites" column in *The Christian Century* entertained and irritated readers for many years, and this little volume contains a selection of the best.

6. For other references including *agon* and *agonizomai*, see: Philippians 1:30; Colossians 1:29, 2:1, and 4:12; 1 Thessalonians 2:2; 1 Timothy 6:12.

7. The three images of the church given in 1 Corinthians 3 — the family (vv. 1-4), the field (vv. 5-9a) and the building (vv. 9b-23) — emphasize different goals in ministry. The goal for the family is *maturity*; for the field it is *quantity*; and for the building it is *quality*. There is an interesting parallel here to Jer. 1:10.

8. See also Ephesians 1:23 and 2:16; Colossians 1:18, 24; 2:19; 3:15.

9. The image of marriage is sometimes used when God warns local churches about their sins. The church at Ephesus had forsaken her first love (Rev. 2:4), a statement that reminds us of Jeremiah 2:2; and "that woman Jezebel" had seduced the believers in Thyatira (Rev. 2:18-25). James 4:4 equates "friendship with the world" with adultery.

10. When Paul expounded a doctrine, he wedded it to a duty; when he admonished God's people, he tied the admonition to a doctrine; and he associated both doctrine and duty with Jesus Christ. This is what it means to "build on Christ" in a local church. Why should God's people give? Because of "the grace of our Lord Jesus Christ" (2 Cor. 8:1-9). Why should they forgive one another? Because Christ has forgiven them (Eph. 4:32). Why should husbands love their wives? Because Christ loved the church (Eph. 5:25ff). Why should believers submit to one another? Because Jesus Christ emptied Himself and became a servant for us (Phil. 2:1-18). Duty without doctrine lacks authority; doctrine without duty lacks practicality; and both without Jesus Christ lack motivation. A local church that is built on a preacher, a program, a tradition, or even the defense of some special teaching, will not survive the fire of God's judgment, no matter how successful it appears to be in this world.

11. One of the best concise discussions of this passage is by Leon Morris in the *Tyndale Bible Commentaries* series, volume 7 on 1 Corinthians (Grand Rapids: Eerdmans, 1970).

12. Versions of the Bible striving to avoid sexist language translate *adelphoi* as "brothers and sisters," recognizing that Paul included the whole church when he used the word. In his hypothetical illustration regarding faith and works, James wrote, "Suppose a brother or sister is without clothes . . . " (James 2:15). Our Lord used both "brother" and "sister" when referring to believers (Matt. 5:22; 12:46-50; 23:8; see Rom. 8:29; Heb. 2:11). Peter called the whole church "the brotherhood of believers" (1 Peter 2:17; and see 5:9).

13. Lesslie Newbigin, *The Good Shepherd* (Grand Rapids: Eerdmans, 1977), 43. An evangelist friend of mine suggested that preachers drop the shepherd image from their thinking and preaching inasmuch as we are living in an urban society that knows little or nothing about sheep. Newbigin's book explains why that suggestion is unwise.

14. Books abound on the shepherd metaphor, most of them of a devotional nature dealing with Psalm 23. A classic is William Allen Knight, *The Song of Our Syrian Guest* (Boston: Pilgrim, 1956). John Stevenson, *The Lord Our*

Shepherd (London: J.H. Jackson, 1853) is an old work that contains a wealth of insight. Two newer works that are helpful are John J. Davis, *The Perfect Shepherd* (Winona Lake, Ind.: BMH Books, 1979), and J. Douglas MacMillan, *The Lord Our Shepherd* (Evangelical Press of Wales, 1988). You will also want to consult Charles Jefferson, *The Minister as Shepherd* (New York: Thomas Crowell, 1912), and Lesslie Newbigin, *The Good Shepherd* which I quoted above.

15. See *Evangelism and the Sovereignty of God* (Chicago: InterVarsity, 1961).

16. On the relationship in God's program between Israel and the church, see: John S. Feinberg, ed., *Continuity and Discontinuity: Perspectives on the Relationship Between the Old and New Testaments* (Wheaton, Ill.: Crossway Books, 1988); Samuel J. Schultz, *The Gospel of Moses* (Chicago: Moody, 1979); Thomas E. McComiskey, *The Covenants of Promise: A Theology of the Old Testament Covenants* (Grand Rapids: Baker, 1985); Stephen Westerholm, *Israel's Law and the Church's Faith* (Grand Rapids: Eerdmans, 1988); Daniel P. Fuller, *Gospel and Law: Contrast or Continuum?* (Grand Rapids: Eerdmans, 1980); Renald E. Showers, *There Really Is a Difference!* (Bellmawr, N.J.: Friends of Israel, 1990); Charles C. Ryrie, *Dispensationalism Today* (Chicago: Moody, 1965); Robert L. Cate, *Old Testament Roots for New Testament Faith* (Nashville: Broadman, 1982); Walter C. Kaiser, Jr., *Toward an Old Testament Theology* (Grand Rapids: Zondervan, 1978); *Toward Rediscovering the Old Testament* (Grand Rapids: Zondervan, 1987); *The Old Testament in Contemporary Preaching* (Grand Rapids: Baker, 1973); F.F. Bruce, *New Testament Development of Old Testament Themes* (Grand Rapids: Eerdmans, 1968); Willis J. Beecher, *The Prophets and the Promise* (Grand Rapids: Baker, 1963).

17. Continuity doesn't necessarily demand identity. In the unfolding of His program, God brings the new out of the old and doesn't always abandon the old. Good and godly people disagree over whether there is a future for *national* Israel, and the choice they make depends on their hermeneutic. But our hermeneutic is an act of faith based on our interpretation of the data we perceive in Scripture. The amillennialist can be just as sincere in his or her approach as the premillennialist, and the approach must never be made a test of orthodoxy or spirituality.

18. The classic study is H. Richard Niebuhr, *Christ and Culture* (New York: Harper and Row, 1951). The emergence of the "religious right" in America has forced "separatists" and "fundamentalists" (I do not use these terms pejoratively) to examine their theology of culture. Traditionally, the separatist/fundamentalist doesn't identify with "the world" or seek to change it. According to their theology, the church is "in the world but not of the world," and the church's main task is to save people "out of " the world. See George M. Marsden, *Fundamentalism and American Culture* (New York: Oxford Univ. Press, 1980); *Religion and American Politics,* ed. Mark A. Noll (New York: Oxford Univ. Press, 1990); Randall Balmer, *Mine Eyes Have Seen the Glory* (New York: Oxford Univ. Press, 1989); Jon Johnson, *Will Evangeli-*

calism Survive Its Own Popularity? (Grand Rapids: Zondervan, 1980). It's worth noting that Abraham was a pilgrim and stranger, yet he had allies among the people of the land (Gen. 14:13, 24) and he risked his life to save the wicked people of Sodom (Gen. 14:14-16). Through it all, however, he maintained his strong testimony as a worshiper of God and didn't force his standards on those who were confederated with him (Gen. 14:17-24). See also the Prophet Jeremiah's counsel to the Jewish exiles in Babylon (Jer. 29:1-23). The New Testament commentary on Jeremiah's letter is the First Epistle of Peter. For a perceptive study of Peter's counsel to the "scattered strangers," see Bruce Winter, " 'Seek the Welfare of the City': Social Ethics According to 1 Peter," *Themelios* 13 (April/May 1988).

19. The "unequal yoke" is an agricultural image and suggests Deuteronomy 22:10. The phrase "have in common" translates *metoche*, a word with "business" connotations involving partnership in common purposes and activities. (See Luke 5:7.) Light and darkness are mutually exclusive (see 1 John 1) and have no *koinonia*. "Harmony" comes from a Greek word that gives us our English word "symphony" (*sumphonesis*, "to agree in sound, to be in harmony") and suggests that believers and unbelievers belong to different orchestras, read different scores and follow different conductors. "Have in common" in 2 Corinthians 6:15 is a translation of *meris*, a word that means "part" or "portion" (see also *meros*). The word has geographical overtones and can refer to real estate such as a division or district of a nation. God's people and the people of the world have different citizenships and live on different ground. "Agreement" in 6:16 is *synkatathesis*, derived from *synkatatithemi*, which means "to agree, to cast one's vote together"; so the word has political connotations (Luke 23:51). The temple of God doesn't support the candidates on the devil's ballot.

Sixteen

1. One of the best surveys of the Book of Revelation that focuses on the imaginative is Eugene H. Peterson, *Reversed Thunder* (San Francisco: Harper and Row, 1988). In *A Rebirth of Images* (Albany: State Univ. Press, 1986), Austin Farrer interprets the imagery of the Apocalypse in the light of the annual Jewish feasts, the signs of the zodiac, the number seven, and the prophecies of Ezekiel, Daniel, and Zechariah. One need not agree with his approach to benefit from all he "sees" in what he calls "John's theological poem." In his "Didsbury Lectures," published as *The Relevance of the Apocalypse*, Donald Guthrie says of Farrer's approach: "But to maintain the theory there is much manipulation of evidence, and it needs to be asked whether the readers would have grasped the symbolism. As an explanation of the structure of the book Farrer's theory is not convincing for it introduces too much subjectivity" (Grand Rapids: Eerdmans, 1987), 23–24. Merrill C. Tenney, *Interpreting Revelation* (Grand Rapids: Eerdmans, 1957) is a helpful handbook to the Apocalypse; and William Hendriksen, *More Than Conquerors* (Grand

Rapids: Baker, 1982) presents the amillennial view in a scholarly and irenic manner, giving full consideration to the symbolism of the book. Paul Minear's *I Saw a New Earth* focuses on the symbolism and takes a non-prophetic point of view. No matter what your eschatological position, you are wise to read widely and learn from those you may disagree with. The exegete must steer cautiously between the crass literalism of some expositors who miss the significance of the symbolism, and the sheer fantasy of others who make it mean whatever they want it to mean.

2. The NIV simply says "He made it known," and the NASB "He sent and communicated it," with the marginal note for "communicated" reading "signified."

3. Robert H. Mounce, *The Book of Revelation* in *New International Commentary of the New Testament* (Grand Rapids: Eerdmans, 1977), 65. Writing in *The Tyndale Bible Commentary,* Leon Morris says, "*Signified* is cognate with 'sign,' and, though the point cannot be pressed, it is natural to associate this with the multiplicity of 'signs' narrated in the book" (Grand Rapids: Eerdmans, 1969), 46.

4. Trumpets or trumpeters are referred to fifteen times in the Apocalypse. According to Numbers 10, the trumpets were used to assemble God's people, declare war, announce the holy days and prepare the people to move, all of which have their application in the Book of Revelation. See also Matthew 24:31, 1 Corinthians 15:52, 1 Thessalonians 4:16, and Hebrews 12:19.

5. See my book *Real Worship* (Nashville: Oliver Nelson, 1986), for a study of these themes and their application to the church's ministry today.

6. The Book of Revelation is the book of the throne. The word is used forty-six times.

Seventeen

1. The metaphor of spoils after the battle ought to arouse your imagination so that you ask yourself, "Who in the Bible had to deal with this kind of situation?" You would probably think of Abraham (Gen. 14:17-24), Achan (Josh. 7) and King Saul (1 Sam. 15); and these examples offer you wide opportunity for exegesis and meditation. The metaphor also suggests that there's no reward in Bible study unless we fight some battles with ourselves and with the enemy.

2. Anne Morrow Lindbergh, *The War Within* (New York: Harcourt Brace Jovanovich, 1980), 171. She was quoting the French sculptor Charles Despiau from whom she learned many lessons while he was sculpting her head in his Paris studio. She marveled at his patience and total disregard of the passing of time. Despiau claimed that if an artist had three minutes of "clear vision" in a day, it was enough for him (p. 91). "But you have to step back—to step back—in order to move forward," he claimed (p. 150). As in the creation of a beautiful work of art, the preparation of a message demands time and patience; and it does the minister good to step back occasionally and examine

what is "growing" under his hands. This isn't to suggest that a sermon is a piece of "artistic literature," a religious essay born to be admired. The "baby" is born to confront our listeners personally and accomplish a specific purpose in their lives and the life of the church. As we shall see in a later chapter, the preacher or teacher can learn much about creativity from gifted artists in many fields.

3. Thomas Merton, *The Monastic Journey* (Garden City, N.Y.: Doubleday Image, 1977), 50.

4. Jill Morgan, *A Man of the Word* (London: Pickering and Inglis, 1951), 188.

5. George W. Truett, *The Prophet's Mantle* (Nashville: Broadman, 1948), 143–54. The sermon is included in volume 8 of *20 Centuries of Great Preaching,* ed. Clyde E. Fant, Jr., and William M. Pinson, Jr. (Waco, Texas: Word, 1971), 174–81. Interestingly enough, George H. Morrison used the same text and preached on "The Perils of the Middle-Aged." See Morrison's *The Wings of the Morning* (London: Hodder and Stoughton, n.d.), 131–44.

6. James S. Stewart, *The Gates of New Life* (Edinburgh: T & T Clark, 1939), 102–11.

7. Willard L. Sperry, *Sermons Preached at Harvard* (New York: Harper & Brothers, 1953), 37–44.

8. Frank Boreham, *A Bunch of Everlastings* (Philadelphia: Judson, 1949), 210–21. William Knibb (1803–1845) was an English missionary to Jamaica and crusader against slavery.

9. See *The New Park Street Pulpit* (Pasadena, Texas: Pilgrim, 1981) 4:473. That other dean of American homiletics professors, Andrew W. Blackwood, wrote, "If Spurgeon had thought about the contents and tone color of Judges, he would not have preached a sermon about Samson as an object lesson of consecration." See Blackwood's *The Preparation of Sermons* (Nashville: Abingdon-Cokesbury, 1958), 52. Spurgeon also used Samson as a type of Christ in the sermon "Our Champion," found in *The Metropolitan Tabernacle Pulpit,* 52:493.

10. John A. Broadus, *A Treatise on the Preparation and Delivery of Sermons* (New York: A.C. Armstrong and Son, 1897), 51.

11. Broadus, *Treatise,* 62.

12. Some seminary professors insist that we must make our own translations of our texts, a task that's especially difficult and time consuming for busy preachers who are not proficient in Bible languages. Certainly we ought to study the text in the original language as best we can, using all the helps we can; but, to paraphrase Emerson, why swim the river when somebody has built a bridge?

13. I was fortunate as a seminary student to study under two gifted homileticians, Dr. Charles W. Koller and Dr. Lloyd M. Perry, both of whom insisted on careful "spade work" as we prepared our messages. They required us to hand in our "factual data" sheets along with our sermon outlines, just so they could be sure we weren't depending more on "inspiration" than information and perspiration. Dr. Koller's book *Expository Preaching*

Without Notes (Grand Rapids: Baker, 1962) and Dr. Perry's *Biblical Sermon Guide* (Grand Rapids: Baker, 1970) both discuss the gathering of factual data and the organizing of the material into expository sermons. The Koller volume also contains fifteen of his best sermons. When Dr. Koller or Dr. Perry preached in seminary chapel, we were all there to listen!

14. I realize that, strictly speaking, there is no such thing as an objective study of anything, because the observer is always a part of the process and can't be completely neutral. Students of the Word need to recognize and identify their prejudices and seek to be as objective as possible as they study the Bible.

15. Leland Ryken has written some valuable books to help the student better understand the significance of the literature of the Bible. See *How to Read the Bible as Literature* (Grand Rapids: Zondervan/Academie, 1984); *The Literature of the Bible* (Grand Rapids: Zondervan, 1974); and *The Christian Imagination* (Grand Rapids: Baker, 1991). Another valuable manual is *The Bible in Its Literary Milieu*, ed. John Maier and Vincent Tollers (Grand Rapids: Eerdmans, 1979). I also highly recommend Roy B. Zuck's *Basic Bible Interpretation* (Wheaton, Ill.: Victor, 1991); chapter 6, "Bridging the Literary Gap," is especially pertinent to this discussion. Also, Sidney Greidanus, *The Modern Preacher and the Ancient Text* (Grand Rapids: Eerdmans, 1988) is an excellent survey of modern literary theory as it relates to biblical hermeneutics and homiletics. The author summarizes a wealth of material and explains how it can be used in the study of the Bible and the preparation of sermons. An older, but still useful, work is E.W. Bullinger, *Figures of Speech Used in the Bible* (Grand Rapids: Baker, 1968).

16. For that matter, the word "literal" is itself a metaphor and means "according to the letter." The image is that of a student with a copy-book, learning to write by imitating the letters on the page. As Emerson said, every word was once a picture.

17. For an excellent survey of various types of "criticism" and their application to biblical hermeneutics, see David Alan Black and David S. Dockery, eds., *New Testament Criticism and Interpretation* (Grand Rapids: Zondervan, 1991).

18. One of the best tools for identifying New Testament "semantic domains" is the *Greek—English Lexicon of the New Testament Based on Semantic Domains*, ed. Johannes P. Louw and Eugene A. Nida, 2 vols. (New York: United Bible Society, 1989).

19. I use "hearers" instead of "readers" because much of the Word was spoken before it was written, or if it was written first, it was written to be read aloud. Furthermore, the written Word as we have it today should be "heard" even when it is read privately. In fact, as a regular part of the study process, the minister would do well to read the text aloud and listen to it. The careless reading of the Scriptures in public is often an evidence that the passage wasn't carefully read in private. It was said that people learned more from Campbell Morgan's public reading of the Bible than from anybody else's *preaching* of the Bible!

20. There is a brief but insightful discussion on preaching and biblical theology in Greidanus, *Modern Preacher*, 67–72. See also Geerhardus Vos, *Biblical Theology, Old and New Testaments* (Grand Rapids: Eerdmans, 1948); Edmund P. Clowney, *Preaching and Biblical Theology* (Grand Rapids: Eerdmans, 1961); Gordon R. Lewis and Bruce A. Demarest, *Integrative Theology* (Grand Rapids: Zondervan/Academie, 1987); and Alan F. Johnson and Robert E. Webber, *What Christians Believe* (Grand Rapids: Zondervan/Academie, 1989). These last two volumes summarize both biblical and historical theology as they explain the major doctrines of the Christian faith.

21. See Louis Berkhof, *The History of Christian Doctrines,* (Grand Rapids: Baker, 1975); Geoffrey W. Bromiley, *Historical Theology: An Introduction* (Grand Rapids: Eerdmans, 1978); Gordon R. Lewis and Bruce A. Demarest, *Integrative Theology* (Grand Rapids: Zondervan/Academie, 1987); and Alan F. Johnson and Robert E. Webber, *What Christians Believe: A Biblical and Historical Summary* (Grand Rapids: Zondervan/Academie, 1989).

22. The Santayana quote is found in his *The Life of Reason*, volume 1, chapter 12. The Whitehead quote is in his *Adventures in Ideas* (New York: Free Press, 1967), 238. In quoting Whitehead, I'm not at all agreeing with either "process philosophy" or "process theology"; but there's a sense in which the way things change helps to determine what will happen in the future. One is reminded of George Orwell's "party slogan" in *1984*, "Who controls the past, controls the future: who controls the present controls the past" (part 1, ch. 3). See Earle E. Cairns, "Christian Faith and History" in *Christianity and the World of Thought*, ed. Hudson T. Armerding (Chicago: Moody, 1968); George A. Buttrick, *Christ and History* (Nashville: Abingdon, 1963); Colin Brown, *History and Faith* (Grand Rapids: Zondervan/Academie, 1987); and Herbert Butterfield, *Christianity and History* (New York: Scribners, 1950). No historian can be purely objective; even the selection of materials has a subjective bias. But the alternative is to have no historians at all, and that would be tragic.

23. See Harry Emerson Fosdick, *The Living of These Days* (New York: Harper, 1956), 230.

24. In his preface to Karl Barth's *Homiletics* (Louisville: Westminster /John Knox, 1991), Geoffrey Bromiley writes: "Theology for him could not be an end in itself. It is not to be done in isolation from the church's supreme ministry. It is itself a secondary ministry It has the servant role of critically and constructively testing the church's proclamation with a view of keeping it in tune with its function as testimony to the revealed Word of God according to the norm of the scriptural Word."

25. Philip Schaff, *The Creeds of Christendom* (Grand Rapids: Baker, 1977), 1: 6.

26. "Few things are more essential to biblical preaching than being aware that the Word addresses pastor and people alike, that the struggle to appropriate the text is common to us all." Leander E. Keck, *The Bible in the Pulpit* (Nashville: Abingdon, 1978), 63.

27. Phillips Brooks, *Lectures on Preaching* (Grand Rapids: Baker, 1969), 8. The edition published by Kregel Publications, *The Joy of Preaching*, contains paragraph headings that help to make it easier to read these long lectures. In my opinion, Brooks's *Lectures on Preaching* is the seminal book on preaching published in the United States, and almost everything we've since published about preaching is a footnote to what Brooks said at Yale in 1877.

28. This is from Emerson's famous "Divinity School Address" which he delivered at Harvard on Sunday evening, July 15, 1838. The fact that Emerson himself was a "ministerial drop-out" didn't endear him to the Divinity School faculty; and he had been invited to speak, not by the school officers, but by the members of the senior class. It would take nearly thirty years for the faculty to get over this address and invite Emerson back to speak. He defined preaching as "the expression of the moral sentiment in application to the duties of life." While his address contains a good deal of "Emersonian transcendental fog," he does say some things about the church and preaching that we could well take to heart today.

29. The experience of Isaiah, recorded in chapter 6 of his prophecy, is often used to illustrate how God prepares us for ministry: Isaiah saw the Lord, he saw himself, and he saw the needs of others. He met the Lord in worship, the Lord met him in cleansing, and then the Lord commissioned him for service. Both Jeremiah and Ezekiel had to experience personal suffering before they could receive and deliver the messages God gave them. When we divorce the messenger from the message, we cease to have "divine truth communicated through human personality."

30. Bonar, *Menoir and Remains,* 36, 40.

31. *The Journal of Henry David Thoreau,* March 18, 1842.

32. Dwight E. Stevenson writes: "Nothing is more central to a genuine ministry than the faculty of feeling one's way into the lives of others. . . . It is more than sympathy; it is *empathy,* the imaginative projection of one's consciousness into another's being." *In the Biblical Preacher's Workshop* (Nashville: Abingdon, 1967), 113.

33. I use the word "myth" to mean a set of beliefs, often nebulous, that hover around persons, events, and institutions. Myths help people to understand life, find their place in society, and cope with what comes their way. An excellent introduction to the subject is K.K. Ruthven's, *Myth* in the "Critical Idiom" series published by Methuen and Co. The section on "The Context of Preaching" in James W. Cox, *Preaching* (San Francisco: Harper & Row, 1985) contains many helpful insights.

34. "I always consider the settlement of America as the opening of a grand scheme and design in Providence for the illumination of the ignorant and the emancipation of the slavish part of mankind all over the earth." John Adams wrote that, and George Washington said in his first inaugural address, "The preservation of the sacred fire of liberty and the destiny of the republican model of government are justly considered, perhaps, as *deeply,* as *finally,* staked on the experiment intrusted to the hands of the American people."

Senator Albert Gore justified the annexation of the Philippines in these words: "God has not been preparing the English-speaking and Teutonic peoples for a thousand years for nothing but vain and idle self-contemplation and self-admiration. No. He made us master organizers of the world to establish a system where chaos reigned. . . . He has marked the American people as His chosen nation to finally lead in the redemption of the world." These quotations are cited from Robert N. Bellah, *The Broken Covenant* (New York: Seabury, 1975), 33–34, 38. A nation that's been through costly unsettled wars in Korea and Vietnam, as well as the upheavals of the '60s and '70s, probably questions some of these noble sentiments. But the "American messianic myth" of progress and conquest is still the guiding light of millions of people. Add to this the "Horatio Alger myth" (or the "log cabin to White House" myth) of success available to anyone who will work hard, and you have the statement of faith for American civil religion, celebrated every Fourth of July and Labor Day. The minister of a WASP church doesn't have the advantages of the minister of a black congregation, who knows that the people look to the exodus from Egypt as their unifying and guiding myth.

35. Following are some helpful books in this area: Samuel Volbeda, *The Pastoral Genius of Preaching* (Grand Rapids: Zondervan, 1960); Charles F. Kemp, *The Preaching Pastor* (St. Louis: Bethany, 1966); David H.C. Read, *Preaching About the Needs of Real People* (Philadelphia: Westminster, 1988); Wayne E. Oates, *The Bible In Pastoral Care* (Philadelphia: Westminster, 1953); Edmund Holt Linn, *Preaching as Counseling: The Unique Method of Harry Emerson Fosdick* (Valley Forge, Pa.: Judson, 1966); and J. Peter Vosteen, "Pastoral Preaching" in *The Preacher and Preaching*, ed. Samuel T. Logan, Jr. (Phillipsburg, N.J.: Presbyterian and Reformed, 1986).

36. See Thomas H. Troeger, *Imagining a Sermon* (Nashville: Abingdon, 1990), and Paul Scott Wilson, *Imagination of the Heart* (Nashville: Abingdon, 1988). Both books contain excellent suggestions for transforming a "standard sermon outline" into a message that is creative.

Eighteen

1. See my *Bible Exposition Commentary* (1989) as well as *Wiersbe's Expository Outlines on the New Testament* (1992), *Wiersbe's Expository Outlines on the Old Testament* (1993), and the individual commentaries in the BE series, all published by Victor Books; also see *With the Word*, published by Oliver-Nelson.

2. I courageously attempted to outline Ecclesiastes in my book *Be Satisfied* (1990), and First John in *Be Real* (1979), both published by Victor Books. The astute reader, however, discovers that in both books I arrived at my outlines by first imposing an overriding theme. I saw Ecclesiastes as a study of satisfaction in this life, and First John as a description of real Christian living. If you selected a different theme, you'd end up with a different outline. In *Be Joyful*, I expounded Philippians as an epistle of Christian joy, but I could just as well

have used the themes of unity and servanthood and developed different outlines. There is no escaping the fact that the student's outlook will largely determine the outcome.

3. The one exception may be the Book of Revelation; that is, if you take Revelation 1:19 as the "inspired outline," as dispensational premillennial expositors do. A case can be made, however, for seeing *two* divisions in the text and not three: "the things you see, namely, what is and what is to come." For a concise discussion, see Mounce, *Revelation*, 81–82. Psalm 119 and other acrostic psalms follow the order of the Hebrew alphabet, but this can hardly be called an outline. The careful expositor should follow the example of Campbell Morgan, who did not say "This is *the* outline of the book" but "This is *an* outline of the book." In my own ministry, I have used the phrase "a suggested outline."

4. I recommend that you index the sermons in your personal library by texts and take time regularly in your studies to compare and contrast the approaches that various preachers take to the same passage. Of course, you *never* read sermons on your text until your own preparation is completed, lest you be tempted either to plagiarize or to follow a "track" that just isn't suited to you. One of Alexander Whyte's assistants once modeled a sermon after Whyte's approach, and Whyte's only comment was, "Preach your own message!" Good advice!

5. T.S. Eliot, *On Poetry and Poets* (London: Faber and Faber, 1957), 27.

6. A lady with pen and notebook in hand stopped me after I had preached a message at a summer Bible conference. She asked, "What was the third subpoint under Roman numeral five?" I really must have done a poor job that morning, because there was no Roman numeral five! I trust she didn't go away from the meeting with her notebook full and her heart empty.

7. Philip Wheelwright, *Metaphor and Reality* (Bloomington, Ind.: Indiana Univ. Press, 1975), 39. For a fascinating discussion of the importance of imagination to scientific research, see Roger Shepard, "The Imagination of the Scientist," in *Imagination and Education,* ed. Kieran Egan and Dan Nadaner (New York: Teachers College Press, 1988), 153–85.

8. Emerson agreed with his friend, for he wrote, "Whoever discredits analogy and requires heaps of facts before any theories can be attempted, has no poetic power, and nothing original or beautiful will be produced by him." See *The Complete Works of Ralph Waldo Emerson* (Boston: Houghton, Mifflin, 1903–1904), 5:239. "The poet/prophet is a voice that shatters settled reality and evokes new possibility in the listening assembly," writes Walter Brueggemann in *Finally Comes the Poet,* 4.

9. Walt Whitman, *Leaves of Grass* (New York: Modern Library, 1950), 217.

10. Since the Enlightenment, the Western world has focused on "reality" and encouraged the "scientific approach." During the Romantic Era, the pendulum began to swing back with the new emphasis on feelings and imagination—the "world" within us; and now, science and imagination are good friends, if not wedded. But the Eastern world has cultivated a different ap-

proach that Western thinkers shouldn't ignore: the "real" world is the world within. See Robert Avens, *Imagination Is Reality* (Dallas, Texas: Spring, 1980) for a brief survey of "Eastern" views of imagination and reality. Thomas Moore's best-selling *Care of the Soul* (New York: Harper-Collins, 1992) blends Jungian psychology with the Eastern philosophy of reality and applies both to pastoral work and spiritual development. Moore says a great deal about the imagination and the role it plays in the making of a life.

11. Hugh Black, *Listening to God* (New York: Revell, 1906), 17. Hugh Black (1868–1953) was Alexander Whyte's associate at Free St. George's Church in Edinburgh and later served as professor of practical theology at Union Seminary, New York City. Because Black was more liberal in his theology than was his senior minister, the congregation facetiously said that in the morning service they were blackened by Whyte and in the evening they were whitewashed by Black! However different they may have been in personality and doctrine, the two men agreed on the importance of imagination in preaching God's Word.

12. Marvin Bell, "Three Propositions: Hooey, Dewey, and Looney," in *Writers on Writing*, ed. Robert Pack and Jay Parini (Hanover, N.H.: Univ. Press of New England, 1991), 7.

13. Nancy Hale, in "The Two-Way Imagination," *Adventures of the Mind: Second Series*, ed. Richard Thruelson and John Kobler (New York: Alfred A. Knopf, 1961), 357. She quotes the nineteenth-century German chemist Friedrich A. Kekule von Stradonitz who said, "If we learn to dream, gentlemen, then we shall perhaps find the truth. We must take care, however, not to publish our dreams before submitting them to proof by the waking mind" (p. 362). Blessed are the balanced! See Northrop Frye's discussion of imagination and science in chapter 1 of his *The Educated Imagination* (Bloomington, Ind.: Indiana Univ. Press, 1964).

14. Kittay, *Metaphor*, 7. See also p. 67: "A model is, in essence, a sustained and systematic metaphor." Physicists smile and tell us that on Mondays, Wednesdays, and Fridays, they envision light as waves, while on Tuesdays and Thursdays, they envision light as particles; and apparently nobody is worse off because of the bargain.

15. Quoted in Derek Jarrett, *The Sleep of Reason* (London: Weidenfeld and Nicolson, 1988), 129.

16. Watchman Nee, *A Table in the Wilderness* (Fort Washington, Pa.: Christian Literature Crusade, 1965), selection for August 13.

17. Terence Hawkes, *Metaphor*, The Critical Idiom Series (London: Methuen, 1972). I haven't referred to it before, but this book is perhaps the best brief introduction to the study of metaphor.

18. Frye, *Educated Imagination*, 32.

19. Peterson, *Answering God*, 73.

20. Edward F. Murphy, *The Crown Treasury of Relevant Quotations* (New York: Crown, 1978), 593. Somewhere, Emerson wrote, "A system-grinder hates the truth." Life is characterized by "spontaneity and variety," and so is

Scripture. Why then should our sermons be characterized by lameness and tameness?

21. Guy Davenport, *The Geography of the Imagination* (San Francisco: North Point, 1981), 43. "No word in a context can have more meaning than the writer thinks into it," he says. "When a writer does not care about the meaning of a word, we know it" (p. 31). In his *Proverbs from Plymouth Pulpit,* Henry Ward Beecher called words "pegs to hang ideas on," which is about as tame a definition as you can get. Joseph Conrad came closer to the truth when he wrote in *Lord Jim:* "A word carries far — very far — deals destruction through time as the bullets go flying through space." In Scripture, when God speaks, something happens. The miracle of preaching God's Word is that the Spirit can take our feeble efforts and accomplish things in His church. "He sent forth his word and healed them; he rescued them from the grave" (Ps. 107:20). "The words I have spoken to you are spirit and they are life" (John 6:63).

22. "O for the touch of the Holy Spirit to make this outline into a living sermon," cried Spurgeon as he launched into a sermon. "Here are the altar and the wood: O Holy Ghost, be thou the fire!" See *The Metropolitan Tabernacle Pulpit,* vol. 27, p. 158.

23. There was a post-resurrection "boat experience" recorded in John 21:1-14; and it too emphasizes the importance of faith. Peter and the other six men didn't wait for Jesus to instruct them, so their efforts were in vain. Jesus said, "Apart from me you can do nothing" (John 15:5).

24. Preachers are generally too hard on Peter because he got his eyes off the Lord and began to sink. But keep four facts in mind: none of the other disciples left the ship; Peter did successfully walk out to Jesus; Peter had faith enough to cry out to Jesus for help; and both Peter and Jesus walked back to the ship. Anybody who's still cowering in the ship has no right to criticize Peter!

25. If an outline comes to you as a seeming inspiration from heaven, write it down and set it aside while you "imagineer" the message. On more than one occasion, I've discovered that the "inspired" outline detoured me from the message I was supposed to prepare; but there have been other times when it became the key to the passage. You never know what will happen, so don't abandon even material that doesn't seem to fit into the message at all.

26. It has been said that the art of expository preaching is the wise use of the wastebasket, and there's some truth to the statement. In a seminar on preaching, one minister confessed that his sermons sounded like Bible commentaries because he tried to include everything he'd learned about the passage. Remember Harry Emerson's Fosdick's admonition that the purpose of preaching is not to explain a subject but to achieve an object. The overriding metaphor you select is governed by the purpose you want to achieve in preaching the message.

27. In my outline, I chose "statement of faith," i.e., a personal creed, and my key word was "affirmations"; but I could just as well have used "anchors"

and maintained the nautical theme. "When you find yourself in the storms of life, lay hold of several anchors of faith . . . " would have been the transitional sentence.

28. Johnson was quoting one of his old college tutors. See Boswell's *Life of Samuel Johnson,* entry for April 30, 1773. What's true of writing is true of preaching: we preach to *express* and not to *impress.* The familiar statement of James Denny still stands: "No man can bear witness to Christ and to himself at the same time. No man can give the impression that he himself is clever and that Christ is mighty to save."

29. Donald Coggan, *Stewards of Grace* (London: Hodder and Stoughton, 1958), 71. Coggan was Bishop of Bradford when he wrote this book; from 1974 to 1980, he served as Archbishop of Canterbury. I also recommend his *Ministry of the Word* (London: Canterbury, 1945), and *Preaching: The Sacrament of the Word* (New York: Crossroad, 1988).

30. Alliteration can be very effective if the way it's used is original and the pictures are more vivid than the frames. Anyone who ever heard Dr. R.G. Lee go down his famous "Alphabet of Sin" heard alliteration at its best ("Man calls sin an accident; God calls it an abomination!"). In his younger years, Spurgeon sometimes alliterated his main points, as in his sermon on the curing of the demonized boy (Luke 9:42). "There are four points for our consideration this morning," he told his New Park Street congregation. "That you may easily remember them I have made them alliterative: the devil's *doings, designs, discovery,* and *defeat.*" (See *The New Park Street Pulpit* (Pasadena, Texas: Pilgrim, 1981), 2:269. In his sermon on "Rahab's faith," Spurgeon pointed out that her faith was saving faith, singular faith, stable faith, self-denying faith, sympathizing faith, and sanctifying faith (*New Park Street,* 3:97–104). He preached the first message in 1856 and the second in 1857; but as late as 1890, he was still occasionally using alliteration in one way or another. "Faith is the fountain, the foundation, and the fosterer of obedience," he said in his introduction to a sermon on Abraham's faith (*Metropolitan Tabernacle Pulpit,* 37:157). He entitled a message based on Psalm 106:7, "Sin: Its Spring-head, Stream and Sea" (*Metropolitan Tabernacle,* 37:264). In a sermon on Luke 7:50, he said, "Salvation, then, is a present thing, in price, in promise, in principles, and in pledge" (*New Park Street,* 48:124). James S. Stewart developed the "drama" of John Mark's life in four alliterated "acts": Recantation, Remorse, Restoration, and Reparation. See his *The Gates of New Life* (Edinburgh: T & T Clark, 1939), 220–31). In the same volume, his excellent sermon entitled "Why Be a Christian?" presents four alliterated reasons: "The Christian life is happier than any other, harder than any other, holier than any other and more hopeful than any other."

If an alliterated outline comes naturally out of the text, and if it doesn't distract from the message, it can be a useful tool to help people remember what you said. But if this is the only way you set the table, your menu may become too predictable; and predictable preaching isn't usually powerful preaching. If our people assemble for worship each week asking themselves,

"What will it be today, all *G's* or all *W's?*" then we're carrying alliteration too far and *form* is destroying *function*. Of course, if the preacher wants the reputation of being a clever fellow with words, then that's another matter altogether.

31. Mark Twain is supposed to have said that "the difference between any word and the right word is the difference between lightning and a lightning bug." Rather than wasting his time thumbing through the thesaurus, the preacher would accomplish more if he spent that time consulting a good dictionary of synonyms to make certain the key words in his outline are accurate. We who preach the Gospel do so by using words; and since words are the tools that we use, we ought to study them and learn how they work. Preachers who neglect to use the dictionary and increase their vocabulary are robbing themselves and their people.

Nineteen

1. Harry Farra, *The Sermon Doctor* (Grand Rapids: Baker, 1989), 55. This very original approach to homiletics deserves more attention than it has received. Perhaps the title frightened off preachers who don't think their sermons need "doctoring." (Some of mine need burying!)

2. A fine example is R.G. Lee's famous sermon "Pay Day Some Day." It is biblical biographical preaching at its best; and if you haven't read it, you should do so soon. You will find it in *25 of the Greatest Sermons Ever Preached*, comp. and ed. Jerry Falwell (Grand Rapids: Baker, 1983), and also in *Great Sermons of the 20th Century*, comp. Peter F. Gunther (Westchester, Ill.: Crossway, 1986).

3. The popular TV series "Life-Styles of the Rich and Famous" gave a pastor friend of mine the idea for a sermon series on the Beatitudes, which he called "The Life-Styles of the *Spiritually* Rich and Famous." That's using your imagination!

4. Let me recommend that you read Daniel J. Boorstin's book *The Image: A Guide to Pseudo-Events in America* (New York: Harper and Row, 1964). "Two centuries ago when a great man appeared," wrote Boorstin, "people looked for God's purpose in him; today we look for his press agent" (p. 45). Instead of producing heroes today, we are manufacturing celebrities; and thanks to media advertising techniques, we can make a nobody into somebody almost overnight. Boorstin's book is an entertaining and enlightening study of the "illusions" that have captured America and what they are doing to us.

5. Arthur M. Schlesinger, Jr. "The Decline of Heroes" in *Adventures of the Mind*, ed. John Kobler and Richard Thruelsen (New York: Alfred A. Knopf, 1960), 95–106. The quotations are from pages 97 and 104 respectively.

6. Ambrose Bierce said that "the world is divided into two classes of people, the righteous and the unrighteous, with the righteous doing the classifying."

7. If you have a problem doing this, I suggest you read Frederick

Buechner's (pronounced "BEEK-ner") *Peculiar Treasures: A Biblical Who's Who* (San Francisco: Harper and Row, 1979). "What struck me more than anything else as I reacquainted myself with this remarkable rag-bag of people," says Buechner in his preface, "was both their extraordinary aliveness and their power to make me feel somehow more alive myself for having known them."

8. "There is one study, my Christian brethren, which never can lose its interest for us so long as we are men: and that is the investigation of human character. The deep interest of Biography consists in this—that it is in some measure the description to us of our own inner history. You cannot unveil the secrets of another heart without at the same time finding something to correspond with, and perchance explain, the mysteries of your own. Heart answers to heart." Frederick W. Robertson, *Sermons: Fourth Series* (London: Kegan Paul, Trench, Trubner, 1900), 160. Robertson was especially gifted at penetrating the human heart as he preached about Bible personalities.

9. Russell Baker, "Life with Mother," in *Inventing the Truth*, ed. William Zinsser (New York: Book-of-the-Month Club, 1987), 49.

10. Catherine Drinker Bowen, *Biography: The Craft and the Calling* (Boston: Little, Brown, 1969). Chapter 6 is the one I'm referring to. While this book is primarily for biographers writing papers, articles, or books, it contains some wise counsel that preachers can apply as they prepare their biographical messages. Bowen points out the subtle pitfalls we should avoid as we gather data and try to understand history. I especially like her quotation from Henry James: "To live over people's lives is nothing, unless we live over their perceptions, live over the growth, the change, the varying intensity of the same—since it was by these things they themselves lived" (p. 35).

11. Some helpful books to supplement your own research are Harold L. Wilmington's *Old Testament People, New Testament People* and *The Life of Christ*, in the series, Wilmington's Complete Guide to Bible Knowledge, (Wheaton, Ill.: Tyndale). The biblical facts are presented in a concise and orderly manner, and the author even tells you how many times the people are named!

12. In recent years, the "dramatic monologue" has become a popular approach to biographical preaching; but before you move in that direction, be sure you have the talent needed to make it succeed. Not every preacher is an actor. Furthermore, the dramatic monologue necessarily involves *assuming* that the character would speak and act in a certain manner, and your assumptions might be wrong. We're sure of ourselves when we quote what the Bible says; but we can't always be sure that what we say, or the way we say it, is true to sacred history. An actor has no more right to declaim a lie than a preacher has to preach a lie. The dramatic monologue must have just as much factual basis as the biographical sermon. Imagination is no substitute for information.

13. I've often wanted to preach a series of sermons on the hands of David. They held among other things, a sling, a sword, a harp, a pen (for writing the

psalms) and a cup of cold water. David made as significant a use of the simple things as he did of the great things.

14. For a fascinating study of names in the contemporary literary world, see Leon Edel's "The Figure Under the Carpet" in *Telling Lives: The Biographer's Art,* ed. Marc Pachter (Washington, D.C.: New Republic, 1979). Leon Edel is a leading advocate of "psycho-biography" (or "literary psychology") and is the author of the monumental biography of Henry James, which won a Pulitzer Prize. His theories are explained and illustrated in his book *Stuff of Sleep and Dreams: Experiments in Literary Psychology* (New York: Harper and Row, 1982). He outlines his approach in the first three chapters, and I recommend them to you. I also recommend his book *Writing Lives: Principia Biographica* (New York: W.W. Norton, 1984). Here and there in this book, the preacher will find hints and principles that apply to the study and preaching of Bible biography. However, let me caution you not to try to become an amateur psychiatrist as you seek to understand the lives of the great men and women of the Bible. A basic knowledge of yourself in particular, and human nature in general, should suffice. For a simple presentation and sane evaluation of this new field, see Milton Lomask, "Psychbiography" in *The Biographer's Craft* (New York: Harper and Row, 1986), chap. 13. For an advanced study, see Peter Gay, *Freud for Historians* (New York: Oxford Univ. Press, 1985). Dorothy F. Zeligs, *Psychoanalysis and the Bible* (New York: Bloch, 1974) contains interesting studies by a Jewish psychoanalyst of seven Old Testament leaders: Abraham, Jacob, Joseph, Samuel, Saul, David and Solomon.

15. Quoted in John A. Garraty, *The Nature of Biography* (New York: Random House/Vintage Books, 1984), 11. A novelist can invent a character and always know what that character is thinking, but a biographer doesn't have that advantage. Why did Judas sell Jesus? Was it for money? Was it to force Him to do something to redeem Israel? Was it because he hated Him for setting up a spiritual kingdom instead of a glorious kingdom for the Jews? Or was it because his own character had so eroded that there was nothing left for him to do but kill himself and Jesus? Perhaps it was a combination of all of these. "The heart is deceitful above all things and beyond cure. Who can understand it?" (Jer. 17:9)

16. We wonder how Judas responded inwardly to all of our Lord's warnings about wealth and covetousness. How did Judas the treasurer feel when Jesus rejected the rich young ruler's shallow offer to become a disciple? When Mary of Bethany anointed Jesus, did our Lord's rebuke of the disciples sting Judas and make him even more determined to listen to the devil?

17. Along with the standard books on Bible characters and the books about the twelve Apostles, you might want to consult these special studies on Judas: S. Pearce Carey, *Judas and Jesus* (London: Hodder and Stoughton, 1931); Bertil Gartner, *Iscariot* (Philadelphia: Fortress "Facet Books," 1971); Jasper A. Huffman, *Judas: The Biography of a Soul* (Marion, Ind.: The Wesley Press, 1958); and Albert Nicole, *Judas The Betrayer* (Grand Rapids: Baker, 1957).

Clarence E. Macartney, *He Chose Twelve* (Grand Rapids: Kregel, 1993) contains an excellent study of Judas by a preacher who majored in preaching Bible biographies.

18. John Bunyan closes the first part of his *Pilgrim's Progress* with the sobering words, "Then I saw that there was a way to hell, even from the gates of heaven, as well as from the City of Destruction."

19. In recent years, much has been done in the area of studying biblical narrative. See: Meir Sternberg, *The Poetics of Biblical Narrative,* (Bloomington, Ind.: Indiana Univ. Press, 1987); *The Bible in its Literary Milieu,* ed. John Maier and Vincent Tollers (Grand Rapids: Eerdmans, 1979), especially the part entitled "Tragedy and the Gospel Narratives" by Roger L. Cox; Leland Ryken, *The Literature of the Bible* (Grand Rapids: Zondervan, 1974), especially chapter 3 on "Heroic Narrative"; and Michael Goldberg, *Theology and Narrative: A Critical Introduction* (Nashville: Abingdon, 1982).

20. See Walter Wangerin, Jr., *Ragman and Other Cries of Faith* (San Francisco: Harper and Row, 1984). Fulghum's books include these: *All I Really Need To Know I Learned in Kindergarten, It Was on Fire When I Lay Down on It,* and *Uh-Oh,* all published by Villard Books. When it comes to Buechner, you have your choice of fiction, theology, autobiography, sermons, and miscellaneous essays. Just check your local bookstore. *Wishful Thinking* and *Whistling in the Dark,* and *Peculiar Treasures* are among my favorites, although I certainly enjoyed *The Clown in the Belfry.* All are published by either Harper and Row or HarperCollins. I find Garrison Keillor easier to listen to than to read or to watch on TV, and you can probably locate his program on your local public radio station on Saturday evenings. Cassette tapes of his monologues ("the news from Lake Wobegon") are available in many tape and record shops. His book *Lake Wobegon Days* is delightful (New York: Viking, 1985), and *Leaving Home* has its moments (New York: Viking, 1987). Michael Fedo has written an unauthorized biography of Keillor that is thought-provoking, *The Man from Lake Wobegon* (New York: St. Martin's Press, 1987). In a brief conversation with Keillor after one of his shows, I suggested to him that he wasn't just telling stories; he was really preaching sermons. He smiled and denied it, but his denial wasn't too enthusiastic. Maybe I read more into what he says than is really there.

21. Just a reminder that while "comedy" may include laughter, the essential ingredient in this type of drama is a happy ending with all turning out well. The stories of Joseph and Ruth are comedic, while those of Samson and Saul are tragic.

22. See E.M. Forster, *Aspects of The Novel* (New York: Harcourt Brace Jovanovich, 1956).

Twenty

1. Andrew W. Blackwood, *The Funeral: A Source Book for Ministers* (Philadelphia: Westminster, 1942), 138. My son David and I encourage this ap-

proach in our book *Comforting the Bereaved* (Chicago: Moody, 1985).

2. I've glanced through my notebook of funeral messages that I've preached, and I'm embarrassed to discover how many of them lack that "sanctified imagination" that I contend is so necessary; but I'm encouraged to see a steady improvement over the years. There is hope.

3. Wiersbe, *Comforting the Bereaved,* 53.

4. This is hinted at in John 11:44, "Take off the grave clothes and let him go." The funeral is not the place for the preacher to try to answer everybody's questions about eschatology. The post-funeral pastoral ministry will provide many opportunities to teach what the Bible says about death, heaven and hell, the new body and the return of the Lord. In the regular course of our preaching ministry, we ought to deal with these subjects so that our people are informed.

5. This is a good place to remind all of us that only God knows the truth about the life of the deceased, and we'd better be careful not to go too far in our eulogies. I once conducted the funeral service for a man everybody thought was a devout Christian and a faithful church worker, only to discover a few weeks later that he was leading a double life. From our limited point of view, the weaving might be beautiful; but to God, it might be ugly and soiled.

6. Does Psalm 23 deal *only* with the shepherd image, or are verses 5-6 describing God as the Host who honors us at a banquet in His house? Expositors are not agreed in their interpretations. Scroggie sees three images in Psalm 23: the shepherd and the sheep (v. 1), the guide and the traveler (vv. 2-4) and the host and the guest (vv. 5-6). (W. Graham Scroggie, *Know Your Bible: The Psalms* [London: Pickering and Inglis, 1948] 1:145–49.) G. Campbell Morgan also took that view. See his *Great Chapters of the Bible* (New York: Fleming H. Revell, 1935), 55. Alexander Maclaren saw two images: the sheep and the shepherd (vv. 1-4) and the host and the guest (vv. 5-6). (See *The Expositor's Bible* [Grand Rapids: Eerdmans, 1940], 3:65–66.) The two-image interpretation is defended by John J. Davis in *The Perfect Shepherd* (Winona Lake, Ind.: BMH, 1979). The classic devotional treatment of Psalm 23, William Allen Knight's *The Song of Our Syrian Guest* (Boston: Pilgrim, 1956), ably presents the single-image approach; and to this agree Phillip Keller, *A Shepherd Looks at Psalm 23* (Grand Rapids: Zondervan, 1970) and J. Douglas MacMillan *The Lord Our Shepherd* (Wales: Evangelical Press, 1983). Both of Keller and MacMillan worked as shepherds. Our Lord's words in Luke 12:32 ("Do not be afraid, little flock, for your Father has been pleased to give you the kingdom") would suggest that the single-image interpretation doesn't violate the shepherd metaphor; for in the East, the sheik is a father, a king and a shepherd. I prefer the single-image view.

7. The "valley of the shadow of death" in verse 4 is an image for any place of danger and fear, which could include the experience of death. The NIV margin note reads "through the darkest valley." John J. Davis translates it, "Even though I should walk in the valley of extreme dangers, I will not be afraid" (Davis, *Perfect Shepherd,* 93). "The valley of death" is a popular

image, based primarily on the KJV (Job 3:5; 10:21-22; 24:17; 34:22; 38:17; Pss. 23:4; 107:10; Isa. 9:2; Jer. 2:6; 13:16; Amos 5:8). In some of these verses, the NIV has moved "shadow of death" to the margin, and in others abandoned it completely. The preacher who pictures death as "a valley that cannot detain us and a shadow that cannot harm us" had better keep in mind that, while the deceased may be safe in the Father's house, the mourners present are still in the gloomy valley. Death is an enemy who often tears homes apart and leaves suffering people behind, and we must not ignore this fact as we use biblical images. The enemy in the valley may be only a shadow, but the fear and grief in the hearts of the sheep are very real.

8. Jesus Christ will still be the Shepherd of His sheep even after they get to glory (Rev. 7:17). The image of a banquet for sheep in the Father's house is not at all grotesque (Ps. 23:5-6). The sheep go to the Father's house; the dogs are outside the city (Rev. 22:15).

9. Some commentators and expositors have concluded that David was a young man when he wrote this psalm, but I seriously question that interpretation. It's possible that Absalom's rebellion is the background for Psalms 22–24: David seemingly abandoned by God (Ps. 22), David trusting God in the wilderness (Ps. 23), and David returning to his throne in victory (Ps. 24). In his delightful *A Psalm of an Old Shepherd*, Morgan defends the view that David wrote it "when he was advanced in years." Morgan says, "The one consideration which led to the adoption of this view was that of the wealth of experience quite evidently possessed by the writer. Surely it would be as impossible to associate such wealth with youth, as it would be unnatural for youth to possess it" (F. Crosley Morgan, *A Psalm of an Old Shepherd* [London: Marshall, Morgan and Scott, n.d.], 20–21). Whether Psalm 23 has anything to do with Absalom's rebellion is not important. That it has everything to do with the believer's life and death is important, and that's where the emphasis should be.

10. See J. Sidlow Baxter, *His Part and Ours* (London: Marshall, Morgan and Scott, 1938), 113–22; and E.W. Bullinger, *Figures of Speech Used in the Bible* (London: Eyre and Spottiswoode, 1898), 737.

11. M'Cheyne used Song of Songs 6:2 to picture the death of a child: "My beloved is gone down into His garden . . . to gather lilies" (KJV) (Robert Murray M'Cheyne, *Memoirs and Remains* [London: Banner of Truth, 1966], 551). This may be spiritualizing the text a bit.

12. For an excellent sermon on this theme, see Ian Macpherson, "What Christ the Carpenter Has Made of His Cross," in *God's Middleman* (London: The Epworth Press, 1965), 149–61.

Twenty-One

1. One of the first things the new pastor should do when he arrives on the field is make a calendar of the important dates in the history of the church. Nothing endears a pastor to the older folks more than seeing his appreciation

for the past, and the younger people need to know about the church's roots. Make a list of the significant dates and start planning your preaching. I have often had frantic phone calls and letters from pastors asking me to speak at a fiftieth or hundredth anniversary of their church—two months before the event! My brethren, such things ought not so to be.

2. For a balanced collection of contemporary sermons for the church year, by twenty-six different preachers, see Richard Allen Bodey, ed. *Good News for All Seasons* (Grand Rapids: Baker, 1987). George Sweeting gives us eighteen of his sermons in his *Special Sermons for Special Days* (Chicago: Moody, 1977), and Clovis G. Chappell's *Chappell's Special Day Sermons* (Grand Rapids: Baker, 1976) contains sixteen sermons for special days. Most "garden variety" sermons can be transformed into special day sermons if you use your imagination and discover how the truth of the sermon relates to the occasion.

3. No lover of ecclesiastical calendars, even Charles Spurgeon knew it was smart to preach about the birth of Christ during the Christmas season. "We venture to assert, that if there be any day in the year, of which we may be pretty sure that it was not the day on which the Saviour was born, it is the twenty-fifth of December. Nevertheless, since the current of men's thoughts is led this way just now, and I see no evil in the current itself, I shall launch the bark of our discourse upon that stream, and make use of the fact, which I shall neither justify nor condemn, by endeavoring to lead your thoughts in the same direction." *The Metropolitan Tabernacle Pulpit* (Pasadena, Texas: Pilgrim, 1984), 17:697. See also the introduction to the sermon "The Great Birthday" in vol. 22, p. 709.

4. See H.P. Liddon, *Sermons*, The Contemporary Pulpit Library (London: Swan Sonnenschein, 1892), 129–88, for an excellent series of messages on "The Magnificat."

5. Mary Elizabeth Coleridge, "I Saw a Stable," in *The Treasury of Religious Verse*, comp. Donald T. Kauffman (Westwood, N.J.: Revell, 1966), 120–21.

6. James Stalker's *The Trial and Death of Jesus Christ* is a classic work that you ought to read, not only for sermon preparation, but, even more, for your own soul's good (London: Hodder and Stoughton, 1894). An equally rich volume is W.M. Clow, *The Day of the Cross* (London: Hodder and Stoughton, 1909). More contemporary volumes are William Sangster, *They Met at Calvary*, (Nashville: Abingdon, 1956), and Clovis G. Chappell, *Faces about the Cross* (Grand Rapids: Baker, 1974). The famous "Schilder Trilogy" by K. Schilder, *Christ in His Suffering, Christ on Trial,* and *Christ Crucified* (Eerdmans), contain a wealth of material, but you must mine it.

7. Clovis G. Chappell, *The Cross Before Calvary* (Nashville: Abingdon, 1960). These six messages deal primarily with "Old Testament figures who reveal the spirit of the cross."

8. While the phrase "lifted up" refers primarily to our Lord's death on the cross (John 12:33), it also carries with it the suggestion of His exaltation (12:23, 28; 13:31-32). The Greek verb literally means "to lift up" and figuratively means "to enhance." Isaiah 52:13 and 53:12 come to mind.

9. Charles W. Koller, *Sermons Preached Without Notes* (Grand Rapids: Baker, 1964). He also called the message "The Plus Sign on the Sky Line."

10. A church elder said to me one day, "I've noticed that my pastor is prone to bash the fathers on Father's Day and bless the mothers on Mother's Day. It isn't fair!" And it isn't. There are godly fathers and worldly mothers as well as worldly fathers and saintly mothers, and sometimes they're married to each other.

11. Even if you aren't trying to work a special day emphasis into your regular course of preaching, this is a good way to handle special day messages. It takes some research to get the facts about famous mothers, fathers, or what have you, but the results are worth it. Give yourself plenty of time!

12. See James Strahan, *Hebrew Ideals in Genesis* (Grand Rapids: Kregel, 1982). This is the best study I have found of the essentials of godly living as illustrated in Genesis, beginning with the call of Abraham. Alexander Whyte advised, "Let that fine piece of evangelical scholarship be in every home."

13. When I was teaching homiletics, I used to warn the students not to fall into the time-honored trap of comparing the decay of our country to the fall of the Roman Empire. In the first place, do you know anybody who wanted the Roman Empire to continue? I don't. It was built on brutality and slavery and deserved to collapse. Furthermore, Daniel had prophesied that the Roman Empire would fall; and God always fulfills His Word.

14. If you want to pursue the study of the place of religion in America, see: Bruce L. Shelley, *The Gospel and the American Dream* (Portland, Ore.: Multnomah, 1989); Mark A. Noll, Nathan O. Hatch, and George M. Marsden, *The Search for Christian America* (Westchester, Ill.: Crossway, 1983); Edwin Scott Gaustad, *A Religious History of America*, rev. ed. (San Francisco: Harper and Row, 1990); Mark A. Noll, ed., *Religion and American Politics* (New York: Oxford Univ. Press, 1990); DeWitte Holland, ed., *Preaching in American History* (Nashville: Abingdon, 1969) and *Sermons in American History* (Nashville: Abingdon, 1971).

15. I note that in some modern hymnals the word "Ebenezer" has been deleted from the second verse of the familiar hymn "Come Thou Fount of Every Blessing," another concession to the biblical illiteracy that is engulfing the church. Pioneer missionary J. Hudson Taylor had the words "Jehovah-Jireh" and "Ebenezer" displayed in his home: "The Lord will provide—Hitherto has the Lord helped us!"

16. For an imaginative anniversary sermon, see Frederick Buechner's, "The Clown in the Belfry," in *The Clown in the Belfry* (San Francisco: HarperCollins, 1992), 107–17. Buechner used Psalm 23 and an incident from the church's history to create a message that is unique among church anniversary sermons.

17. This prayer has been quoted so often that both the original wording and the authorship have faded into oblivion. Niebuhr wrote the prayer in 1934 and a friend introduced it to Alcoholics Anonymous who made it their official motto. See June Bingham, *Courage To Change* (New York: Charles Scribner's

Sons, 1972). In the popular comic strip "Calvin and Hobbes," Calvin gives his own version: "I pray for the strength to change what I can, the inability to accept what I can't, and the incapacity to tell the difference."

Twenty-Two

1. "Poetry . . . takes its origin from emotion recollected in tranquillity." Wordsworth wrote this in a letter to Lady Beaumont, 21 May 1807.
2. *New York Post*, 29 February 1960.
3. Kittay, *Metaphor*, 4.
4. Mel Brooks said, "Tragedy is if I cut my finger. Comedy is if I walk into an open sewer and die." *The New Yorker*, 30 October 1978.
5. For interesting studies of American humor and comedians, see Steve Allen's *Funny People* (Briarcliff Manor, N.Y.: Stein and Day, 1981), *More Funny People* (Briarcliff Manor, N.Y.: Stein and Day, 1982), and *How to Be Funny* (N.Y.: McGraw Hill, 1987). The last book he wrote with Jane Wollman. Steve Allen is not only a very funny man himself but also a well-educated man who reads widely and can discuss philosophy and history as intelligently as humor and entertainment. His award-winning television program "Meeting of Minds" proved that.
6. This is also true in biblical humor where exaggerated contrast is the basis for humor. When Jesus suggested that a camel go through the eye of a needle, His listeners certainly smiled or even laughed out loud. See Elton Trueblood, *The Humor of Christ* (New York: Harper and Row, 1964), and Cal Samra, *The Joyful Christ: The Healing Power of Humor* (San Francisco: Harper and Row, 1986).
7. Keane, *Christian Ethics*, 67. Reinhold Niebuhr makes a similar observation in his sermonic essay entitled "Humour and Faith." He says, "The intimate relation between humour and faith is derived from the fact that both deal with the incongruities of our existence. Humour is concerned with the immediate incongruities of life and faith with the ultimate ones." The essay is found in Reinhold Niebuhr, *The Signs of the Times* (New York: Charles Scribner's Sons, 1946), 111–31.
8. E.B. White, *A Subtreasury of American Humor* (New York: Coward McCann, 1941), xvii.
9. For a study of the relationship between humor and creativity, with an emphasis on Freud's views of humor, see chapter 7 of Silvano Arieti, *Creativity: The Magic Synthesis* (New York: Basic Books, 1976).
10. "The total absence of humour from the Bible," remarked Whitehead, "is one of the most singular things in all literature." See Lucien Price, *Dialogues of Alfred North Whitehead* (Boston: Little, Brown, 1954), 199. As with so many other things relating to the Bible and the Christian faith, the learned philosopher/mathematician was wrong.
11. See E.W. Bullinger, *Figures of Speech Used in the Bible* (Grand Rapids: Baker, 1968), 806–15.

12. Brooks, *Lectures*, 56. But Brooks warns the preacher against becoming a "clerical jester . . . [who] lays his hands on the most sacred things, and leaves defilement upon all he touches. He is full of Bible jokes. He talks about the Church's sacred symbols in the language of stale jests that have come down from generations of feeble clerical jesters before him. . . . There are passages in the Bible which are soiled forever by the touches which the hands of ministers who delight in cheap and easy jokes have left upon them" (p. 56).

13. Helmut Thielicke, *Encounter with Spurgeon*, trans. John W. Doberstein (Philadelphia: Fortress, 1963), 25–26.

14. William Jewett Tucker, *The Making and the Unmaking of the Preacher* (Boston: Houghton Mifflin, 1898), 122.

15. *Oswald Chambers: His Life and Work*, comp. and ed. Gertrude Chambers (London: Simkin Marshall, 1933), 276. See also Warren W. Wiersbe, *Victorious Christians You Should Know* (Grand Rapids: Baker), 53–59.

Twenty-Three

1. Two of the best studies of biblical evangelism are David Watson, *I Believe in Evangelism* (Grand Rapids: Eerdmans, 1976) and Michael Green, *Evangelism in the Early Church* (Grand Rapids: Eerdmans, 1970). See also David Watson's *Called and Committed: World-Changing Discipleship* (Wheaton, Ill.: Harold Shaw, 1982). The entire book is relevant to our theme, but chapter 9 deals primarily with evangelism.

2. According to Deuteronomy 21:18-21, the rebellious son, having brought disgrace to family and village, could have been stoned to death; but the father got there first!

3. When he was five years old, John Wesley was rescued from the burning parsonage at Epworth; and all his life, he called himself "a brand plucked from the burning."

4. The word "Gehenna" is a modified transliteration of the Aramaic phrase *ge-ben-hinnom* "valley of the son of Hinnom." It was a valley southwest of Jerusalem where Ahaz and Manasseh sacrificed their sons to the god Molech (2 Chron. 28:3; 33:6; see Jer. 7:31-32; 32:35). Godly King Josiah defiled the site by turning it into a place for waste and garbage (2 Kings 23:10). It's interesting that Paul never uses the word "gehenna" in his epistles, although he does teach eternal punishment (2 Thes. 1).

5. "In all discussions of hell we should keep steadily before our eyes the possible damnation, not of our enemies or our friends (since both these disturb the reason) but of ourselves" (C.S. Lewis, *The Problem of Pain* [London: Geoffrey Bles, 1950], 116). Lewis' discussion of hell in chapter 8 of this book is significant to the work of the evangelist. I recommend you read it.

6. According to Patterson and Kim, 82 percent of the American public believes in life after death, including both heaven and hell; but only 4 percent of the people think they're going to hell. Nearly half (46 percent) believe they're going to heaven. Only 55 percent believe in the existence of Satan. James

Patterson and Peter Kim, *The Day America Told the Truth* (New York: Prentice Hall, 1991), 204.

7. Of course, we all know that people want justice to fall on others but not on themselves. The person who cheats on his income tax complains when he's caught and fined, but he insists that the salesman who cheated him be punished to the nth degree.

8. Listen to Spurgeon at age twenty-one: "Thine heart beating high with fever; thy pulse rattling at an enormous rate in agony; thy limbs cracking like the martyrs in the fire, and yet unburnt; thyself, put in a vessel of hot oil, pained, yet coming out undestroyed; all thy veins becoming a road for the hot feet of pain to travel on; every nerve a string on which the devil shall ever play his diabolical tune of Hell's Unutterable Lament; thy soul forever and ever aching, and thy body palpitating in unison with thy soul" (*The New Park Street Pulpit*, vol. 2, 105). At age fifty-six, Spurgeon said this: "You are hanging over the mouth of hell by a single thread, and that thread is breaking. Only a gasp for breath, only a stopping of the heart for a single moment, and you will be in an eternal world, without God, without hope, without forgiveness. Oh, how can you face it?" (*Metropolitan Tabernacle Pulpit*, vol. 37, 527.) In his famous sermon "Sinners in the Hands of an Angry God," Jonathan Edwards said: "You hang by a slender thread, with the flames of divine wrath flashing about it, and ready every moment to singe it, and burn it asunder." He also said in this sermon: "Your wickedness makes you as it were heavy as lead, and to tend downwards with great weight and pressure towards hell; and if God should let you go, you would immediately sink and swiftly descend and plunge into the bottomless gulf." See John Gerstner, *Jonathan Edwards on Heaven and Hell* (Grand Rapids: Baker, 1980). I have a feeling that both Spurgeon and Edwards, if ministering today, would still preach passionately on eternal punishment, but, without minimizing the awfulness of hell, would probably take a different approach.

9. Lewis, *Problem of Pain*, 115.

10. The verse can also be translated "able to keep what he has entrusted to me," as in the RSV, NEB, and PH. But I prefer the translation in the NIV, NRSV, NKJV, and NASB. The image is that of a person going on a journey who entrusts his valuables to a friend. Paul is about to "depart," and he is sure that his salvation and the fruit of his ministry are safe in the hands of the Lord who called him. The theme of "a committed deposit" is important in Paul's letters to Timothy (1 Tim. 6:20; 2 Tim. 1:12, 14; 2:2; 4:7).

11. Users of the *Authorized Version* should note that the word is *strait*, not *straight*, and means "narrow, hemmed in." It comes from the Latin *strictus*, "to bind." The words of Lloyd-Jones explain the image well: "When worldly wisdom and carnal motives enter into evangelism, you will find that there is no 'strait gate.' Too often the impression is given that to be a Christian is after all very little different from being a non-Christian, that you must not think of Christianity as a narrow life, but as something most attractive and wonderful and exciting, and that you come in in crowds. . . . The Christian way of life is

not popular. It never has been popular, and it is not popular today" (Martyn Lloyd-Jones, *Studies in the Sermon on the Mount* [Grand Rapids: Eerdmans, 1960], 2:220–21).

Twenty-Four

1. Books on creativity are many and of varied quality, covering the spectrum from erudite psychology texts to pop culture how-to-do-it books. I suggest you investigate the following: James I. Adams, *Conceptual Blockbusting: A Guide to Better Ideas* (Reading, Mass.: Addison-Wesley, 1986); Silvano Areti, *Creativity: The Magic Synthesis* (New York: Basic Books, 1976); Henri Bergson, *The Creative Mind* (New York: Philosophical Library, 1946); Robert Fritz, *Creating* (New York: Fawcett Columbine, 1991); Brewster Ghiselin, ed., *The Creative Process* (Berkeley: Univ. of California Press, 1985); Robert Gruden, *The Grace of Great Things: Creativity and Innovation* (New York: Ticknor and Fields, 1990); Robert B. Heywood, ed., *The Works of the Mind* (Chicago: Univ. of Chicago Press, 1966); Vera John-Steiner, *Notebooks of the Mind* (New York: Harper and Row, 1985); Rollo May, *The Courage to Create* (New York: W.W. Norton, 1975); Alex F. Osborn, *Applied Imagination* (New York: Charles Scribner's Sons, 1953); Denise Shekerjian, *Uncommon Genius: How Great Ideas Are Born* (New York: Viking, 1990); Jerome L. Singer and Ellen Switzer, *Mind-Play: The Creative Uses of Fantasy* (Englewood Cliffs, N.J.: Prentice-Hall, 1980); Anthony Storr, *The Dynamics of Creation* (New York: Atheneum, 1985); John Wonder and Priscilla Donovan, *Whole-Brain Thinking* (New York: Morrow, 1984).

2. According to the experts, some of the more obvious "marks" of the creative person are these: courage to go it alone; a willingness to take risks and even fail; a good sense of humor; curiosity; confidence in hunches and intuition; persistence; and a positive attitude toward change. Education and IQ aren't that important, although creative people want to master their field and continue learning. So-called "inspiration" doesn't play a big part in being creative. It appears that "creativity" isn't a single isolated skill but a combination of abilities and "ways of thinking" about things.

3. For a perceptive discussion of this important topic see chapter 3, "Intellect and Imagination," in William Temple, *Mens Creatrix* (London: Macmillan, 1917). The book is a stimulating discussion of "the mind creative"; and even if you don't totally agree with Archbishop Temple's Platonism, you will benefit from being exposed to his creative thinking. Temple confessed that the three most formative influences on his mind were Plato, St. John, and Robert Browning. Interestingly enough, Temple sat up very late the night before his wedding to finish writing *Mens Creatrix!* See F.A. Iremonger, *William Temple: Archbishop of Canterbury* (London: Geoffrey Cumberlege, 1948). Chapter 28, "The Philosopher," was written by Dorothy Emmet. For a general summary of Temple's theology and philosophy, see A.E. Baker, ed., *William Temple's Teaching* (London: James Clarke, n.d.).

4. Eudora Welty, *One Writer's Beginnings* (New York: Warner, 1985), 83. I highly recommend this book as a record of how one creative person cultivated a creative gift in spite of what some people would consider difficult obstacles.

5. Ciardi's statement is, "The poet's trade is not to talk about experience, but to make it happen." See his essay "The Art of Language" in Thruelson and Kobler, *Adventures of the Mind*, 587. What Thoreau wrote in his journal about writing is true of preaching: "The forcible writer stands bodily behind his words with his experience. He does not make books out of books, but he has been there in person" (3 February 1852). "How vain it is to sit down and write when you have not stood up to live!" (19 August 1851) Thoreau's friend Emerson agreed with him: "If you would learn to write, 'tis in the street you must learn it. . . . The people, and not the college, is the writer's home." See *Society and Solitude* (Boston: Houghton, Mifflin and Co., 1883), 16. The minister who comfortably studies behind the lines of battle will not have much to say to the troops.

6. "What is experience but a wealth of parallels upon which our imagination can draw?" That question was asked by Alex Osborn, co-founder of Batten, Barton, Durstine and Osborn, in his fascinating book *Your Creative Power* (New York: Dell, 1961), 87. I recommend the book to you.

7. See Gary Jackson Oliver, *Real Men Have Feelings Too* (Chicago: Moody, 1993).

8. William Wordsworth's poem "Lines Composed A Few Miles Above Tintern Abbey" wrestles with the problem of how to re-create beautiful experiences when you remember delightful events. I suggest you read the poem and note especially the sensory language: I hear, I behold, I see, etc. Writing about his experiences enjoying nature, the poet says:

But oft, in lonely rooms, and 'mid the din
Of towns and cities, I have owed to them,
In hours of weariness, sensations sweet,
Felt in the blood, and felt along the heart;
And passing even into my purer mind,
With tranquil restoration: —feelings too
Of unremembered pleasure. . .

9. "There's a strange paradox about writing novels. It is simply this: there's no occupation in the universe that is lonelier and that at the same time depends more radically on a community, a commonwealth of other writers." Walker Percy, *Sign-Posts in a Strange Land* (New York: Farrar, Strauss and Giroux, 1991), 199.

10. A report in the *New Yorker* magazine (7 March 1959), stated that a survey of sixty-seven people with "the world's greatest minds" revealed that most of them had their "greatest ideas" either just before they went to sleep or immediately upon awakening. When I was in high school, I discovered that

my mind worked all night on geometry problems I had wrestled with before going to bed, and often I awakened with the solutions just waiting to be written down. I've had similar experiences with sermon texts I've meditated on before dozing off. Ideas are like seeds: after they're planted, they need time to grow. "The Genius of Poetry must work out its own salvation in a man," wrote the English poet John Keats. "It cannot be matured by law and precept, but by sensation and watchfulness in itself—that which is creative must create itself" (8 October 1818, *Letters*, 1:374). A survey of 200 college students revealed that 86 percent of the most creative students fell asleep at night within twenty minutes or less of retiring, while the least creative students took thirty minutes or more to go to sleep (*USA Today*, 26 September 1985). If this is true, creative people don't have much time at night to give birth to those great ideas!

11. Albert Einstein asked a friend at Princeton, "Why is it I get my best ideas in the morning while I'm shaving?" Rollo May's reply is that "the insight comes at a moment of transition between work and relaxation." See Rollo May, *The Courage to Create*, 66–67.

12. See Robert L. Short's *The Gospel According to Peanuts* (Richmond, Va.: John Knox, 1965) and *The Parables of Peanuts* (New York: Harper and Row, 1968). I may be wrong, but I get the impression that "good ol' Charlie Brown" has been replaced recently by uncontrollable and unpredictable Calvin of "Calvin and Hobbes," one of the most imaginative comic strips to appear in decades. Whether the contrast in personalities between Charlie and Calvin represents a significant change in the outlook of the American child, I'll leave to the sociologists and psychologists to figure out.

13. James Elphinston asked Samuel Johnson if he had read a certain new book that was popular, and Johnson replied, "I have looked into it." "What," said Elphinston, "have you not read it *through*?" Johnson replied, "No, Sir; do you read books through?" (See Boswell, *Life of Johnson*, 1:463.) If I feel that a book I'm reading isn't really helping me, no matter how highly it was recommended, I mark the place where I stopped reading, scan the rest of the book, and set it aside until later. When I read a book, I underline what's important to me and make my own index at the back of the book. If the book is biographical, I construct a chronology of the person's life (unless there's already one in the book) and make a list of the important people in the subject's life, the influential books the person read, and other significant data that will help me use the book later on. If you want to improve your reading skills, consult: Mortimer Adler and Charles Van Doren, *How to Read a Book* (New York: Simon and Schuster 1972); James Sire, *The Joy of Reading* (Portland, Ore.: Multnomah, 1978); and Ben E. Johnson, *Rapid Reading with a Purpose* (Glendale, Ca.: Regal, 1973). The classic book on rapid reading is Norman Lewis, *How to Read Better and Faster*, 3rd ed. (New York: Thomas Y. Crowell, 1959).

14. Mark Twain defined a classic as "a book which people praise and don't read," and Daniel J. Boorstin defined a best-seller as "a book which somehow

sold well simply because it was selling well. . . . It is known primarily (sometimes exclusively) for its well-knownness." See *Writers on Writing,* comp. Jon Winokur (Philadelphia: Running Press, 1990), 40–41.

15. When pastors ask me what classics they ought to read, I usually refer them to the revised edition of Clifton Fadiman, *The Lifetime Reading Plan* (New York: Thomas Y. Crowell, 1978). Fadiman lists over 100 books that have stood the test of time, and he tells you what they're about and why they're important. Charles Van Doren performs a similar service on a wider scale in *The Joy of Reading* (New York: Harmony Books, 1985). In *Classics Revisited,* Kenneth Rexroth introduces you to sixty classic writers and their writings (New York: New Directions, 1986); and in *The Harvard Guide to Influential Books,* ed. by Devine, Dissel and Parrish (New York: Harper and Row, 1986), 113 Harvard professors list the books that have "shaped their thinking." Beatrice Batson, *A Reader's Guide to Religious Literature* (Chicago: Moody, 1968), is a guide to the best in religious literature from the middle ages to the mid-twentieth century. When it comes to selecting books to read, especially in the realm of "great literature," don't let anybody intimidate you. It's your time you're investing and you must make the most of it. Some "great books" we have to grow into; others we read simply because we need to know what they say; and others we can ignore. Before you rush out and buy *The Great Books of the Western World* or *The Harvard Classics,* or you start collecting the classics in paperback, buy a good anthology of great literature and give yourself a chance to get acquainted with the classic authors and their works. The literature anthologies published by W.W. Norton and Company, New York, are used as textbooks in many colleges and universities and can often be purchased used at campus bookstores. For a contemporary collection, see Frye, Baker, Perkins and Perkins, eds., *The Practical Imagination* (Harper and Row). An anthology enables you to get acquainted quickly and inexpensively with a wide variety of writers, and you can soon learn which ones really speak to you. Since a classic is a book that doesn't have to be rewritten, it can always speak to us and the age in which we live. That's what makes classics important: they deal with matters that are timeless and essential. Much of what is being written about ecology today was anticipated by Thoreau in *Walden;* and Thoreau's *Civil Disobedience,* published in 1849, is the primer for the modern civil rights movement.

16. For years, I've been telling pastors that when it comes to reading the classics, they have the advantage because of their knowledge of the Bible. Classical art, music, and literature are saturated with biblical allusions and images that the average person might not recognize. Many university students read the first sentence of the first chapter of Melville's *Moby Dick*—"Call me Ishmael"—but have no idea how significant that name is to the plot. Some years ago, while rereading *Moby Dick,* I marked all the biblical allusions and quotations. I found over 100 of them, and I know I overlooked some. See *A Dictionary of Biblical Tradition in English Literature,* ed. David Lyle Jeffrey (Grand Rapids: Eerdmans, 1992), and Walter B. Fulghum, Jr., *A Dictionary of*

Biblical Allusions in English Literature, (New York: Holt, Rinehart and Winston, 1965).

17. When reading printed sermons, keep in mind that the material has been edited and the statements that might best reveal the heart of the preacher have sometimes been removed. "But it is impossible to print a sermon," wrote Charles E. Jefferson. "The most fully reported sermon is nothing but a skeleton. The life of the sermon lies in the tones and accents, in the subtle fire that burns in the syllables, and the spiritual heat which radiates from the man himself. A sermon is a man, and you cannot print a man." Charles E. Jefferson, *The Minister as Prophet* (New York: Grosset and Dunlap, 1905), 62.

18. If you're rusty in this area of literature, start with chapter 3 of Leland Ryken's *The Liberated Imagination* (Wheaton, Ill.: Harold Shaw, 1989) and enjoy his exposition of ee cummings' poem about the balloonman. John Ciardi and Miller Williams, *How Does a Poem Mean* (Boston: Houghton, Mifflin, 1975), Laurence Perrine, *Sound and Sense: An Introduction to Poetry* (New York: Harcourt Brace Jovanovich, 1973), and Elizabeth Drew, *Discovering Poetry* (New York: W.W. Norton, 1933) are good introductions to the understanding and enjoyment of poetry. If you have children in your home — or even if you don't — secure Lee Bennett Hopkins, *Pass the Poetry, Please!* (New York: Harper and Row, 1987) and look at poetry from the child's point of view. Kathleen E. Morgan, *Christian Themes in Contemporary Poetry* (London: SCM, 1965) discusses six twentieth century poets, and Stopford A. Brooke, *Theology in the English Poets* (London: J.M. Dent, in the "Everyman Series") is the classic study of Cowper, Coleridge, Wordsworth and Burns, with the emphasis on Wordsworth. *Four Ways of Modern Poetry,* edited by Nathan A. Scott, Jr. (Richmond, Va.: John Knox, 1965) is a brief introduction from a Christian perspective to the poetry of Wallace Stevens, Robert Frost, Dylan Thomas, and W.H. Auden. I found Richard Hugo, *The Triggering Town* (New York: W.W. Norton, 1979) both enlightening and entertaining. Hugo is a contemporary poet and teacher of "creative writing" who can both write and teach with skill and imagination. C.F. Main and Peter J. Seng, eds., *Poems: Wadsworth Handbook and Anthology* (Belmont, Ca.: Wadsworth, 1961), is the ideal introductory text for somebody just getting started in reading poetry. The selections are balanced and the introductions and expositions are scholarly without being academic. The classic anthologies of religious poetry are Donald T. Kauffman, ed., *The Treasury of Religious Verse* (Westwood, N.J.: Revell, 1962) and James Dalton Morrison, ed., *Masterpieces of Religious Verse* (New York: Harper and Brothers, 1948). Merle Meeter, comp., *The Country of the Risen King* (Grand Rapids: Baker, 1978) is one of the best anthologies of Christian poetry that includes a fine selection of contemporary poets along with the historic "greats." A.W. Tozer, comp., *The Christian Book of Mystical Verse* (Harrisburg, Pa.: Christian Pub., 1963) reflects Dr. Tozer's love for the mystics and is a good supplement to the standard D.H.S. Nicholson and A.H.E. Lee, comps., *Oxford Book of English*

Mystical Verse (Oxford: Clarendon, 1917). Lord David Cecil, ed., *Oxford Book of Christian Verse* (Oxford: Clarendon, 1940). A fascinating anthology of religious poetry is Robert Atwan and Laurance Wieder, eds., *Chapter into Verse: Poetry in English Inspired by the Bible* (Oxford: Oxford Univ. Press, 1993). Volume 1 contains poetry based on Old Testament passages, and volume 2, poetry based on the New Testament. Both volumes follow the biblical order of books.

19. Listen to Luci Shaw: "The Christian poet offers the Church what the Bible has always offered, but has too often been ignored or perceived incorrectly. God thinks metaphorically. The Bible is full of striking metaphors, but we've become too familiar with them to realize how vivid they are. . . . When we have a real image, a picture, we can understand better what God is talking about. This is what poetry should do. It shows us a picture. It focuses in on a small area of life and sees it from a fresh angle. This is how poets and other artists can call Christians to a new understanding of God." Etta Worthington, "Creative Christianity: An Interview with Luci Shaw" *Sunday Digest*, 10 June 1984. Luci Shaw's poetry is published by Harold Shaw Publishers, Wheaton, Ill., and includes the following titles: *Listen to the Green* (1971), *The Secret Trees* (1976), *The Sighting* (1981), *A Widening Light: Poems of the Incarnation* (1984), *Postcard from the Shore* (1985), and *Polishing the Petoskey Stone* (1990), which includes all the previous titles except the anthology, *A Widening Light*.

20. "Poetry Considered," *Atlantic Monthly*, March 1923.

21. Did you know that the English words "erudite" and "rude" are first cousins? They both come from the Latin root *rudis*, which means "unformed, rough, uncultivated, unskilled." The verb *erudio* means "to free from roughness, to instruct, to educate"; hence, an erudite person is one whose rough edges have been polished by education. Late Latin had the verb *eruderare*, "to clear of rubbish." Sometimes we have to clear away the rubbish of wrong ideas before we can plant the seeds of new ideas. Words are fascinating!

22. I can't urge you enough to become a student of words. If you've studied Hebrew and Greek, you have a head start; and if you were exposed to a modern language sometime during your educational career, this training will help you even if you think you've forgotten what you studied. If you haven't studied any foreign languages, it's still never too late to start studying English. To get started becoming an effective "word detective," lay hands on the books by William Safire, such as *Take My Word for It* (New York: Henry Holt, 1984), *What's The Good Word?* (New York: Times Books, 1982), *On Language* (New York: Times Books, 1981), and *I Stand Corrected* (New York: Times Books, 1984). Edward Newman's *Strictly Speaking* (New York: Bobbs-Merrill, 1974) and *A Civil Tongue* (New York: Bobbs-Merrill, 1975) are both entertaining and enlightening. Poet John Ciardi gave us *A Browser's Dictionary* (New York: Harper and Row, 1980), *A Second Browser's Dictionary* (New York: Harper and Row, 1983), and *Good Words to You* (New York: Harper and Row, 1987), all of which are delightful treasuries of etymological

lore. Charles Earle Funk, *Thereby Hangs a Tale* (New York: Harper and Row, 1950) is a charming collection of facts about the origins of words and phrases, and so is *Word Mysteries & Histories*, by the Editors of *The American Heritage Dictionary* (New York: Houghton Mifflin, 1986). Owen Barfield, *History in English Words* (Grand Rapids: Eerdmans, 1967) is a more academic treatment of selected words, but a book worth studying. Chapter 11 on "Imagination" is worth the price of the book. Of course, every serious reader needs a copy of *Brewer's Dictionary of Phrase and Fable* to help identify the many persons, objects, events, and ideas that have wormed their way into the English language from mythology and other literature. My copy was revised by Ivor H. Evans and published in 1970 by Harper and Row. Raymond Williams, *Keywords: A Vocabulary of Culture and Society* (New York: Oxford Univ. Press, 1983) is a fascinating discussion of 155 words that are important to modern thinking and speaking; and William Lutz, *Double-Speak* (New York: Harper and Row, 1989) records and analyzes the frightening "language pollution" taking place in America today.

23. Gerald Kennedy, *For Preachers and Other Sinners* (New York: Harper and Row, 1964), 91.

Twenty-Five

1. Bliss Perry, *The Heart of Emerson's Journals* (Boston: Houghton Mifflin Co., 1926), 150. On April 1, 1838, after a visit with some Harvard Divinity School students, Emerson wrote in his journal: "A minister nowadays is plainest prose, the prose of prose. He is a warming-pan, a night-chair at sickbeds and rheumatic souls; and the fire of the minstrel's eye and the vivacity of his word is exchanged for intense, grumbling enunciations of the Cambridge sort, and for Scripture phraseology" (p. 126). He described one sermon he heard as a speech that had "much the style of a problem in geometry, wholly uncoloured and unimpassioned" (p. 91). In spite of the fact that Emerson rejected biblical theology and had no great love for the organized church, his assessment of dull preaching is worth considering.

2. Charles H. Spurgeon, *Lectures to My Students*, 308, 310.

3. Lloyd-Jones, *Preaching and Preachers*, 97.

4. Boswell, *Life of Johnson*, 2:27.

5. Samuel Johnson, *Lives of the Poets* (London: Oxford Univ. Press, 1977), 1:117.

6. Samuel Butler (d. 1902) said that "definitions are a kind of scratching and generally leave a sore place more sore than it was before." That may be so; but until somebody finds a better way to do it, we'll have to keep scratching.

7. Martyn Lloyd-Jones warns us, "We are not going to fight this modern battle successfully by repeating the sermons of the Puritans verbatim, or adopting their classifications and sub-divisions, and their manner of preaching. That would be futile. We must learn to hold on to the old principles but

we must apply them, and use them, in a manner that is up-to-date. . . . The moment we become slaves to any system—I do not care how good it was in its age and generation—we are already defeated, because we have missed this whole principle of adaptability." *The Christian Soldier* (Grand Rapids: Baker, 1978), 290–91.

8. Donald Coggan argues that the rural biblical images are so radically different from modern industrial and scientific images that the preacher must translate the ancient images into contemporary thought-forms if he hopes to be understood. I'm not so sure. While there may be modern equivalents to some of the biblical images, most of them really transcend time and can be understood by people today: birth, death, bread, light, disease, burdens, bondage, guilt and punishment, warfare, drowning, etc. The specifically Jewish images can easily be explained (e.g., leprosy, shepherds, vines, marriage customs). The danger is that we dilute the original revelation, and Coggan recognizes this. See Donald Coggan, *Preaching: The Sacrament of the Word* (New York: Crossroads, 1988), 113–14, 152–55. Henri J.M. Nouwen has some helpful insights on this problem in chapter 1 of *The Wounded Healer* (Garden City, N.Y.: Doubleday "Image Books," 1979). On page 39, Nouwen reminds us that "preaching means much more than handing over a tradition; it is rather the careful and sensitive articulation of what is happening in the community so that those who listen can say: 'You say what I suspected, you express what I vaguely felt, you bring to the fore what I fearfully kept in the back of my mind. Yes, yes—you say who we are, you recognize our condition.' " Remember that images are pictures (we see life) that become mirrors (we see ourselves) and then windows (we see God). If people reach out by faith, then the sermon becomes a door through which they can move to meet God personally.

9. I've forgotten which famous preacher it was, but a listener accosted him after a service with, "Your sermon went over my head!" The preacher replied, "Raise your head!" Preaching is difficult work because in our communicating we have to reach down in order to lift people up; and if we aren't careful, we'll replace proclamation with accommodation and accomplish neither.

10. Brooks, *Lectures on Preaching*, 46–47.

11. Atkinson, *Ralph Waldo Emerson*, 77.

12. F.W. Dillistone in Donald Coggan, *Stewards of Grace* (London: Hodder and Stoughton, 1958), 120.

Appendix B

1. The best treatment of this topic is Richard Kearney's *The Wake of Imagination* (Minneapolis: Univ. of Minnesota, 1988), and I gratefully acknowledge my indebtedness to this book in the preparation of this brief summary.

2. See Plato *Republic*, bk. 10.

3. See Francis A. Schaeffer, *Art and the Bible* (Downers Grove, Ill.: Inter-Varsity, 1973).

4. The NIV translates several Hebrew words as "imagine," depending on the context, including *lev* (heart), *mahasabah* (thoughts), *hasab* (to think), *dabar* (to speak).

5. In his *The Origins of Knowledge and Imagination* (New Haven: Yale Univ. Press, 1978), Jacob Bronowski says: "In my view, which not everybody shares, the central problem of human consciousness depends on this ability to imagine" (p. 18). "The act of imagination is the opening of the system so that it shows new connections" (p. 109). This is a fascinating series of lectures revealing how "unscientific" science can occasionally be used to arrive at truth.

6. See Roberts Avens, *Imagination Is Reality* (Dallas, Texas: Spring, 1980). The schools of psychology of Carl Jung and James Hillman draw upon the ideas of the Eastern philosophers, especially their concepts of myths and archetypes. The growing fascination in the West for Eastern philosophies and religions suggests that we may have a new "romantic" movement on our hands. People are weary of sterile cerebral doctrinaire philosophies and theologies and want something that will excite the imagination and warm the heart. Moore, *Care of the Soul* draws upon this Eastern tradition as filtered through Jung and Hillman.

Appendix C
1. Joseph Campbell's books include: *The Hero with a Thousand Faces* (Princeton Univ. Press, 1968); *The Masks of God: Creative Mythology,* 4 vols. (Penguin, 1983); *Myths to Live By* (Bantam, 1973); *Historical Atlas of World Mythology: The Way of the Seeded Earth,* 3 vols. and *The Way of the Animal Powers,* 2 vols., all published by Harper and Row. The Campbell-Moyers conversations on mythology, "The Power of Myth," are available on video cassette or in book form, published by Doubleday in 1988. Joseph Campbell also edited *Myths, Dreams and Religion* (Dallas, Texas: Spring, 1970). David Adams Leeming, *The World of Myth* (New York: Oxford Univ. Press, 1990), is an excellent one-volume anthology of texts from many peoples. Rex Warner, *The Stories of the Greeks* (New York: Farrar, Straus and Giroux, 1967) is a satisfying retelling of the Greek myths. For a more academic approach, see Robert Graves, *The Greek Myths* (Mt. Kisco, N.Y.: Moyer Bell, 1988). The classic *Bulfinch's Mythology* is available in a "Modern Library" edition as well as an edition from Thomas Y. Crowell. Stewart Perowne, *Roman Mythology* was published in New York by Peter Bedrick Books in 1984. If you want to go back to the originals, read Ovid's *Metamorphoses;* Homer's *Iliad* and *Odyssey;* the plays of Aeschylus, Sophocles, Aristophanes, and Euripides; Hesiod's *Works and Days* and *Theogony;* Plutarch's *Lives;* and *The Histories* by Herodotus. For guidance through the mythological maze, see Michael Stapleton, *The Illustrated Dictionary of Greek and Roman Mythology* (New York: Peter Bedrick, 1986). *Myth and Mythmaking,* ed. Henry A. Murray (Boston: Beacon, 1968) is a comprehensive anthology; and John Ferguson, *Greek and*

Roman Religion: A Source Book (Park Ridge, N.J.: Noyes, 1980) is "an anthology amplified by essays." For an interesting study not only of mythology but also of imagination and faith, see Paul Veyne, *Did the Greeks Believe in Their Own Myths?* (Chicago: Univ. of Chicago Press, 1988).

2. Tom McArthur, "Myth" in *The Oxford Companion to the English Language,* ed. Tom McArthur (Oxford: Oxford Univ. Press, 1992), 675–76.

3. See the article on *muthos* by G. Stahlin in *Theological Dictionary of the New Testament,* ed. Gerhard Kittel and trans. Geoffrey W. Bromiley (Grand Rapids: Eerdmans, 1967), 4:762–95. Also see F.F. Bruce's article on myth in *The New International Dictionary of New Testament Theology,* ed. Colin Brown (Grand Rapids: Zondervan, 1977), 3:643–47.

4. Kittel, *Theological Dictionary,* 4:793.

5. J.A. Cuddon, *Dictionary of Literary Terms and Literary Theory* (Oxford: Blackwell, 1991), 562.

6. See E.A. Bennet, *What Jung Really Said* (New York: Schocken, 1966).

7. For examples of this kind of therapy, see Moore, *Care of the Soul.* See also Rollo May, *The Cry for Myth* (New York: W.W. Norton, 1991). On p. 9, May says, "Many of the problems of our society, including cults and drug addiction, can be traced to the lack of myths which will give us as individuals the inner security we need in order to live adequately in our day."

8. The Associated Press obituary of Frye called him "the influential literary critic who tracked myths and symbols to their biblical sources."

9. Northrup Frye, *The Great Code: The Bible and Literature* (New York: Harcourt Brace Jovanovich, 1982).

10. Malcolm Muggeridge, *Confessions of a Twentieth-Century Pilgrim* (San Francisco: Harper and Row, 1988), 107.

11. May, *The Cry for Myth,* 15.

12. C.S. Lewis, "Myth Became Fact" in *God in the Dock* (Grand Rapids: Eerdmans, 1970), 63–67. The quotation is found on page 66.

Selected Bibliography

Achtemeier, Elizabeth. *Creative Preaching*. Nashville: Abingdon, 1980.

_____. *Preaching as Theology and Art*. Nashville: Abingdon, 1984.

Arieti, Silvano. *Creativity: The Magic Synthesis*. New York: Basic Books, 1976.

Atkinson, Brooks. *The Complete Essays and Other Writings of Ralph Waldo Emerson*. New York: The Modern Library, 1950.

Avens, Robert. *Imagination Is Reality*. Dallas, Texas: Spring Publications, 1980.

Barr, James. *The Semantics of Biblical Language*. London: SCM, 1983.

Beecher, Henry Ward. *Yale Lectures on Preaching: First, Second and Third Series*. New York: Fords, Howard and Hulbert, 1881.

Bellah, Robert N. *The Broken Covenant*. New York: Seabury, 1975.

Boswell, James. *The Life of Samuel Johnson*. 2 vols. London: James M. Dent and Sons, 1906.

Bowen, Catherine Drinker. *Biography: The Craft and the Calling*. Boston: Little, Brown and Co., 1969.

Brooks, Phillips. *Lectures on Preaching*. Grand Rapids: Baker, 1969.

Brueggmann, Walter. *Finally Comes the Poet: Daring Speech for Proclamation*. Minneapolis: Fortress, 1989.

_____. *The Prophetic Imagination*. Philadelphia: Fortress, 1978.

Buechner, Frederick. *The Clown in the Belfry*. San Francisco: Harper/Collins, 1992.

―――. *Peculiar Treasures*. San Francisco: Harper and Row, 1979.

―――. *Telling the Truth: The Gospel as Tragedy, Comedy & Fairy Tale*. San Francisco: Harper and Row, 1977.

―――. *Whistling in the Dark: An ABC Theologized*. San Francisco: Harper and Row, 1988.

―――. *Wishful Thinking: A Theological ABC*. New York: Harper and Row, 1973.

Bullinger, E.W. *Figures of Speech Used in the Bible*. Grand Rapids: Baker, 1968.

Bullock, C. Hassell. *An Introduction to the Old Testament Poetical Books*. Chicago: Moody, 1988.

Buttrick, David. *Homiletic: Moves and Structures*. Philadelphia: Fortress, 1987.

Caird, G.B. *The Language and Imagery of the Bible*. Philadelphia: Westminster, 1980.

Cherry, Conrad. *Nature and Religious Imagination*. Philadelphia: Fortress, 1980.

Ciardi, John, and Miller Williams. *How Does a Poem Mean?* Boston: Houghton, Mifflin Co., 1975.

Coulson, John. *Religion and Imagination*. Oxford: The Clarendon, 1981.

Crabtree, Harriet. *The Christian Life*. Minneapolis: Fortress, 1991.

Dale, Robert W. *Nine Lectures on Preaching*. London: Hodder and Stoughton, 1877.

Davis, H. Grady. *Design for Preaching*. Philadelphia: Fortress, 1958.

Dixon, John W., Jr. *Art and the Theological Imagination*. New York: Seabury, 1978.

Egan, Kieran. *Imagination in Teaching and Learning*. Chicago: Univ. of Chicago, 1992.

Egan, Kieran, and Dan Nadaner, eds. *Imagination and Education*. New York: Teachers College Press, Columbia Univ., 1988.

Ellul, Jacques. *The Humiliation of the Word*. Grand Rapids: Eerdmans, 1985.

Elwell, Walter A. *Topical Analysis of the Bible.* Grand Rapids: Baker, 1991.

Emerson, Ralph Waldo. *Nature.* Boston: Beacon, 1985.

Farra, Harry. *The Sermon Doctor.* Grand Rapids: Baker, 1989.

Frye, Northrop. *The Educated Imagination.* Bloomington, Ind.: Indiana Univ., 1964.

————. *The Great Code: The Bible and Literature.* New York: Harcourt Brace Jovanovich, 1982.

————. *Myth and Metaphor: Selected Essays 1974–1988.* Edited by Robert D. Denham. Charlottesville, Va.: Univ. of Virginia, 1990.

————. *Words with Power.* New York: Harcourt Brace Jovanovich, 1990.

Gale, Herbert M. *The Use of Analogy in the Letters of Paul.* Philadelphia: Westminster, 1964.

Ghiselin, Brewster, ed. *The Creative Process.* Berkeley: Univ. of California, 1985.

Goldberg, Michael. *Theology and Narrative: A Critical Introduction.* Nashville: Abingdon, 1982.

Greidanus, Sidney. *The Modern Preacher and the Ancient Text.* Grand Rapids: Eerdmans, 1988.

Gruden, Robert. *The Grace of Great Things: Creativity and Innovation.* New York: Ticknor and Fields, 1990.

Hale, Nancy. "The Two-Way Imagination." In *Adventures of the Mind: Second Series,* edited by Richard Thruelson and John Kobler. New York: Alfred A. Knopf, 1961.

Hawkes, Terence. *Metaphor.* London: Methuen, 1972.

Hendriksen, William. *More Than Conquerors.* Grand Rapids: Baker, 1940.

Heywood, Robert B., ed. *The Works of the Mind.* Chicago: Univ. of Chicago, 1966.

Holmes, Urban T., III. *Ministry and Imagination.* New York: Seabury, 1976.

Howson, John S. *The Metaphors of St. Paul.* London: Hodder and Stoughton, 1883.

Huttar, Charles, ed. *Imagination and the Spirit.* Grand Rapids: Eerdmans, 1971.

Jeffrey, David Lyle, ed. *A Dictionary of Biblical Tradition in*

English Literature. Grand Rapids: Eerdmans, 1992.

Johnson, Mark. *Moral Imagination: Implications of Cognitive Science for Ethics.* Chicago: Univ. of Chicago, 1993.

Johnson, Samuel. *Lives of the English Poets.* 2 vols. Oxford: Oxford Univ., 1977.

John-Steiner, Vera. *Notebooks of the Mind.* New York: Harper and Row, 1985.

Keane, Philip. *Christian Ethics and Imagination.* New York: Paulist, 1984.

Kearney, Richard. *The Wake of Imagination.* Minneapolis: Univ. of Minnesota, 1988.

Keel, Othmar. *The Symbolism of the Biblical World.* New York: Seabury, 1978.

Kilby, Clyde S. *Christianity and Aesthetics.* Chicago: Inter-Varsity, 1961.

Kittay, Eva Feder. *Metaphor: Its Cognitive Force and Linguistic Structure.* Oxford: Clarendon, 1987.

Kuhlman, Edward. *The Master Teacher.* Old Tappan, N.J.: Revell, 1987.

Lakoff, George. *Women, Fire and Dangerous Things.* Chicago: Univ. of Chicago, 1987.

Lakoff, George, and Mark Johnson. *Metaphors We Live By.* Chicago: Univ. of Chicago, 1980.

———. *More Than Cool Reason: A Field Guide to Poetic Metaphor.* Chicago: Univ. of Chicago, 1989.

Luccock, Halford. *In the Minister's Workshop.* New York: Abingdon, 1944.

McFague, Sallie. *Metaphorical Theology.* London: SCM, 1983.

Maier, John, and Vincent Tollers, eds. *The Bible in Its Literary Milieu.* Grand Rapids: Eerdmans, 1979.

Mander, Jerry. *Four Arguments for the Elimination of Television.* New York: Quill, 1978.

May, Rollo. *The Courage to Create.* New York: W.W. Norton, 1975.

———. *The Cry for Myth.* New York: W.W. Norton, 1991.

Minear, Paul S. *Images of the Church in the New Testament.* Philadelphia: Westminster, 1977.

Moore, Thomas. *Care of the Soul.* New York: Harper-Collins, 1992.

Muggeridge, Malcolm. *Christ and the Media*. Grand Rapids: Eerdmans, 1977.

Ortony, Andrew, ed. *Metaphor and Thought*. Cambridge: Cambridge Univ., 1979.

Osborn, Alex. *Applied Imagination*. New York: Charles Scribner's Sons, 1953.

_____. *Your Creative Power*. New York: Dell, 1961.

Ozick, Cynthia. "The Moral Necessity of Metaphor." *Harper's*, May 1986.

Payne, Robert. *The Roman Triumph*. London: Abelard-Schuman, 1962.

Percy, Walker. *Signposts in a Strange Land*. New York: Farrar, Straus and Giroux, 1991.

_____. *The Message in the Bottle*. New York: Farrar, Straus and Giroux, 1990.

Peterson, Eugene H. *Answering God*. San Francisco: Harper and Row, 1989.

_____. *Reversed Thunder*. San Francisco: Harper and Row, 1988.

Postman, Neil. *Amusing Ourselves to Death*. New York: Viking, 1985.

Radmacher, Earl D. *What the Church Is All About*. Chicago: Moody, 1972.

Reddy, Michael J. "The Conduit Metaphor—A Case of Frame Conflict in Our Language about Language." In *Metaphor and Thought*, edited by Andrew Ortony. Cambridge: Cambridge Univ., 1979.

Rice, Charles L. *Interpretation and Imagination*. Philadelphia: Fortress, 1970.

Ryken, Leland, ed. *The Christian Imagination*. Grand Rapids: Baker, 1981.

_____. *How to Read the Bible as Literature*. Grand Rapids: Zondervan, 1984.

_____. *The Liberated Imagination*. Wheaton, Ill.: Harold Shaw, 1989.

_____. *The Literature of the Bible*. Grand Rapids: Zondervan, 1974.

_____. *Triumphs of the Imagination*. Downers Grove, Ill.: InterVarsity, 1979.

Sacks, Sheldon, ed. *On Metaphor.* Chicago: Univ. of Chicago, 1979.

Sayers, Dorothy. *Christian Letters to a Post-Christian World.* Grand Rapids: Eerdmans, 1969.

————. *The Mind of the Maker.* San Francisco: Harper and Row, 1987.

Schultze, Quentin J. *Redeeming Television.* Downers Grove, Ill.: InterVarsity, 1992.

Schlesinger, Arthur M., Jr. "The Decline of Heroes." In *Adventures of the Mind,* edited by Richard Thruelson and John Kobler. New York: Alfred A. Knopf, 1960.

Shekerjian, Denise. *Uncommon Genius: How Great Ideas Are Born.* New York: Viking, 1990.

Siegelman, Ellen Y. *Metaphor and Meaning in Psychotherapy.* New York: Guildford, 1990.

Soskice, Janet Martin. *Metaphor and Religious Language.* Oxford: Clarendon, 1985.

Spurgeon, Charles Haddon. *Lectures to My Students.* London: Marshall, Morgan, and Scott, 1954.

————. *The Metropolitan Tabernacle Pulpit.* 63 vols. Pasadena, Texas: Pilgrim Publications, 1981.

Stevenson, Dwight E. *In the Biblical Preacher's Workshop.* Nashville: Abingdon, 1967.

————. *Faith Takes a Name.* New York: Harper, 1954.

Sternberg, Meir. *The Poetics of Biblical Narrative.* Bloomington, Ind.: Indiana Univ., 1987.

Storr, Anthony. *The Dynamics of Creation.* New York: Atheneum, 1985.

Stott, John R.W. *Between Two Worlds.* Grand Rapids: Eerdmans, 1982.

Temple, William. *Mens Creatrix.* London: Macmillan, 1917.

Tenney, Merrill C. *Interpreting Revelation.* Grand Rapids: Eerdmans, 1957.

Thruelson, Richard, and John Kobler, eds. *Adventures of the Mind: Second Series.* New York: Alfred A. Knopf, 1961.

Tozer, A.W. *Of God and Man.* Harrisburg, Pa.: Christian Publications, 1960.

Troeger, Thomas H. *Imagining a Sermon.* Nashville: Abingdon, 1990.

Trueblood, Elton. *The Humor of Christ.* New York: Harper and Row, 1964.

Wangerin, Walter, Jr. *Ragman and Other Cries of Faith.* San Francisco: Harper and Row, 1984.

Warnock, Mary. *Imagination.* London: Faber and Faber, 1976.

Welty, Eudora. *One Writer's Beginnings.* New York: Warner, 1985.

Wheelwright, Philip. *Metaphor and Reality.* Bloomington, Ind.: Indiana Univ., 1975.

Whyte, Alexander. *Biblical Characters from the Old and New Testaments.* Grand Rapids: Kregel, 1990.

Wilson, Paul Scott. *Imagination of the Heart.* Nashville: Abingdon, 1988.

Wuellner, Wilhelm H. *The Meaning of "Fishers of Men."* Philadelphia: Westminster, 1967.

Young, Robert D. *Religious Imagination: God's Gift to Prophets and Preachers.* Philadelphia: Westminster, 1979.

Zuck, Roy B. *Basic Bible Interpretation.* Wheaton, Ill.: Victor, 1991.

Zuck, Roy B., ed. *Sitting with Job.* Grand Rapids: Baker, 1992.

Index of Subjects

Index of Persons

Index of Major Biblical Images

71239224R00224

Made in the USA
San Bernardino, CA
13 March 2018